6th

Blue Book Dolls & Values™

by Jan Foulke

photographs by Howard Foulke

Published by HOBBY HOUSE PRESS, INC.
Cumberland, Maryland 21502

Other Titles by Author:

Blue Book of Dolls & Values™
2nd Blue Book of Dolls & Values™
3rd Blue Book of Dolls & Values™
4th Blue Book of Dolls & Values™
5th Blue Book of Dolls & Values™
Focusing on Effanbee Composition Dolls
Focusing on Treasury of Mme. Alexander Dolls
Focusing on Gebrüder Heubach Dolls
Kestner: King of Dollmakers
Simon & Halbig Dolls: The Artful Aspect

The doll prices given within this book are intended as value guides rather than arbitrarily set prices. Each doll price recorded here is actually a compilation. The retail prices in this book are recorded as accurately as possible but in the case of errors, typographical, clerical or otherwise, the author and publisher assume no liability nor responsibility for any loss incurred by users of this book.

ADDITIONAL COPIES AVAILABLE @ $12.95 FROM
HOBBY HOUSE PRESS, INC.
900 FREDERICK STREET
CUMBERLAND, MARYLAND 21502

Printed in the United States of America

ISBN: 0-87588-228-5

Introduction

Rare pouty-faced Schoenhut doll, all original and in excellent condition. *H&J Foulke, Inc.*

Little did we realize when the very first *BLUE BOOK OF DOLLS AND VALUES*™ was published in 1974 that we would eventually be writing a 6th edition of our book, greatly expanded from the original 194 pages to a volume with over three times as much information and more than 600 photographs. Through the years our objectives have always remained the same. Our first objective has been to present a book which will help collectors identify dolls and learn more about them. These may be dolls that they already own, dolls that they might like to own from the large variety shown, dolls that they are considering as additions to their collection, or dolls which they just might be curious about. Our second objective has been to provide retail prices of the dolls discussed as a guide for the prospective buyer and seller.

The dolls presented in this book are listed alphabetically by the maker, the material, the type of doll, or sometimes the name or trade name of the individual doll. An extensive index has been provided at the back of the book for the reader's convenience in locating a specific doll. Of course, in a volume of this size, it would be impossible to include every doll ever made and even all sizes of those discussed, but we have tried to include those which are either available, desirable, interesting, or popular, and even some which are very rare. For each doll we have provided historical information, a description of the doll, a copy of the mark or label, the retail selling price of the doll, and, in most cases, a photograph. The historical information given for some of the dolls would have been much more difficult to compile were it not for the

Tiny German bisque-head doll on composition body, all original, with trunk and additional outfits, a very choice ensemble. *H&J Foulke, Inc.*

original research already published by Dorothy, Elizabeth and Evelyn Coleman and Johana G. Anderton.

The data on the retail prices, which was gathered from January to July 1984, was obtained from antique shops and shows, auctions, doll shops and shows, advertisements in collectors' periodicals, lists from doll dealers, and purchases and sales reported by both collectors and dealers. For some of the rarer dolls we had to dip back into 1983. The information was sorted, indexed, cataloged, and finally computed into the range of prices shown in this book. Hence, the prices used here are not merely our own valuations and judgments, although they must necessarily enter in, they are the results of our research as to the actual retail prices at which these dolls were either sold or offered for sale.

In setting down a price, we use a range to allow for the variables discussed later which must affect the price of any doll. The range used in this edition is wider than that allowed in previous editions because of the greater fluctuation in the current doll market. Collectors are becoming more sophisticated in their purchases by giving higher consideration to originality, quality, and condition. Fine examples of a doll can bring a premium of up to 50 percent more than ordinary versions of the same doll. This is especially true of Schoenhuts, Lencis, *Shirley Temples,* and American composition babies. Faded and dusty played-with models are waiting to be sold, while collectors eagerly vie for excellent examples. Fine quality bisque dolls which are all original or with period clothes are bringing much higher prices than the same models with poor bisque and new clothing. This trend is also noticeable in the early papier-mâché and wooden dolls where period clothing and condition are very important and command a premium.

All prices given for antique dolls are for those of good quality and condition, appropriately dressed, but showing normal wear, unless specifically noted in the description accompanying that particular doll. Bisque and china heads should not be cracked, broken or repaired. The especially outstanding doll in absolutely mint condition, never played with, dressed in original clothes, perhaps even in the original box, would command a much higher price than those quoted. Prices given for modern dolls are for those in overall very good to excellent condition with original hair and clothes except as noted. Again, a never-played-with doll in original box with tagged clothes would bring a higher price than noted.

Certain dolls are becoming increasingly difficult to find and are seldom offered at a show or advertised. If we could not find a sufficient number of these rare dolls offered to be sure of giving a reliable range, we reported the information which we could find and marked those prices "**." In a very few instances, we could find none of a certain doll offered, so we resorted to estimates from reliable established dealers and collectors. These, too, are noted individually with "**."

The users of this book must keep in mind that no price guide is the final word — it cannot provide the absolute answer of what to pay. It should be used only as an aid in purchasing a doll. The final decision must be yours, for only you are on the scene actually

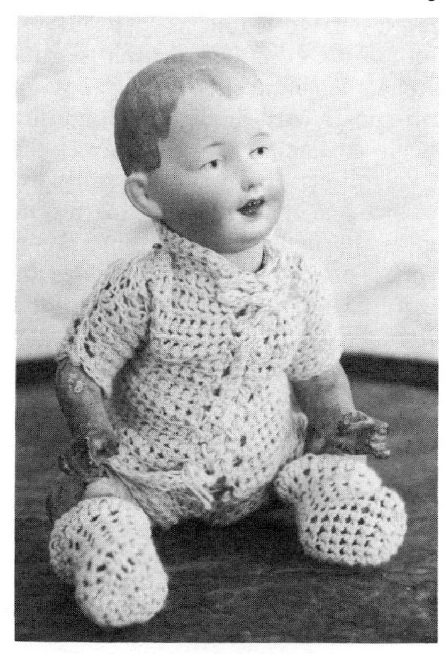

Unusual German bisque-head character baby on very crude bent-limb baby body, wearing original crocheted outfit. *Richard Wright Antiques.*

examining the specific doll in question. No book can take the place of actual field experience. Doll popularity can cycle, and prices can fluctuate. Even though there are national periodicals and shows, price variations can still occur regionally. Before you buy, do a lot of looking. Ask questions. You will find that most dealers and collectors are glad to talk about their dolls and pleased to share their information with you.

It is interesting to note areas of significant price change in this *6th Blue Book*. American cloth dolls have become especially popular during the past two years. The rare Izannah Walker dolls have reached record prices, Babyland Rag dolls have soared, Columbian and "Philadelphia Baby" dolls are over $1000. This interest in cloth dolls has carried over into the German Käthe Kruse and Italian Lenci market. Both types are bringing record prices with condition being particularly important with the Lenci dolls. Early dolls, especially papier-mâché, woodens, and bisque and china ladies with rare molded hair styles are also bringing increased prices. In the German bisque "dolly-faced" category, the larger dolls have increased in price. Nice examples of medium and small sized "dolly faces" are moving slowly and sometimes can be found for less than "book price." But choice or all original examples can go much beyond. Collectors are also willing to pay higher for an unusual face, but not necessarily for an unusual mark if the face is ordinary.

Acknowledgements

A book of this type is the result of not only the talents and energies of the author, but also the encouragement and assistance of many people.

My thanks and appreciation therefore, is given:

To Howard for his lovely photographs and infinite general assistance.

To our many supportive friends among doll collectors and dealers who have given suggestions and encouraged us in our work.

To those people who allowed us to use photographs of their dolls or who provided special information for aspects of this edition: Yvonne Baird, Edna Black, Nancy Schwartz Blaisure, Miriam Blankman, Anna May Case, Pearl Church, Barbara Crescenze, Zelda Cushner, Rosemary Dent, Marceil Drake, Beth Foulke, Kathy George, Carol Green, Ralph Griffith, Betty Harms, Virginia Ann Heyerdahl, Gladyse Hills Hilsdorf, Mimi Hiscox, Lesley Hurford, Wayne and Kay Jensen, Ann Lessey, Lorna Lieberman, Elizabeth McIntyre, Betty McSpadden, Alice Mahoney, Glenn Mandeville, Pearl D. Morley, Lynn Murray, Sheila Needle, Ruth Noden, Joanna Ott, Jimmy and Faye Rodolfos, Mary Lou Rubright, Paula Ryscik, Esther Schwartz, Rhoda Shoemaker, India Stoessel, Z. Frances Walker, Emma Wedmore, Mike White, Zona Wickham, Richard Wright, Alice Pat Young, Jane Young, Carol Stoessel Zvonar, C. C. Collection, Crandall Collection and Roberts Collection.

To the Colemans who allowed some of the doll marks to be reproduced from their book, *The Collector's Encyclopedia of Dolls*.

To Virginia Ann Heyerdahl, my editor, as well as Gary Ruddell and the staff of Hobby House Press, Inc., who worked on this book.

All of these people helped to make this *6th Blue Book of Dolls & Values*™ a reality.

Determining Doll Prices

Doll collecting has become an extremely popular hobby. In the last few years the number of doll collectors has grown by leaps and bounds. This large group of people entering the doll market is reflected within the field in quite a few different ways: there are more dealers in dolls now than ever before; there are more doll shows being organized; there are more doll books and magazines being written. However, the most significant effect this great expansion has is on the increased demand for old dolls. And, of course, since the number of old dolls available is limited, the increased demand necessarily raises the prices of old dolls, as a larger number of collectors are vying for the same number of dolls. It is true that some dolls are still turning up from long-time storage in basements and attics, and these are certainly welcome additions to the doll market, yet this increase in numbers of dolls available is insignificant when compared to the numbers of new collectors entering the marketplace.

With the average doll representing a purchase of at least several hundred dollars, it follows that collectors must be as well-informed as possible about the dolls they are considering as additions to their collections. It follows also that if a collector is not particularly well-informed about the doll in question, he should not purchase it unless he has confidence in the person selling it to him. With today's prices, the assembling of a doll collection becomes rather costly and purchases must be made wisely. Actually, very few people buy dolls strictly as an investment, but most collectors expect to at least break even when they eventually sell their dolls. Unfortunately, there is no guarantee that any particular doll will appreciate consistently year after year. However, the track record on old or antique dolls is fairly good. If you are thinking of future sale of your collection, be wary of buying expensive reproduction dolls. They have no track record and little resale value.

Although many collectors rationalize their purchases by saying that they are making a good investment, they are still actually buying the doll because they like it — it has appeal to them for some reason: perhaps as an object of artistic beauty, perhaps because it evokes some kind of sentiment, perhaps it fills some need that they feel, or perhaps it speaks to something inside them. It is this personal feeling toward the doll which makes it of value to the collector. To what monetary extent a collector will go to obtain the yearned-for dolls, however, is dictated by his financial resources and his willingness to part with them. Unfortunately for most of us, there are enough collectors with the funds available who can afford to purchase the very rare and desirable dolls which cost thousands of dollars each. The rest of us will be content to collect the dolls we can comfortably afford, and even some we cannot comfortably afford, but go out on a limb to buy. Because most of us have only limited funds for purchasing dolls, we must be sure that we are spending our dollars to the best advantage. There are many factors to consider when buying a doll, and this chapter will give some suggestions about what to look for and what to consider when purchasing a doll.

MARKS

Fortunately for collectors a good number of the antique bisque, some of the papier-mâché, cloth, and other types of antique dolls are marked or labeled. This is particularly helpful to the beginning collector who is trying to sort out the doll spectrum. It also gives the buyer confidence: he or she knows exactly what has been purchased because of the mark or label which has given a trade name or identified the maker or the country of origin or even given a patent date or a style or mold number. With a little study a collector will soon discover that a doll marked "A. M. 390," even though she is in good condition and well-dressed, is plentiful and should not cost as much as the harder-to-find S & H 1039 doll in the same size and condition. Going one step further, an S & H 1279 girl would be even higher in cost because she has a more unusual character face. Dolls by some makers are more desirable than those by another maker: a Kestner doll, always known for especially high quality, brings a higher price than a comparable doll made by Recknagle. There are even gradations of dolls by the same maker: a Greiner doll with a '58 label is more desirable than one with a '72 label. A *Bourgoin* Steiner is higher in price than a *Le Parisien* one.

Sweet-faced doll of fine quality bisque, incised: "DEP" on stamped Jumeau body. *Betty Harms Collection.*

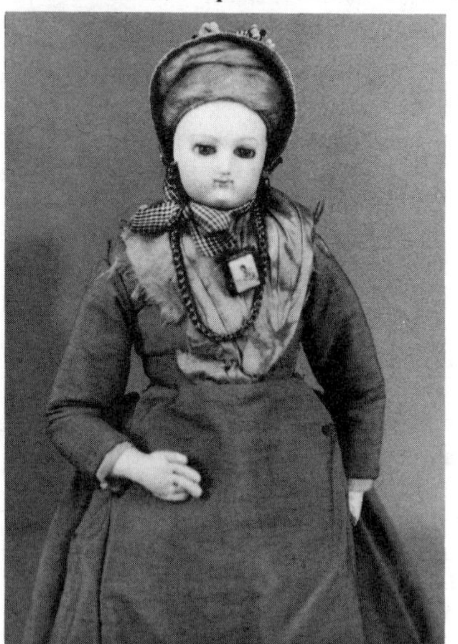

French Fashion lady on original cloth body with kid arms, totally original wig and outfit of simple handmade clothes. *H&J Foulke, Inc.*

Again, fortunately for collectors most of the composition and modern dolls are marked with the maker's name and sometimes also the trade name. A *Jane Withers* doll is higher in price and harder to find than one marked *Patsy*. With so many imitations prevalant in the American doll industry, it is important for a *Shirley Temple* doll to be marked as assurance that the high price being paid is for the genuine article and not for a lookalike doll. Many modern dolls have other methods of identification beside marks on the doll. Some, especially those by Madame Alexander, have tagged clothes, and many still retain their original wrist hang tags.

Of course, many dolls are unmarked, but after you have seen quite a few dolls, you begin to notice their individual characteristics, so that you can often determine what a doll possibly is. After a collector has some experience buying dolls, he or she begins to recognize an unusual face or an especially fine quality doll. Then there should be no hesitation about buying a doll marked only with a mold number or no mark at all. Many fine and unusual dolls do not carry a maker's name or any identifying number or symbol. The doll has to speak for itself, and price must be based upon the collector's frame of doll reference. That is, one must relate the face and quality to those of a known doll maker and make price judgments from that point.

QUALITY

But even the mark does not tell all about a doll. Two examples from exactly the same mold could look entirely different and carry vastly different prices because of the quality of the work done on the doll. To command top price, a bisque doll should have lovely bisque, decoration, eyes and hair. A collector studying many dolls will soon see that the quality varies from head to head, even with dolls made from the same mold by one firm. Before purchasing a doll, the collector should determine whether the example is the best to be found of that type. Even the molding of one head can be much sharper with more delineation of details such as dimples or locks of hair. This molding detail is especially important to notice when purchasing dolls with character faces or dolls with molded hair.

The quality of the bisque should be smooth and silky; dolls with bisque which is rough, pimply, or peppered with tiny black specks would be second choices. However, collectors must also keep in mind that many heads were put out from the factories with small manufacturing defects as companies were in business for profit and were producing play items, not works of art. The tinting of the complexion should be subdued and even, not harsh and splotchy, although the amount of color acceptable is often a matter of personal preference, some collectors liking very pale white bisque and others preferring a little more pink.

Since doll heads are hand-painted, one of good quality should show artistic skill in the portrayal of the expression on the face and in details, such as the lips, eyebrows and eyelashes. On a doll with molded hair, individual brush marks to give the hair a more realistic look would be a desired detail.

If a doll has a wig, the hair should be appropriate if not old. Dynel or synthetic wigs are not appropriate for antique dolls; a human hair or good quality mohair wig should be used. Another important feature is the doll's eyes which should have a natural and lifelike appearance. If they are glass, they should have good natural color and threading in the irises. If they are painted, they should show highlights and shading.

If a doll does not meet all of these standards, it should be priced lower than one that does. Furthermore, an especially fine example with original or contemporary old clothes would bring a premium over an ordinary but nice model.

CONDITION

Another factor which is important when pricing a doll is the condition. A bisque doll with a crack on the face or extensive professional repair would sell for considerably less than a doll with only normal wear; a hairline or a small professional repair in an inconspicuous place would decrease the value somewhat, but not nearly so much. Sometimes a head will have a factory flaw which occurred in the making, such as a cooking crack, scratch, piece of kiln debris or a ridge not smoothed out. Since the factory was producing toys for a profit and not creating works of art, all heads with slight flaws were not discarded, especially if they were in an inconspicuous place or could be covered. If these factory defects are slight and not detracting, they have little or no affect on the value of the doll, and whether or not to purchase such a doll would be a matter of personal opinion.

It is to be expected that an old doll will show some wear: perhaps there is a rub on the nose or cheek, or maybe a chipped earring hole; a Schoenhut doll or a Käthe Kruse may have some scuffs; an old papier-mâché may have a few age cracks; a china head may show wear on the hair; an old composition body may have scuffed toes or missing fingers. These are to be expected and do not necessarily affect the value of the doll. However, collectors are now paying particular attention to the condition of Lencis, Schoenhuts, and *Shirley Temples* as well as other composition dolls. A fine example will bring three times more than a played-with model. Certainly, an old doll in never-played-with condition with original hair and clothes,

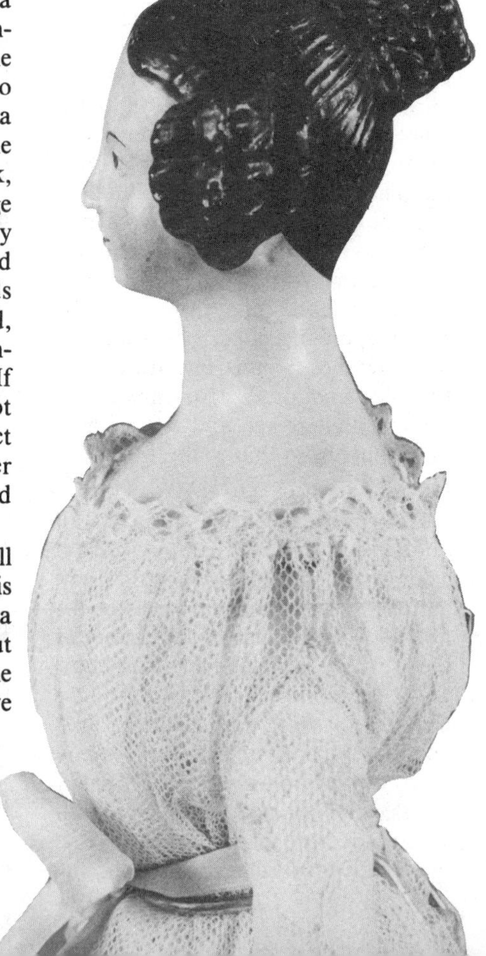

Large molded hair papier-mâché lady with interesting hairdo featuring side curls and a coiled braid bun, kid body with wooden lower limbs, totally original. *Pearl D. Morley Collection.*

perhaps even in its original box is every collector's dream — and would carry the highest of all prices for that type of doll.

Unless an antique doll is rare or you particularly want it, do not pay top price for a doll which needs extensive work: restringing, setting eyes, repairing fingers, replacing body parts, new wig, dressing — all of these repairs add up to a considerable sum at the doll hospital, possibly making the total cost of the doll more than it is really worth.

Composition dolls in perfect condition are becoming harder to find. As their material is so susceptible to the atmosphere, their condition can deteriorate literally overnight. Even in excellent condition, a composition doll nearly always has some fine crazing or perhaps slight fading. It is very difficult to find a composition doll in mint condition and even harder to be sure that it will stay that way. However, if a composition doll is at top price, there should be little or no crazing, excellent coloring, original uncombed hair, and original clothes in excellent condition; the doll should be unplayed with. Pay less for a doll which does not have original clothes and hair or one which may be all original but shows extensive play wear. Pay even less for one which has heavy crazing and cracking or other damages.

The hard plastic and vinyl dolls must be in mint condition if they are at top price. The hair should be perfect in the original set; clothes should be completely original and unfaded. Skin tones should be natural with good cheek color; avoid dolls which have turned yellow.

BODY

A buyer should inspect not only the head of an antique doll, but also the body. In order to command a top price, an old doll should have the original or an appropriate old body in good condition. If a doll does not have the correct type of body, the buyer ends up not with a complete doll, but with two parts — head and body — not worth as much as one whole doll. Fortunately for collectors makers such as H. Handwerck, Kestner, Koenig & Wernicke, Jumeau, and J. Steiner, did mark their bodies, helping to remove some of the guesswork from their dolls. As dolls are becoming harder to find, more are turning up with "put together" bodies; therefore, it is necessary for the buyer to check all of the body parts of make sure that they are all appropriate to each other. A body which has mixed parts from several makers or types of bodies is not worth as much as one which has parts original to each other.

Minor damage or repair to an old body parts to make sure that they are antique doll. An original body carefully repaired, recovered or even completely refinished, if necessary, is preferable to a new one. An antique head on a new body would be worth only the value of its parts, whatever the price of the head and the new body, not the full price of an antique doll. It is just a rule of thumb that an antique head is worth about one-third to one-half the price of a complete doll.

If there is a choice of body types for the same bisque head, a good quality ball-jointed composition body is more desirable than a crudely made five-piece body or a stick-type body with just pieces of turned wood for upper arms and legs. This is often the case for heads made by Armand Marseille and Gebrüder Heubach as well as other companies which made only heads and not bodies. Unfortunately, many of the small German character heads came on these crude bodies, and collectors just have to live with them. J. D. Kestner was the only German firm to make both heads and bodies. Other doll factories bought their heads from porcelain factories, some of which were Armand Marseille, Ernst Heubach, Simon & Halbig, Kling & Co, Gebrüder Heubach, Bähr & Pröschild, and Alt, Beck & Gottschalck.

Occasionally, the body adds value to the doll. For instance, in the case of bisque heads, a small doll with a completely jointed body, a French fashion-type with a wood-jointed body, a *Tête Jumeau* head on an adult body or a character baby head on a jointed toddler-type body would all be higher in price because of their special bodies.

As for the later modern dolls, a composition doll on the wrong body or on a body in poor condition which was cracked and peeling would have a greatly reduced value. The same is true of a vinyl doll with replaced parts, body stains, or chewed-off fingers.

CLOTHING

A buyer should look at the clothing critically in considering the value of the doll. Because as the years go by fabrics deteriorate, it is becoming increasingly difficult to find dolls in old clothes. As a result, collectors are paying more for an antique doll if it has old clothes. When the clothing has been replaced on an antique doll, it should be appropriately styled for the age of the doll, made in fabrics which would have been used when the doll was produced. Original clothes are, of course, highly desirable and even faded, somewhat worn, or carefully mended ones are preferable to new clothes. However, it is often difficult to determine whether or not the clothes are original or simply just old ones. Many antique dolls came undressed or clad only in a chemise and were dressed at home.

A doll with original clothes is certainly more valuable and higher in price than one with replaced clothes. Unfortunately, because these clothes are sometimes faded or worn or not of a style preferred by the buyer, they are removed and the doll is redressed while the original clothes are lost. This is certainly an unfortunate circumstance, and it is hoped that collectors who feel that they must redress their dolls will show respect for the original clothes and keep them in a labeled bag or box for giving to the next owner should the dolls ever be sold or passed down to another family member. Dolls are heirlooms and part of their charm is their clothing which is also part of social history. Present owners are only custodians for a short time in history.

For the first time, antique dolls are just now beginning to attract the attention of the buyers in the art market. As these people enter the doll field, they will be looking for the top-of-the-line dolls with original clothing for which they are willing to pay record prices. Doll collectors must realize that some of their dolls are truly works of art. They must be treated as such, and in the future many will be sold as such. The art market is currently beginning to buy early French dolls, rare German character dolls, pre-Greiners, Izannah Walkers, and other early types. These buyers want the dolls in pristine condition with original clothes.

To bring top price, a modern doll must have original clothes. It is usually fairly easy to determine whether or not the clothing is original and factory made. Many makers, such as Madame Alexander, placed tags in the doll's clothing. Replaced clothing greatly reduces the price of modern dolls. Also without the clothing it is often impossible to identify a modern doll as so many were made using the same face mold.

TOTAL ORIGINALITY

Having already discussed body, wig, eyes and clothes, this would seem to be a good place to put in a word about the total originality of an antique doll. An antique doll which has all original parts and clothes is much more valuable than one which has replaced wig, body parts, eyes, pate, clothes, and so on. Collectors try to ascertain that the head and body and all other parts are not only appropriate, but have always been together. Of course, this is not always possible to determine when a doll has seen hard play for several generations or has passed through many hands before reaching the collector. However, sometimes if the original source of the doll is known, the collector can be reasonably sure by using a little knowledge as well as common sense. Totally original dolls nowadays are few and far between, but the determined searcher can still be rewarded.

SIZE

The size of the doll is always taken into account when determining a price. Usually the price and size are related for a certain type of doll — a smaller size is lower, a larger size is higher. The greatest variances of price to size occur at the extremes, either a very small or a very large doll. On the large side, bisque head dolls, especially over 30in (76cm) are in demand and have risen in price; the large 36in (91cm) vinyl *Shirley Temple* and the 30in (76cm) *Patsy Mae* are very difficult to find. On the tiny side, the small closed-mouth Jumeau, tiny German dolly-faced dolls on fully-jointed bodies, and the composition *Wee Patsy* and 11in (28cm) *Shirley Temple* are examples of dolls which bring higher prices than dolls in their series which may be larger.

AGE

Another important point to consider in pricing a doll is its age. An early Queen Anne wood doll is more greatly valued than a late 19th century penny wooden one. However, curiously enough to beginners, the oldest dolls do not necessarily command the highest prices. A lovely old china head with exquisite decoration and very unusual hairdo would bring a good price, but not as much as a 20th century S.F.B.J. 252 pouty. Many desirable composition dolls of the 1930s and fairly recent but discontinued Alexander dolls are selling at prices higher than older bisque dolls of 1890 to 1920. So, in determining price, the age of the doll may or may not be significant, according to the specific type.

AVAILABILITY

The availability of a doll is based on how easy or difficult it is to find. Each year brings more new doll collectors than it brings newly-discovered desirable old dolls; hence the supply is diminished. As long as the demand for certain antique and col-

Effanbee ***Barbara Ann***, totally original and in mint condition. *Beth Foulke Collection.*

Käthe Kruse doll with wig, totally original and in mint condition. *Rosemary Dent Collection.*

lectible dolls is greater than the supply, prices will rise. This explains the great increase in prices of less common dolls, such as the K & R and S.F.B.J. characters, the early French and German closed-mouth dolls, googlies, composition personality dolls, and some Alexander dolls which were made for only a limited period of time. Dolls which are fairly common, primarily the German girl or child dolls and the china-head dolls which were made over a longer period of time, show a more gentle increase in price. The price of a doll is comensurate and directly related to its availability.

POPULARITY

Sometimes, it is the popularity of a certain doll which makes the price rise. There are fads in dolls just like in clothes, food, and other aspects of life. Dolls which are rising in price because of their popularity are the American cloth dolls, Käthe Kruse dolls, and large German bisque "dolly-faced" dolls. Some dolls are popular enough to tempt collectors to pay prices higher than the availability factor warrants. Although *Shirley Temples*, Jumeaus, *Bye-Los,* Heubach pouty characters, S & H 1249s, and most hard plastic and vinyl Alexanders are not rare, the high prices they bring are due to their popularity.

UNIQUENESS

Sometimes the uniqueness of a doll makes price determination very difficult. If a collector has never seen a doll exactly like it before, and it is not given in the price guide or even shown in any books, deciding what to pay can be a problem. In this case, the buyer has to use all of his available knowledge as a frame of reference in

Vogue ***Ginny*** doll, mint in original box with extra wardrobe items. *Beth Foulke Collection.*

which to place the unknown doll. Perhaps a doll marked "A.M. 2000" or "S & H 1289" has been found, but is not listed in the price guide. The price is 25 percent higher than for the more commonly found numbers by that maker and the collector must decide on his own whether or not the doll is worth the price. (Of course, if would be!) Perhaps a dealer offers a black *Kamkins* for twice the price of a white one, but she is not listed in the price guide. A collector must use his own judgment to determine what the doll is worth to him.

RETAIL PRICE

An important factor which helps determine what asking price goes on the doll in a dealer's stock is the price which the dealer himself had to pay for it. In buying a doll, a dealer has to consider all aspects of the doll discussed in this chapter in addition to whether or not there is a possibility of making a reasonable profit on the doll. A dealer, when buying stock, cannot pay the prices listed in the price guide; he must buy somewhat lower if he expects to make a profit. In order to obtain stock, a dealer looks to disbursement of estates, auctions, collectors and other dealers as possible doll sources — all of which are also available to collectors who can purchase from these sources at the same prices that dealers can. Contrary to what many collectors believe, dealers in antique dolls do not make enormous profits. Their margin of profit is not nearly so high as that of the proprietor of a shop which sells new items. This is primarily due to the availability factor already discussed. Old dolls cannot be ordered from a wholesale catalog. Most are coming from estates or collections, whose owners, understandably enough, want to get as much as they can for their dolls. Expenses involved in exhibiting at shows include booth rent and travel costs which are quite high. To the price which he must pay for a doll, a dealer must figure in his costs and percentage of profit to come up with a dollar amount for the price tag.

The price for a doll which is listed in the price guide is the retail value of a doll fulfilling all of the criteria discussed if it is purchased from a dealer. Collectors, however, sometimes have other sources of dolls where the price could be somewhat lower. Sometimes collectors will sell to each other at less than "book price" or sometimes a dealer will undersell a doll if he wants to turn stock fast or if he obtains a type of doll which he does not usually carry. Then, too, collectors just might get a lucky price at an antique shop, garage sale, flea market or just about anywhere that there might be an old doll!

A.T.

Maker: Possibly by A. Thuillier, Paris, France
Date: 1875—1890
Material: Bisque socket head on wooden, kid or composition body
Size: Size 1 is usually 9in (23cm); size 14 is 29in (74cm)
Mark: "A.T." and size number (1-14 known) incised as shown or with size number between the A and T

AT•N° 8

Marked A. T. Child: Perfect bisque head, cork pate, good wig, paperweight eyes, pierced ears, closed mouth; body of wood, kid or composition in good condition; appropriate clothes.

20in (51cm) **$16,500—18,500 up**

16in (41cm) A. T. *Rhoda Shoemaker Collection. Photograph courtesy of the owner.*

Alabama Indestructible Doll

Maker: Ella Smith Doll Co., Roanoke, AL., U.S.A.
Date: 1904—on
Material: All-cloth
Size: 11½—22½in (29—57cm) known
Mark: On torso or leg, sometimes both:

PAT. NOV. 9, 1912
NO. 2
ELLA SMITH DOLL CO.
or
"MRS. S. S. SMITH
Manufacturer and Dealer to
The Alabama Indestructible Doll
Roanoke, Ala.
PATENTED Sept. 26, 1905"
(also 1907 on some)

Alabama Baby: All-cloth, painted with oils, tab-jointed shoulders and hips, painted hair and features, molded face, applied ears, painted stockings and shoes; appropriate clothes; all in good condition.
17—19in (43—48cm) **$800—850**

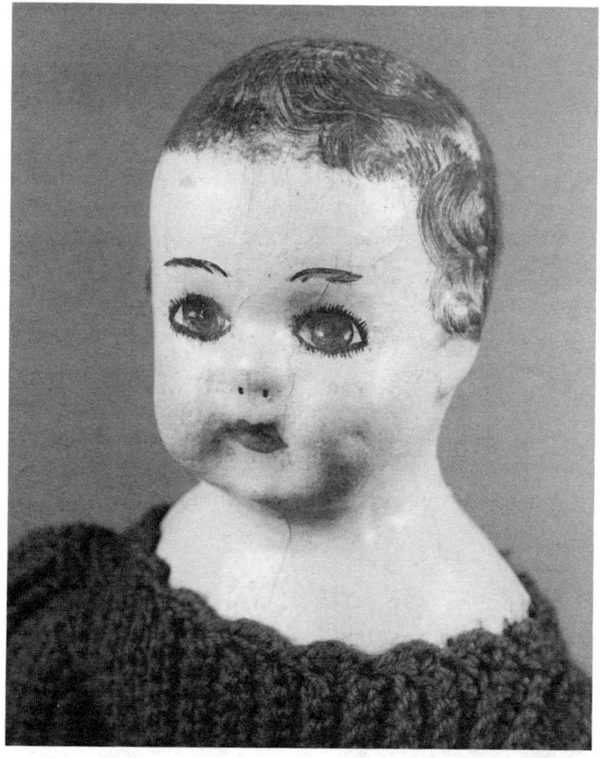

18in (46cm) ***Alabama Baby.*** *Dr. Carole Stoessel Zvonar Collection.*

Madame Alexander

Maker: Alexander Doll Co., New York, N.Y., U.S.A.
Date: 1923—on
Mark: Dolls themselves marked in various ways, usually "ALEXANDER". Clothing has a white cloth label with blue lettering sewn into a seam which says "MADAME ALEXANDER" and usually the name of the specific doll.

CLOTH

Alice in Wonderland: Ca. 1930. All-cloth with one-piece arms and legs sewn on; yellow yarn hair, flat face with hand-painted features, large round eyes, O-shaped mouth; later dolls had molded mask face; original blue and white dress with apron; all in good condition.
16in (41cm) **$350—400****

Cloth Character Dolls: Ca. 1933 through the 1930s. All-cloth with one-piece arms and legs sewn on; mohair wig, molded mask face of felt or flocked fabric, painted eyes to the side; original clothes tagged with name of particular doll. Produced characters from *Little Women*, Charles Dickens, Longfellow and other literary works as well as storybook characters.
16in (41cm) Good **$300—350**
Mint **500—600**

Cloth Dionne Quintuplet: Ca. 1936. All-cloth with molded felt or flocked mask face, soft-stuffed pink stockinette body with flexible arms and legs; brown human hair wig, painted brown eyes with long upper and lower eyelashes; original tagged clothes; all in good condition. Came in sizes 13in (33cm), 17in (43cm) and 21in (53cm). Gold-colored name pin or necklace.
17in (43cm) **$450—500****

**Not enough price samples to compute a reliable range.

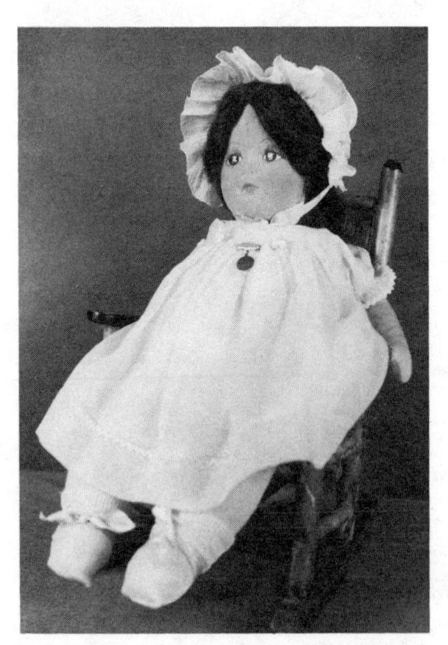

17in (43cm) all-cloth Dionne Quintuplet ***Marie***, all original with pin. *Miriam Blankman Collection.*

Madame Alexander continued

Susie Q. & Bobby Q.: Ca. 1938. All-cloth with turning head, yellow or red yarn braids, mask face, large side-painted googly eyes, button nose, tiny closed mouth; striped stocking legs, white felt spats; original tagged clothes including hat, coat and cardboard suitcase; all in good condition. Came in sizes 12—13in (31—33cm) and 15—16in (38—41cm).

All Sizes **$500****

**Not enough price samples to compute a reliable range.

15in (38cm) ***Susie Q***, all original, but missing her hat.

Little Shaver: 1942. Stuffed pink stocking body, curved arms, tiny waist; floss wig glued on; mask face with large painted eyes to the side, tiny mouth; original clothes, all in good condition. Various sizes.

MARK: Cloth dress tag:

"Little Shaver
Madame Alexander
New York
All Rights Reserved."

7in (18cm)	**$225—250**
10—12in (25—31cm)	**225—250**
16in (41cm)	**325—375**

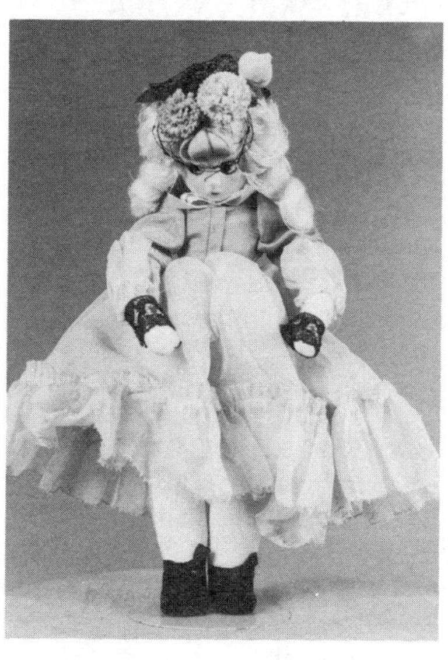

10in (25cm) ***Little Shaver***, all original.
H&J Foulke, Inc.

Madame Alexander continued

COMPOSITION

Tony Sarg Marionettes: 1934. Composition character faces, composition torso, arms and legs with painted shoes, cloth upper limbs; original clothes; all in good condition.

MARK: On torso:
"TONY SARG
ALEXANDER"
On head:
"TONY
SARG"
On clothing: "Madame Alexander"; sometimes with the name of the character.

10—12in (25—31cm) **$150**

12in (31cm) Tony Sarg ***Snow White*** marionette. *H&J Foulke, Inc.*

Dionne Quintuplets: 1935. All-composition with swivel head, jointed hips and shoulders, toddler or bent-limb legs; wigs or molded hair, sleep or painted eyes; original clothing, all in good condition.

MARK: "ALEXANDER"
sometimes "DIONNE"
Clothing label:
"GENUINE
DIONNE QUINTUPLET DOLLS
ALL RIGHTS RESERVED
MADAME ALEXANDER, N.Y."
or
"DIONNE QUINTUPLET
(her name)
EXCLUSIVE LICENSEE
MADAM [sic] ALEXANDER
DOLL CO."

7—8in (18—20cm) **$175—200**
10in (25cm) baby **300**
11in (28cm) toddler **350**
14in (36cm) toddler **450**
16in (41cm) baby **400**
Pins **$75 each**

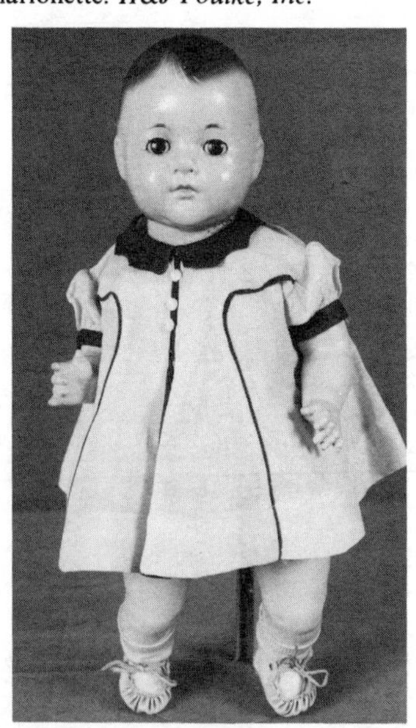

17in (43cm) Dionne Quintuplet baby, all original. *H&J Foulke, Inc.*

Madame Alexander continued

7in (18cm) Dionne Quintuplet baby *Cecile*, all original. *H&J Foulke, Inc.*

Dr. Dafoe: 1936. All-composition with swivel head, jointed hips and shoulders; gray wig, painted eyes, smiling face; original tagged doctor's outfit; all in good condition; doll unmarked.

14in (36cm) **$550—650**

Foreign and Storyland: Ca. 1935 to mid 1940s. All-composition with one-piece head and body on smaller ones and separate head on larger ones, jointed shoulders and hips; mohair wig, painted eyes; original tagged clothes; all in good condition. Made children to represent foreign lands as well as storybook characters.

MARK: On back: "Mme. Alexander"

7—9in (18—23cm) **$150—200***

*More for special characters.

14in (36cm) ***Dr. Dafoe***, all original. *India Stoessel Collection.*

7in (18cm) ***January*** Birthday Doll, all original. *H&J Foulke, Inc.*

Madame Alexander continued

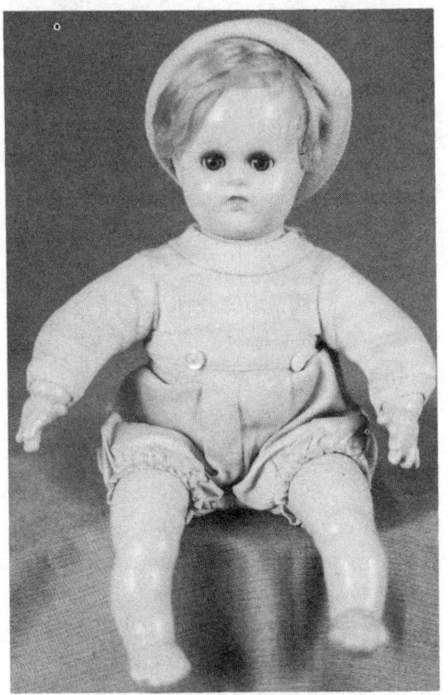

Babies: 1936—on. Composition head, hands and legs, cloth bodies; molded hair or wigged, sleep eyes, open or closed mouth; original clothes; all in good condition.

MARK: On dolls:
"ALEXANDER"
On clothing: "Little Genius", "Baby McGuffey", "Pinky", "Precious", "Butch", "Bitsey" and so on.

11—12in (28—31cm)	**$150—175**
16—18in (41—46cm)	**200**
24in (61cm)	**250**

12in (31cm) ***Butch***, all original. *H&J Foulke, Inc.*

Dopey: 1938. Composition character head, cloth body; original felt outfit.

13in (33cm) **$200—225**

Little Colonel: 1935. All-composition with swivel head, jointed hips and shoulders; mohair wig, sleep eyes, closed mouth, dimples; original clothes; all in good condition.

MARK: On head:
"ALEXANDER"
or none
On dress tag:
"Madame Alexander"

13—14in (33—36cm) **$500—550**

13in (33cm) ***Little Colonel***, all original. *H&J Foulke, Inc.*

Madame Alexander continued

13in (33cm) ***Princess Elizabeth***, all original. *H&J Foulke, Inc.*

13in (33cm) ***Snow White***, all original. *H&J Foulke, Inc.*

Princess Elizabeth: 1937. All-composition, jointed at neck, shoulders and hips; mohair wig, sleep eyes, open mouth; original clothes; all in good condition.
MARK: On head:
"PRINCESS ELIZABETH
ALEXANDER DOLL CO."
On dress tag:
"Princess Elizabeth"

13in (33cm) **$275**
16in (41cm) **300—325**
20in (51cm) **350—400**

Snow White: 1937. All-composition, jointed neck, shoulders and hips; black mohair wig, brown sleep eyes, very pale complexion, closed mouth; original clothes; all in good condition.
MARK: On head:
"PRINCESS ELIZABETH
ALEXANDER DOLL CO."
On dress tag: "Snow White"

13in (33cm) **$250**
16—18in (41—46cm) **300—350**

Baby Jane: 1935. All-composition with swivel head, jointed hips and shoulders; mohair wig, sleep eyes, open mouth; original clothes; all in good condition.
MARK: On head:

"Baby Jane
Reg Mme. Alexander"

16in (41cm) **$550—600**

Madame Alexander continued

Flora McFlimsey: 1938. All-composition, jointed at neck, shoulders and hips; red human hair wig with bangs, sleep eyes, open mouth, freckles on nose; original clothes; all in good condition.
MARK: On head:
"PRINCESS ELIZABETH
ALEXANDER DOLL CO."
On dress:
"Flora McFlimsey
of Madison Square
by Madame Alexander, N.Y."
13—15in (33—38cm) **$500—600**

16in (41cm) ***McGuffey Ana***, all original.
H&J Foulke, Inc.

Kate Greenaway: 1938. All-composition with swivel head, jointed shoulders and hips; blonde wig, sleep eyes with eyelashes, open mouth; original clothes; all in good condition.
MARK: On head:
"PRINCESS ELIZABETH
ALEXANDER DOLL CO."
On dress tag: "Kate Greenaway"
15—18in (38—46cm) **$400—450**

McGuffey Ana: 1937. All-composition, jointed at shoulders, hips and neck; blonde human hair or mohair pigtails, sleep eyes, open mouth, original clothes; all in good condition.
MARK: On Head:
"PRINCESS ELIZABETH
ALEXANDER"
On dress tag: "McGuffey Ana"

9in(23cm)	**$200—225**
12—13in (31—33cm)	**300—325**
16—18in (41—46cm)	**375—400**
20in (51cm)	**425**

Wendy-Ann: 1936. All-composition with swivel head, jointed at neck, shoulders, hips and **waist**; human hair wig, sleep eyes, closed mouth; original clothes; all in good condition.
MARK:
"WENDY-ANN
MME ALEXANDER"

9in (23cm) painted eyes	**$200—225**
14in (36cm)	**325—350**
21in (53cm)	**400—450**

Madame Alexander continued

Scarlet O'Hara: 1937. All-composition, jointed at neck, shoulders and hips; original black wig, green sleep eyes, closed mouth; original clothes; all in good condition.

MARK: On dress tag:
"Scarlet O'Hara
Madame Alexander
N.Y. U.S.A.
All Rights reserved"

Note: Sometimes the name is spelled "Scarlet" and other times it is spelled "Scarlett".

11in (28cm) **$350—375**
14in (36cm) **400—450**
18in (46cm) **450—500**

18in (46cm) ***Scarlet O'Hara***, all original.
H&J Foulke, Inc.

Jane Withers: 1937. All-composition with swivel head, jointed shoulders and hips; dark mohair wig, sleep eyes, open smiling mouth; original clothes; all in good condition.

MARK: On dress:
"Jane Withers
All Rights Reserved
Madame Alexander, N.Y."

12in (31cm)
closed mouth **$650—700**
15—16in (38—41cm) **750—850**
21in (53cm) **900—1000**

14in (36cm) ***Wendy-Ann***, all original.
H&J Foulke, Inc.

Madame Alexander continued

Sonja Henie: 1939. All-composition, jointed at neck, shoulders and hips; human hair or mohair wig, sleep eyes, smiling open mouth with teeth; original clothes; all in good condition. Various sizes. 14in (35.6cm) can be found on the WENDY-ANN body with swivel waist.

MARK: On back of neck:
"MADAME ALEXANDER-
SONJA HENIE"
On dress: "Sonja Henie"

13—14in (33—36cm) **$275—325**
18in (46cm) **375—400**
21in (53cm) **425**

Madelaine: 1940. All-composition, jointed at neck, shoulders and hips; dark wig, sleep eyes, closed mouth; original clothes; all in good condition.

MARK: On head:
"ALEXANDER"
On dress tag: "Madelaine" or
"Madelaine Du Baine"

14in (36cm) **$325**
18in (46cm) **400—450**

14in (36cm) ***Bridesmaid***, all original. *H&J Foulke, Inc.*

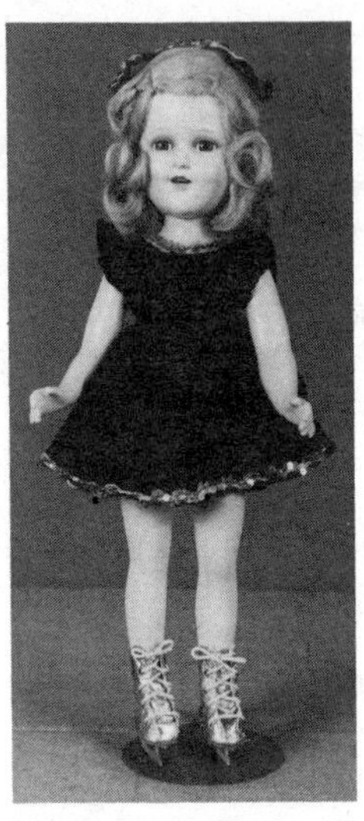

18in (46cm) ***Sonja Henie***, all original. *H&J Foulke, Inc.*

Bride and Bridesmaids: 1940—on. All-composition, jointed at neck, shoulders and hips; mohair wig, sleep eyes, closed mouth; original clothes; all in good condition.

MARK: On head:
"MME ALEXANDER"
On dress: "Madame Alexander"

14in (36cm) **$225**
18in (46cm) **275**
21in (53cm) **300**

Portrait Dolls: 1940s. All-composition, jointed at neck, shoulders and hips; mohair or human hair wig, sleep eyes, closed mouth, painted fingernails; original clothes; all in good condition. Came with green cloverleaf wrist tag.

MARK: None on doll; label inside dress: "Madame Alexander"

21in (53cm) **$450—500**

Madame Alexander continued

Jeannie Walker: 1941. Composition, jointed at neck, shoulders and hips, with walking mechanism; human hair or mohair wig, sleep eyes, closed mouth; original clothes; all in good condition.

MARK: On body:
"ALEXANDER/PAT. NO. 2171281"
On dress:
"Jeannie Walker —
Madame Alexander — N.Y., U.S.A.
All rights reserved"

13—14in (33—36cm) **$350—400**
18in (46cm) **500**

Carmen (Miranda): 1942. Composition, jointed at neck, shoulders and hips; black mohair wig, sleep eyes, closed mouth; original clothes including turban and gold-hoop earrings; all in good condition.

MARK: On head:
"MME. ALEXANDER"
On dress:
"Carmen
Madame Alexander, N.Y. U.S.A.
All Rights Reserved"

9in (23cm) **$200**
14—15in (36—38cm) **300**

Fairy Princess: 1942. Composition, jointed at neck, shoulders and hips; mohair wig, sleep eyes, closed mouth; original clothes including tiara and necklace; all in good condition.

MARK: On head:
"MME ALEXANDER"
On dress: "Fairy Princess"

14in (36cm) **$250**
18in (46cm) **300**

Special Girl: 1942. Composition head, shoulder plate, arms and legs, cloth torso; blonde braids. Doll unmarked; clothing tagged: "Madame Alexander".

22in (56cm) **$300—325**

Margaret O'Brien: 1946. All-composition, jointed at neck, shoulders and hips; dark wig in braids, sleep eyes, closed mouth; original clothes; all in good condition.

MARK: On head:
"ALEXANDER"
On dress tag:
"Madame Alexander
'Margaret O'Brien' "

14in (36cm) **$400—450**
18—21in (46—53cm) **600—700**

18in (46cm) ***Margaret O'Brien***, all original. *Rosemary Dent Collection.*

Madame Alexander continued

Karen Ballerina: 1946. All-composition, jointed at neck, shoulders and hips; blonde wig with coiled braids and flowers, sleep eyes, closed mouth; original clothes; all in good condition.
MARK: On head:
"ALEXANDER"
On dress tag:
"Madame Alexander"
18—21in (46—53cm) **$400—450**

Alice in Wonderland: 1947. All-composition, jointed at neck, shoulders and hips; blonde wig, sleep eyes, closed mouth; original clothes; all in good condition.
MARK: On head:
"ALEXANDER"
On dress tag:
"Alice in Wonderland"
13—14in (33—36cm) **$250—275**
18—21in (46—53cm) **300—350**

14in (36cm) ***Margaret Rose***, all original. *H&J Foulke, Inc.*

14in (36cm) ***Nina Ballerina***, all original. *H&J Foulke, Inc.*

HARD PLASTIC

Margaret Face: 1948—on. All-hard plastic, jointed at neck, shoulders and hips; lovely wig, sleep eyes, closed mouth; original clothes tagged with name of doll; all in excellent condition. All prices for the 14in (36cm) size except ***Wendy-Ann*** and ***Prince Phillip*** which are 18in (46cm).

Nina Ballerina, 1949—1951	**$250—300**
Fairy Queen, 1947—1948	**250—275**
Babs, 1948—1949	**250—275**
Margaret Rose, 1948—1953?	**250—275**
Margaret O'Brien, 1948	**450—500**
Wendy-Ann, 1947—1948	**275—325**
Wendy Bride, 1950	**250—275**
Cinderella, 1950	**425—450**
Prince Charming, 1950	**500**
Cynthia (black), 1952—1953	**500**
Story Princess, 1954—1956	**325—350**
Wendy (from Peter Pan set), 1953	**450**
Prince Phillip, Ca. 1950	**500—600**

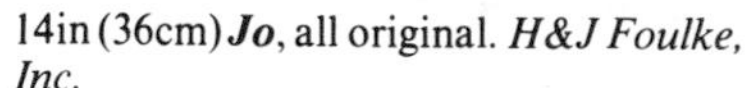

14in (36cm) ***Jo***, all original. *H&J Foulke, Inc.*

14in (36cm) ***Meg***, all original. *H&J Foulke, Inc.*

Little Women: 1948—1956. All-hard plastic, jointed at neck, shoulders and hips; synthetic wig, sleep eyes, closed mouth; original clothes; all in good condition. Some models have jointed knees.

MARK: On head:

"ALEXANDER" (used both "Maggie" and "Margaret" faces)

On clothes tag: "Meg", "Jo", "Beth", "Amy" and "Marme"

14—15in (36—38cm):

Floss hair, 1948—1950	**$300**
Dynel wig	**250—275**
Amy with loop curls	**350—375**
Little Men	**500**

Godey Ladies: 1950. All-hard plastic, jointed at neck, shoulders and hips; lovely wigs, sleep eyes; original period costumes; all in excellent condition.

14in (36cm) **$450—500**

Glamour Girls: 1953. All-hard plastic, jointed at neck, shoulders and hips, walkers; lovely human hair wigs; original period costumes; all in excellent condition.

18in (46cm) **$500—600**

14in (36cm) ***Peter Pan*** and ***Wendy***, all original. *Paula Ryscik Collection.*

Maggie Face: 1948—1956. All-hard plastic, jointed at neck, shoulders and hips; good quality wig, sleep eyes, closed mouth; original clothes tagged with the name of the doll; all in excellent condition.

Maggie, 1948—1953:
14in (36cm) **$225—250**
17in (43cm) **250—275**

Polly Pigtails, 1949:
14in (36cm) **275—300**

Kathy, 1951:
14in (36cm) **300**

Alice in Wonderland, 1950—1951:
14in (36cm) **225—250**
17in (43cm) **300—325**

Annabelle, 1952:
17in (43cm) **300—325**

Peter Pan, 1953 **450**

21in (53cm) ***Polly Pigtails***, all original. *Paula Ryscik Collection.*

Winnie and Binnie: 1953—1955. All-hard plastic, walking body, later with jointed knees and vinyl arms; lovely wig, sleep eyes, closed mouth; original clothes; all in excellent condition.

15in (38cm) **$200—225**
18in (46cm) **225—250**
24in (61cm) **300**

Cissy: 1955—1959. Head, torso and jointed legs of hard plastic, jointed vinyl arms; synthetic wig, sleep eyes, closed mouth, pierced ears; original clothes; all in excellent condition.

MARK: On head:
"ALEXANDER"
On dress tag: "Cissy"

21in (53cm) **$225 up***
Queen Elizabeth II **350—400**

Elise: 1957—1964. All-hard plastic with vinyl arms, completely jointed; lovely wig, sleep eyes, closed mouth; original clothes; all in excellent condition.

16½—17in (42—43cm) **$225 up***

*Depending upon costume.

Sleeping Beauty: 1959. All-hard plastic with vinyl arms, completely jointed; blonde wig, sleep eyes, closed mouth; original clothes; all in excellent condition.
16½in (42cm) **$450—500**

21in (53cm) ***Cissy***, all original. *H&J Foulke, Inc.*

Shari Lewis: 1959. All-hard plastic with slim fashion body; auburn hair, brown eyes, closed mouth; original clothes; all in excellent condition.
14in (36cm) **$350**
21in (53cm) **450**

16½in (42cm) ***Elise***, all original. *Virginia Ann Heyerdahl Collection.*

12in (31cm) ***Lissy***, all original. *H&J Foulke, Inc.*

Lissy: 1956—1958. All-hard plastic, jointed at neck, shoulders, hips, elbows and knees; synthetic wig, sleep eyes, closed mouth; original clothes; all in excellent condition.
MARK: None on doll
On dress tag: "Lissy"
or name of character
12in (31cm) **$350**

Kelly: 1959. Same doll as ***Lissy*** but does not have jointed elbows and knees; original clothes; all in excellent condition.
12in (31cm) **$350—400**

Little Women, 1957—1967 **$300**

Laurie, 1967 **500**

Katie, 1962 **1000—1200**

Tommy, 1962 **1000—1200**

Cissette: 1957—1963. All-hard plastic, jointed at neck, shoulders, hips and knees; synthetic wig, sleep eyes, closed mouth, pierced ears; original clothes; all in excellent condition.

MARK: None on doll
On dress tag: "Cissette"

10in (25cm) **$185 up***

Margot, 1961	**350**
Sleeping Beauty, 1960s	**350**
Jacqueline, 1962	**550**

Portrettes

Southern Belle, 1968	**$400**
Melinda (turquoise), 1968	**500**
Renoir (navy), 1968	**500**
Agatha, 1968	**500**
Godey, 1968—1970	**500**
Melinda (pink lace), 1969	**400**
Melanie (yellow lace), 1970	**400**
Jenny Lind, 1969—1970	**550**
Renoir (aqua), 1970	**500**
Scarlett, 1968—1973	**400**
Queen, 1972—1973	**400**
Southern Belle, 1969—1973	**400**

*Depending upon costume.

Maggie Mixup: 1960—1961. All-hard plastic, fully-jointed; red straight hair, green eyes, closed mouth, freckles; original clothes; all in excellent condition.

16½—17in (42—43cm) **$325—350**

16½in (42cm) ***Maggie Mixup***, all original. *H&J Foulke, Inc.*

10in (25cm) ***Scarlett***, all original. *Virginia Heyerdahl Collection.*

10in (25cm) ***Queen***, all original. *H&J Foulke, Inc.*

10in (25cm) ***Melinda***, 1968, all original. *H&J Foulke, Inc.*

Madame Alexander continued

Alexander-Kins: All-hard plastic, jointed at neck, shoulders and hips; synthetic wig, sleep eyes, closed mouth; original clothes; all in excellent condition.

7½—8in (19—20cm)
1953, straight leg non-walker
1954—1955, straight leg walker
1956—1964, bent-knee walker
1965—1972, bent knee
1973—current, straight leg
1978, face change
1981, white face

MARK: On back of torso:
"ALEX"
After 1978:
"MADAME ALEXANDER"
On dress tag:
"Madame Alexander"
"Alexander-Kins" or specific name of doll

Wendy in dresses	**$200 up**
Wendy Ballerina	**200 up**
Quizkin	**400**
Little Lady	**400**

Special Outfits:

Scarlett O'Hara, print dress	**350—400**
Enchanted Doll	**350—375**
Korea, Africa, Hawaii, Vietnam, Spanish Boy, Greek Boy, Morocco, Equador, Bolivia	**400—425**
Amish Boy and Girl, Cowboy, Cowgirl, English Guard, Pocahontas, Hiawatha	**500**
Bent-knee	
Internationals	**110—125**
Storybooks	**125—150**
Little Women	**135—150**
Maggie Mixup	**375**

8in (20cm) Alexander-Kin ***Cherry Blonde***, all original. *H&J Foulke, Inc.*

8in (20cm) Alexander-Kin ***Beth***, all original. *H&J Foulke, Inc.*

8in (20cm) ***Bo-Peep***, all original. *H&J Foulke, Inc.*

Madame Alexander continued

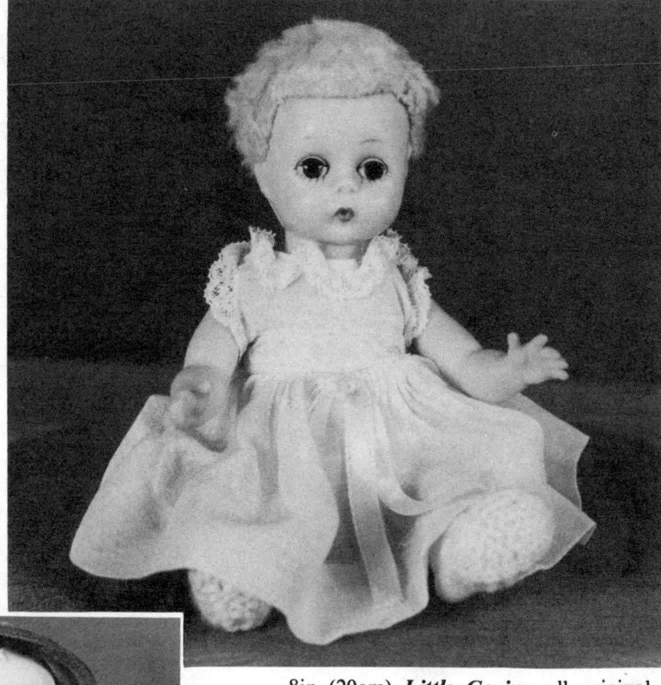

8in (20cm) ***Little Genius***, all original.
H&J Foulke, Inc.

10in (25cm) ***Little Boy Blue***, all original.
H&J Foulke, Inc.

Little Genius: 1956—1962. Hard plastic head with short curly wig, sleep eyes, drinks and wets; vinyl torso, arms and legs; original clothes; all in good condition.
8in (20cm) **$185**

Little Boy Blue: Ca. 1950. Vinyl head, molded and painted hair and eyes; stuffed "magic skin" body; original clothes; all in very good condition.
9—10in (23—25cm) **$150—175**

Sonja Henie: 1951. Vinyl character face with open smiling mouth and dimples, rooted hair; body of hard plastic; original clothes; all in excellent condition.
18in (46cm) **$500**

Madame Alexander continued

Madelaine: 1952, 1953, 1961. Vinyl character face with rooted hair; ball-jointed hard plastic body; original clothes; all in excellent condition.
18in (46cm) **$300—325**

Kathy: 1956—1962. All-vinyl, jointed at neck, shoulders and hips; molded or rooted hair, sleep eyes, drinks and wets; original clothes; all in good condition.
MARK: On dress tag: "Kathy";
also called "Kathy Cry Dolly" and "Kathy Tears"
Various sizes.
15in (38cm) **$100-125**

21in (53cm) ***Jacqueline***, all original. *H&J Foulke, Inc.*

Kelly Face: 1958—on. Vinyl character face with rooted hair, vinyl arms, hard plastic torso and legs, jointed waist; original clothes; all in excellent condition.
MARK: On head: MME © ALEXANDER

Kelly, 1958—1959:
15in (38cm) **$200—225**
Pollyana, 1960—1961:
15in (38cm) **225—250**
Marybel, 1959—1965:
15in (38cm), in case **275**
Edith, 1958—1959:
15in (38cm) **225—250**

Jacqueline: 1961—1962. Vinyl and hard plastic; rooted dark hair, sleep eyes, closed mouth; original clothes; all in excellent condition.
21in (53cm) **$700—750**

Madame Alexander continued

Caroline: 1961—1962. Hard plastic and vinyl; rooted blonde hair, smiling character face; original clothes; in excellent condition.
15in (38cm) **$300—350**

Miss Melinda: 1962—1963. Vinyl character face with smiling open/closed mouth and two painted upper teeth; swivel waist, vinyl arms, hard plastic torso and legs; original clothes; all in excellent condition.
MARK: On head:

"ALEXANDER
19©62"

16in (41cm) **$300**

Smarty: 1962—1963. Hard plastic and vinyl, smiling character face with rooted hair, knock-kneed and pigeon-toed; original clothes; in excellent condition.

12in (31cm)	**$250**
Katie (black), 1965	**400**

Littlest Kitten: 1963—1964. All-vinyl with rooted hair, jointed at neck, shoulders and hips; original tagged clothes; all in excellent condition.
8in (20cm) **$185**

Janie: 1964—1966. Vinyl and hard plastic with rooted hair, impish face, pigeon-toed and knock-kneed; original tagged clothes; all in excellent condition.

12in (31cm)	**$275**
Lucinda, 1969—1970	**375**
Rozy, 1969	**400**
Suzy, 1970	**400**

12in (31cm) ***Smarty***, all original. *H&J Foulke, Inc.*

Madame Alexander continued

14in (36cm) ***Brigitta***, all original. *H&J Foulke, Inc.*

Sound of Music: Large set 1965—1970; small set 1971-1973. All dolls of hard plastic and vinyl with appropriate synthetic wigs and sleep eyes; original clothes; all in excellent condition.
MARK: Each doll tagged as to character.

Small set	
8in (20cm) ***Friedrich***	**$225**
8in (20cm) ***Gretl***	**200**
8in (20cm) ***Marta***	**200**
10in (25cm) ***Brigitta***	**225**
12in (31cm) ***Maria***	**300**
10in (25cm) ***Louisa***	**400**
10in (25cm) ***Liesl***	**325**
Large set*	
11in (28cm) ***Friedrich***	**275**
11in (28cm) ***Gretl***	**225**
11in (28cm) ***Marta***	**225**
14in (36cm) ***Brigitta***	**225**
17in (43cm) ***Maria***	**350**
14in (36cm) ***Louisa***	**300**
14in (36cm) ***Liesl***	**250**

*Allow considerably more for sailor outfits.

11in (28cm) ***Friedrich***, all original. *H&J Foulke, Inc.*

Madame Alexander continued

14in (35cm) ***Renoir Girl***, 1967—1968, all original. *H&J Foulke, Inc.*

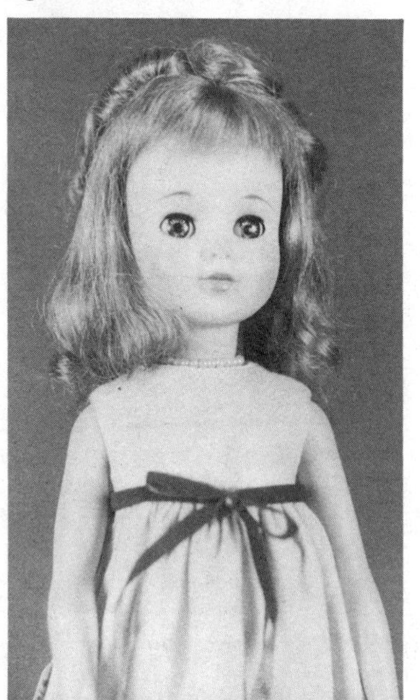

17in (43cm) ***Polly***, all original. *H&J Foulke, Inc.*

Mary Ann Face: Introduced in 1965 and used widely to present a variety of dolls. Only discontinued dolls are listed here. Vinyl head and arms, hard plastic torso and legs; appropriate synthetic wig, sleep eyes; original clothes; all in excellent condition.

MARK: On head:

"ALEXANDER
19©65"

14in (35cm) only:

Madame, 1967—1975	**$350**
Mary Ann, 1965	**300**
Orphant Annie, 1965—1966	**350**
Gidget, 1966	**300**
Little Granny, 1966	**250**
Riley's Little Annie, 1967	**350**
Renoir Girl, 1967—1971	**300**
Easter Girl, 1968	**1500**
Scarlett #1495, 1968	**450**
Jenny Lind & Cat, 1969—1971	**400**
Jenny Lind, 1970	**500**
Grandma Jane, 1970—1972	**250**
Disney Snow White, to 1977	**500**
Goldilocks, 1978-1982	**125**

Polly Face: All-vinyl with rooted hair, jointed at neck, shoulders and hips; original tagged clothes; all in excellent condition.

17in (43cm):

Polly, 1965	**$250**
Leslie (black), 1965—1971	**300**

Madame Alexander continued

21in (53cm) ***Melanie***, 1980, all original. *Virginia Ann Heyerdahl Collection.*

Portrait Dolls: Jacqueline face. 1965 to present. Vinyl and hard plastic; rooted hair with elaborate hair styles; lovely original clothes; all in excellent condition.

21in (53cm) **$350 and up***

*Depending upon individual doll.

Elise: 1966 to present. Vinyl face, rooted hair; original tagged clothes; all in excellent condition.

17in (43cm)	**$150***
Portrait Elise, 1973	**300**
Marlo, 1967	**500****
Maggie, 1972—1973	**300**

*Discontinued styles only.

**Not enough price samples to compute a reliable range.

Madame Alexander continued

Peter Pan Set: 1969. Vinyl and hard plastic with appropriate wigs and sleep eyes; original clothes; all in excellent condition.

14in (36cm) ***Peter Pan*** ("Mary Ann" face) **$300—325**
14in (36cm) ***Wendy*** ("Mary Ann" face) **300—325**
12in (31cm) ***Michael*** ("Janie" face) **350**
11in (28cm) ***Tinker Bell*** ("Cissette") **325—350**

Nancy Drew Face: Introduced in 1967 and used widely to present a variety of dolls. Only discontinued dolls are listed here. Vinyl head and arms, hard plastic torso and legs; appropriate synthetic wig, sleep eyes; original clothes; all in excellent condition.

12in (31cm) only:
Nancy Drew, 1967 **$275—300**
Renoir Child, 1967 **300**
Blue Boy, 1972—1983 **125**
Lord Fauntleroy, 1981—1983 **140**

Coco: 1966. Vinyl and hard plastic, rooted blonde hair, jointed waist, right leg bent slightly at knee; original clothes; all in excellent condition. This face was also used for the 1966 portrait dolls.

21in (53cm) **$1800 up**

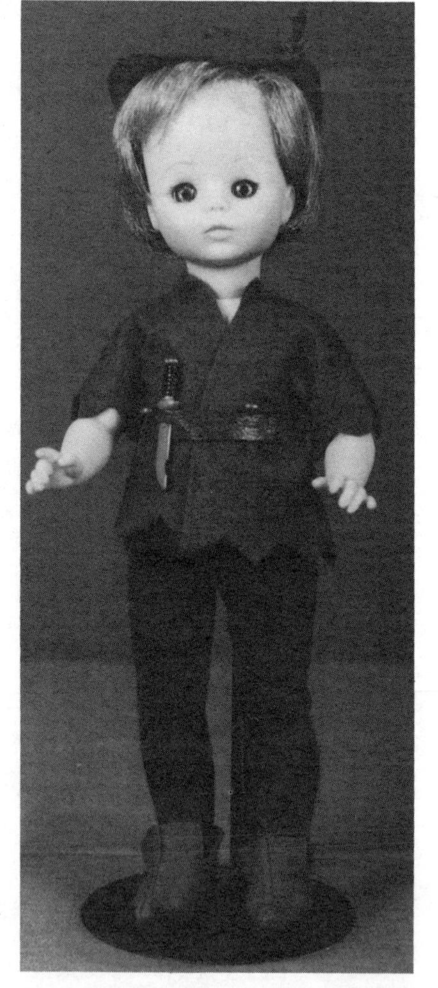

14in (35cm) ***Peter Pan***, all original. *H&J Foulke, Inc.*

Madame Alexander continued

First Ladies: Hard plastic and vinyl with rooted synthetic hair individually styled and sleep eyes; original tagged clothes; in mint condition.

14in (36cm)

1976—1978

Martha Washington
("Martha" face)
Abigail Adams
("Mary Ann" face)
Martha Randolph
("Martha" face)
Dolley Madison
("Martha" face)
Elizabeth Monroe
("Mary Ann" face)
Louisa Adams
("Martha" face)

Set Price **$1600—1700**
Individual doll **250**
Martha Washington **400**

1979—1981

Sarah Jackson
("Martha" face)
Angelica Van Buren
("Martha" face)
Jane Findlay
("Mary Ann" face)
Julia Tyler
("Martha" face)
Sarah Polk
("Martha" face)
Betty Taylor Bliss
("Mary Ann" face)

Set Price **$800—850**
Individual doll **140**

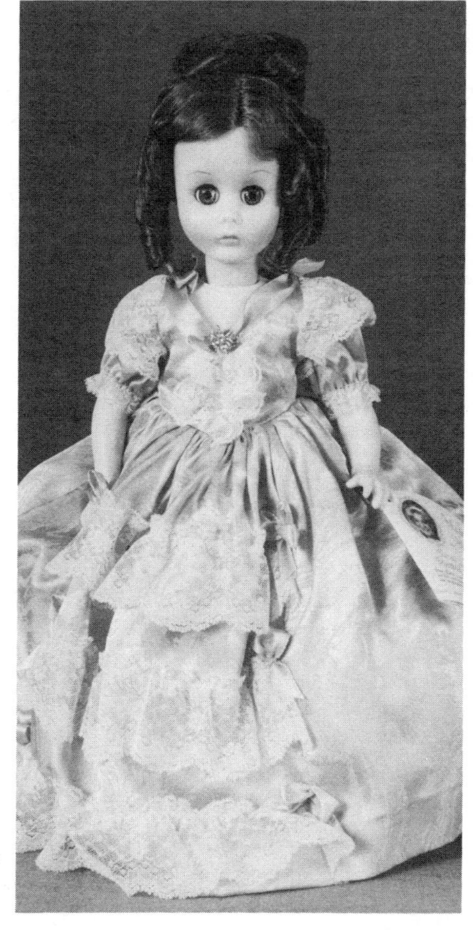

14in (36cm) ***Sarah Polk***, all original. *H&J Foulke, Inc.*

All-Bisque Dolls
(French)

Maker: Various French firms
Date: Ca. 1880—on
Material: All-bisque
Size: Various small sizes, under 12in (31cm)
Mark: None, sometimes numbers

All-Bisque French Doll: Jointed at shoulders and hips, swivel neck, slender arms and legs; good wig, glass eyes, closed mouth; molded shoes or boots and stockings; dressed or undressed; all in good condition.

4½—5in (12—13cm)	**$600—650**
5½—6in (14—15cm)	**650—700**
With bare feet, 5—6in (13—15cm)	**700—800**
With jointed elbows and knees, 5—6in (13—15cm)	**2200****
With jointed elbows, 5—6in (13—15cm)	**1500****
SFBJ, 6in (15cm)	**375**

**Not enough price samples to compute a reliable range.

6in (15cm) French doll, all original. *Jan Foulke Collection.*

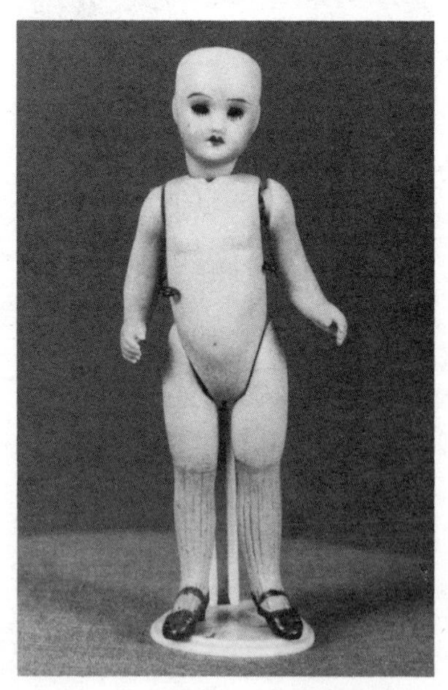

6in (15cm) French doll incised "SFBJ." *H&J Foulke, Inc.*

All-Bisque Dolls
(German)

Maker: Various German firms
Date: Ca. 1880—on
Material: Bisque
Size: Various small sizes, most under 12in (31cm)
Mark: Some with "Germany" and/or numbers; some with paper labels on stomachs

---

All-Bisque with molded clothes: Ca. 1880—on. Jointed only at shoulders, molded and painted clothes or underwear; molded and painted hair, sometimes with molded hat, painted eyes, closed mouth; molded shoes and socks (if in underwear often barefoot); good quality work; all in good condition.

Children:	
3—4in (8—10cm)	**$ 85—110**
5in (13cm)	**110—135**
6—7in (15—18cm)	**175—225**
Black, 5in (13cm)	**325—350**
Early-style characters, jester and clown	**250—300**
Punch and ***Judy*** and other white bisque characters	**85—95**

4in (10cm) ***Judy***. *H&J Foulke, Inc.*

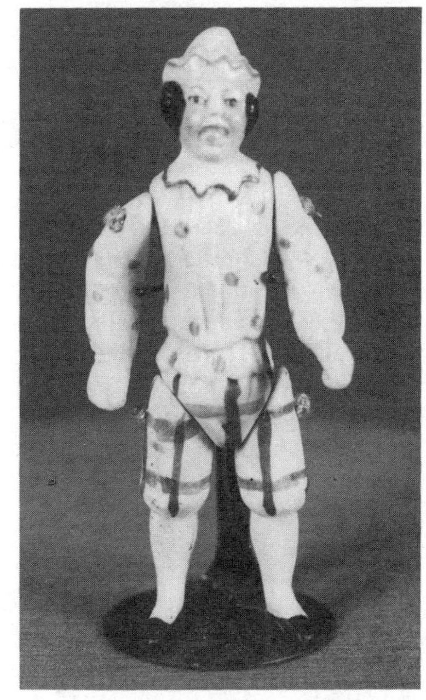

4½in (12cm) clown. *H&J Foulke, Inc.*

3¼in (8cm) French-type, all original. *H&J Foulke, Inc.*

All-Bisque French-type: Ca. 1880—on. Jointed usually by wire or pegging at shoulders and hips, slender arms and legs; good wig, glass eyes, closed mouth; molded shoes or boots and stockings; dressed or undressed; all in good condition.

3—4in (8—10cm)	**$150—175**
6—6½in (15—17cm)	**275—300**
Swivel Neck:	
3½—4in (9—10cm)	**250—300**
6—6½in (15—17cm)	**350—400**

4in (10cm) French-type, black fired-on mustache; all original. *H&J Foulke, Inc.*

All-Bisque with painted eyes: Ca. 1880—on. Jointed at shoulders and hips, stationary neck; molded and painted hair or mohair wig, painted eyes, closed mouth; molded and painted shoes and stockings; fine quality work; dressed or undressed; all in good condition.

1¼in (3cm)	**$ 50—60**
1½—2in (4—5cm)	**50—60**
4—5in (10—13cm)	**100—125**
6—7in (15—18cm)	**150—175**
Swivel neck:	
2½in (9cm)	**125**
4—5in (10—13cm)	**150—175**

5in (13cm) girl 620, swivel neck, all original. *H&J Foulke, Inc.*

All-Bisque Dolls (German)

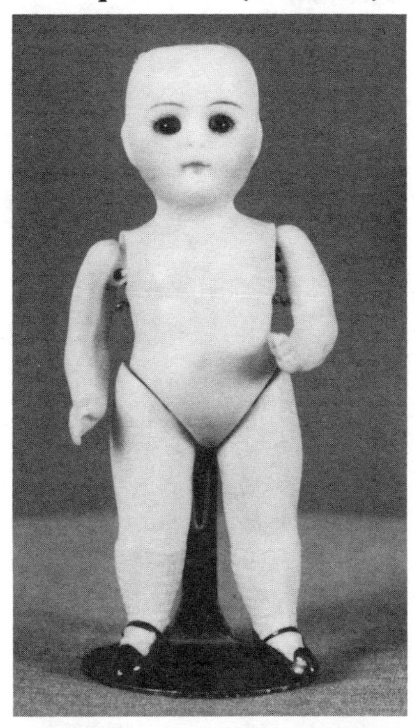

All-Bisque with glass eyes: Ca. 1890—on. Very good quality bisque, jointed at shoulders and hips; good wig, glass eyes, closed mouth; molded and painted shoes and stockings; dressed or undressed; all in good condition.

3in (8cm)	**$165**
4—5in (10—13cm)	**150—175**
6—7in (15—18cm)	**225—275**
8in (20cm)	**325—375**
9in (23cm)	**500—550**
11in (28cm)	**750**
12in (31cm)	**850**

Above Left: 4in (10cm) girl 184.2, yellow boots; all original. *H&J Foulke, Inc.*

Above Right: 4½in (12cm) girl 30.3, pink stockings. *H&J Foulke, Inc.*

Below Right: 7in (18cm) unmarked girl. *H&J Foulke, Inc.*

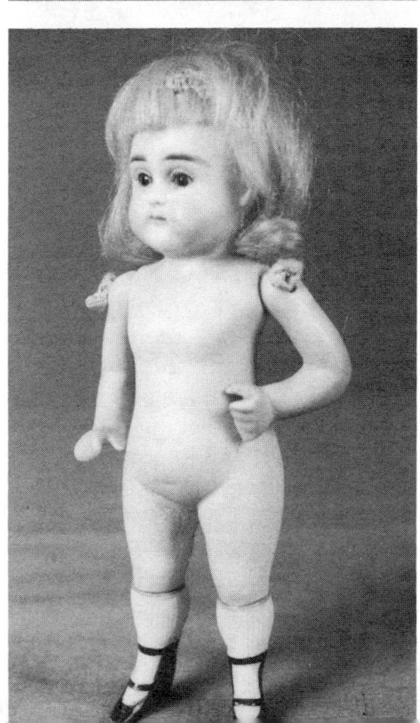

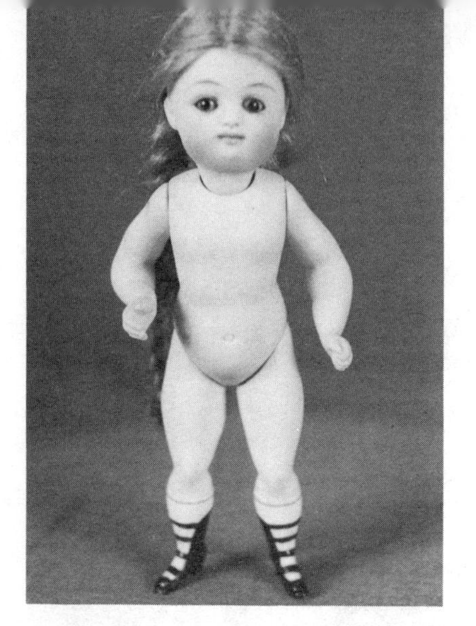

Left: 6½in (17cm) unmarked girl, early fine quality. *H&J Foulke, Inc.*

Below: 6½in (17cm) girl incised "3," pegged joints. *H&J Foulke, Inc.*

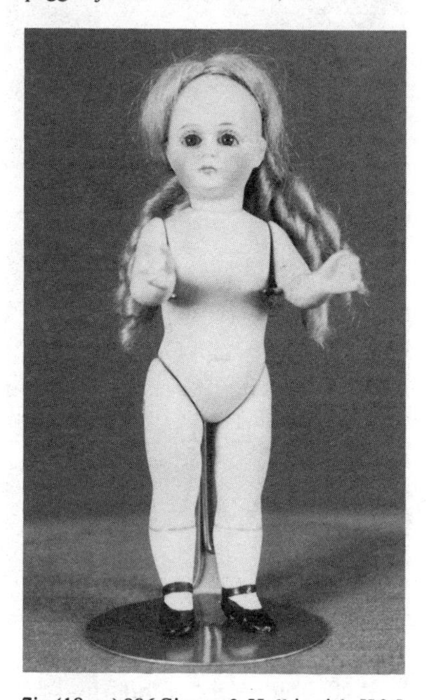

7in (18cm) 886 Simon & Halbig girl. *H&J Foulke, Inc.*

All-Bisque with swivel neck and glass eyes: Ca. 1890—on. Swivel neck, pegged shoulders and hips; good wig, glass eyes, closed mouth; molded and painted shoes and stockings; dressed or undressed; all in good condition.

4in (10cm)	**$ 225—250**
5—6in (13—15cm)	**300—325**
7in (18cm)	**350—375**
8in (20cm)	**500—550**
10in (25cm)	**800—850**
Early Kestner-type:	
6—7in (15—18cm)	**800—850**
9—10in (23—25cm)	**1200—1500**

All-Bisque with long black or blue stockings: Ca. 1890—on. Jointed at neck, shoulders and hips; good wig, glass sleep eyes, open mouth with teeth; molded brown shoes and molded long black or blue stockings; dressed or undressed; all in good condition. Sometimes marked "S & H 886" or "890".

5—6in (13—15cm)	**$375—475**
7—7½in (18—19cm)	**550—600**
10in (25cm)	**900—950**

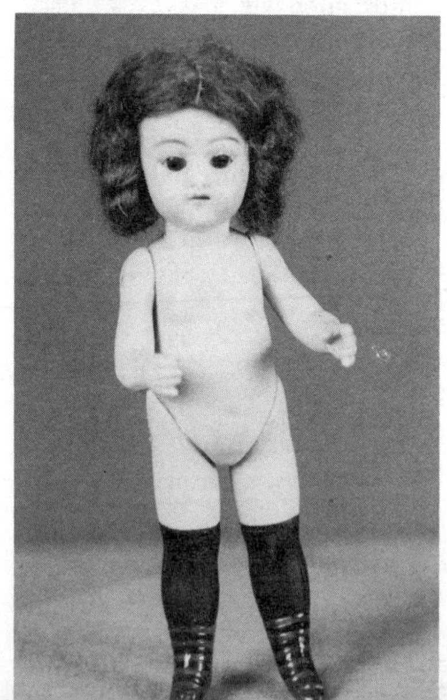

All-Bisque Dolls (German) continued

All-Bisque with glass eyes: Ca. 1910. Jointed at shoulders and hips; good wig, glass eyes, closed or open mouth; molded and painted black one-strap shoes and stockings; undressed or dressed; all in good condition.

4—5in (10—13cm)	**$125—150**
7in (18cm)	**175—200**
8in (20cm)	**225—250**
11in (28cm)	**500**

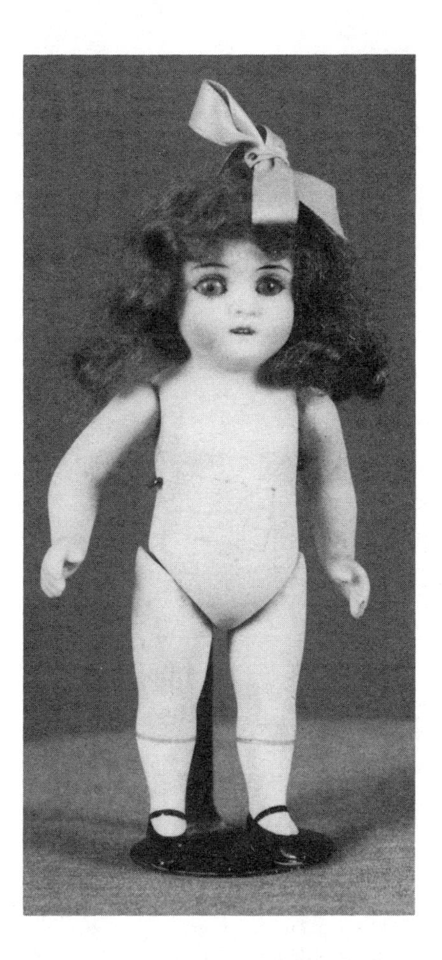

Above Left: 10in (25cm) girl 83/225/24. *Joanna Ott Collection.*

Below Left: 5¾in (15cm) girl 150, all original. *H&J Foulke, Inc.*

Above: 5½in (14cm) girl 100, open mouth. *H&J Foulke, Inc.*

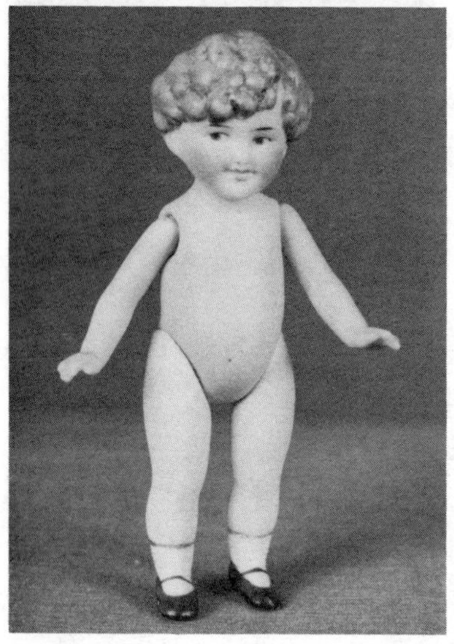

Above Left: 6in (15cm) 150/4 character. *H&J Foulke, Inc.*

Left: 5in (13cm) 167-2 character. *H&J Foulke, Inc.*

Above: 6in (15cm) girl, blue slippers. *H&J Foulke, Inc.*

All-Bisque with character face: Ca. 1915. Jointed at shoulders and hips; good wig, smiling character face, closed or open mouth; molded and painted black one-strap shoes and stockings; dressed or undressed; all in good condition.

5—5½in (13—14cm)

Painted eyes	**$125—150**
Glass eyes	**250—275**
#150 open/closed mouth with two painted teeth, 5½—6in (14—15cm)	**200—250**

All-Bisque with painted eyes: Ca. 1920. Jointed at shoulders and hips, stationary neck; mohair wig or molded hair, painted eyes, closed mouth; molded and painted one-strap shoes and white stockings; dressed or undressed; all in good condition.

4½—5in (12—13cm)	**$ 75—85**
6—7in (15—18cm)	**100—135**

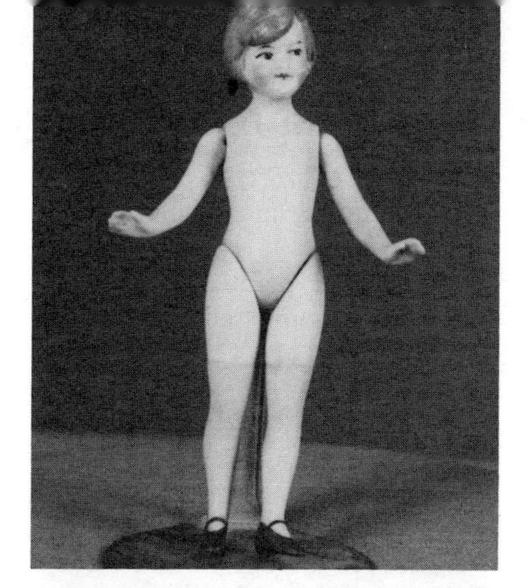

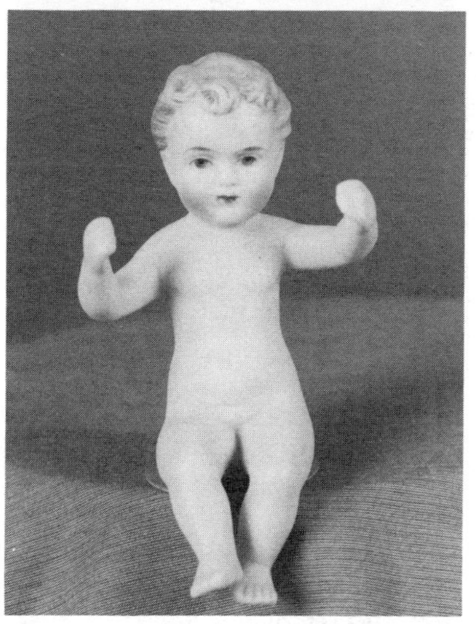

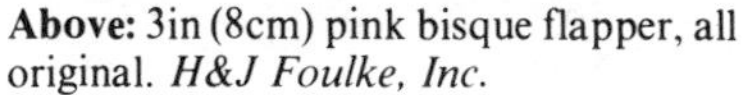

Above: 3in (8cm) pink bisque flapper, all original. *H&J Foulke, Inc.*

Above Right: 6½in (17cm) tinted bisque flapper, yellow stockings. *H&J Foulke, Inc.*

Right: 5½in (14cm) unjointed fine early quality baby. *H&J Foulke, Inc.*

All-Bisque "Flapper": Ca. 1920. Pink bisque with wire joints at shoulders and hips; molded bobbed hair and painted features; painted shoes and socks; original factory clothes; all in good condition.

3in (8cm) **$40—45**

All-Bisque "Flapper" (tinted bisque): Jointed at shoulders and hips; molded bobbed hair with loop for bow, painted features; long yellow stockings, one-strap shoes with heels; undressed or dressed; all in good condition.

4—5in (10—13cm) **$200—250**
6—7in (15—18cm) **300—350**

All-Bisque Baby: 1900—on. Jointed at shoulders and hips with curved arms and legs; molded and painted hair, painted eyes; very good workmanship; not dressed; all in good condition.

2½—3½in (6—9cm)	**50—65**
4—5in (10—13in)	**95—110**
Fine early quality, 4½in (12cm)	**125—135**
Unjointed, 4—5in (10—13cm)	**65—85**

All-Bisque Baby: Pink bisque, jointed at shoulders and hips, curved arms and legs; painted hair, painted eyes; original factory clothes; all in good condition.

2½—3in (6—8cm) **$60—65**

All-Bisque Dolls (German) continued

All-Bisque Character Baby: Ca. 1910. Jointed at shoulders and hips, curved arms and legs; molded hair, painted eyes, character face; undressed; all in good condition.

4in (10cm) **$100—110**
6in (15cm) **175**
With glass eyes,
4—5in (10—13cm) **225—250**
Swivel neck,
5—6in (13—15cm) **375—400**

All-Bisque Character Dolls: 1913—on. Character faces with painted features and molded hair; usually jointed only at arms. Also see individual listings.

Chin Chin (Heubach),
4in (10cm) **$225—250**
Small pink bisque characters,
up to 3in (8cm) **30—40**
Oriental,
6in (15cm) **300**
Baby Bud,
7in (18cm) **275**
Our Fairy,
6in (15cm) **850**
Little Imp,
6in (15cm) **200**
Boy with removable hat,
6in (15cm) **135**
Our Fairy-type, painted eyes, molded hair,
4½in (12cm) **110**
Kewpie,
4—5in (10—13cm) **100—125**
Molded Clothes Immobiles,
4in (10cm) **75—85**

Right: Character baby incised "833", painted eyes. *H&J Foulke, Inc.*
Left: Character baby incised "833", glass eyes. *H&J Foulke, Inc.*

All-Bisque Nodder Characters: Ca. 1920. Nodding heads, elastic strung, molded clothes; all in good condition.

3—4in (8—10cm) **$40—45**
German Comic Characters,
3—4in (8—10cm) **60 up**

All-Bisque Immobiles: Ca. 1920. All-bisque figures with molded clothes, molded hair and painted features. Decoration is not fired, so it wears and washes off very easily.

Tinies: adults and children,
1½—2¼in (4—6cm) **$25—30**
Children,
3¼in (8cm) **30—35**
Bride & Groom,
4—5in (10—13cm) **50—60**

2½in (6cm) pink bisque baby. *H&J Foulke, Inc.*

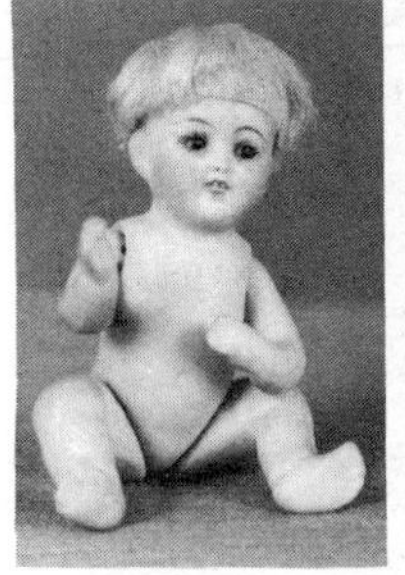

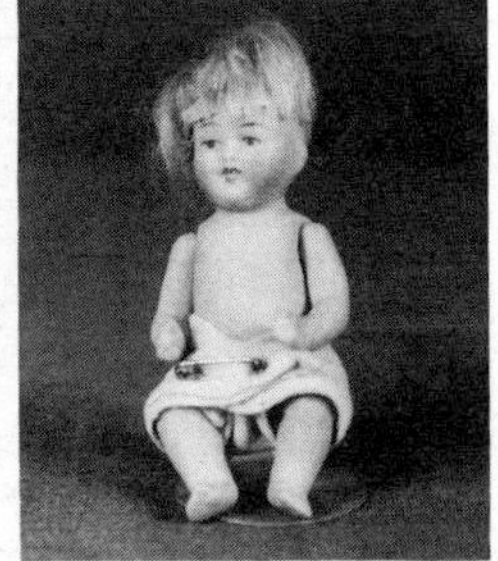

All-Bisque Dolls (German) continued

4½in (12cm) Gebrüder Heubach character girl with blue molded bow. *H&J Foulke, Inc.*

5¾in (15cm) rare Oriental character. *H&J Foulke, Inc.*

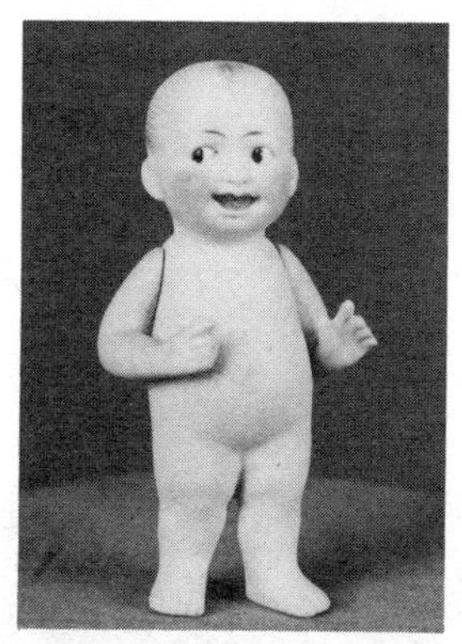

6¼in (16cm) character. *H&J Foulke, Inc.*

3½in (9cm) character with molded removable hat, orange shoes. *H&J Foulke, Inc.*

3½in (9cm) nodder girls. *H&J Foulke, Inc.*

3½in (9cm) immobile children. *H&J Foulke, Inc.*

All-Bisque Dolls
(Made in Japan)

Maker: Various Japanese firms
Date: Ca. 1915—on
Material: Bisque
Size: Various small sizes
Mark: "Made in Japan" or "NIPPON"

Baby Doll with bent limbs: Jointed shoulders and hips; molded and painted hair and eyes; not dressed; all in good condition.
White, 4in (10cm) **$20**
Black, 4in (10cm) **25**

Betty Boop-type, 4—5in (10—13cm)	**$15—20**
Child, 4—6in (10—15cm)	**20—25**
Comic Characters, 3—4in (8—10cm)	**25 up***
Stiff Characters, 3—4in (8—10cm)	**5— 7**
Cho-Cho San, 4½in (12cm)	**65—75**
Nodders, 4in (10cm)	**20—25**
Orientals, 3—4in (8—10cm)	**20—25**
Queue San, 4in (10cm)	**65—75**
Marked "Nippon" Characters, 4—5in (10—13cm)	**35—45**

*Depending upon rarity.

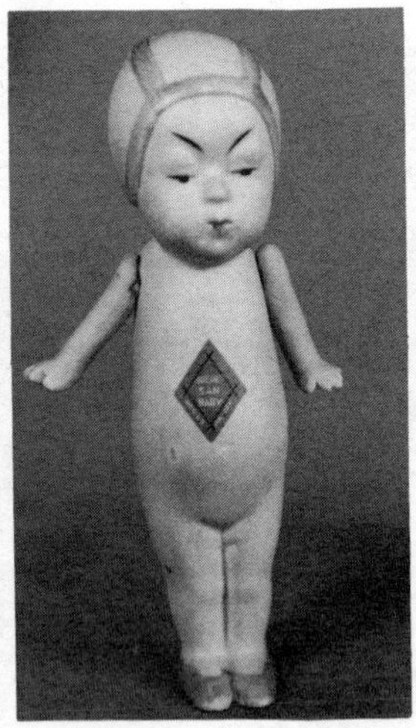

Left: 5in (13cm) girl incised "Nippon". *H&J Foulke, Inc.* **Middle:** 5in (13cm) ***Queue San Baby.*** *H&J Foulke, Inc.* **Right:** 3in (8cm) black baby. *H&J Foulke, Inc.*

Farnell's Alpha Toys

Maker: J. K. Farnell Co., Ltd., Acton, London, England
Date: 1930s
Material: Felt and cloth
Size: Various
Mark: Cloth label on foot:

FARNELL'S
ALPHA TOYS
MADE IN ENGLAND

Alpha Toys Child: All-cloth with felt face, painted features, mohair wig; cloth body jointed at neck, shoulders and hips; original clothes; all in good condition.

Child, 14in (36cm) **$200—225**

Alpha Toys Coronation Doll of King George VI, 16in (41cm) **350**

14in (36cm) child, all original.
H&J Foulke, Inc.

Alt, Beck & Gottschalck

Maker: Alt, Beck & Gottschalck, porcelain factory, Nauendorf, Thüringia, Germany
Date: 1854—on
Material: Bisque head, composition body
Size: Various
Mark: plus mold number

Child Doll: Ca. 1893—on. Mold number 1362. Perfect bisque head, good wig, sleep eyes, open mouth; ball-jointed body in good condition; appropriate clothes.

17—19in (43—48cm)	**$ 350—400**
22—24in (56—61cm)	**450—500**
30—33in (76—84cm)	**1000—1200**
39—42in (99—107cm)	**2200—2500**

Character Baby: 1910—on. Mold numbers 1361, 1352. Perfect bisque head, good wig, sleep eyes, open mouth, open nostrils; composition baby body with bent limbs in good condition; suitable clothes.

10—12in (25—31cm)	**$350—400***
15—17in (38—43cm)	**450—500***
21—22in (53—56cm)	**700—750***

*Allow extra for flirty eyes or toddler body.

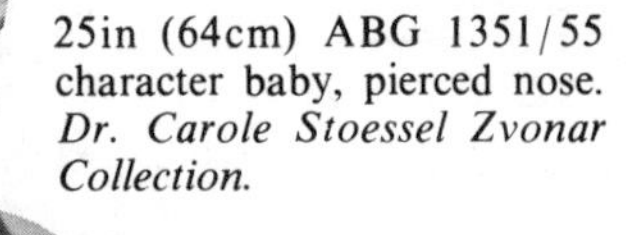

25in (64cm) ABG 1351/55 character baby, pierced nose. *Dr. Carole Stoessel Zvonar Collection.*

Louis Amberg & Son

Maker: Louis Amberg & Son, New York, N.Y., U.S.A.
Date: 1911—on (although Amberg had been in the doll business under other names since 1878)

New Born Babe: 1914, reissued 1924. Designed by Jeno Juszko. Bisque head of an infant with painted hair, sleep eyes, closed mouth; soft cloth body with celluloid, rubber or composition hands; appropriate clothes; all in good condition.

MARK: "© L.A.&S. 1914, G 45520 Germany #4", also

"Heads copyrighted by
LOUIS AMBERG and Son",
also
"© L. Amberg & Son Germany
886/2"

8in (20cm)	**$300—325**
10—11in (25—28cm)	**350—400**
12—13in (31—33cm)	**450—500**

Charlie Chaplin: 1915. Composition portrait head with molded and painted hair, painted eyes to the side, closed full mouth, molded mustache; straw-filled cloth body with composition hands; original clothes; all in good condition.

MARK: cloth label on sleeve:

"CHARLIE CHAPLIN DOLL
World's Greatest Comedian
Made exclusively by Louis Amberg
& Son, N.Y.
by Special Arrangement with
Essamay Film Co."

14in (36cm) **$225—250**

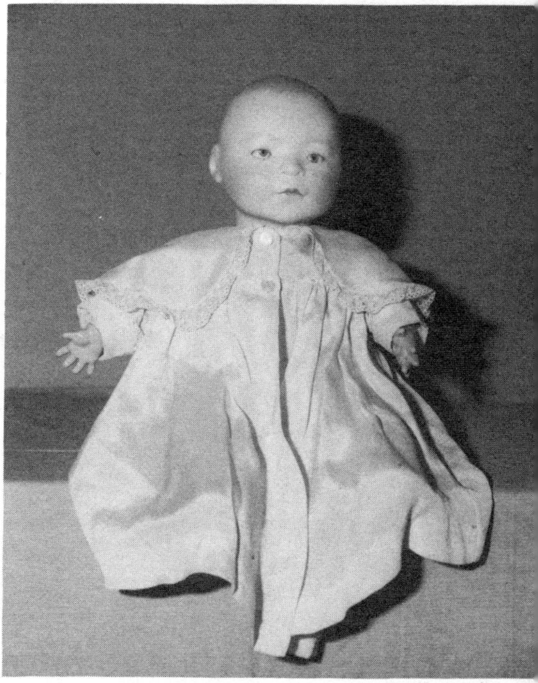

16in (41cm) long Amberg baby. *Dr. Carole Stoessel Zvonar Collection.*

Composition Mibs: 1921. Composition shoulder head with wistful expression, molded and painted blonde or reddish hair, blue painted eyes, closed mouth; cloth body with composition arms and legs with painted shoes and socks; appropriate old clothes; all in good condition.

MARK: None on doll; paper label only:

"Amberg Dolls
Please Love Me
I'm Mibs"

16in (41cm) **$400**

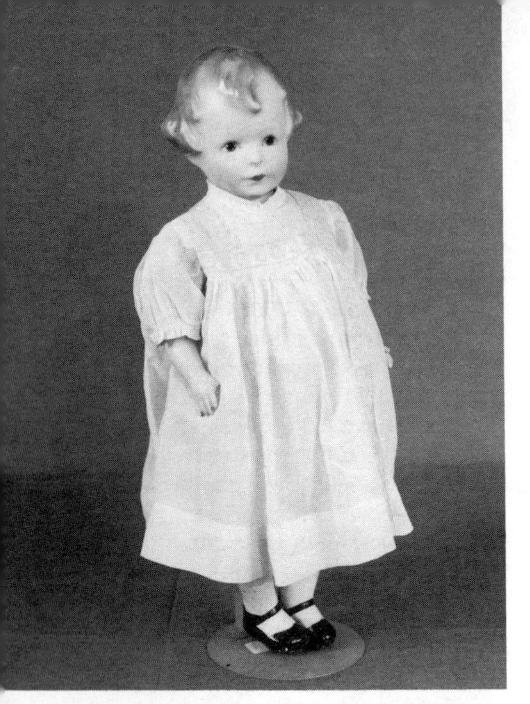

17in (43cm) ***Mibs***, replaced dress. *Beth Foulke Collection.*

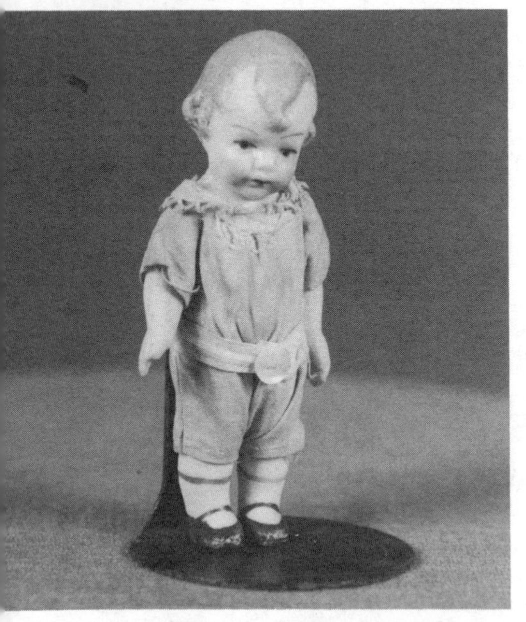

3in (8cm) ***Mibs***, all original. *H&J Foulke, Inc.*

All-Bisque Mibs: 1921. Molded and painted features, jointed at shoulders and sometimes hips; painted shoes and socks; undressed; all in good condition.

MARK: Sometimes on back:

"©
LA&S 1921
Germany"

or paper label on chest:

'Please
Love Me
I'm
MIBS"

3in (8cm) **$225**

Baby Peggy: 1924. Bisque head with smiling character face, brown bobbed mohair wig, brown sleep eyes, closed mouth; composition or kid body, fully jointed; dressed or undressed; all in very good condition.

MARK:

"19 © 24
LA & S NY
Germany
—50—
982/2"

also: 973 (smiling socket head)
972 (pensive socket head)
983 (smiling shoulder head)
982 (pensive shoulder head)

17—19in (43—48cm) **$2300—2600**

Baby Peggy: 1923. Composition head, arms and legs, cloth body; molded brown bobbed hair, painted eyes, smiling closed mouth; appropriately dressed; all in good condition.

20in (51cm) **$200—250****

**Not enough price samples to compute a reliable range.

21in (53cm) ***Baby Peggy*** with composition head. *Betty Harms Collection.*

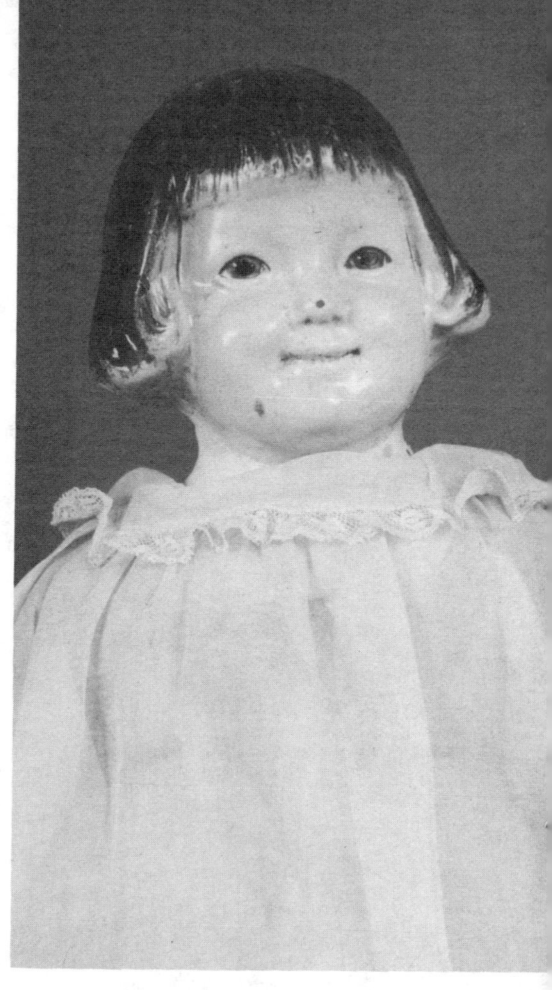

All-Bisque Baby Peggy: 1924. Smiling face with painted brown bobbed hair, painted eyes, closed mouth; jointed arms and legs; brown strap shoes and socks; undressed; all in excellent condition. Unmarked, but had a paper label on stomach.
5½in (14cm) **$275—300**

Vanta Baby: 1927. A tie-in with Vanta baby garments. Composition or bisque head with molded and painted hair, sleep eyes, open mouth with two teeth (closed mouth and painted eyes in all-composition small dolls); muslin body jointed at hips and shoulders, curved composition arms and legs; suitably dressed; all in good condition.
MARK:
"VANTA BABY -- AMBERG"
20in (51cm):

Composition head	**$175—200**
Bisque head	**650—675**

Sue or Edwina: 1928. All-composition with molded and painted hair, painted eyes; jointed neck, shoulders and hips, a large round ball joint at waist; dressed; all in very good condition.
MARK:
"AMBERG
PAT. PEND.
L.A. & S. © 1928"
14in (36cm) **$275**

Tiny Tots Body Twists: 1928. All-composition with jointed shoulders and a large round ball joint at the waist; molded and painted hair in both boy and girl styles, painted eyes; painted shoes and socks; dressed; all in good condition.
MARK: tag on clothes:
"An Amberg Doll with
BODY TWIST
all its own
PAT. PEND. SER. NO.
32018"
8in (20cm) **$165**

14in (36cm) ***Sue*** or ***Edwina*** with ball joint at waist. *Betty Harms Collection.*

American Character

Maker: American Character Doll Co., New York, N.Y., U.S.A.
Date: 1919—on
Mark: Various for each doll

19in (48cm) Petite girl, contemporary dress. *H&J Foulke, Inc.*

Puggy: 1931. All-composition chubby body jointed at neck, shoulders and hips; molded and painted hair, painted eyes to the side, closed mouth, pug nose, frowning face; original clothes; all in good condition.
MARK: "A PETITE DOLL"
12in (31cm) **$375—400**

Sally: 1927. Composition head, arms and legs, cloth torso; molded and painted hair, tin sleep eyes, closed mouth; appropriate old clothes; all in good condition.
MARK:
"PETITE
SALLY"

12in (31cm), all-composition	**$115—125**
16—18in (41—46cm)	**175—200**
24in (61cm)	**300**

Marked Petite Girl Dolls: 1930s. Composition head, arms and legs, cloth torso or all-composition; mohair or human hair wig, sleep eyes, closed mouth; appropriate old clothes; all in good condition.
24in (61cm) **$175—200**

Tiny Tears: 1950. Hard plastic head with sleep eyes and tear ducts, molded hair, drinks, wets; rubber body; original clothes; all in good condition. (Later dolls had inset hair and vinyl body; still later dolls were all vinyl.) Various sizes.
MARK:
"Pat No. 2675644
Ame—Character"

Early one, 12in (31cm)	**$ 85—95**
21in (53cm)	**150**

18in (46cm) ***Sweet Sue***, all original. *H&J Foulke, Inc.*

21in (53cm) ***Alice in Wonderland***, all original. *Paula Ryscik Collection.*

8in (20cm) ***Betsy McCall***, all original. *H&J Foulke, Inc.*

Sweet Sue: 1953. Hard plastic and vinyl, some with walking mechanism, some fully-jointed including elbows, knees and ankles; original clothes; all in excellent condition.

MARKS: Various, including: "A.C.", "Amer. Char. Doll", "American Character" in a circle.

18in (46cm) **$125—150**
24in (53cm) **150—175**

Betsy McCall: 1957. All-hard plastic with vinyl arms, legs jointed at knees; rooted saran hair, round face with sleep eyes, plastic eyelashes; original clothes; all in good condition.

MARK: McCALL © CORP

8in (20cm) **$75—85**

Betsy McCall: 1960. All-vinyl with rooted hair, lashed sleep eyes, round face, turned-up mouth; slender arms and legs; original clothes; all in excellent condition.

14in (36cm)	**$125—135**
20in (51cm)	**150—165**
30—36in (76—91cm)	**200—250**

Arranbee

Maker: Arranbee Doll Co., New York, N.Y., U.S.A.
Date: 1922—1960
Mark: "ARRANBEE" or "R & B"

Baby: 1924. Perfect solid dome bisque head with molded and painted hair, sleep eyes, open mouth with teeth, dimples; cloth body with celluloid or composition hands, may have a molded celluloid bottle in hand; dressed; all in good condition.
Head circumference:
11—13in (28—33cm) **$350—400**

My Dream Baby: 1924. Perfect bisque head with solid dome and painted hair, sleep eyes, closed or open mouth; all-composition or cloth body with composition hands; dressed; all in good condition. Heads made by Armand Marseille, mold 341 or 351.
Head circumference:
12—13in (31—33cm) **$325—400**

Bottletot: 1926—on. All-composition baby with bent arms and legs; molded and painted hair, sleep eyes, open mouth; celluloid hand with molded bottle. Doll is unmarked; bottle is marked "Arranbee/Pat Aug. 10, 26". Original clothes; all in good condition.
13—14in (33—36cm) **$125**

Storybook Dolls: 1930s. All-composition with swivel neck, jointed arms and legs; molded and painted hair, painted eyes; all original storybook costumes; all in good condition.
10in (25cm) **$150**

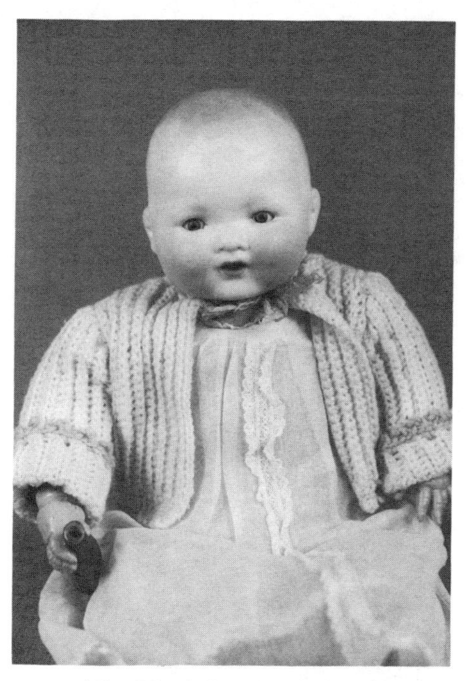

13in (33cm) Arranbee baby with open mouth, holding molded bottle. *Jimmy & Faye Rodolfos Collection.*

Debu' Teen: 1938—on. All-composition or composition swivel shoulder head and limbs on cloth torso; mohair or human hair wig, sleep eyes, closed mouth; original clothes; all in good condition.
MARK: "R & B"

14in (36cm)	**$135—150**
18in (46cm)	**175—185**
21in (53cm)	**200—225**
Skating doll, 14in (36cm)	**150**

Arranbee continued

16in (41cm) ***Nancy***, all original. *H&J Foulke, Inc.*

17in (43cm) ***Nanette***, all original. *H&J Foulke, Inc.*

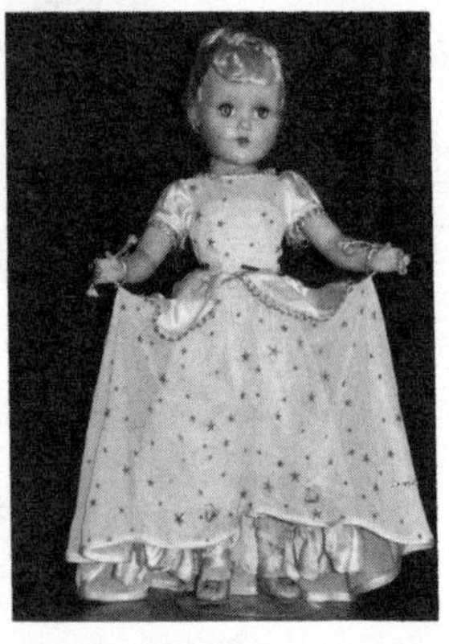

18in (46cm) ***Cinderella***, all original. *Paula Ryscik Collection.*

Nancy: Up to 1940. All-composition or composition swivel shoulder head and limbs on cloth torso; molded hair or original mohair or human hair wig, sleep eyes and open mouth with teeth (smaller dolls have painted eyes and closed mouth); original or appropriate clothes; all in good condition.
Sizes: 12—20in (31—51cm)
MARK: "ARRANBEE" or "NANCY"

12in (31cm) **$125**
18in (46cm) **175—200**

Nancy Lee: 1940s. All-composition with jointed neck, shoulders and hips; mohair or human hair wig, sleep eyes, closed mouth; original clothes; all in good condition. This face mold was also used for dolls which were given other names.
MARK: "R & B"

14in (36cm) **$135—150**

Nanette: 1950s. All-hard plastic, jointed at neck, shoulders and hips; synthetic wig, sleep eyes, closed mouth; original clothes; all in excellent condition. This face mold was also used for dolls which were given other names.
MARK: "R & B"

18—21in (46—53cm) **$150—175**

Mabel Lucie Attwell

Maker: Chad Valley Co., Harbourne, England
Date: 1924—on
Material: All-fabric
Size: 14—19in (36—38cm)
Designer: Mabel Lucie Attwell
Mark: Cloth label usually on foot:

"HYGENIC TOYS
Made in England by
CHAD VALLEY CO. LTD."

Cardboard tag:

"The 'Mabel Lucie Attwell' Doll Regd & Patented Sole Makers Chad Valley Co. Ltd."	or	"THE CHAD VALLEY HYGENIC TEXTILE TOYS Made in England"

Chad Valley Attwell Doll: Felt head with molded features, curly mohair wig, glass inset side-glancing eyes, smiling water-melon mouth, full cheeks; velveteen body with jointed shoulders and hips; original clothes; all in excellent condition.
14in (36cm) **$400—450**

14in (36cm) Chad Valley doll of the type designed by Mabel Lucie Attwell. Shoes and possibly hat are replacements. His jointed velvet dog is ***Bonzo***.

B.F.

Maker: Possibly Jumeau or Danel & Cie, as Bébé Française or Ferté as Bébé Ferté, Paris, France
Date: Ca. 1880s—1890s
Material: Bisque head, composition body
Size: Various
Mark: "B.F." with size number

B. F. marked Bébé: Perfect bisque head with good wig, paperweight eyes, closed mouth, pierced ears; jointed composition body; appropriate clothes; all in good condition.
12—14in (31—36cm) **$2000—2200**
19—22in (48—56cm) **3000—3200**
25—26in (64—66cm) **3500—3700**

24in (61cm) B.F. *Betty Harms Collection.*

B.S.

(Fashion-type Lady Doll)

Maker: Unidentified French firm
Date: Ca. 1860s
Material: Bisque shoulder head, kid body
Size: Various
Mark: "B 3 S" (Size number in center may vary; 0, 2, 3 and 4 reported)

Marked B.S. Lady Doll: Very pale perfect bisque shoulder head with stiff neck, good old wig, inset paperweight eyes, closed mouth; shapely kid body, sometimes with kid over wood upper arms and bisque lower arms; appropriate clothes; all in good condition with perfect head.
17in (43cm) **$1500—1600**

15in (39cm) French fashion-type lady incised "B 3 S" with stiff neck.

Baby Bo Kaye

Maker: Composition heads by Cameo Doll Co.; bisque heads made in Germany, possibly by Alt, Beck, & Gottschalck; bodies by K & K Toy Co., New York, N.Y., U.S.A.

Date: 1925

Material: Bisque, composition or celluloid head with flange neck; composition or celluloid limbs, cloth body

Size: About 18in (46cm)

Designer: J. L. Kallus

Mark:

"Copr. by
J. L. Kallus
Germany
1394/30"

Baby Bo Kaye: Perfect bisque head marked as above, molded hair, glass eyes, open mouth with two lower teeth; body as above; dressed; all in good condition.

16in (41cm):

Bisque	**$2000****
Celluloid or composition	**550****

**Not enough price samples to compute a reliable range

All-Bisque Baby Bo Kaye: Molded hair, glass sleep eyes, open mouth with two teeth; swivel neck, jointed shoulders and hips; molded shoes and socks; unmarked.

MARK:

6in (15cm) **$1250—1500**

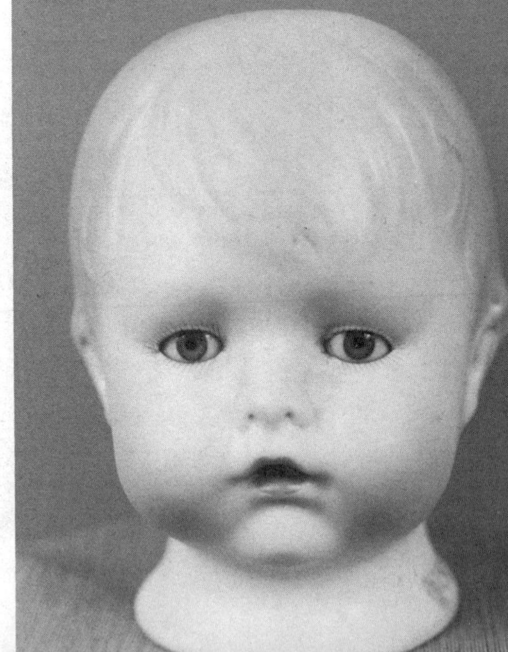

Baby Bo Kaye head. *Dr. Carole Stoessel Zvonar Collection.*

Babyland Rag

Maker: E. I. Horsman, New York, N.Y., U.S.A
Date: 1904—1920
Material: All-cloth
Size: 12—30in (31—76cm)
Mark: None

Babyland Rag: Cloth face with hand-painted features, later with printed features, sometimes mohair wig; cloth body jointed at shoulders and hips; original clothes; all in good condition.

13—15in (33—38cm) **$350—400**
30in (76cm) **900—1000**

Topsy Turvy,
13—15in (33—38cm) **350—400**

Black,
20in (51cm) **650**

12in (31cm) Babyland Rag ***Topsy Turvy***, all original. *H&J Foulke, Inc.*

Bähr & Pröschild

Maker: Bähr & Pröschild, porcelain factory, Ohrdruf, Thüringia, Germany
Date: 1871—on
Material: Bisque head, composition bent-limb baby or toddler body
Size: Various
Mark: BP

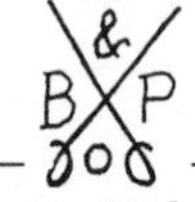

with "Germany" and numbers 585, 604, 624, 678, 619

Marked B. P. Character Baby: Ca. 1910. Perfect bisque socket head, good wig, sleep eyes, open mouth; composition bent-limb baby body; dressed; all in good condition.

12—15in (31—38cm) **$400—450**
18—20in (46—51cm) **550—650**
24—26in (61—66cm) **900—1000**

Toddler:
16in (41cm) **700—750**
24in (61cm) **1250**

Marked B. P. Character Child: Ca. 1910. Perfect bisque socket head, good wig, sleep eyes, closed mouth; toddler or jointed composition body; dressed; all in good condition.

19—20in (48—51cm) **$3000—3500**

15in (38cm) B. P. character baby 585. *H&J Foulke, Inc.*

19in (48cm) B. P. character child 2072. *Richard Wright Antiques.*

Bathing Beauty

Maker: Various German firms
Date: 1920s
Material: All-bisque
Size: Up to about 7in (18cm) tall or long
Mark: Sometimes "Germany" and/or numbers

Bathing Beauty: All-bisque lady, either nude or partially dressed in painted-on clothing, in various sitting, lying or standing positions; painted features and molded hair, possibly with bathing cap, sometimes a bald head with mohair wig; may be dressed in bits of lace.

Common type,
3—4in (8—10cm) **$ 55—75**
Fine quality:
4—6in (10—15cm) **250**
8in (20cm) **400**

5in (13cm) bathing beauty with mohair wig and original bathing suit.

Belton-type
(So-called)

Maker: Various French and German firms
Date: 1875—on
Material: Bisque socket head, ball-jointed wood and composition body with straight wrists
Size: Various
Mark: None, except sometimes numbers

Belton-type Child Doll: Perfect bisque socket head, solid but flat on top with two or three small holes, paperweight eyes, closed mouth, peirced ears; wood and composition ball-jointed body with straight wrists; dressed; all in good condition.

12—13in (31—33cm) $ **800—900**
16—18in (41—46cm) **1200—1500**
22—24in (56—61cm) **1700—1900**
Early, fine quality:
11—13in (28—33cm) **1100—1300**
15—17in (38—43cm) **1500—1800**
20—22in (51—56cm) **2000—2300**
Tiny with five-piece body,
8in (20cm) **550—600**

10in (25cm) Belton-type child with skin wig. *Richard Wright Antiques.*

C. M. Bergmann

Maker: C. M. Bergmann of Waltershausen, Thüringia, Germany; heads manufactured for this company by Armand Marseille, Simon & Halbig and perhaps others.
Date: 1889—on
Material: Bisque head, composition ball-jointed body
Size: Various
Mark:

C.M. BERGMANN
4/0

C. M. Bergmann
Waltershausen
Germany
1916
6½a

Bergmann Child Doll: Ca. 1889-on. Marked bisque head, composition ball-jointed body; good wig, sleep or set eyes, open mouth; dressed; all in nice condition.

21—23in (53—58cm)	**$ 425—475**
28—30in (71—76cm)	**700—850**
35—36in (89—91cm)	**1200—1300**
39in (99cm)	**2000**

Bergmann Character Baby: 1909—on. Marked bisque socket head, mohair wig, sleep eyes, open mouth; composition bent-limb baby body; dressed; all in good condition.

12—15in (31—38cm) **$400—450****
#612,
14—16in (36—41cm) **700—800****

**Not enough price samples to compute a reliable range.

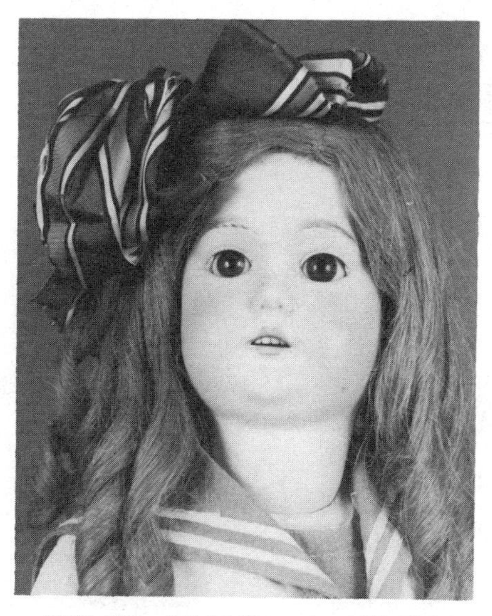

23½in (60cm) C. M. Bergmann/ / II child, all original. *Anna May Case Collection.*

Black Dolls

Black Bisque Doll: Ca. 1880—on. Various French and German manufacturers from their regular molds or specially designed ones with Negroid features. Perfect bisque socket head either painted dark or with dark coloring mixed in the slip, this runs from light brown to very dark; composition or sometimes kid body in a matching color, cloth bodies on some baby dolls; appropriate clothes; all in good condition.

Bru, Circle & Dot, 16in (41cm)	**$12000**
Jules Steiner, open mouth, 14in (36cm)	**2500—2700**
Jumeau, open mouth, 12—14in (31—36cm)	**1600—1800**
S.F.B.J. 34-27, 16in (41cm)	**3800—4200**
34-17, 7½in (19cm) fully-jointed	**350**
S.F.B.J./Unis 60, 11—13in (28—33cm)	**250—300**
German, unmarked, good quality	
10—13in (25—33cm) jointed body	**350—400**
8—9in (20—23cm) five-piece body	**250—275**
5in (13cm) closed mouth	**225**
Simon & Halbig/Handwerck, 16in (41cm)	**750—850**
22in (56cm)	**1000**
S & H 1358, 18in (46cm)	**4200—4500**
AM 341 or ***351***, 11—13in (28—33cm) long	**375—475**
17—18in (43—46cm) long	**775—875**
K★R 116A, 16in (41cm)	**2500**
Kestner 134, 10—11in (25—28cm)	**450—500**
AM 1894, 13—14in (33—36cm)	**450**
Hanna, 8—10in (20—25cm)	**225—250**
K★R 100, 15—16in (38—41cm)	**1000**
HK 463 toddler, 10in (25cm)	**550**
K★R 126, 17in (43cm)	**750**
Heubach 7671, 8in (20cm)	**800**

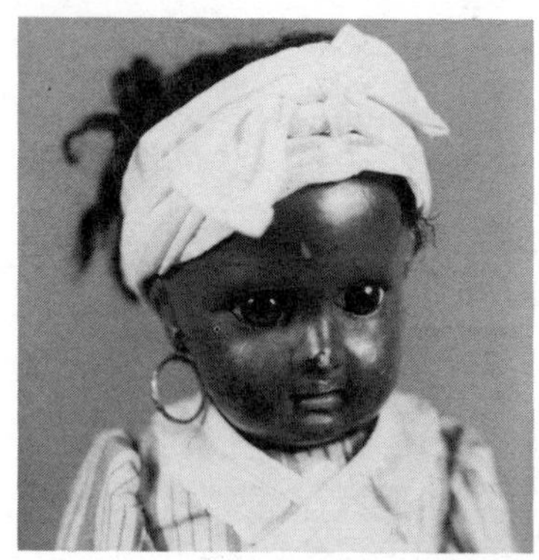

11½in (29cm) E 3 J//DEPOSE black bisque girl. *Dr. Carole Stoessel Zvonar Collection.*

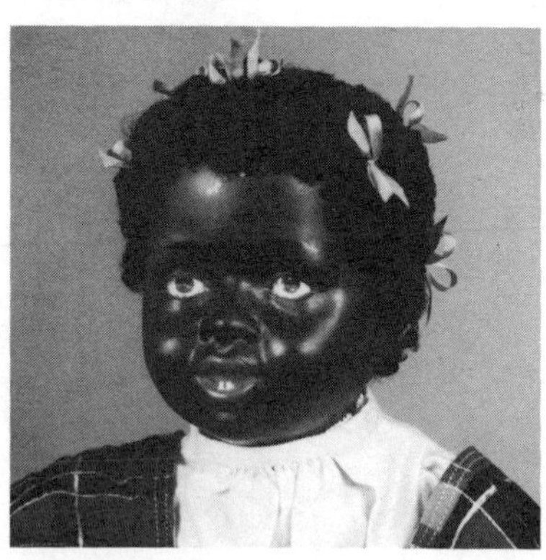

20in (51cm) R X 6//R.A. black character, intaglio eyes. *Richard Wright Collection.*

Black Dolls continued

28in (71cm) S & H 1039 black girl, French body. *Betty Harms Collection.*

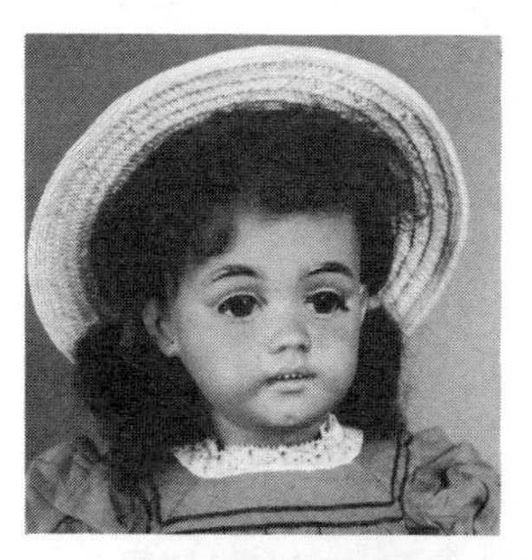

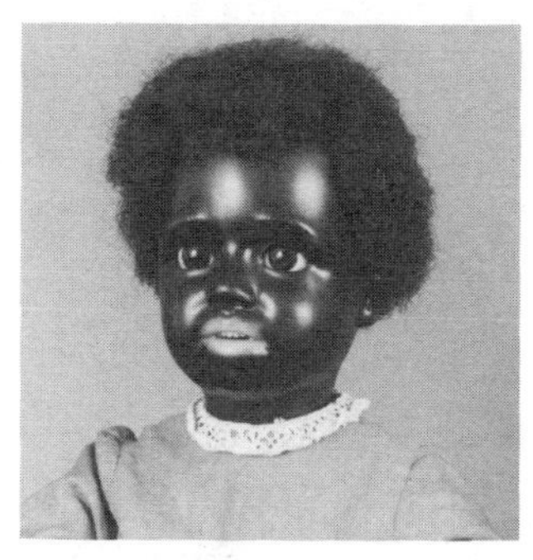

Very black S & H 1358 character girl. *Richard Wright Collection.*

6½in (17cm) S PB H ***Hanna*** toddler, Schoenau Hoffmeister. *H&J Foulke, Inc.*

4in (10cm) tiny girl, closed mouth, all original. *H&J Foulke, Inc.*

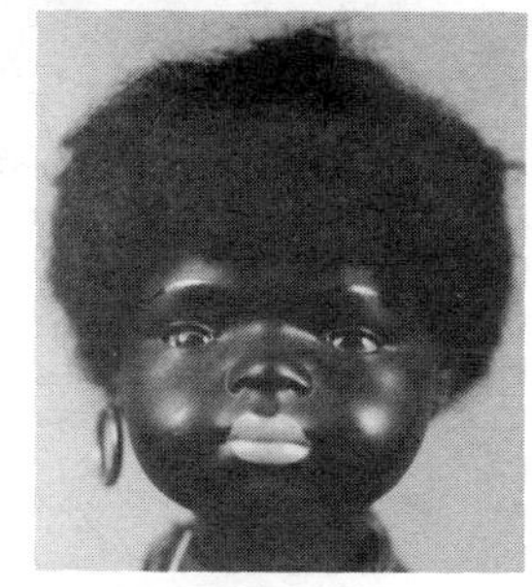

13½in (34cm) Heubach Köppelsdorf 444 character baby. *India Stoessel Collection.*

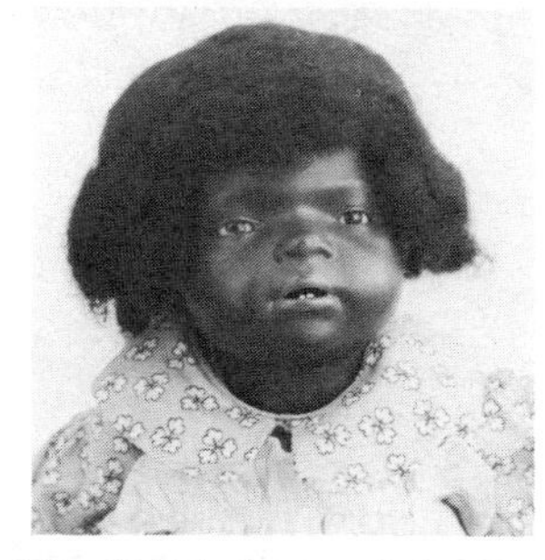

15in (38cm) black character baby. *Richard Wright Antiques.*

12½in (32cm) black bisque shoulder head with Horseshoe 1900, Heubach Köppelsdorf. *India Stoessel Collection.*

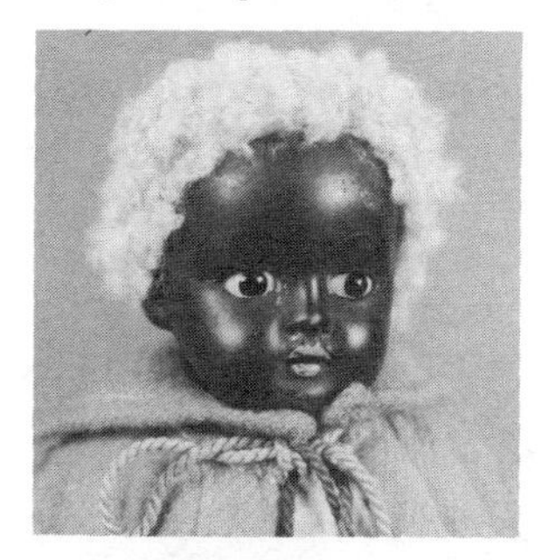

Black Dolls continued

27in (69cm) black papier-mâché shoulder head girl, cloth body, composition lower arms and legs. *Betty Harms Collection.*

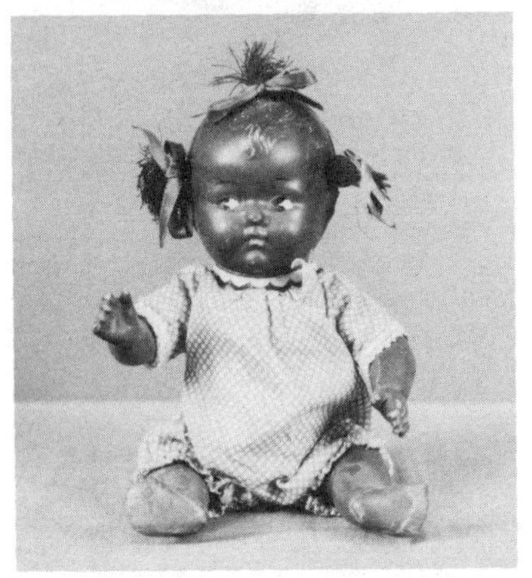

9in (23cm) black composition ***Topsy*** by GEM, all original with cloth label. *Betty Harms Collection.*

Tony Sarg's Mammy Doll: Composition character face with wide smiling mouth, painted features; large composition hands and molded shoes; cloth body; original clothes, carrying a white baby; all in good condition.

18in (46cm) **$425—475**

Papier-mâché Black Doll: Ca. 1890. By various German manufacturers. Papier-mâché character face, arms and legs, cloth body; glass eyes; original or appropriate clothes; all in good condition.

10—12in (25—31cm) **$250—275**
22—25in (56—64cm) **750—850****

**Not enough price samples to compute a reliable range.

Black Composition Doll: Ca. 1930. American-made bent-limb baby or mama-type body, jointed at hips, shoulders and perhaps neck; molded hair, painted or sleep eyes; original or appropriate clothes; some have three yarn tufts of hair on either side and on top of the head; all in good condition.

Baby,
10—12in (25—31cm) **$ 65—85**
Mama Doll,
20—22in (51—56cm) **125—150**

18in (46cm) Tony Sarg ***Mammy***, all original.

Black Dolls continued

Black Composition Doll: Ca. 1920 on. German made character doll, all-composition, jointed at neck, shoulders and hips; molded hair or wig, glass eyes (sometimes flirty); appropriate clothes; all in good condition.
17—18in (43—46cm) **$400—500**

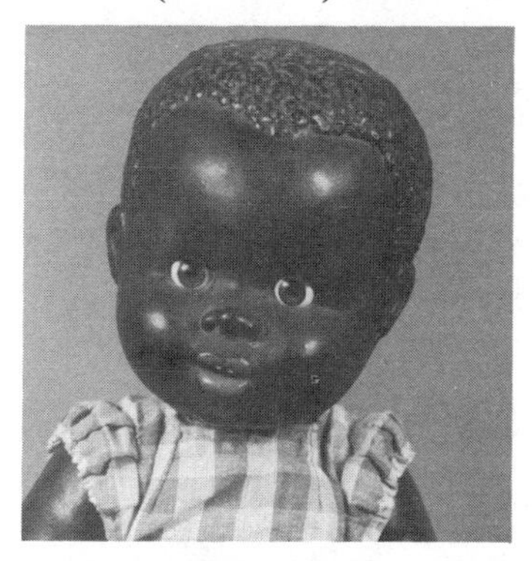

17in (43cm) unmarked black composition baby with molded kinky hair, appears German. *Betty Harms Collection.*

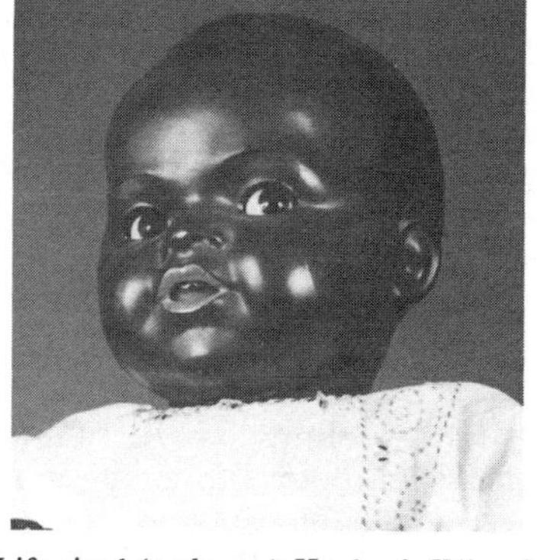

Life-sized (or larger) Heubach Köppelsdorf black composition baby. *Betty Harms Collection.*

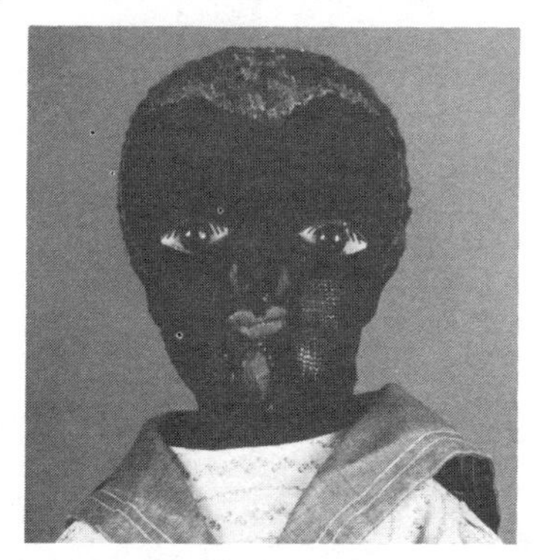

20in (51cm) black cloth stockinette boy with black bead eyes.

14in (36cm) handmade black cloth doll, later dress. *H&J Foulke, Inc.*

Cloth Black Doll: Ca. 1910. American-made cloth doll with black face, painted, printed or embroidered features; jointed arms and legs; original clothes; all in good condition.

Mammy-type, 14—16in (36—41cm) **$200 up***
Babyland Rag-type, 19in (48cm) **500—600**
Beecher-type, 19in (48cm) **850—900****
1930s Mammy, 14—16in (36—41cm) **125—150**

*Depending upon appeal.
**Not enough price samples to compute a reliable range.

Bonnie Babe

Maker: Bisque heads by Alt, Beck & Gottschalck of Nauendorf, Thüringia, Germany; Cloth bodies by George Borgfeldt & Co. of New York, N.Y., U.S.A. Dolls sold by K & K Toy Co. of New York, N.Y., U.S.A.
Date: 1926
Material: Bisque head with cloth body or all-bisque.
Size: Various
Designer: Georgene Averill
Mark:

Copr. by
Georgene Averill
Germany

1005/3652 plus another number, such as 1402 or 1368

Marked Bonnie Babe: Perfect bisque head with molded hair, glass sleep eyes, open mouth with two lower teeth, smiling face; cloth body with composition extremities often of poor quality; all in good condition.

Head circumference:

11—13in (28—33cm)	**$700—750**
15in (38cm)	**900—1000**
Celluloid head, 16in (41cm) tall	**400—450**

16in (41cm) ***Bonnie Babe*** with celluloid head, all original. *Richard Wright Antiques.*

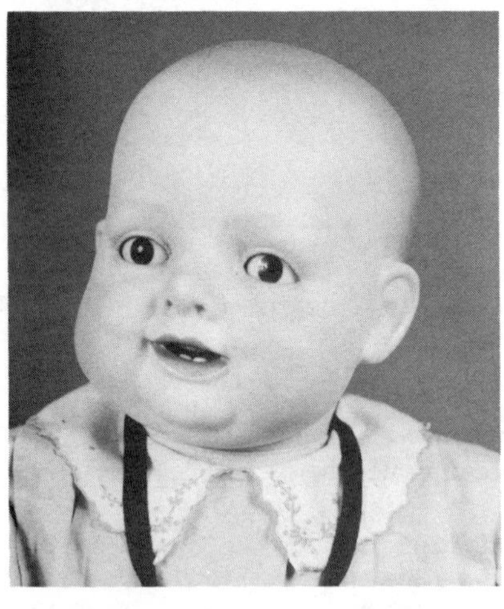

22in (56cm) ***Bonnie Babe*** 1005/3652 with bisque head. *Betty Harms Collection.*

All-Bisque Bonnie Babe: Molded hair, glass eyes, open mouth with two lower teeth; pink or blue molded slippers; jointed at neck, shoulders and hips; unmarked except for round paper label as shown.

4½in (12cm) **$750**

Boudoir Dolls

Maker: Various French, U.S. and Italian firms
Date: Early 1920s into the early 1930s
Material: Heads of composition and other materials; bodies mostly cloth but also of composition and other substances.
Size: Many 24—36in (61—91cm); some smaller
Mark: Mostly unmarked

Boudoir Doll: Head of composition, cloth or other material, painted features, composition or cloth stuffed body, unusually long extremities, usually high heeled shoes; original clothes elaborately designed and trimmed; all in good condition.

28—30in (71—76cm) **$75—95***

*More depending upon style of costume.

32in (81cm) Boudoir doll with cloth face, all original. *Betty Harms Collection.*

Bru

Maker: Bru Jne. & Cie, Paris, France
Date: 1866—1899
Material: Bisque swivel head on body as indicated below
Size: 10in (25cm) and up; size 0 is the smallest
Mark: On head, shoulder plate and body as shown below

Marked Brevete Bébé: Ca. 1870s. Bisque swivel head on shoulder plate, cork pate, skin wig, paperweight eyes with shading on upper lid, closed mouth with white space between lips, full cheeks, pierced ears; gusseted kid body pulled high on shoulder plate and straight cut with bisque lower arms (no rivet joints); dressed; all in good condition.

MARK: Size number only on head.

Oval sticker on body: BÉBÉ Breveté SGDG PARIS

13—14in (33—36cm) **$5500—6500**
17—18in (43—46cm) **8000—8500**

Marked Crescent or Circle Dot Bébé: Ca. late 1870s. Bisque swivel head on a deep shoulder plate with molded breasts, cork pate, attractive wig, paperweight eyes, closed mouth with slightly parted lips, plump cheeks, pierced ears; gusseted kid body with bisque lower arms (no rivet joints); dressed; all in good condition.

MARK: ◠ ⊙

Sometimes with "BRU Jne"

17—19in (43—48cm) **$ 9000—10000**
16in (41cm) Black **12000**

Marked Nursing Bru (Bébé Teteur): 1878—1898. Bisque head, shoulder plate and lower arms, kid body; upper arms and upper legs of metal covered with kid, lower legs of carved wood, or jointed composition body; attractive wig, lovely glass eyes, open mouth with hole for nipple, mechanism in head sucks up liquid, operates by turning key; nicely clothed; all in good condition.

18in (46cm) Bru Jne **$7000—7500**

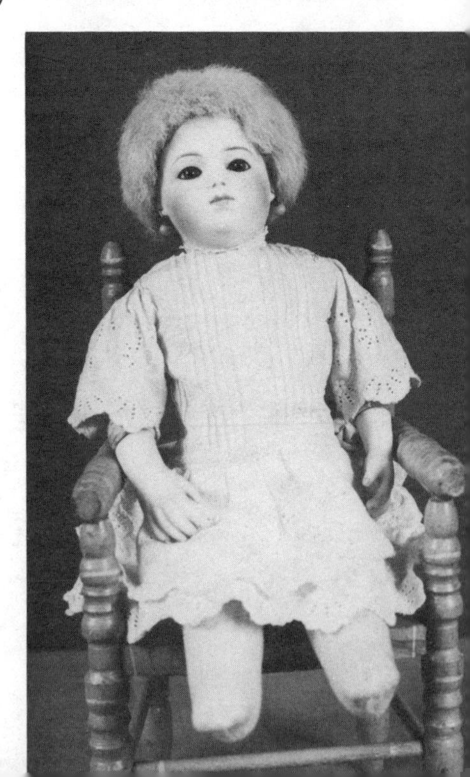

12in (31cm) Brevete Bébé.

Bru continued

Marked Bru Jne Bébé: Ca. 1880s. Bisque swivel head on deep shoulder plate with molded breasts, cork pate, attractive wig, paperweight eyes, closed mouth, pierced ears; gusseted kid body with scalloped edge at shoulder plate, bisque lower arms with lovely hands, kid over wood upper arms, hinged elbow, wooden legs (sometimes on a jointed composition body); dressed; all in good condition.

MARK: "BRU Jne"

Body Label:

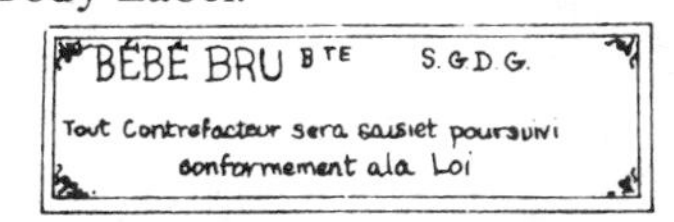

12in (31cm)	**$ 6000**
15in (38cm)	**7000**
18—19in (46—48cm)	**8000—9000**
20—22in (51—56cm)	**9000—10000**
26—27in (66—69cm)	**12500—15000**

Marked Bru Jne R Bébé: Ca. Early 1890s. Bisque head on a jointed composition body; attractive wig, paperweight eyes, closed mouth, pierced ears; dressed; all in good condition.

MARK: BRU Jne R
11

Body Stamp: "Bebe Bru" with size number

22in (56cm):

Very pretty	**$6000—6500**
Ugly	**4500**

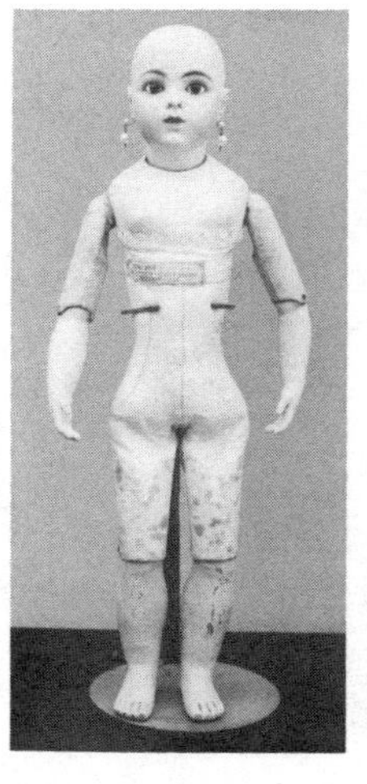

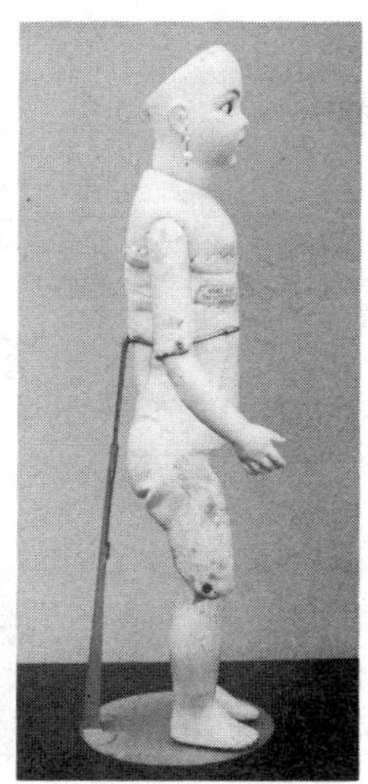

20in (51cm) Bru Jne 7 with labeled kid body, kid over wood upper arms, bisque lower arms and carved wooden legs. *H&J Foulke, Inc.*

Side view of the 20in (51cm) Bru Jne 7. *H&J Foulke, Inc.*

Marked Bru Bébé with open mouth: Ca. 1895. Bisque head on a jointed composition body with kiss-throwing and walking mechanism; attractive wig, sleep eyes, open mouth with upper teeth, pierced ears; dressed; all in good condition.

MARK: "BRU Jne"

23in (58cm):

Very pretty	**$4500**
Ugly	**3500**

17in (43cm) Bru Jne, all original except wig. *Ruth Noden Collection.*

Brückner Rag Doll

Maker: Albert Brückner, Jersey City, N.J., U.S.A.
Date: 1901—on
Material: All-cloth with stiffened mask face
Size: About 12—15in (31—38cm)
Mark: On right front shoulder: PAT'D. JULY 8TH 1901

Marked Brückner: Cloth head with printed features on stiffened mask face, cloth body flexible at shoulders and hips; appropriate clothes; all in good condition.

12in (31cm) White	**$150**
12in (31cm) Black	**175**
12in (31cm) ***Topsy Turvy***	**250**

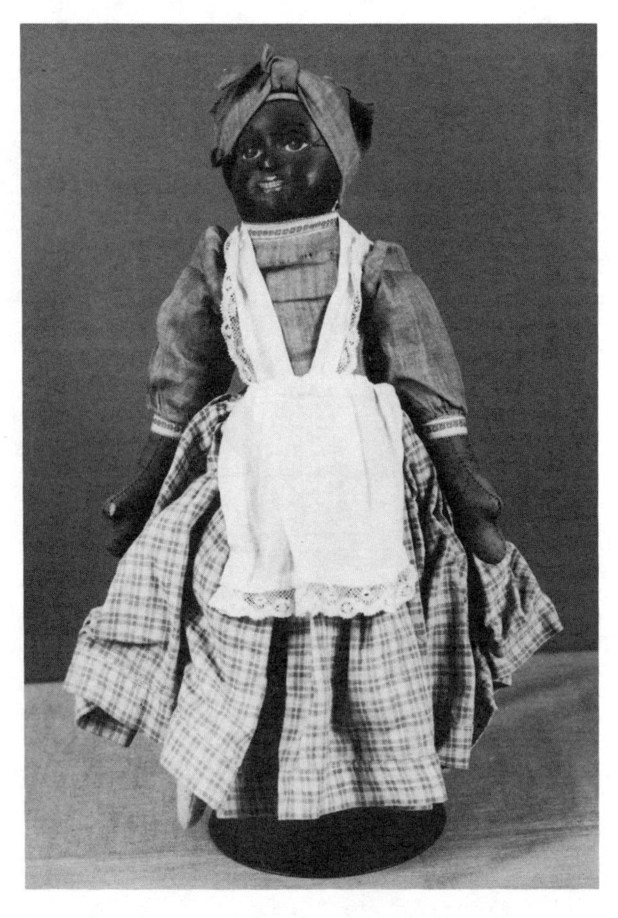

12in (31cm) Brückner ***Topsy Turvy***, all original.

Bye-Lo Baby

Maker: Bisque heads — J. D. Kestner; Alt, Beck & Gottschalck; Kling & Co.; Hertel Schwab & Co.; all of Thüringia, Germany.
Composition heads — Cameo Doll Co., New York, N.Y., U.S.A.
Celluloid heads — Karl Standfuss, Saxony, Germany
Wooden heads (unauthorized) — Schoenhut of Philadelphia, PA., U.S.A.
All-Bisque Baby — J. D. Kestner
Cloth Bodies and Assembly — K & K Toy Co., New York, N.Y., U.S.A.

Date: 1922—on

Size: Bisque head - seven sizes 9—20in (23—51cm)
All-bisque - up to 8in (20cm)

Designer: Grace Storey Putnam, U.S.A.

Distributor: George Borgfeldt, New York, N.Y., U.S.A.

Mark: See various marks below

Bisque Head Bye-Lo Baby: Ca. 1923. Perfect bisque head, cloth body with curved legs (sometimes with straight legs), composition or celluloid hands; sleep eyes; dressed. (May have purple "Bye-Lo Baby" stamp on front of body.)

MARK: © 1923 by
Grace S. Putnam
MADE IN GERMANY

Head Circumference:

8—10in (20—25cm)	**$ 375—425**
12—13in (31—33cm)	**475—550**
14in (36cm)	**650—675**
15in (38cm)	**800**
17in (43cm)	**1000—1100**
18in (46cm)	**1250—1500**
Composition body, 13in (33cm) long	**1100—1200**
Rare smiling face	**4500****

**Not enough price samples to compute a reliable range.

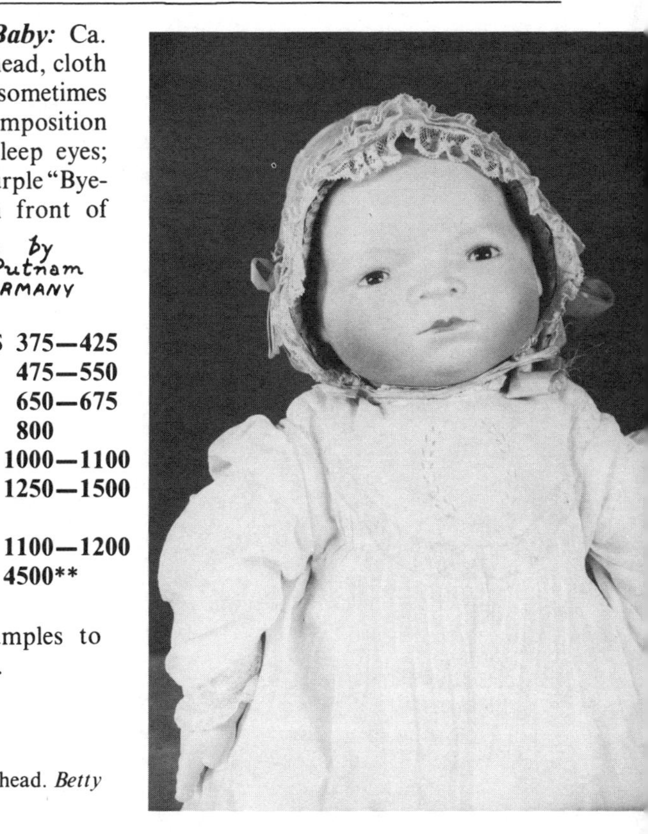

Life-size ***Bye-Lo*** with bisque head. *Betty Harms Collection.*

Bye-Lo Baby continued

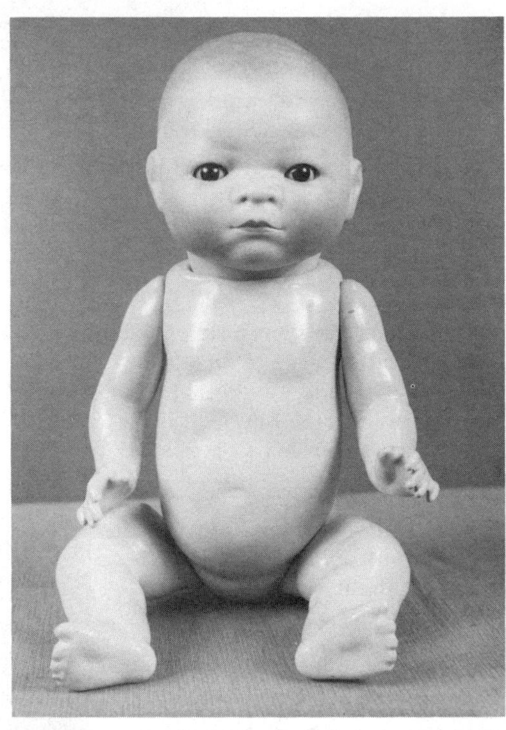

15in (38cm) ***Bye-Lo Baby*** incised "1369/45 © 1923 by Grace S. Putnam." Composition body marked "K & W". *Dr. Carole Stoessel Zvonar Collection.*

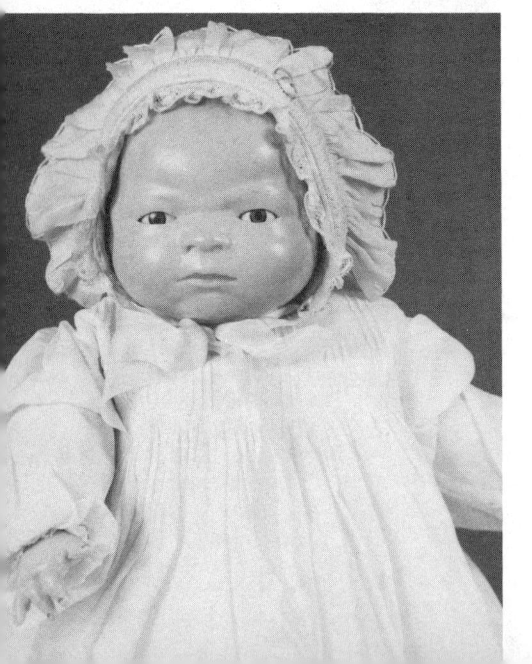

15in (38cm) head circumference ***Bye-Lo Baby*** with composition head. *Joanna Ott Collection.*

Composition Head Bye-Lo Baby: Ca. 1924. Cloth body with curved legs, composition hands; sleep eyes; nice clothes; all in good condition.

Head Circumference:

13in (33cm)	**$350**
Mint-in-box	**450**

Bye-Lo Baby continued

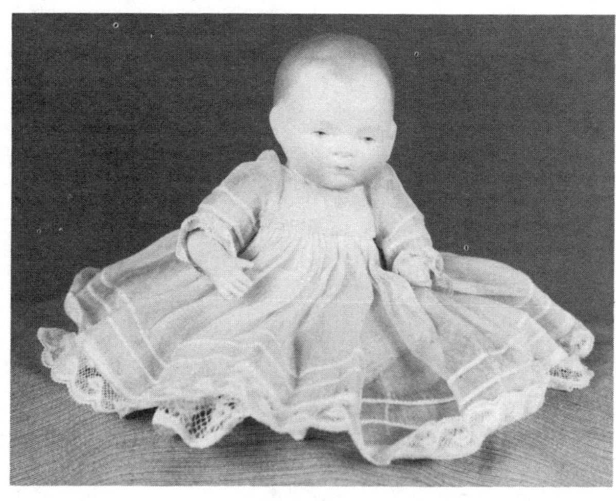

6½in (17cm) all-bisque ***Bye-Lo Baby*** with painted eyes, all original. *H&J Foulke, Inc.*

Marked All-Bisque Bye-Lo Baby:
1925—on.

MARK: Dark green paper label on front torso often missing; incised on back "20-12" (or other stock and size number)

BYE-LO BABY
©
GERMANY
G.S. PUTNAM

"Copr. by
G.S. Putnam"

a. Solid head with molded hair and painted eyes, jointed shoulders and hips.

4in (10cm)	**$275**
5in (13cm)	**375**
With booties, 4in (10cm)	**350**

b. Solid head with swivel neck, glass eyes, jointed shoulders and hips.

5—6in (13—15cm)	**550—650**

c. Head with wig, glass eyes, jointed shoulders and hips.

4—5in (10—13cm)	**550—650**

d. Action ***Bye-Lo Baby***, immobile in various positions, painted features.

3in (8cm)	**325—375**

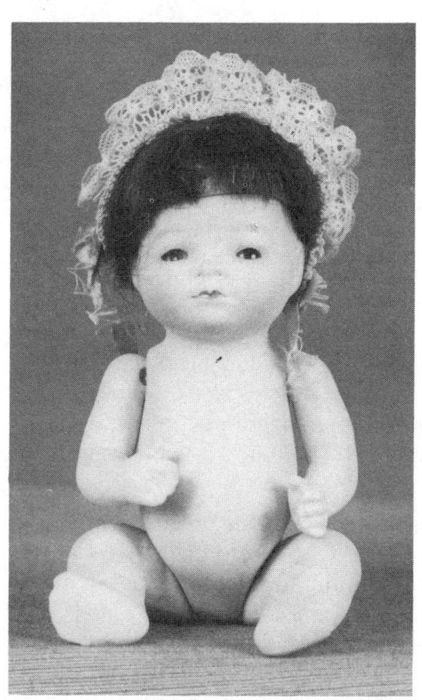

5in (13cm) all-bisque ***Bye-Lo Baby*** with glass eyes and wig, original bonnet. *Richard Wright Collection.*

Bye-Lo Baby continued

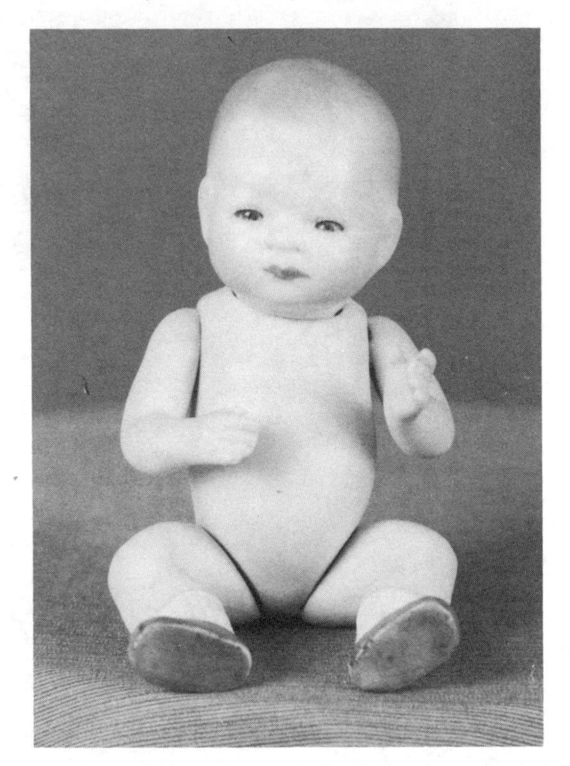

5in (13cm) all-bisque ***Bye-Lo Baby*** with glass eyes, swivel neck, molded blue booties. *H&J Foulke, Inc.*

Schoenhut Bye-Lo Baby: Ca. 1925. Wooden head with sleep eyes; cloth body; nice clothes; all in good condition.
$1200 up

Painted Bisque Head Bye-Lo Baby: Ca. late 1920s. Head has coating of flesh-colored paint, not baked in, washes and rubs off easily, sleep eyes; cloth body with composition hands; dressed; all in good condition.
Head Circumference:
13in (33cm) **$325—375**

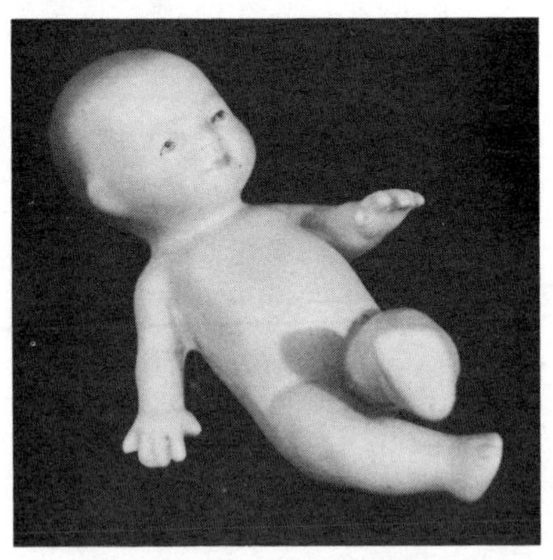

3½in (9cm) immobile ***Bye-Lo Baby*** often referred to as an ***Action Bye-Lo***. *H&J Foulke, Inc.*

Cameo Doll Company

Maker: Cameo Doll Company, New York, N.Y. U.S.A.; later Port Allegany, PA., U.S.A.
Date: 1922—on
Material: Wood-pulp composition and wood

(See also ***Kewpie*** and ***Baby Bo Kaye***)

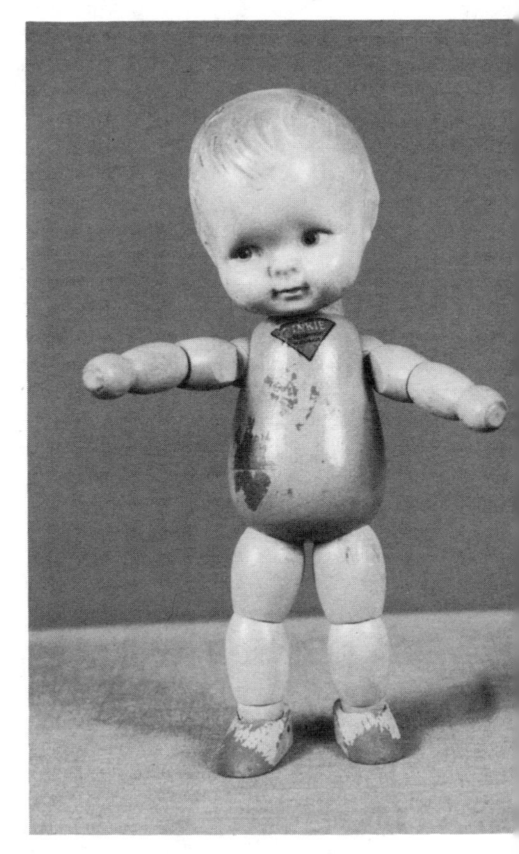

10in (25cm) ***Pinkie***. Betty Harms Collection.

Pinkie: 1930. Designed by J. L. Kallus. Composition head, molded hair, painted eyes, closed mouth; segmented wood body; undressed; all in good condition.

MARK: Triangle on chest:
"PINKIE
Des. & Copyright
by Jos. Kallus"

10in (25cm) **$275—325****

**Not enough price samples to compute a reliable range.

All-Bisque Little Annie Rooney: 1925. Designed by Jack Collins. Molded clothes, jointed arms: yellow yarn hair with braids, painted features with large round eyes and watermelon mouth; red felt hat; excellent condition.

MARK: Germany
LITTLE ANNIE ROONEY
REG. U.S. PAT. OFF
CORP. BY JACK COLLINS

4in (10cm) **$200—225**

Composition Little Annie Rooney: 1925. Designed by Jack Collins. All-composition, jointed at neck, shoulders and hips, legs as black stockings, feet with molded shoes; braided yarn wig, painted round eyes, watermelon mouth; original clothes; all in good condition.

MARK: None

16in (41cm) **$650****

**Not enough price samples to compute a reliable range.

Cameo Doll Company continued

10in (25cm) ***Margie.*** *Betty Harms Collection.*

Margie: 1929. Designed by J. L. Kallus. Composition head with smiling face, molded hair, painted eyes, closed mouth with painted teeth; segmented wood body; undressed; all in good condition.
MARK: Red triangle label on chest:
"MARGIE
Des. & Copyright
by Jos. Kallus"
10in (25cm) **$225—250**

Joy: 1932. Designed by J. L. Kallus. Composition head with smiling face, molded curls with loop for a bow, blue side-glancing eyes, watermelon mouth; wood segmented body; undressed; all in good condition.
MARK: Round label on chest:
"JOY
Des. & Copy't
J. L. Kallus"
10in (25cm) **$275—325**

All-Bisque Scootles: 1925. Jointed at shoulders only, very good detail modeling in torso and legs; molded yellow hair, blue eyes looking to the side; smiling face.
MARK: "Scootles" on red and gold chest label;
"Scootles" and "Rose O'Neill" on feet
5—6in (13—15cm):
Germany **$450—500**
Japan **200—225**

Scootles: 1925. Designed by Rose O'Neill. All-composition, unmarked, jointed at neck, shoulders and hips; molded hair, blue or brown painted eyes looking to the side, closed smiling mouth; not dressed; all in good condition.
MARK: Wrist tag only
Rare 7—8in (18—20cm) **$225—250**
12in (31cm) **350—375**
16in (41cm) **400—450**
14in (36cm), Black **500—550**

16in (41cm) ***Scootles***, all original. *Betty Harms Collection.*

Cameo Doll Company continued

Betty Boop: 1932. Designed by J. L. Kallus. Composition swivel head, painted and molded black hair, large goo-goo eyes, tiny closed mouth; composition torso with molded-on and painted bathing suit, wood segmented arms and legs; all in good condition. (Also made in a rare form without the molded bathing suit and with composition legs; wearing a cotton print dress.)

MARK: Heart-shaped label on chest:

"BETTY—BOOP
Des. & Copyright
by Fleischer
Studios"

12in (31cm) **$450—500**

Giggles: 1946. Designed by Rose O'Neill. All-composition, unmarked, jointed at neck, shoulders and hips, molded hair with bun in back, large painted side-glancing eyes, closed mouth; original romper; all in good condition.

MARK: Paper wrist tag only

14in (36cm) **$425—450**

12in (31cm) ***Betty Boop.*** *Mike White Collection.*

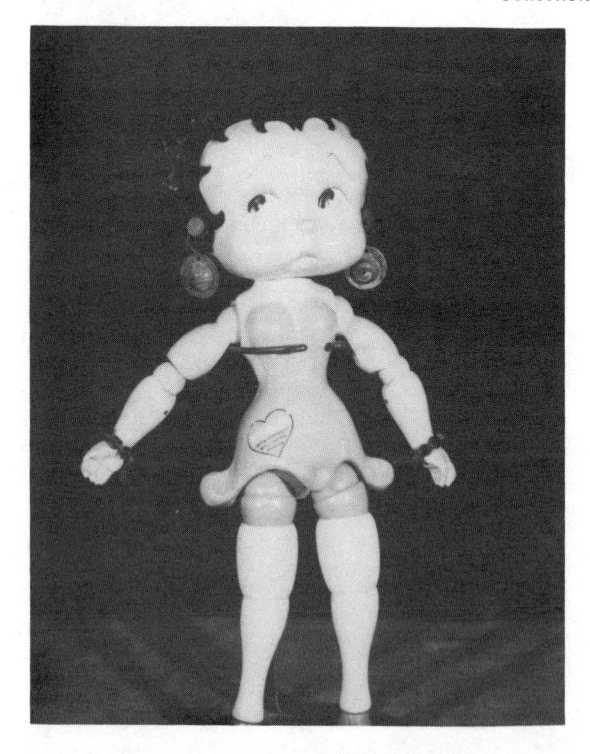

Campbell Kid

Maker: E. I. Horsman Co., Inc., New York, N.Y., U.S.A.; American Character Doll Co., New York, N.Y., U.S.A.
Date: 1910—on
Material: Composition head and arms, cloth body and legs; or all-composition
Size: Usually 10—16in (25-41cm)
Designer: Grace G. Drayton

Campbell Kid: 1910-1914. By Horsman. Marked composition head with flange neck, molded and painted bobbed hair, painted round eyes to the side, watermelon mouth; original cloth body, composition arms, cloth legs and feet; original romper suit; all in fair condition.
MARK: On head: E.I.H. © 1910

Cloth label on sleeve:

The Campbell Kids
Trademark by
Joseph Campbell
Mfg. by E. I. HORSMAN Co.

10—13in (25—33cm) **$150.**

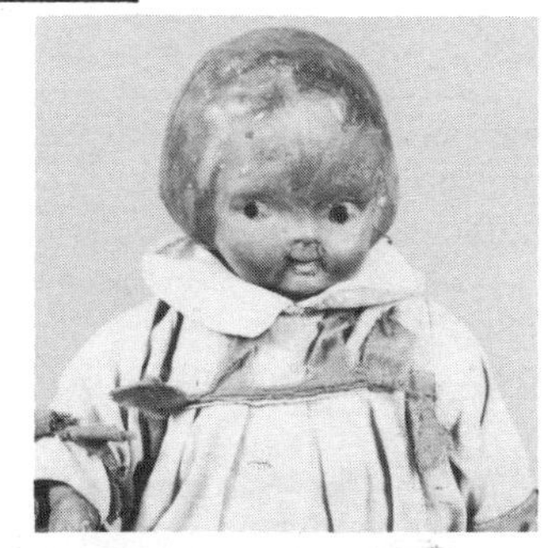

9½in (24cm) brown ***Campbell Kid***, 1910. *Betty Harms Collection.*

Campbell Kid: 1923. By American Character, sometimes called "Dolly Dingle". All-composition with swivel head, jointed shoulders and hips; molded and painted hair, eyes to the side, watermelon mouth; original clothes; all in good condition.
MARK: On back:
"A PETITE DOLL"
12in (31cm) **$400—450**

Campbell Kid: 1948. By Horsman. Unmarked all-composition, molded painted hair, painted eyes to the side, watermelon mouth; painted white socks and black slippers; original clothes; all in good condition.
12in (31cm) **$250—275**

12in (31cm) ***Campbell Kid***, 1948, all original. *Betty Harms Collection.*

Catterfelder Puppenfabrik

Maker: Catterfelder Puppenfabrik, Catterfeld, Thüringia, Germany
Heads by J. D. Kestner and other porcelain makers
Date: 1902—on
Material: Bisque head; composition body
Size: Various
Mark: "C.P." or "Catterfelder Puppenfabrik" and mold #201, 208, 209, or 264

C.P. Child Doll: Ca. 1902—on. Perfect bisque head, good wig, sleep eyes, open mouth with teeth; composition jointed body; dressed; all in good condition.

#264 22—24in (56—61cm) **$650—750**

C.P. Character Baby: Ca. 1910—on. Perfect bisque character face with wig or molded hair, painted or glass eyes; jointed baby body; dressed; all in good condition.

#263, 208, 209
15—18in (38—46cm) **$450—500**
20—22in (51—56cm) **600—700**

C.P. Character Child: Ca. 1910—on. Perfect bisque character face with wig, painted eyes; composition jointed body; dressed; all in good condition.

15in (38cm) **$2650****

**Not enough price samples to compute a reliable range.

17in (43cm) 264 child *Sheila Needle Collection.*

25in (64cm) 263 character baby with retractable tongue. *Dr. Carole Stoessel Zvonar Collection.*

Celluloid Dolls

Makers: Germany:
Rheinische Gummi und Celluloid Fabrik Co. (Turtle symbol)
Buschow & Beck. *Minerva* trademark. (Helmet symbol)
E. Maar & Sohn. *Emasco* trademark. (3 M symbol)
Cellba. (Mermaid symbol)
Poland:
P.R. Zask, (ASK in triangle)
France:
Petitcolin. (Eagle symbol)
Société Nobel Francaise. (SNF in diamond)
Neumann & Marx. (Dragon symbol)

Date: 1900—1940s for dolls discussed here

Material: All-celluloid or celluloid head with jointed kid, cloth or composition body.

Size: up to 25in (64cm)

Marks: Various as indicated above; sometimes also in combination with the marks of J. D. Kestner, Kämmer & Reinhardt, Bruno Schmidt, Käthe Kruse and König & Wernicke

---

Celluloid shoulder head Child doll: Ca. 1900—on. Molded hair or wig, painted or glass eyes, open or closed mouth; cloth or kid body, celluloid or composition arms; dressed; all in good condition.

Painted eyes:
12—14in (31—36cm) $ **90—110**
Glass eyes:
16—18in (41—46cm) **150—175**
22—24in (56—61cm) **200—225**

12in (31cm) K ★ R 701 character girl, painted eyes, jointed composition body. *Richard Wright Antiques.*

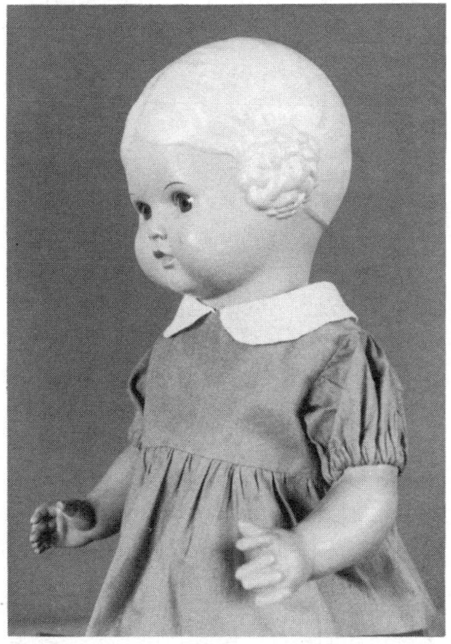

18in (46cm) all-celluloid girl with turtle trademark, molded hair, inset eyes. *H&J Foulke, Inc.*

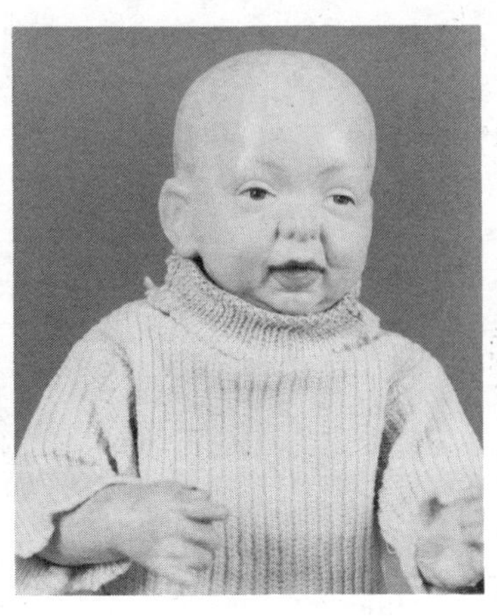

Left to right: 12½in (32cm) all-celluloid boy with turtle trademark, all original. *H&J Foulke, Inc.* 10in (25cm) French all-celluloid baby. *H&J Foulke, Inc.* 13in (33cm) K ★ R 700 character baby. *Richard Wright Antiques.*

Celluloid socket head Child Doll: Ca. 1910—on. Wig, glass eyes, sometimes flirty, open mouth with teeth; ball-jointed or bent-limb composition body; dressed; all in good condition.

15—18in (38—46cm)	**$200—225**
22—24in (56—61cm)	**300—325**
***Characters*:**	
K★R 701, 12—13in (31—33cm)	**550—600**
K★R 717, 24in (61cm)	**400—425**
K★R 728, 12in (31cm) baby	**275**
K★R 700 baby, 13in (31cm)	**400**

All-Celluloid Child Doll: Ca. 1900—on. Jointed at neck, shoulders, and hips; molded hair or wig, painted eyes; dressed; all in good condition.

5—6in (13—15cm)	**$ 25—35**
9—10in (23—25cm)	**60—75**
12—13in (31—33cm)	**85—95**
Glass eyes:	
12—13in (31—33cm)	**125—135***
16—18in (41—46cm)	**175—225***

*Add more for K★R dolls.

All-Celuloid Baby: Ca. 1910—on. Bent-limb baby, molded hair, painted eyes, closed mouth; jointed arms and/or legs; no clothes; all in good condition.

8—10in (20—25cm)	**$ 65**
14—15in (36—38cm)	**95**
Glass eyes, 14—15in (36—38)	**125**

Century Doll Co.

Maker: Century Doll Co., New York, N.Y., U.S.A.; bisque heads by J.D. Kestner, Germany
Date: 1909—on
Material: Bisque head, cloth body, composition arms (and legs)
Size: Various
Mark: "Century Doll Co." Sometimes ⟨K⟩ (for Kestner). "Germany"

Marked Century Infant: Ca. 1925. Perfect bisque solid-dome head, molded and painted hair, sleep eyes, open/closed mouth; cloth body, composition hands or limbs; dressed; all in good condition.
Head Circumference:
12—13in (31—33cm) **$600—650**
14—15in (36—38cm) **700—800**

13in (33cm) head circumference Century baby. *Richard Wright Collection.*

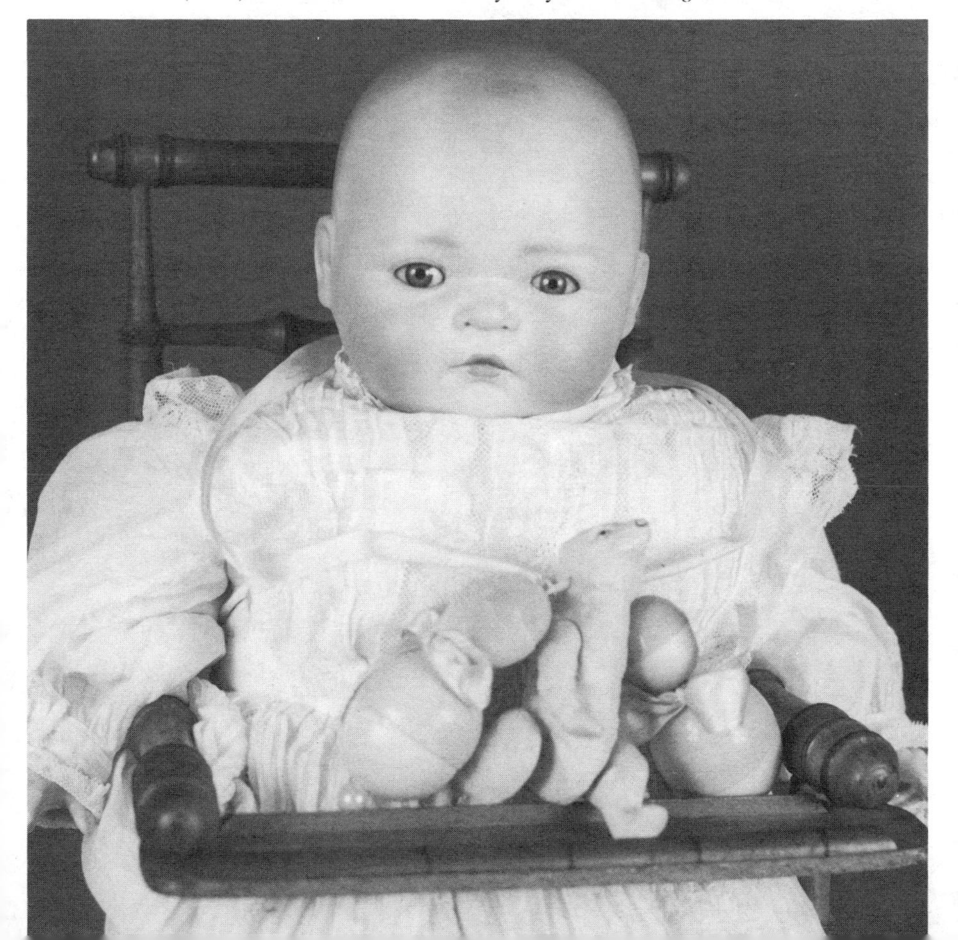

Chad Valley

Maker: Chad Valley Co. (formerly Johnson Bros., Ltd.), Birmingham, England
Date: 1923—on
Material: All-cloth
Size: Various
Mark: Paper or cloth label

(See also Mabel Lucie Attwell)

Chad Valley Doll: All-cloth, usually felt face and velvet body, jointed neck, shoulders and hips; mohair wig, glass or painted eyes; original clothes; all in good condition.

Characters, painted eyes,
10—12in (25—31cm) **$ 55—75**

Children, painted eyes,
11—13in (28—33cm) **125—150**
16—18in (41—46cm) **300—400**

Children, glass eyes,
16—18in (41—46cm) **400—500**

Royal Children,
16—18in (41—46cm) **800—1000**

18in (46cm) child with painted eyes, original clothes. *H&J Foulke, Inc.*

Martha Chase

Maker: Martha Jenks Chase, Pawtucket, R.I., U.S.A.
Date: 1893 to present
Material: Stockinette and cloth, painted in oils; some fully painted washable models; some designed for hospital training use.
Size: 9in (23cm) to life-size
Designer: Martha Jenks Chase
Mark: "Chase Stockinet Doll" stamp on left leg or under left arm, paper label on back (usually gone)

Chase Doll: Pre-1930. Head and limbs of stockinette, treated and painted with oils, rough-stroked hair to provide texture, cloth bodies jointed at shoulders, hips, elbows and knees, later ones only at shoulders and hips; some bodies completely treated; not in perfect condition.

Baby, 16—20in (41—51cm)	**$500—550**
Child, molded bobbed hair, 15—16in (38—41cm)	**725—775**
Lady, 15in (38cm)	**1200—1300**
Black, 27in (69cm)	**3000****

**Not enough price samples to compute a reliable range.

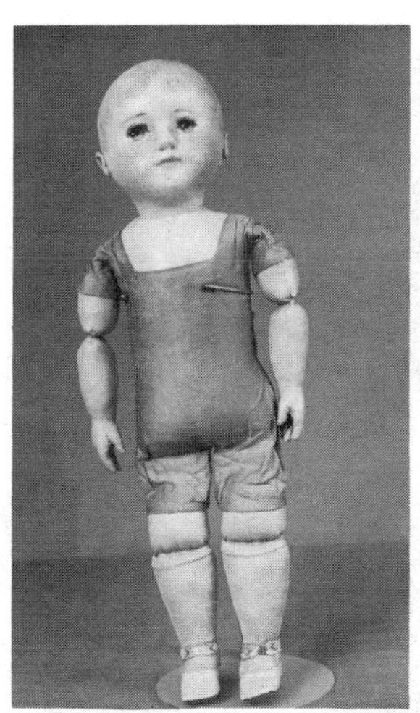

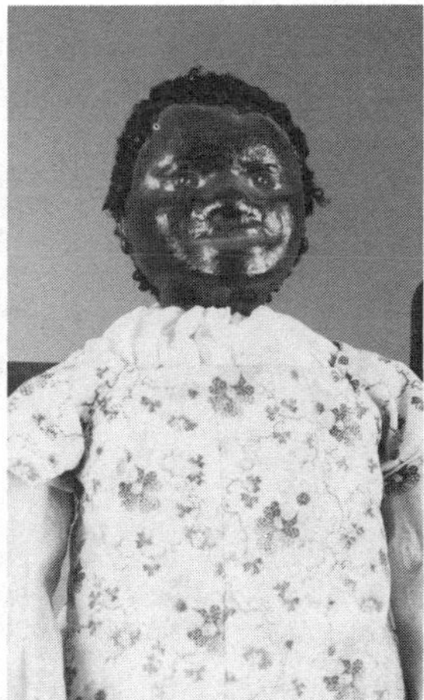

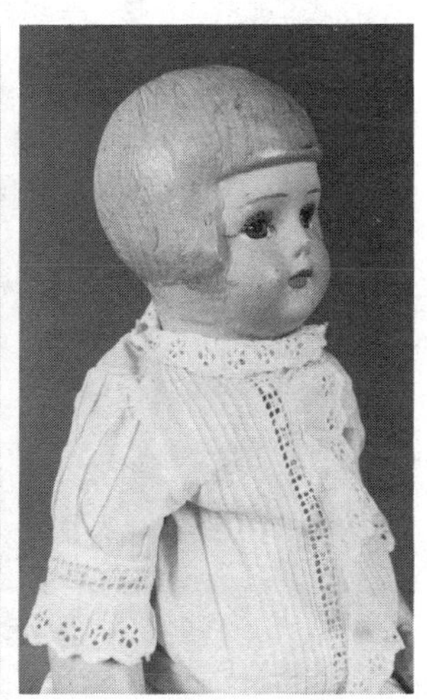

Left to right: 20in (51cm) Chase child, tan sateen body. *H&J Foulke, Inc.* 27in (69cm) black Chase doll, very rare. 17in (43cm) Chase girl with bobbed hair. *H&J Foulke, Inc.*

China Heads
(German)

Maker: Often unknown
Date: Various
Material: China head, cloth or kid body, china or leather arms
Size: Various
Mark: Often unmarked, sometimes marked with numbers and/or "Germany"

Adelina Patti (so-called): Ca. 1870. Black-haired china shoulder head with high forehead, white center part with wings on each side, short overall curls, brush marks at temple; cloth body with leather arms or china arms and legs.
MARK: None
20—24in (51—61cm) **$450—550**

Bald (so-called Biedermeier): Ca. 1840. China shoulder head with bald head, some with black areas on top of head, proper wig, blue painted eyes; cloth body, bisque, china or leather arms; nicely dressed; all in good condition.
15—18 (38—46cm) **$375—475**

11½in (29cm) bald china with orignial mohair wig.

Bangs: Ca. 1880. Black- or blonde-haired china shoulder head with bangs on forehead; cloth body with china arms and legs to kid body; dressed; all in good condition.
MARK: Some marked "Germany" or Kling & Co: [bell with K mark]
17—18in (43-46cm) **$300—325**
22—24in (56—61cm) **350—400**

5in (13cm) 1096 #8 china head with curly bangs. *H&J Foulke, Inc.*

China Heads (German) continued

15in (38cm) blonde-haired child with bangs. *H&J Foulke, Inc.*

27in (69cm) blonde-haired china boy. *Dr. Carole Stoessel Zvonar Collection.*

Boy or Child: Ca. 1880s. Black- or blonde-haired china shoulder head with short wavy hair and exposed ears; cloth body with china limbs; dressed; all in good condition.

16—18in (41—46cm) **$225—250**
23—25in (58—64cm) **325—375**

Brown Eyes: Ca. 1850. Black hair parted in center, smooth to the head, pulled behind the ears; cloth body with leather arms; dressed; all in good condition.

MARK: None

Greiner-style hairdo:
13—15in (33—38cm) **$375—425**
19—21in (48—53cm) **650—700**

Flat-top style,
16—20in (41—51cm) **250—300**

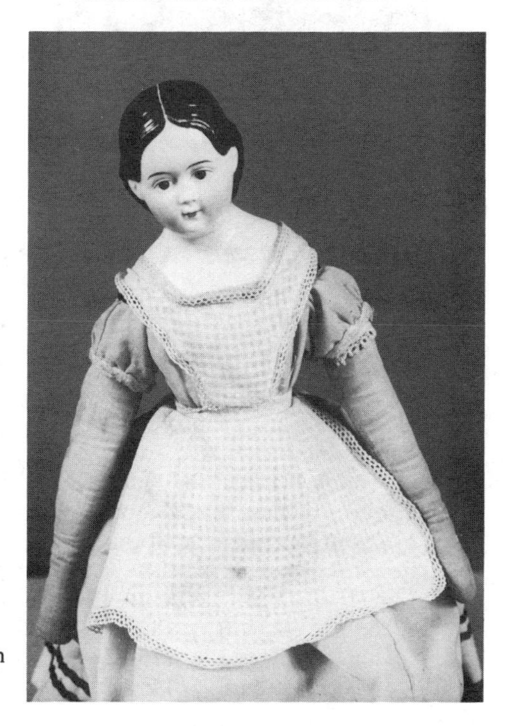

16in (41cm) china head with brown painted eyes, Greiner-style hairdo.

China Heads (German) continued

Bun: Ca. 1840s. Black-haired china shoulder head with pink tint, hair pulled back into braided bun, ears sometimes exposed; old cloth body; dressed; all in good condition.

18—21in (46—53cm) **$750 and up**

19in (48cm) rare brown-haired china head with bun and exposed ears.

Common or Low Brow: Ca. 1890s—on. Black or blonde wavy hair style on china shoulder head, blue painted eyes; old cloth or kid body with stub, leather, bisque or china limbs; appropriate clothes; all in good condition.

7—8in (18-20cm)	**$60—65**
10—12in (25—31cm)	**85—95**
14—16in (36—41cm)	**125—150**
20—24in (52—61cm)	**175—225**

Child, Motschmann-type with swivel neck: Ca. 1850. China head and flange neck with shoulder plate, midsection and lower limbs of china; black painted hair, blue painted eyes; with or without clothes; all in good condition.

MARK: None

11in (28cm) **$1550—1650**

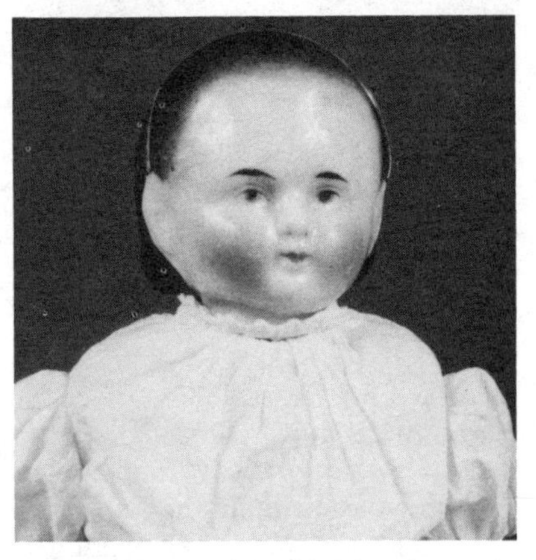

10½in (27cm) child with Motschmann-type body, Alice hairdo.

16in (41cm) blonde-haired china with common hairdo, all original. *H&J Foulke, Inc.*

China Heads (German) continued

Covered Wagon (so-called): 1850—1870. Black-haired china shoulder head with pink tint, hair parted in middle and close to head with vertical sausage curls; old cloth body with varied extremities; well dressed; all in good condition.

MARK: None

11—12in (28—31cm) **$300—325**
16—18in (41—46cm) **450—500**
23in (58cm), brown eyes **950**

Curly Top (so-called): Ca. 1860. Black- or blonde-haired shoulder head with distinctive large horizontal curls around forehead and face; old cloth body with leather arms or china arms and legs; nicely dressed; all in good condition.

MARK: None

18—20in (46—51cm) **$450-500**

Dolley Madison (so-called): 1875—1895. Black-haired china shoulder head with molded ribbon bow in front and molded band on back of head, blue painted eyes; old cloth body with leather arms; nicely dressed; in good condition.

MARK: None

17—21in (43—53cm) **$350—400**

Fancy Hairdo: Ca. 1860. China shoulder head with black hair, brush marks, elaborate style with braids, wings, ornaments, blue painted eyes; old cloth body; appropriate clothes; all in good condition.

20—24in (51—61cm) **$450 up**

7in (18cm) pink tint china head with covered wagon hairdo. *H&J Foulke, Inc.*

20in (51cm) china head lady with variation of Dolley Madison hairdo, molded flowers painted black. *Dr. Carole Stoessel Zvonar Collection.*

16in (41cm) china head laby with elaborate hairdo, brush marks, molded beads. *Dr. Carole Stoessel Zvonar Collection.*

China Heads (German) continued

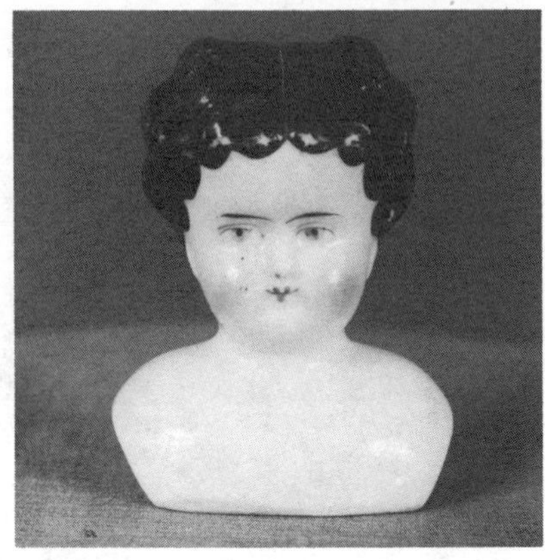

3½in (9cm) china head with flat top hairdo. *H&J Foulke, Inc.*

Glass Eyes: Ca. 1850. Black-haired china shoulder head with hair parted in middle and styled very close to head, dark glass eyes; cloth body with leather arms; appropriate clothes; all in good condition.

MARK: None

14in (36cm)	**$1850**
20in (51cm)	**2350**

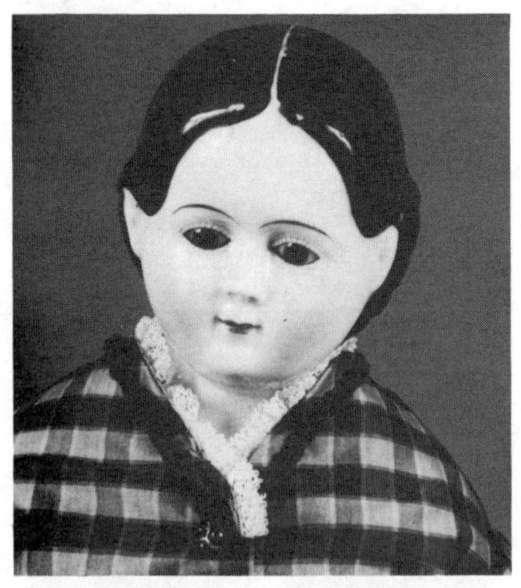

16in (41cm) china head with brown glass eyes and Greiner-style hairdo.

Flat Top (so-called): Ca. 1860-1870. China shoulder head with black hair parted in middle, smooth on top with short curls, blue painted eyes; old cloth body, extremities of leather or china; appropriate clothes; all in good condition.

MARK: None

16—18in (41—46cm)	**$175—200**
22—24in (56cm)	**225—250**
28in (71cm)	**300—325**

12in (31cm) very rare china head wearing molded white bonnet with pink trim.

Hatted China Head: Ca. 1880. Black or blonde hair with molded hat or bonnet; cloth body, stone bisque limbs; dressed; all in good condition.

Poke bonnet, 11in (28cm)	**$200—225**

China Heads (German) continued

High Brow (so-called): Ca. 1860-1870. China shoulder head with black painted hair, high forehead, center part, smooth top, curls clustered above ears; cloth body, china arms; dressed; all in good condition.

15—19in (38—48cm)	**$200—250**
22—24in (56—61cm)	**275-300**
Molded necklace, 23in (58cm)	**500**

Man: Ca. 1850. Black-haired china shoulder head with short hair, brush marks around face, blue painted eyes, cloth body; appropriate clothes; all in good condition.

MARK: None

Early fine quality, 22in (56cm)	**$1000 up**
20—22in (51—56cm)	**450—500**

10½in (27cm) ***Helen*** Pet Name china. *H&J Foulke, Inc.*

20in (51cm) china head with high brow hair style. *H&J Foulke, Inc.*

20in (51cm) china head man with brown eyes.

Pet Name: Ca. 1905. China shoulder head, molded yoke with name in gold; black or blonde painted hair (one-third were blonde), blue painted eyes; old cloth body (some with alphabet or other figures printed on cotton material), china limbs; properly dressed; all in good condition. Used names such as ***Agnes, Bertha, Daisy, Dorothy, Edith, Esther, Ethel, Florence, Helen, Mabel, Marion*** and ***Pauline***.

9—10in (23—25cm)	**$125—135**
16—18in (41—46cm)	**200—225**

China Heads (German) continued

10½in (27cm) china head with pierced ears, brush marks.

Pierced Ears: Ca. 1860. China shoulder head with black hair styled with curls on forehead and pulled back to curls on lower back of head, blue painted eyes, pierced ears; original cloth body with leather arms or china arms and legs; apropriate clothes; all in good condition.

MARK: None

20—22in (51—56cm) **$650 up***

*Depending upon rarity of hairdo.

Snood: Ca. 1860. China shoulder head with black painted hair, slender features, blue painted eyes, molded eyelids, gold-colored snood on hair; cloth body with leather arms or china limbs; appropriate clothes; all in good condition.

MARK: None

21—22in (53—56cm) **$700 up**

21in (53cm) ***Grape Lady*** **1250**

Spill Curl: Ca. 1870. China shoulder head with café-au-lait or black painted hair, massed curls on top spilling down back and sides onto shoulders, brush marks around the forehead and temples, exposed ears; cloth body with china arms and legs; appropriate clothes; all in good condition.

MARK: None

20—22in (51—56cm) **$550—650**

Wood-Body: Ca. 1840. Head with early hair style mounted on a peg-wooden body; usually with china lower limbs; undressed; in good condition.

5—6in (13—15cm)
Rare hairdo **$1400—1500**

6—7in (15—18cm)
Covered Wagon **800—1000**

15in (38cm)
Covered Wagon **1600—1700**

15in (38cm)
Rare hairdo **2200—2500**

20in (51cm) china with molded snood and brush marks. *Dr. Carole Stoessel Zvonar Collection.*

13in (33cm) china head on pegged wood body, rare hairdo with long curls.

Cloth, Printed

Maker: Various American companies, such as Cocheco Mfg Co., Lawrence & Co., Arnold Print Works, Art Fabric Mills and Selchow & Righter.
Date: 1896—on
Material: All-cloth
Size: 6—30in (15—76cm)
Mark: Mark could be found on fabric part which was discarded after cutting, Art Fabric Mills marked on foot.

Cloth, Printed Doll: Face, hair, underclothes, shoes and socks printed on cloth; all in good condition, some soil acceptable. Dolls in printed underwear are sometimes found dressed in old petticoats and frocks. Names such as: ***Dolly Dear, Merry Marie***, and so on.

6—7in (15—18cm) **$ 75**
16—18in (41—46cm) **150—160**
24—26in (61—66cm) **185—215**

Brownies: 1892. Designed by Palmer Cox; marked on foot. 8in (20cm) **95**

Boys and Girls with printed outer clothes, Ca. 1903, 12in (31cm) **150—175**

Darkey Doll, uncut **150**

Aunt Jemima Family (four dolls) **75—85 each**

Punch & Judy **150—175**

Santa **150**

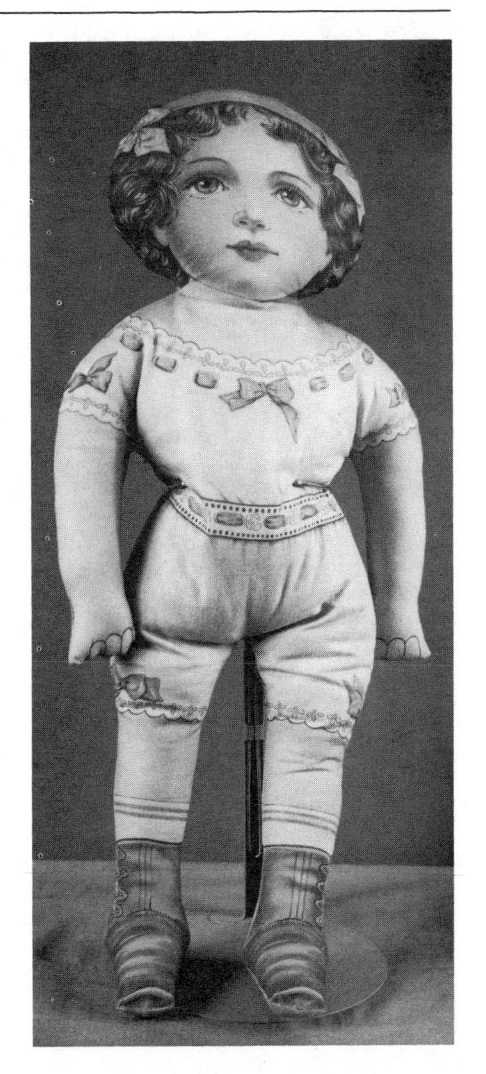

24in (61cm) ***Merry Marie.***

Cloth, Printed continued

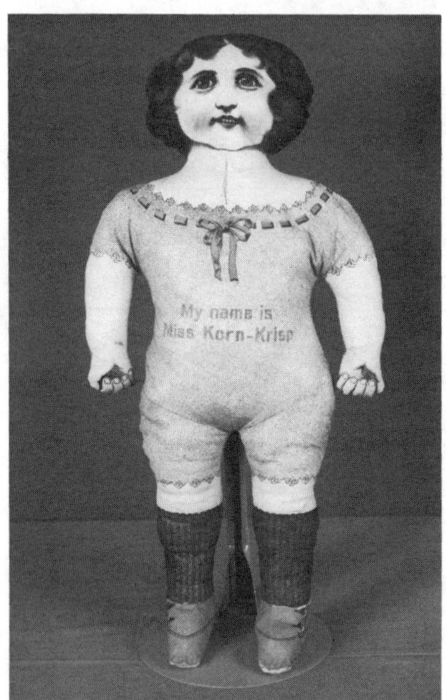

26in (66cm) ***Miss Korn Krisp.*** *H&J Foulke, Inc.*

12in (31cm) ***Harold Lloyd.*** *H&J Foulke, Inc.*

16in (41cm) ***Uncle Mose.*** *H&J Foulke, Inc.*

Cloth, Russian

Maker: Unknown craftsmen
Date: Ca. 1930
Material: All-cloth
Size: 13—15in (33—38cm)
Mark: "Made in Soviet Union" with indentification of doll, such as "Ukranian Woman,", "Village Boy", "Smolensk Districk Woman"

Russian Cloth Doll: All-cloth with stockinette head and hands, molded face with hand-painted features; authentic regional clothes; all in very good condition.
13—15in (33—38cm) **$80-90**

15in (38cm) **Ukranian Woman,** all original. *H&J Foulke, Inc.*

Cloth Shoulder Head

Maker: Unknown
Date: Ca. 1850
Material: All-cloth
Size: 22in (56cm)

Cloth Shoulder Head: Cloth shoulder head with molded features, painted black hair, glass or painted eyes, closed mouth; cloth body; appropriate old clothes. Very rare.

22in (56cm) **$1200—1500 up****

**Not enough price samples to compute a reliable range.

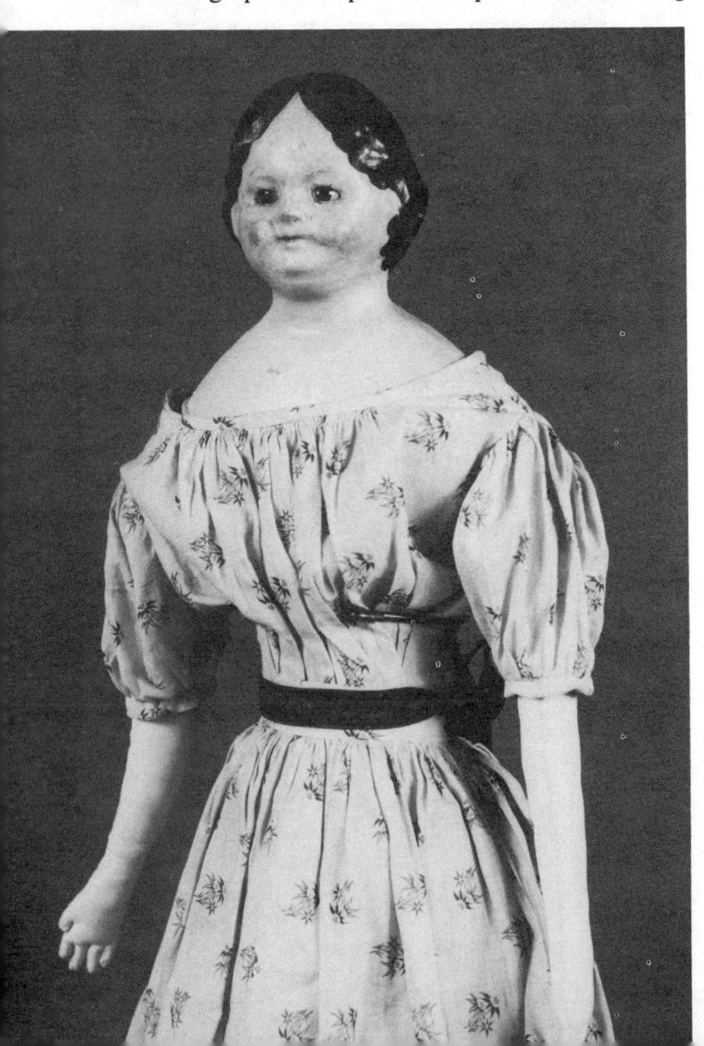

22in (56cm) cloth shoulder head doll with glass eyes.

Clowns

Maker: Various French and German firms
Date: 1890—on
Material: Bisque or papier-mâché head, composition body
Size: Usually small
Mark: Various

Molded Bisque: Clown with molded bisque smiling face, molded hair or wig, painted or glass eyes, clown paint on face; composition body; clown costume.
12—14in (31—36cm) **$600—650**

Standard Bisque: Clown having standard bisque head painted with clown make-up, wig, glass eyes, open mouth; composition body; clown costume.
12—14in (31—36cm) **$350—400**

Papier-mâché: Molded papier-mâché character face with painted features, wooden limbs; squeeze stomach and hands clap; original clothes.
12—14in (31—36cm) **$250—300**
Composition body, original clothes, glass eyes, 14in (36cm) **400-450**

Papier-mâché clown marionette.
Betty Harms Collection.

Dewees Cochran

Maker: Dewees Cochran, Fenton, CA., U.S.A.
Date: 1940—on
Material: Latex
Size: 9—18in (23—46cm)
Designer: Dewees Cochran
Mark: Signed under arm or behind right ear

Dewees Cochran Doll: Latex with jointed neck, shoulders and hips; human hair wig, painted eyes, character face; dressed; all in good condition.

15—16in (38—41cm) ***Cindy,*** 1947-1948.	**$550—650**
Grow-up Dolls: Stormy, Angel, Bunnie, J.J. and ***Peter Ponsett*** each at ages 5, 7, 11, 16 and 20, 1952-1956.	**900—1000**
Look-Alike Dolls (6 different faces)	**900—1000**
Baby, 9in (23cm)	**800—850**
Composition American Children (See Effanbee)	

12in (31cm) ***Veronica*** Portrait Child, 1962. *Pearl D. Morley Collection.*

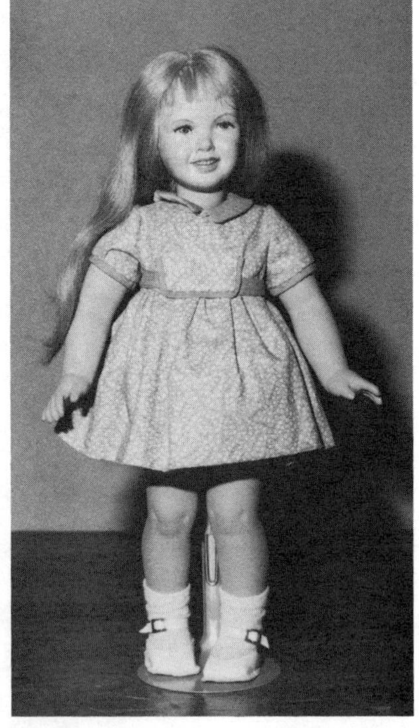

Small ***Look-Alike*** dolls. *Glenn Mandeville Collection.*

Columbian Doll

Maker: Emma and Marietta Adams
Date: 1891—1910 or later
Material: All-cloth
Size: 15—29in (38—74cm)
Mark: Stamped on back of body

Before 1900:
"COLUMBIAN DOLL
EMMA E. ADAMS
OSWEGO CENTRE
N.Y."

After 1906:
"THE COLUMBIAN DOLL
MANUFACTURED BY
MARIETTA ADAMS RUTTAN
OSWEGO, N.Y."

Columbian Doll: All-cloth with hair and features hand-painted; treated limbs; appropriate clothes; all in fair condition showing wear.

19in (48cm)	**$1050—1250**
15—16in (38—41cm)	**850—950**
Columbian-type, 16—18in (41—46cm)	**450—500**

16in (41cm) ***Columbian*** rag doll.

Composition
(American)

Maker: Various American firms, such as Bester Doll Co., New Era Novelty Co., New Toy Mfg. Co., Superior Doll Mfg. Co., Colonial Toy Mfg. Co.
Date: 1912—on
Material: Composition heads, ball-jointed composition bodies or bent-limb baby bodies
Size: Various
Mark: Various, according to company

All-Composition Character Baby: Composition with good wig, sleep eyes, open mouth with teeth; bent-limb baby body; appropriate clothes; all in good condition.

14—15in (36—38cm)	**$125—150**
18in (46cm)	**175—200**
22—25in (56—64cm)	**250—300**

All-Composition Child Doll: Composition with mohair wig, sleep eyes, open mouth; jointed composition body; appropriate clothes; all in good condition.

22—25in (56-64cm)	**$225—275**

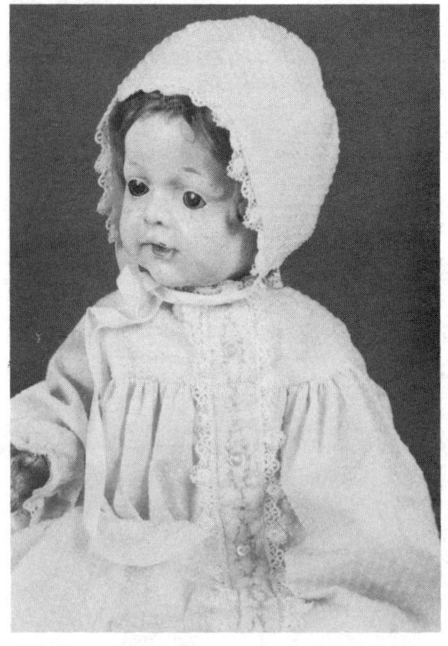

15in (38cm) all-composition baby. *Betty Harms Collection.*

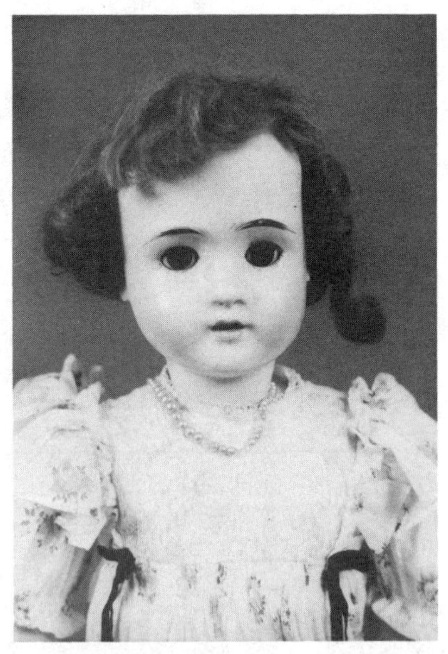

27in (69cm) all-composition doll by Bester Doll Co. *Richard Wright Antiques.*

Composition
(German)

Maker: Various German firms, such as König & Wernicke, Kämmer & Reinhardt and others
Date: Ca. 1925
Material: All-composition
Size: Various

All-Composition Child Doll: Socket head with good wig, sleep (sometimes flirty) eyes, open mouth with teeth; jointed composition body; appropriate clothes; all in good condition.

12—14in (31—36cm) **$150—175**
22—25in (56—64cm) **250—300**

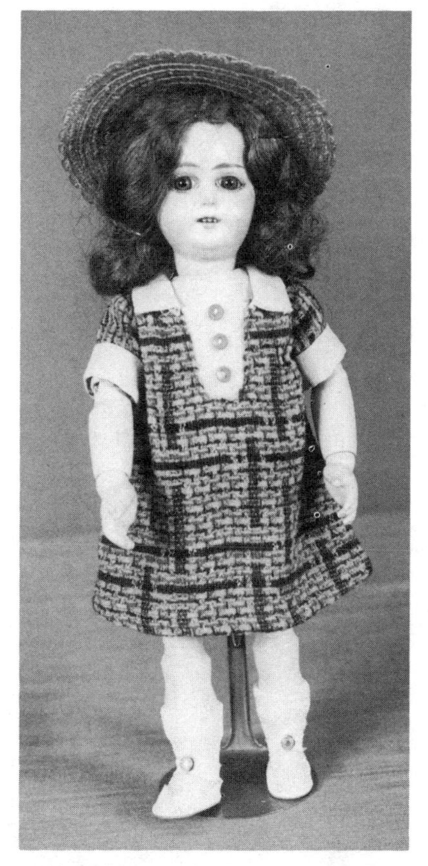

12in (31cm) all-composition child doll, unmarked. *H&J Foulke, Inc.*

All-Composition Character Baby: Composition socket head with good wig, sleep eyes, open mouth with teeth; bent-limb baby body; appropriate clothes; all in good condition.

14—15in (36—38cm) **$125—150**
20—22in (51—56cm) **225—250**
Toddler, 18in (46cm) **225—250**

18in (46cm) ***Our Pet*** character toddler. *H&J Foulke, Inc.*

Composition, Miscellaneous
(American)

Maker: Various United States firms, many unidentified
Date: 1912—on
Material: All-composition or composition head and cloth body, some with composition limbs
Size: 6in (15cm) up
Mark: Various according to company; most unmarked

Girl-type Mama Dolls: Ca. 1920-on. Made by various American companies. Composition head with lovely hair wig, sleep eyes, open mouth with teeth; composition shoulder plate, arms and legs, cloth body; original clothes; all in good condition. Dolls of very good quality.

18—20in (46—51cm)	**$125—150**
22—25in (56—64cm)	**175—225**

25in (64cm) girl-type mama doll, all original. *H&J Foulke, Inc.*

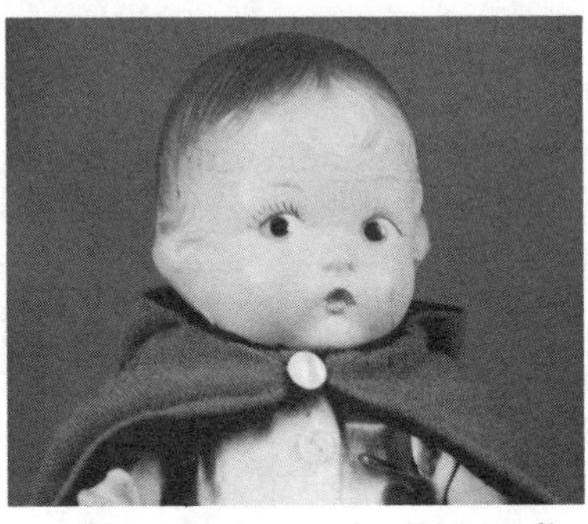

10in (25cm) ***Patsy***-type girl. *H&J Foulke, Inc.*

Patsy-type Girl: Ca. 1930s. All-composition with molded bobbed hair, sleep or painted eyes, closed mouth; jointed at neck, shoulders and hips; appropriate clothes; all in very good condition.

14—16in (36—41cm)	**$100—125**
9—10in (23—25cm)	**75—85**

Early Composition Head: Ca. 1912. Composition head with molded hair and painted features; cloth body with composition hands; appropriate clothes; all in fair condition.

12—15in (31cm)	**$100—125**

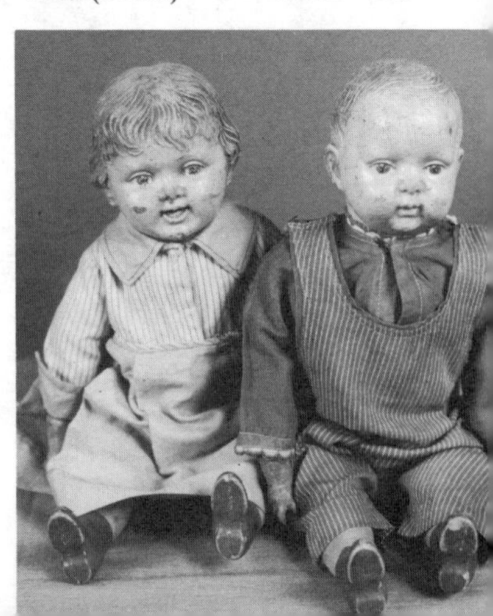

14in (36cm) boy and girl marked ***MTC Co.,*** composition shoes over cloth feet. *Betty Harms Collection.*

Composition (Miscellaneous) continued

Dionne-type Doll: Ca. 1935. All-composition with molded hair or wig, sleep eyes (painted in small dolls), closed or open mouth; jointed at neck, shoulders and hips; original clothes; all in very good condition.

7in (18cm) baby **$50—60**
18in (46cm) toddler **125—150**

20in (51cm) Dionne-type toddler, all original. *H&J Foulke, Inc.*

Shirley Temple-type Girl: Ca. 1935—on. All-composition, jointed at neck, shoulders and hips; blonde curly mohair wig, sleep eyes, open smiling mouth with teeth; original clothes; all in excellent condition.

15—18in (38—46cm) **$125—150**

16in (41cm) ***Shirley Temple***-type girl, all original. *H&J Foulke, Inc.*

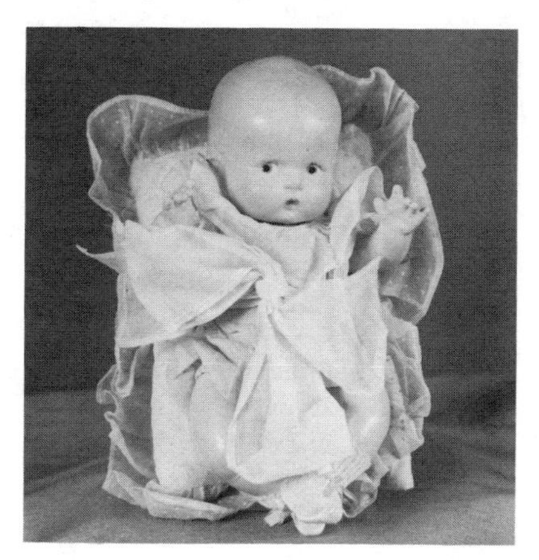

11in (28cm) baby, all original. *H&J Foulke, Inc.*

Composition Baby: Ca. 1930. All-composition with molded and painted hair, painted or sleep eyes, closed mouth; jointed at neck, shoulders and hips with curved limbs; original clothes; all in very good condition.

12—14in (31—36cm) **$60—70**
18—20in (46—51cm) **100—125**

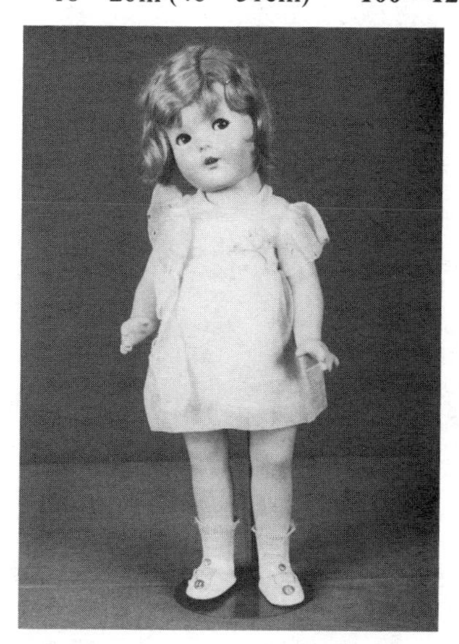

Composition (Miscellaneous) continued

Bobbi-Mae, Swing & Sway Doll: Ca. 1940. Wondercraft Co., N.Y., U.S.A. All-composition of three pieces, molded clothes; torso rocks from side to side, legs function as a stand.

11in (28cm) **$125**

Martiann: Ca. 1940. Composition head with molded yellow hair, movable disc eyes, watermelon mouth; cloth body; dressed; all in good condition.

18in (46cm) **$75—85****

**Not enough price samples to compute a reliable range.

Trudy, Three-faced Doll: 1946. Three-in-One Doll Corp., N.Y., U.S.A. Designed by Elsie Gilbert. Composition head, arms and legs, cloth body; composition knob turns head to three different faces—smiling, crying and sleeping; original clothes; all in good condition.

14in (36cm) **$175—200**

Mint-in-box **300—325**

11in (28cm) ***Bobbi-Mae,*** all original. *H&J Foulke, Inc.*

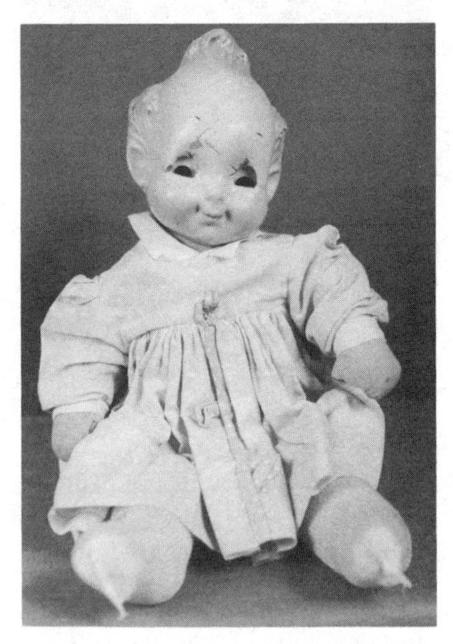

18in (46cm) ***Martiann,*** replaced dress. *Betty Harms Collection.*

16in (41cm) ***Trudy,*** all original. *Betty Harms Collection.*

Composition Shoulder Head

Maker: Various German firms
Date: 1890—1915
Material: Composition shoulder head, cloth body, composition lower limbs
Size: Various

Composition Shoulder Head: Good quality composition with mohair or skin wig, glass eyes, closed or open mouth; cloth body with composition arms and lower legs, sometimes with molded boots; appropriately dressed; all in good condition.

12—14in (31—36cm)	**$200—225**
16—18in (41—46cm)	**250—275**
22—24in (56—61cm)	**300—350**

12in (31cm) composition shoulder head on pink kid body.

Creche Figures

Maker: Various European craftsmen, primarily Italian.
Date: 18th and 19th centuries
Material: Wood and terra-cotta on a wire frame
Size: Various
Mark: None

Creche Figures of various people in a Christmas scene: Early 19th century. Gesso over wood head and limbs, fabric-covered wire frame body; beautifully detailed features with carved hair and glass inset eyes, lovely hands; original or appropriate replacement clothes; all in good condition.

11—13in (28—33cm) **$200—250***
20in (51cm) **400—450***

*Allow more for wood-jointed body.

Mid 19th Century: Later doll with terra-cotta head and limbs, painted eyes; fabric-covered wire frame body; workmanship not as detailed; original or appropriate clothes; all in good condition.

11—13in (28—33cm) **$150—200**

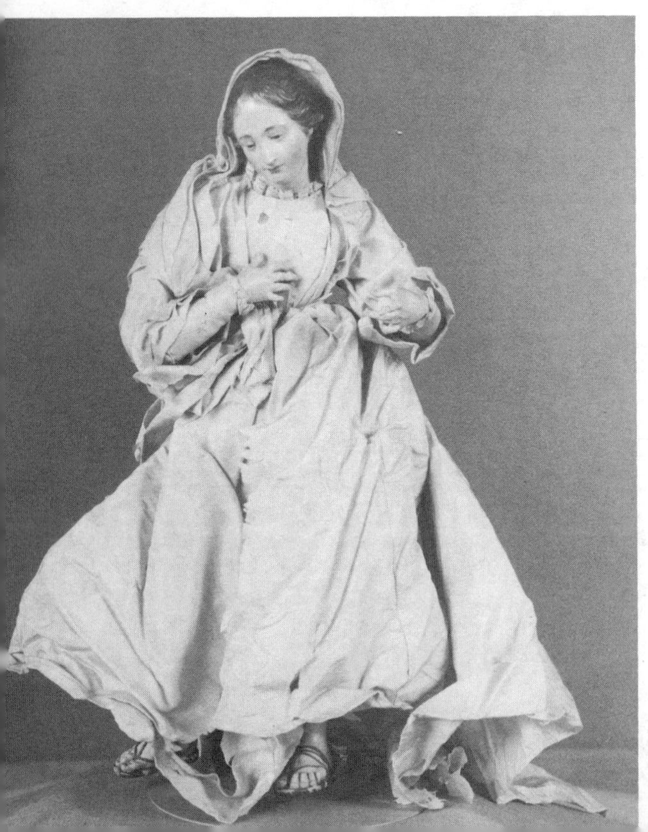

14in (36cm) creche Madonna.
Joanna Ott Collection.

D E P*

Maker: Maison Jumeau, Paris, France; (heads possibly by Simon & Halbig, Gräfenhain, Thüringia, Germany)

Date: Late 1890s

Material: Bisque socket head, French jointed composition body (sometimes marked Jumeau)

Size: About 12—33in (31—84cm)

Mark: "DEP" and size number (up to 16 or so); sometimes stamped in red "Tete Jumeau"; body sometimes with Jumeau stamp or sticker

DEP
8

DEP: Perfect bisque socket head, human hair wig, sleep eyes, painted lower eyelashes only, upper hair eyelashes (sometimes gone), deeply molded eye sockets, open mouth, pierced ears; jointed French composition body; lovely clothes; all in good condition.

13—15in (33—38cm)	**$ 675—775**
18—20in (46—51cm)	**900—1000**
24—26in (61—66cm)	**1200—1300**
33in (84cm)	**1800**

*The letters DEP appear in the mark of many dolls, but the particular dolls priced here have only "DEP" and a size number (unless they happen to have the red stamp "Tete Jumeau"). The face is characterized by deeply molded eye sockets and no painted upper eyelashes.

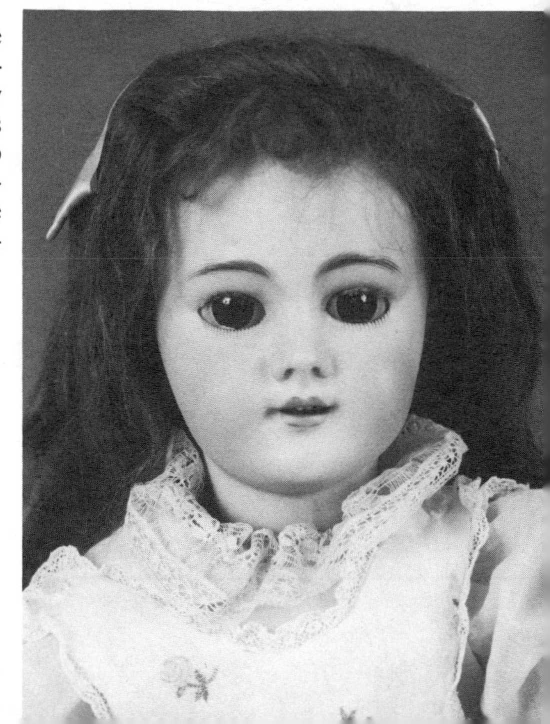

21in (53cm) DEP with French body. *H&J Foulke, Inc.*

Doll House Dolls

Maker: Various German firms
Date: Ca. 1890—1920
Material: Bisque shoulder head, cloth body, bisque arms and legs
Size: Various small sizes
Mark: Sometimes "Germany"

Doll House Doll: Man or lady 5½—7in (14—18cm), as above with molded hair, painted eyes; original clothes or suitably dressed; all in nice condition.

Man or lady	**$150—165***
With molded hair and painted eyes, ca. 1920	**100—125**
Lady with glass eyes and wig	**300—325**

*Allow more for molded hats, grandfathers and unusual characters.

5in (13cm) doll house father with molded mustache, all original. *H&J Foulke, Inc.*

5½in (14cm) doll house nanny. *H&J Foulke, Inc.*

Door of Hope

Maker: Door of Hope Mission, China; heads by carvers from Ning-Po
Date: 1917—on
Material: Wooden heads; cloth bodies, sometimes with carved wooden hands
Size: Various; usually under 13in (33cm)
Mark: Sometimes "Made in China" label

Door of Hope: Carved wooden head with painted and/or carved hair, carved features; cloth body, sometimes carved hands; original handmade clothes, exact costuming for different classes of Chinese people; all in good condition. 25 dolls in the series.

11—13in (28—33cm) ***Adult***	**$200—300**
6—7in (15—18cm) ***Child***	**350**
11in (28cm) ***Mother*** and ***Baby***	**450**
9in (23cm) ***Boy***	**300**

11in (28cm) Door of Hope young gentleman, all original. *H&J Foulke, Inc.*

11in (28cm) Door of Hope Chinese lady. *H&J Foulke, Inc.*

Grace G. Drayton

Maker: Various companies
Date: 1909—on
Material: All-cloth, or composition and cloth combination, or all-composition
Size: Various
Designer: Grace G. Drayton
Mark: Usually a cloth label or a stamp

(See also ***Campbell Kids***)

Chocolate Drop. *Jan Foulke Collection.*

Puppy Pippin: 1911. Horsman Co., New York, N.Y., U.S.A. Composition head with puppy dog face, plush body with jointed legs; all in good condition. Cloth label.
About 8in (20cm) sitting **$300****

Peek-a-Boo: 1913—1915. Horsman Co., New York, N.Y., U.S.A. Composition head, arms, legs and lower torso, cloth upper torso; character face with molded hair, painted eyes to the side, watermelon mouth; dressed in striped bathing suit, polka dot dress or ribbons only; cloth label on outfit; all in good condition.
7½in (19cm) **$125****

Hug-Me-Tight: 1916. Colonial Toy Mfg. Co., New York, N.Y., U.S.A. Mother Goose characters and others in one piece, printed on cloth; all in good condition.
11in (28cm) **$150**

Chocolate Drop: 1923. Averill Manufacturing Co., New York, N.Y., U.S.A. Brown cloth doll with movable arms and legs; painted features, three yarn pigtails; appropriate clothes; all in good condition. Stamped on front torso and paper label.
11in (28cm) **$250—300****

Dolly Dingle: 1923. Averill Manufacturing Co., New York, N.Y., U.S.A. Cloth doll with painted features and movable arms and legs; appropriate clothes; all in good condition. Stamped on front torso and paper label.
11in (28cm) **$250—300****

**Not enough price samples to compute a reliable range.

Dressel

Maker: Cuno & Otto Dressel of Sonneberg, Thüringia, Germany
Date: 1700—on
Material: Bisque head, jointed kid or cloth body or ball-jointed composition body
Size: Various
Mark:

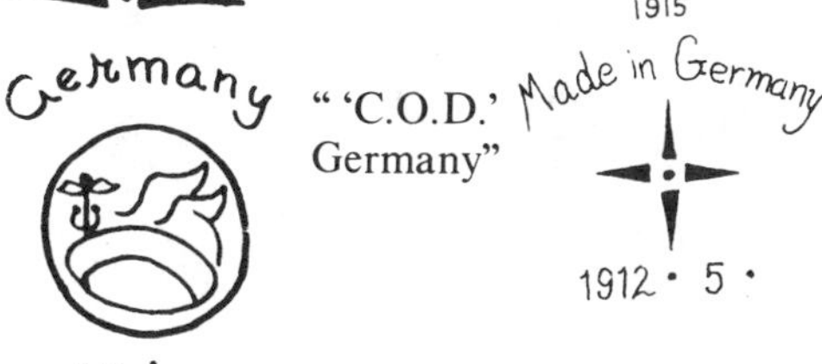

13/0

Child Doll: 1895—on. Perfect bisque head, original jointed kid or composition body; good wig, glass eyes, open mouth; suitable clothes; all in good condition.

Composition body:

15—17in (38—43cm)	**$250—300**
22—24in (56—61cm)	**350—400**
30in (76cm)	**550—600**

Kid body:

13—15in (33—38cm)	**200—225**
22—24in (56—61cm)	**325—375**

Marked Jutta Child: Ca. 1906—1921. Perfect bisque socket head, good wig, sleep eyes, open mouth, pierced ears; ball-jointed composition body; dressed; all in good condition. Head made by Simon & Halbig.
Mold 1348 or 1349

MARK: 1349
Jutta
S & H
11

16—18in (41—46cm)	**$425—475**
22—24in (56—61cm)	**525—600**
28in (71cm)	**850**

25in (64cm) Dressel child incised "1912".
India Stoessel Collection.

Character Doll: 1909—on. Perfect bisque socket head, ball-jointed composition body; mohair wig, painted eyes, closed mouth; suitable clothes; all in good condition. Glazed inside of head.

14—16in (36—41cm) **$2500****

**Not enough price samples to compute a reliable range.

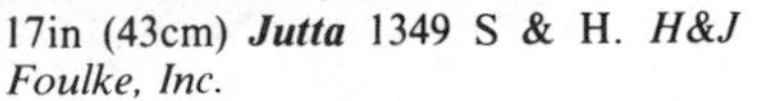

17in (43cm) ***Jutta*** 1349 S & H. *H&J Foulke, Inc.*

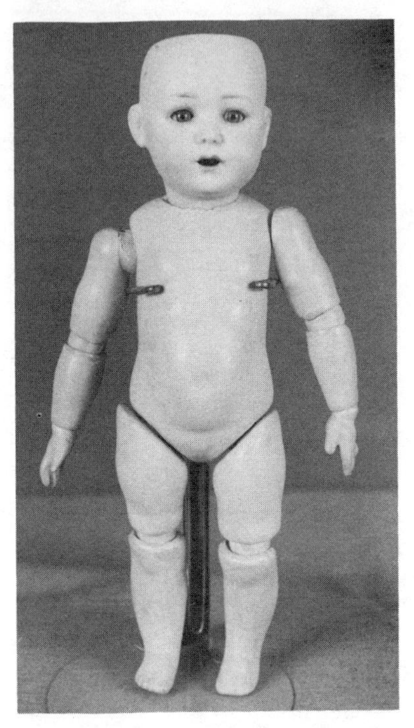

13in (33cm) ***Jutta*** 1914 toddler. *H&J Foulke, Inc.*

Marked Jutta Character Baby: Ca. 1910—1921. Perfect bisque socket head, good wig, sleep eyes, open mouth; bent-limb composition baby body; dressed; all in good condition.

MARK:

Jutta
1914
8

14—16in (36—41cm)	**$475—525**
20—22in (51—56cm)	**700—800**
24in (61cm)	**950—1000**
Toddler, 16in (41cm)	**650—700**

C.O.D. Character Baby: Ca. 1910—on. Perfect bisque character face with wig or molded hair, painted or glass eyes; jointed baby body; dressed; all in good condition.

13—15in (33—38cm)	**$325—375**
18—20in (46—51cm)	**425—475**
22—24in (56—61cm)	**575—675**

Lady Doll: Ca. 1920s. Mold #1469. Bisque socket head with young lady face, good wig, sleep eyes, closed mouth; jointed composition body in adult form with molded bust, slim waist and long arms and legs, feet modeled to wear high-heeled shoes; appropriate clothes; all in good condition.

14in (36cm) **$1200—1400**

E. D. Bébé

Maker: Unknown as yet but *possibly* by E. Denamur of Paris, France
Date: Ca. 1885 into 1890s
Material: Bisque head, wood and composition jointed body
Size: Various
Mark: E 8 D
DEPOSÉ

Marked E. D. Bébé: Perfect bisque head, wood and composition jointed body; good wig, beautiful blown glass eyes, pierced ears; nicely dressed; good condition. Often found on a marked Jumeau body.

Closed mouth:

14—16in (36—41cm)	**$2200—2400**
21—23in (53—58cm)	**2900—3100**
29in (74cm)	**4000**

Open mouth:

17—18in (43—46cm)	**1500—1600**
23—24in (58—61cm)	**2100—2300**

19in (48cm) E. D. *Betty Harms Collection.*

Eden Bébé

Maker: Fleischmann & Bloedel of Fürth, Bavaria, and Paris, France
Date: Founded in Bavaria in 1873. Also in Paris by 1890, then on into S.F.B.J. in 1899
Material: Bisque head, composition jointed body
Size: Various
Mark: "EDEN BÉBÉ, PARIS"

Marked Eden Bébé: Ca. 1890. Perfect bisque head, fully-jointed or five-piece composition jointed body; beautiful wig, large set paperweight eyes, closed or open/closed mouth, pierced ears; lovely clothes; all in nice condition.

Closed mouth, 21—23in (53—58cm)	**$2600—2800**
Open mouth, 18—20in (46—51cm)	**1700—1900**

19in (48cm) ***Eden Bébé*** with open mouth. *H&J Foulke, Inc.*

EFFanBEE

Maker: EFFanBEE Doll Co., New York, N.Y., U.S.A.
Date: 1912—on
Marks: Various, but nearly always marked "EFFanBEE" on torso or head.

EFFANBEE
DURABLE
DOLLS

Wore a metal heart-shaped bracelet; later a gold paper heart label.

Metal Heart Bracelet: **$45**

Baby Dainty: 1912—1922. Composition shoulder head, painted molded hair, painted facial features (sometimes with tin sleep eyes); cloth stuffed body jointed at shoulders and hips, with curved arms and straight legs of composition; original or appropriate old clothes; all in good condition. Came with metal heart bracelet.
MARK: First Mold:

Effanbee

Second Mold:

EFFANBEE
BABY DAINTY

15in (38cm) **$150—175**

Baby Grumpy: 1912—1939. Composition shoulder head with frowning face, molded and painted hair, painted eyes, closed mouth; composition arms and legs, cloth body; original or appropriate old clothes; all in good condition. Came with metal heart bracelet.
MARK:

EFFANBEE
DOLLS
WALK-TALK-SLEEP

12in (31cm) **$165—185**

12in (31cm) black and white versions of ***Baby Grumpy***. *H&J Foulke, Inc.*

Marilee: 1924. Composition shoulder head, arms and legs, cloth torso; human hair wig, sleep eyes, open mouth with teeth; original clothes; all in good condition. Various sizes. Came with metal heart bracelet.
MARK:

EFFANBEE
MARILEE
COPYR.
DOLL

22in (56cm) **$175—200**

EFFanBEE continued

Bubbles: 1924—on. Composition head with blonde molded and painted hair, sleep eyes, open mouth with teeth, smiling face; cloth body, curved composition arms and legs; original or appropriate old clothes; all in good condition. Came with metal heart bracelet or necklace.

MARK:

19 © 24
EFFANBEE
DOLLS
WALK-TALK-SLEEP
MADE IN U.S.A.

EFFANBEE
BUBBLES
COPYR. 1924
MADE IN U.S.A.

16—20in (41—51cm) **$175—200**
22—24in (56—61cm) **$250—300**

Rosemary: 1925. Composition shoulder head, human hair wig, open mouth, tin sleep eyes; cloth torso, composition arms and legs; original or appropriate old clothes; all in good condition. Various sizes. Came with metal heart bracelet.

MARK:

EFFANBEE
ROSEMARY
WALK-TALK-SLEEP

14in (36cm) **$175—185**

27in (69cm) ***Bubbles***, replaced clothes. *Betty Harms Collection.*

14in (36cm) ***Rosemary***, all original. *H&J Foulke, Inc.*

Mae Starr: 1928. Composition shoulder head with human hair wig, sleep eyes, open/closed mouth; cloth body, composition limbs; talking device in center of torso with records.

MARK:

MAE
STARR
DOLL

29—30in (74—76cm) **$400—450**

Mary Ann and Mary Lee: 1928—on. Composition head on ***Lovums*** shoulder plate, composition arms and legs, cloth torso; human hair wig, sleep eyes, open smiling mouth; appropriate clothes; in good condition. Later version came on an all-composition body marked "Patsy-Ann" for ***Mary Ann*** and "Patsy-Joan" for ***Mary Lee***. Came with metal heart bracelet.

MARK: ©
MARY-ANN

16in (41cm) ***Mary Lee*** **$175—200**
19in (48cm) ***Mary Ann*** **185—225**

9in (23cm) ***Patsyette*** as Anne Shirley in *Anne of Green Gables*, all original. *H&J Foulke, Inc.*

7in (18cm) ***Baby Tinyette***, all original. *H&J Foulke, Inc.*

14in (36cm) ***Patsy*** with sleep eyes and wig, replaced clothes. *H&J Foulke, Inc.*

Lovums: 1928—1939. Composition swivel head on shoulder plate, arms and legs; molded painted hair or wig, pretty face, sleep eyes, smiling open mouth with teeth; cloth body; original or appropriate clothes; all in good condition. Various sizes. Came with metal heart bracelet. Note: The "Lovums" shoulder plate was used for many other dolls as well.

MARK: EFFANBEE
LOVUMS
©
PAT. NO. 1,283,558

18—21in (46—53cm) **$200—250**

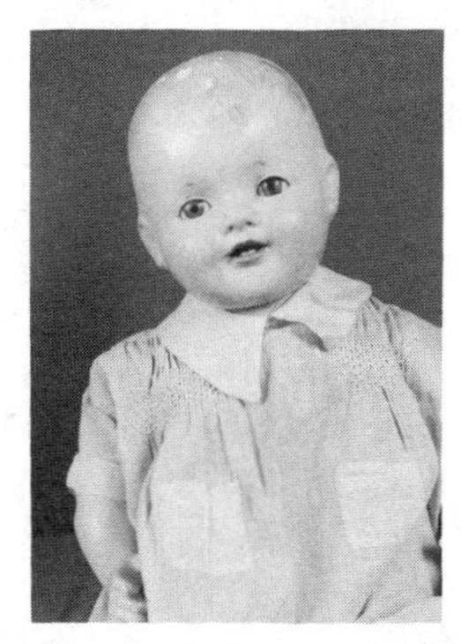

25in (64cm) ***Lovums*** with two rows of teeth, replaced dress. *Betty Harms Collection.*

Patsy Family: 1928—on. All-composition, jointed at neck, shoulders and hips; molded hair (sometimes covered wth wig), bent right arm on some members, painted or sleep eyes; original or appropriate old clothes; may have some crazing. Came with metal heart bracelet.

MARK: Bracelet

EFFANBEE
PATSY
BABY KIN

EFFANBEE
PATSY
DOLL

EFFANBEE
PATSY JR.
DOLL

8in (20cm) ***Patsy Babyette***, all original. *H&J Foulke, Inc.*

9in (23cm) ***Patsyette*** Brother, all original. *H&J Foulke, Inc.*

6in (15cm) ***Wee Patsy***, all original	**$300**
7in (18cm)	
Baby Tinyette	**165—175**
8in (20cm)	
Patsy Babyette	**165—185**
9in (23cm)	
Patsyette	**175—195**
11in (28cm)	
Patsy Baby	**175—200**
Patsy Jr.	**225—250**
Patricia Kin	**225—250**
14in (36cm)	
Patsy	**250—275**
Patricia	**250—275**
16in (41cm)	
Patsy Joan	**275—300**
19in (48cm)	
Patsy Ann	**300—325**
22in (56cm)	
Patsy Lou	**375—400**
26in (66cm)	
Patsy Ruth	**500 up**
30in (76cm)	
Patsy Mae	**500 up**

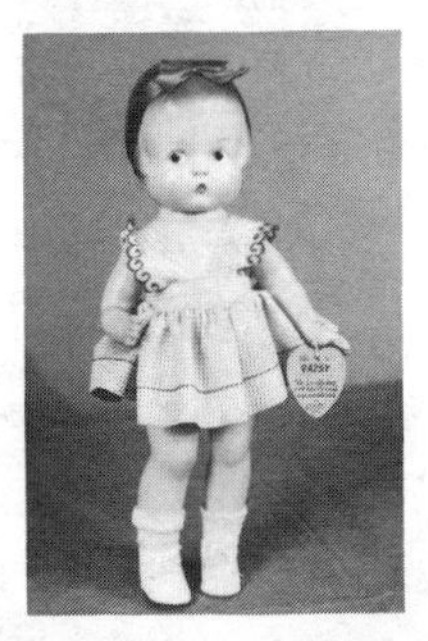

14in (36cm) 1948 ***Patsy***, all original. *H&J Foulke, Inc.*

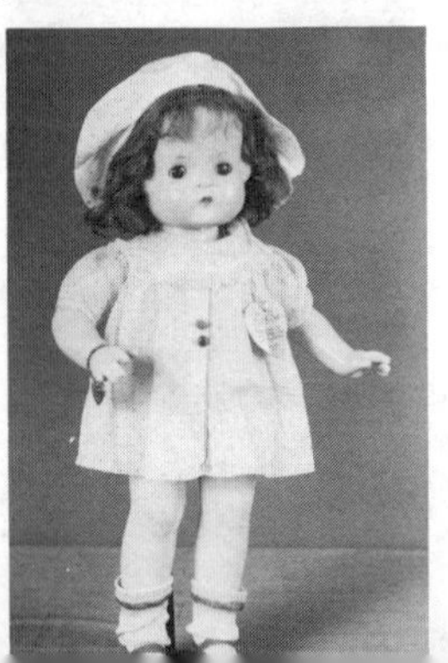

19in (48cm) ***Patsy Ann*** with wig, all original. *H&J Foulke, Inc.*

EFFanBEE continued

Skippy: 1929. All-composition, jointed at neck, hips and shoulders, (later a cloth torso, still later a cloth torso and upper legs with composition molded boots for lower legs); molded hair, painted eyes to the side; original or appropriate clothes; all in good condition. Came with metal heart bracelet.

MARK: EFFANBEE
SKIPPY
©
P.L. Crosby

14in (36cm) **$275—300**

W. C. Fields: 1930. Composition head, hands and feet, cloth body; painted hair and eyes; strings at back of head to open mouth; original clothes; all in good condition.

MARK:
"W.C. FIELDS
AN EFFANBEE PRODUCT"

17—20in (43—51cm) **$750—800**

Lamkin: 1930s. Composition head, arms and legs with very deep and detailed molding, cloth body; molded hair, sleep eyes, bow mouth; original or appropriate clothes; all in good condition.

MARK: On head:
"LAMBKINS"
(note spelling)
Paper heart tag: "Lamkin"

16in (41cm) **$200—225***
Mint-in-box **350**

*In fair condition.

14in (36cm) ***Skippy***, all original. *Miriam Blankman Collection.*

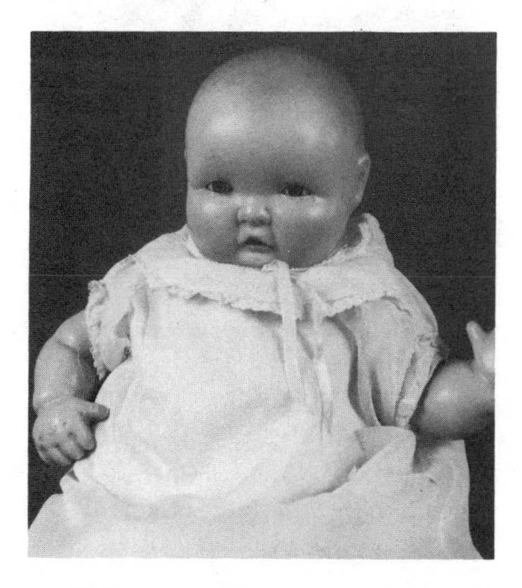

15in (41cm) ***Lamkin***. *Miriam Blankman Collection.*

EFFanBEE continued

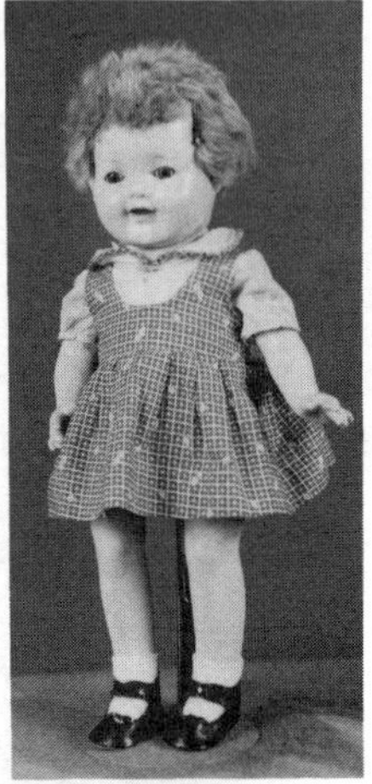

16½in (42cm) ***Betty Brite***, all original. *H&J Foulke, Inc.*

Dy-Dee Baby: 1933—on. First dolls had hard rubber head with soft rubber body, caracul wig or molded hair, open mouth for drinking, soft ears (after 1940). Later dolls had hard plastic heads with rubber bodies. Still later dolls had hard plastic heads with vinyl bodies. Came with paper heart label. Various sizes from 9—20in (23—51cm),

MARK:
"EFF-AN-BEE
DY-DEE BABY
US PAT.-1-857-485
ENGLAND-880-060
FRANCE-723-980
GERMANY-585-647
OTHER PAT PENDING"

Rubber body:
14—16in (36—41cm) **$ 90—100**
24in (61cm) **200—250**

15in (38cm) ***Anne Shirley***, contemporary clothes. *H&J Foulke, Inc.*

Betty Brite: 1933. All-composition, jointed at neck, shoulders and hips; caracul wig, sleep eyes, open mouth with teeth; original or appropriate clothes; all in good condition.

MARK: On torso:
"EFFANBEE
BETTY BRITE"

16½in (42cm) **$225**

Anne Shirley: 1935—1940. All-composition, jointed at neck, shoulders and hips; human hair wig, sleep eyes, closed mouth; original clothes; all in good condition. Various sizes. Came with metal heart bracelet. "Anne Shirley" body used on other dolls as well.

MARK: On back:
"EFFanBEE/ANNE SHIRLEY."

15—16in (38—41cm) **$175—200**
20—21in (51—53cm) **250—275**
27in (69cm) **400—450**

EFFanBEE continued

Sugar Baby: 1936. Composition head, curved arms and toddler legs, cloth body; molded hair or caracul wig, sleep eyes, closed mouth; appropriately dressed; all in good condition.

MARK:

"EFFanBEE
SUGAR BABY"

16—20in (41—51cm) **$175—200**

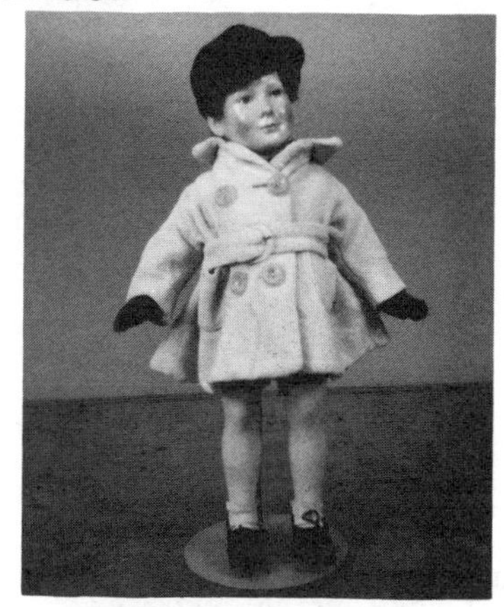

17in (43cm) American Child boy. *H&J Foulke, Inc.*

American Children: 1936-1939. Composition swivel head on composition ***Anne Shirley*** body, jointed at shoulders and hips. Four different faces designed by Dewees Cochran with either open or closed mouths, human hair wigs, painted or sleep eyes; original clothes; all in good condition. Came with metal heart bracelet and paper heart label. Sizes: 15in (38cm), 17in (43cm), 19in (48cm) and 21in (53cm).

MARK: On head:

"EFFANBEE//
AMERICAN//CHILDREN"

On body:

"EFFANBEE//
ANNE SHIRLEY"

The boy and the open-mouth girl are not marked.

21in (53cm) American Child girl with painted eyes, all original. *Rosemary Dent Collection.*

Open mouth:

15in (38cm)

Barbara Joan **$ 600—650**

17½in (45cm)

Barbara Ann **650—700**

21in (53cm)

Barbara Lou **750—800**

Closed mouth:

19—21in (48—53cm) **1000—1200**

17in (43cm) boy **1000—1200**

17in (43cm) ***Barbara Ann*** American Child, open mouth. *Beth Foulke Collection.*

EFFanBEE continued

20in (51cm) ***Charlie McCarthy***, all original. *Miriam Blankman Collection.*

14in (36cm) Historical Doll Replica ***1685—Later Carolina Settlement***, all original. *Rosemary Dent Collection.*

Pennsylvania Dutch Dolls: 1936-1940s. Used ***Baby Grumpy*** shoulder head,
position arms and legs; dressed in costumes to represent "Amish", "Mennonite" or "Brethren". Green wrist tag with black stamp indicated sect.
MARK:

12—13in (31—33cm) **$165—185**

9in (23cm) ***Button Nose***, all original. *H&J Foulke, Inc.*

Charlie McCarthy: 1937. Composition head, hands and feet, cloth body; painted hair and eyes; strings at back of head to operate mouth; original clothes; all in good condition.
MARK:
"EDGAR BERGEN'S CHARLIE McCARTHY, AN EFFanBEE PRODUCT"
17—20in (43—51cm) **$250—300**

Historical Dolls: 1939. All-composition, jointed at neck, shoulders and hips. Three each of 30 dolls portraying the history of American fashion, 1492—1939. "American Children" heads used with elaborate human hair wigs and painted eyes; elaborate original costumes using velvets, satins, silks, brocades, and so forth; all in good condition. Came with metal heart bracelet.
MARKS: On head:
"EFFANBEE AMERICAN CHILDREN"
On body:
"EFFANBEE ANNE SHIRLEY"
21in (53cm) **$1200—1500 up**

EFFanBEE continued

Historical Doll Replicas: 1939. All-composition, jointed at neck, shoulders and hips. Series of 30 dolls, popular copies of the original historical models (see previous page). Human hair wigs, painted eyes; original costumes all in cotton, copies of those on the original models. Came with metal heart bracelet.

MARK: On torso:
"EFFanBEE
ANNE SHIRLEY"

14in (36cm) **$375—400**
Mint-in-box **425—450**

11½in (29cm) ***Suzette***, all original. *H&J Foulke, Inc.*

Button Nose: Ca. 1939. All-composition with swivel head, joints at shoulders and hips; brown molded hair, painted eyes, closed mouth; appropriately dressed; all in good condition.

MARK: "EFFANBEE"

9in (23cm) **$175—200**

Suzette: 1939. All-composition, jointed at neck, shoulders and hips; mohair wig, eyes painted to the side, closed mouth; original clothes; all in good condition. Came with metal heart bracelet.

MARK: SUZETTE
EFF AN BEE
MADE IN
U.S.A.

11½in (29cm) **$150—175**

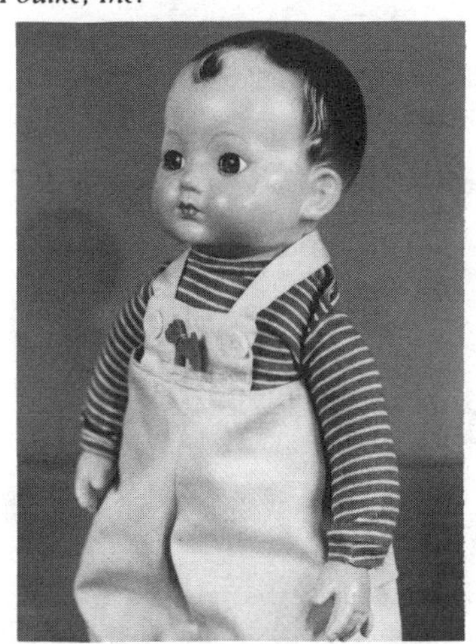

16in (41cm) ***Tommy Tucker***, all original. *Glenn Mandeville Collection.*

Suzanne: 1940. All-composition jointed at neck, shoulders and hips; mohair wig, sleep eyes, closed mouth; original clothes; all in good condition. Came with metal heart bracelet.

MARK: SUZANNE
EFFANBEE
MADE IN U.S.A

14in (36cm) **$175—200**

EFFanBEE continued

Tommy Tucker: 1939—1949. Composition head with painted hair or mohair wig, flirting eyes, closed mouth, chubby cheeks; composition hands, stuffed body; original clothes; all in good condition. Also called ***Mickey*** and ***Baby Bright Eyes***. Came with paper heart tag. Sizes: 15—24in (38—61cm)

MARK: On head: "EFFANBEE
U.S.A."

16—18in (41—46cm) **$175—200**
20—22in (51—56cm) **225—250**

Portrait Dolls: 1940. All-composition, jointed at neck, shoulders and hips; mohair wigs, sleep eyes; in costumes, such as ballerina, Bo-Peep, Gibson Girl, bride and groom, dancing couple; all original, in good condition.

MARK: None

11in (28cm) **$175—225**

11in (28cm) Portrait Doll ballerina, all original. *H&J Foulke, Inc.*

Storybook-type or Sewing Doll: Ca. 1940. All-composition, jointed at shoulders and hips; the same doll as ***Wee Patsy*** sometimes with added mohair wig, painted eyes, molded shoes and socks; all original; in good condition. Sewing doll comes with fabric and patterns for making clothes.

6in (15cm) **$200 up**

Little Lady: 1940—1949. All-composition, jointed at neck, shoulders and hips, separated fingers; mohair or human hair wig, sleep eyes, closed mouth; same face as ***Anne Shirley***; original clothes; all in good condition. (During "war years" some had yarn wigs and/or painted eyes.) Various sizes.

MARK: On back:
"EFFanBEE
U.S.A.
Paper heart:
'I am Little Lady' "

15—16in (38—41cm) **$175—200**
20—21in (51—53cm) **250—275**

Brother and Sister: 1942. Composition swivel heads and hands, stuffed cloth body, arms and legs; yarn wig, painted eyes. Original pink (sister) and blue (brother) outfits.

MARK: "EFFANBEE"

12in (31cm) ***Sister*** **$150**
16in (41cm) ***Brother*** **175**

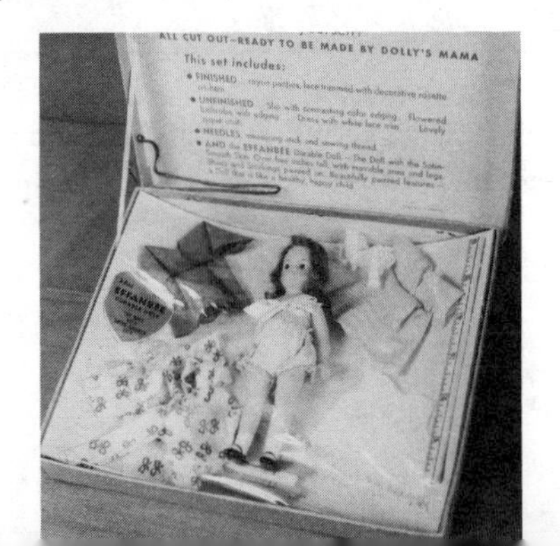

6in (15cm) Sewing doll, all original. *H&J Foulke, Inc.*

EFFanBEE continued

Sweetie Pie: 1942. Composition head and limbs, cloth torso; caracul wig, flirty eyes, closed mouth; original clothes; all in good condition. Available in 16in (41cm), 20in (51cm) and 24in (61cm).

MARK:

"EFFANBEE © 1942"

20—24in (51—61cm) **$150—200**

Sweetie Pie, replaced clothes. *Barbara Crescenze Collection.*

Candy Kid: 1946. All-composition toddler, jointed at neck, shoulders and hips; molded hair, sleep eyes; original clothes; all in good condition. Came with paper heart tag.

MARK: "EFFanBEE"

12in (31cm) **$200—225**

14in (36cm) ***Honey***, all original. *H&J Foulke, Inc.*

Honey: 1949—1955. All-hard plastic, jointed at neck, shoulders and hips; synthetic, mohair or human hair, sleep eyes; original clothes; all in good condition.

MARK: EFFANBEE

14in (36cm) **$135**
18in (46cm) **175**
24in (61cm) **250**

14in (36cm) ***Little Lady***, all original. *H&J Foulke, Inc.*

15in (38cm) ***Honey Walker*** as ***Prince Charming*** and ***Cinderella***, all original. *Paula Ryscik Collection.*

EFFanBEE continued

Effanbee Limited Edition Dolls: 1975—on. All-vinyl jointed doll; original clothes; excellent condition.

1975 ***Precious Baby***	**$350**
1976 ***Patsy***	**325—350**
1977 ***Dewees Cochran***	**175—200**
1978 ***Crowning Glory***	**150—175**
1979 ***Skippy***	**200—250**
1980 ***Susan B. Anthony***	**150**
1981 ***Girl with Watering Can***	**150**
1982 ***Princess Diana***	**125**
1983 ***Sherlock Holmes***	**125**
Legend Series:	
1980 ***W. C. Fields***	**150—175**

25in (64cm) ***Honey Walker***, all original.
H&J Foulke, Inc.

EFFanBEE continued

1977 ***Dewees Cochran Self-Portrait***, all original. *H&J Foulke, Inc.*

Joel Ellis

Maker: Co-operative Manufacturing Co., Springfield, VT., U.S.A.
Date: 1873 and 1874
Material: All-wood, fully-jointed; metal feet and hands
Size: 12in (31cm), 15in (38cm) and 18in (46cm)
Mark: None - unless black paper band around waist still exists with patent date printed on it.

Joel Ellis Wooden Doll: All-wood with mortise and tenon joints; molded hair, painted eyes; metal hands and feet;, undressed; in good condition.
12in (31cm) **$800—850**
15in (38cm) **900—1000**

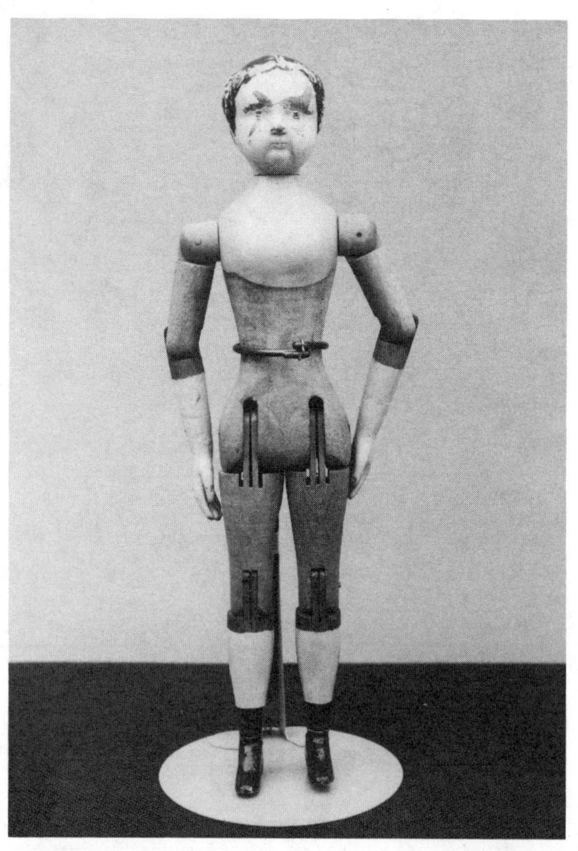

13in (33cm) doll by Joel Ellis with metal hands and feet. *Richard Wright Antiques.*

Maude Tousey Fangel

Maker: Averill Manufacturing Co. and Georgene Novelties, New York, N.Y., U.S.A.
Date: 1938
Material: All-cloth
Size: 10in (25cm) and up
Designer: Maude Tousey Fangel
Mark: "M.T.F.©" at side of face on hair, but often inside the seam

---

Maude Tousey Fangel Doll: All-cloth with printed face in several variations which came dressed as a baby or child; some bodies are of printed cloth, some plain; soft stuffed, flexible arms and legs; original or appropriate clothes; all in good condition.

12in (31cm) **$325—350**
Baby with removable clothes,
14—16in (36—41cm) **450****

**Not enough price samples to compute a reliable range.

Maude Tousey Fangel ***Sweets***, all original with tag. *Jan Foulke Collection.*

French Bébé
(Unmarked)

Maker: Numerous French firms
Date: Ca. 1880—1925
Material: Bisque head, jointed composition body
Size: Various
Mark: None, except perhaps numbers, Paris, or France

Unmarked French Bébé: Perfect bisque head, swivel neck, lovely wig, set paperweight eyes, closed mouth, pierced ears; jointed French body; pretty costume; all in good condition.

14—15in (36—38cm) **$1900—2000**
20—22in (51—56cm) **2500—2600**

Very early face:
12—14in (31—36cm) **3000—3500**
17—19in (43—48cm) **4000—4500**

Open Mouth:
1890s:
16—18in (41—46cm) **1500—1600**
25—26in (64—66cm) **2000—2200**
1920s:
18—20in (46—51cm) **750—800**

18in (46cm) French bébé incised "Bte. SGDG," rare blown kid jointed child body.

23in (58cm) unmarked French bébé with Jumeau body. *Dr. Carole Stoessel Zvonar Collection.*

French Fashion-Type
(Unmarked)

Maker: Various French firms
Date: Ca. 1860—1930
Material: Bisque shoulder head, jointed kid body, some with bisque lower limbs.
Size: Various
Mark: None, except possibly numbers or letters

French Fashion: Perfect unmarked bisque shoulder head, swivel neck, kid body, kid arms -- some with wired fingers, or old bisque arms; original or good wig, lovely blown glass eyes, closed mouth, earrings; appropriate clothes; all in good condition.

Early fine quality:	
12in (31cm)	**$1200 and up***
14—15in (36—38cm)	**1400—1600 and up***
18in (46cm)	**1850—2000 and up***
21in (53cm)	**2200—2500 and up***
Later models:	
12in (31cm)	**900—950**
14in (36cm)	**1000**
20in (51cm)	**1300—1500**

*Greatly depending upon the appeal of the face.

20in (51cm) French Fashion, stationary neck, all original.

17in (43cm) French Fashion lady with cup and saucer neck joint, kid body, bisque arms, redressed.

16in (41cm) French Fashion man, kid body, all original. *Betty Harms Collection.*

French Fashion-Type

(Wood Body)

Maker: Unknown
Date: Ca. 1860—on
Material: Bisque head, fully-jointed wood body
Size: Various
Mark: Size numbers only

Wood Body Lady: Perfect bisque swivel head on shoulder plate, good wig, paperweight eyes, closed mouth, pierced ears; wood body, fully-jointed at shoulders, elbows, wrists, hips and knees; dressed; all in good condition. Rare with ball-joint at waist and ankle joints.

16—18in (41—46cm) **$3000—3500 and up**

15in (38cm) F. G. fashion lady with jointed wood body, all original. *Pearl D. Morley Collection.*

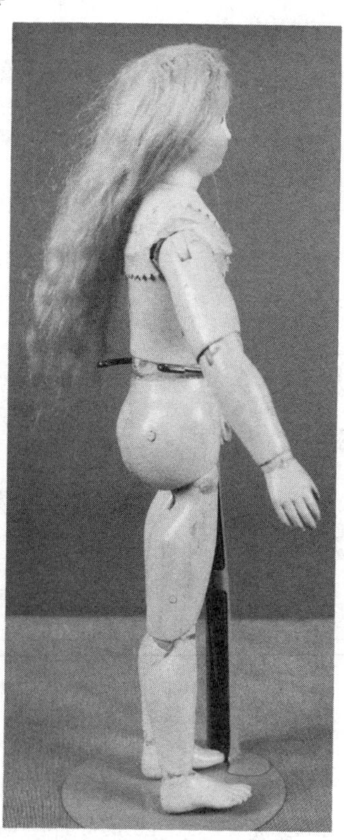

14in (36cm) French Fashion lady with jointed wood body including swivel waist and ankles; incised "B. Jne et Cie." *Dr. Carole Stoessel Zvonar Collection.*

Freundlich

Maker: Freundlich Novelty Corp., New York, N.Y., U.S.A.
Date: 1923—on
Material: All-composition

General Douglas MacArthur: Ca. 1942. All-composition portrait doll, molded hat, painted features, one arm to salute if desired; jointed shoulders and hips; original khaki uniform; all in good condition.
MARK: Cardboard tag: "General MacArthur"
18in (46cm) **$175—200**

15in (38cm) soldier with molded cap, all original. *H&J Foulke, Inc.*

Military Dolls: Ca. 1942. All-composition with molded hats, jointed shoulders and hips, character face, painted features; original clothes. Soldier, Sailor, Wac, and Wave, all in good condition.
MARK: Cardboard tag
15in (38cm) **$125—150**

Baby Sandy: 1939—1942. All-composition with swivel head, jointed shoulders and hips, chubby toddler body; molded hair, smiling face, larger sizes have sleep eyes, smaller ones painted eyes; appropriate clothes; all in good condition.
MARK: On head:
"Baby Sandy"
On pin:
"The Wonder Baby
Genuine Baby Sandy Doll"
8in (20cm) **$110—135**
14in (36cm) **200—250**

Frozen Charlotte

Maker: Various German firms
Date: Ca. 1850s—early 1900s
Material: Glazed china; sometimes untinted bisque
Size: 1—18in (3—46cm)
Mark: None, except for "Germany", or numbers or both

Frozen Charlotte: All-china doll, black or blonde molded hair parted down the middle, painted features; hands extended, legs separated but not jointed; no clothes; perfect condition.

2in (5cm)	**$ 25—35***
4in (10cm)	**65—75***
6in (15cm)	**90—100***
8in (20cm)	**140—165***
11in (28cm)	**225—250***
14—15in (36—38cm)	**325—350***
Pink tint,	
4in (10cm)	**125—150**
Pink tint with bonnet,	
4½in (12cm)	**275—300**
Parian-type (untinted bisque),	
5in (13cm)	**125—150**

*Allow extra for pink tone, especially fine decoration and modeling and unusual hairdos.

4½in (12cm) pink tint Frozen Charlotte with molded bonnet. *H&J Foulke, Inc.*

5in (13cm) Parian-type Frozen Charlotte, blonde hair, all original. *H&J Foulke, Inc.*

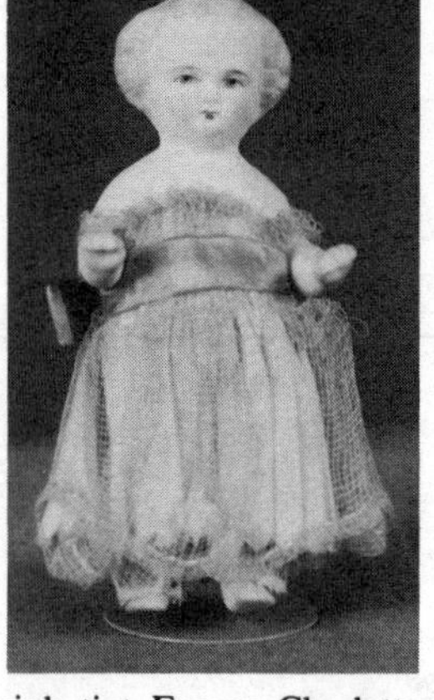

4in (10cm) pink tint Frozen Charlotte with covered wagon hairdo. *H&J Foulke, Inc.*

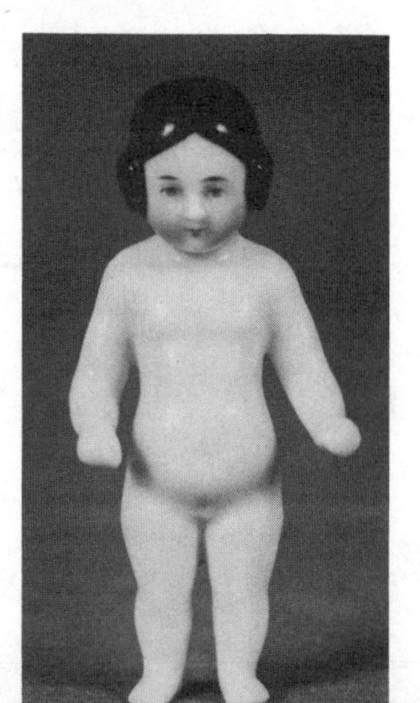

Fulper

Maker: Heads by Fulper Pottery Co. of Flemington, N.J., U.S.A.
Bodies by other companies, often Amberg or Horsman
Date: 1918—1921
Material: Bisque heads; composition ball-jointed or jointed kid bodies
Size: Various
Mark: "Fulper—Made in U.S.A." and others

FULPER

Fulper Child Doll: Perfect bisque head, good wig; kid jointed or composition ball-jointed body; set or sleep eyes, open mouth; suitably dressed; all in good condition.

Kid body,
14—16in (36—41cm) **$325—375**
Composition body,
18—20in (46—51cm) **475—525**

Fulper Baby or Toddler: Same as above, but with bent-limb or jointed toddler body.

14—16in (36—41cm) **$450—500**
20—22in (51—56cm) **600—700**

Kewpie: All-bisque standing figure with legs together, arms jointed, "starfish" hands (fingers outspread); three tufts of hair, painted eyes to side, watermelon mouth; naked; perfect condition.
MARK:

FULPER
MADE IN
USA

7in (18cm) **$300—350****

**Not enough price samples to compute a reliable range.

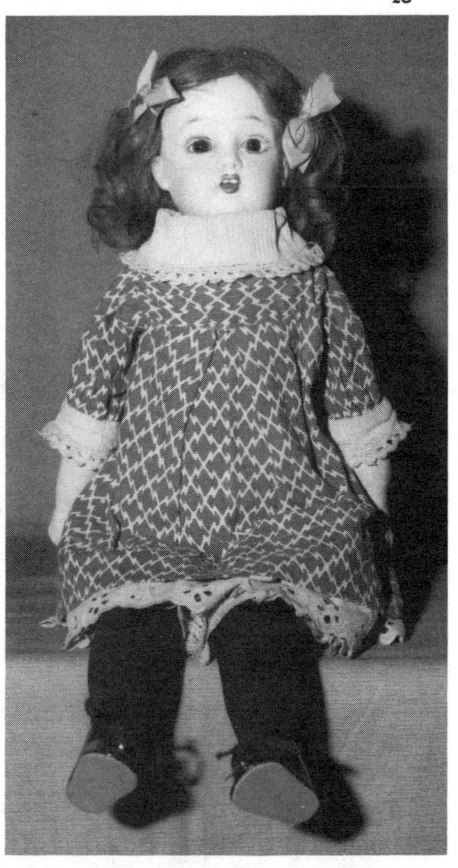

19in (48cm) Fulper child shoulder head on pink cloth body. *Dr. Carole Stoessel Zvonar Collection.*

Fulper continued

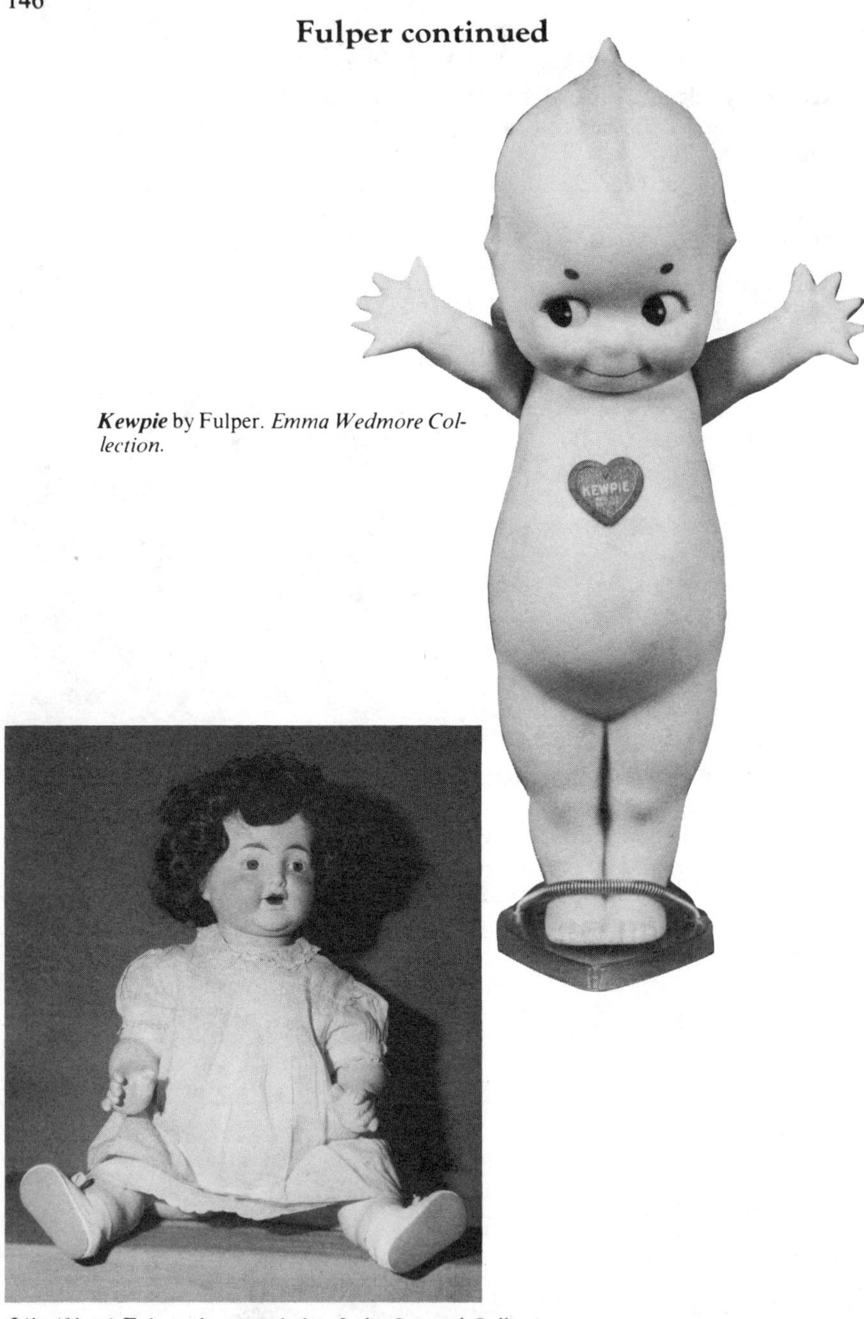

Kewpie by Fulper. *Emma Wedmore Collection.*

24in (61cm) Fulper character baby. *India Stoessel Collection.*

Gaultier

Maker: Francois Gauthier name changed to Gaultier in the early 1870s; St. Maurice, Charenton, Seine, Paris, France (This company made only porcelain parts, not bodies.)
Date: Late 1860s—on
Material: Bisque head; kid or composition body
Size: Various
Mark: As indicated below

Marked F. G. Fashion Lady: Late 1860s to 1930. Bisque swivel head on bisque shoulder plate, original kid body, kid arms with wired fingers or bisque lower arms and hands; original or good French wig, lovely large stationary eyes, closed mouth, ears pierced; dressed; all in good condition.

MARK: "F.G."
on side of shoulder

12—14in (31—36cm) **$1000—1200***
16—18in (41—46cm) **1400—1650***
20in (51cm) **1800—2000***

Late doll in ethnic costume:
12—14in (31—36cm) **850—950**

*Greatly depending upon the appeal of the face.

21in (53cm) F. G. fashion lady. *Betty Harms Collection.*

Marked F. G. Bébé: Ca. 1879—1887. Bisque swivel head on shoulder plate and gusseted kid body with bisque lower arms or chunky jointed composition body; good wig, large bulgy paperweight eyes, closed mouth, pierced ears; dressed; all in good condition.

MARK: "F. 7 G." (or other size number)

14—15in (36—38cm) **$2500—2600**
18—20in (46—51cm) **2800—3000**
25in (64cm) **3750**

Gaultier continued

Marked F. G. Bébé: Ca. 1887—1900 and probably later. Bisque head, composition jointed body; good French wig, beautiful large set eyes, closed mouth, pierced ears; well dressed; all in good condition.
MARK:

F.G

15—17in (38—43cm)	**$1800—2000***	Open mouth:		
20—22in (51—56cm)	**2200—2400***		15in (38cm)	**1150—1250**
27in (69cm)	**3000—3100***		20in (51cm)	**1600—1700**

*Greatly depending upon appeal of face.

24in (61cm) F. G. bébé with scroll mark. *Betty Harms Collection.*

Georgene Novelties

Maker: Georgene Novelties (Georgene Averill, Madame Hendren), New York, N.Y., U.S.A.
Date: 1930s—on
Material: All-cloth or composition and cloth
Size: Various
Designer: Many dolls by Georgene Averill; also see Maude Tousey Fangel, Grace Drayton and Madame Hendren
Mark: Usually a paper tag

Internationals and Children: Mask face with painted features, yarn hair, some with real eyelashes; cloth body with movable arms and legs; attractive original clothes; all in excellent condition.

Foreign costume:	
12in (31cm)	**$ 45—55**
Mint-in-box with wrist tag	**65—75**
24—26in (61—66cm)	**110—125**
Children:	
12—14in (31—36cm)	**90—100**
10in (25cm) ***Topsy & Eva***	**85—95**
14in (36cm) ***Little Lulu***, 1944	**250****
14in (36cm) ***Nancy***, 1944	**300****
14in (36cm) ***Sluggo***, 1944	**300****
14in (36cm) ***Tubby Tom***, 1951	**300****

**Not enough price samples to compute a reliable range.

13in (33cm) cloth child of the type made by Georgene Novelties. *H&J Foulke, Inc.*

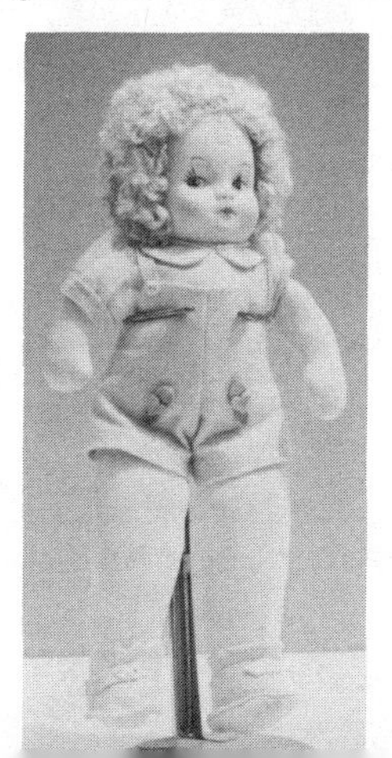

10in (25cm) ***Topsy & Eva***, all original. *H&J Foulke, Inc.*

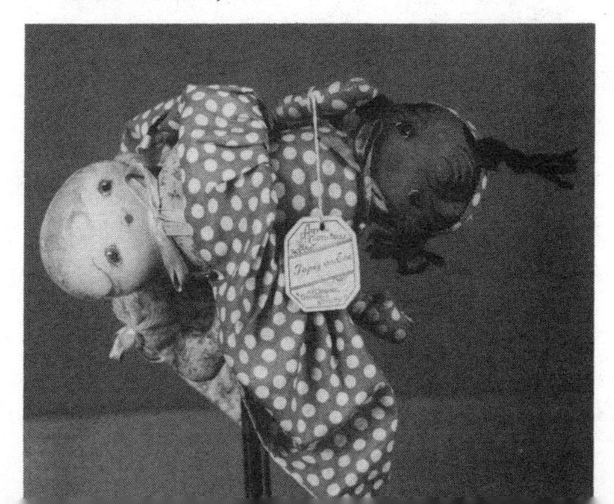

German Bisque Hatted or Bonnet Dolls

Maker: Various German firms
Date: Ca. 1880—1920
Material: Bisque shoulder heads (usually stone bisque), cloth bodies, china or stone bisque extremities
Size: Usually 12in (31cm) and under
Mark: Some with numbers and/or "Germany"

12in (31cm) doll with molded butterfly bonnet. *Richard Wright Antiques.*

9½in (24cm) doll with molded Kate Greenaway bonnet. *Richard Wright Antiques.*

Hatted or Bonnet Doll: Bisque head with painted molded hair and molded fancy bonnet with bows, ribbons, flowers, feathers, and so forth; painted eyes and facial features; original cloth body with original arms and legs; good old clothes or newly dressed; all in good condition.

7—8in (18—20cm)	**$125—150***
12—15in (31—38cm)	**200—250***
16—18in (41—46cm)	**300—350***

*Allow more for unusual styles.

All-bisque, 5—6in (13—15cm):

Common-type	**75—85**
More unusual style	**175—225**

All-bisque flappers,

3—4in (8—10cm)	**125—150**

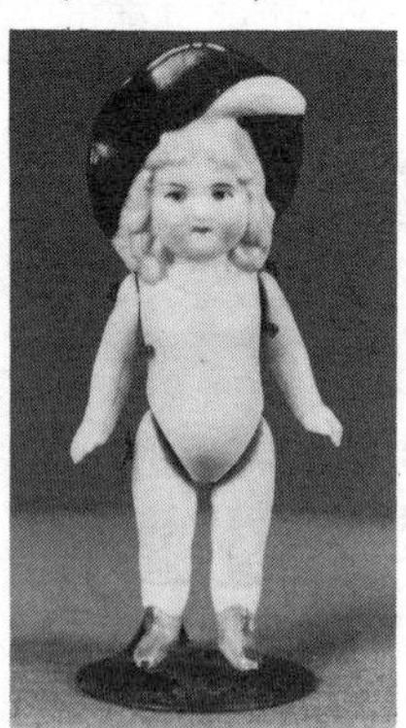

4½in (12cm) all-bisque with molded hat. *H&J Foulke, Inc.*

German Bisque Molded Hair
(Tinted Bisque)

Maker: Various German firms
Date: Last quarter 19th century
Material: Tinted bisque shoulder head, kid or cloth body
Size: Various
Mark: Sometimes numbers and/or "Germany"

Molded Hair Doll: Tinted bisque shoulder head with beautifully molded hair (usually blonde), painted eyes (sometimes glass), closed mouth; original kid or cloth body; appropriate clothes; all in good condition.

15—16in (38—41cm) **$225—275***
18—20in (46—51cm) **325—375***
22—24in (56—61cm) **425—475***
Glass eyes,
18—20in (46—51cm) **500—600**
Tiny doll,
5—7in (13—18cm) **85—95**
All original **125**

*Allow extra for glass eyes or unusual hairdo.

18in (46cm) bisque molded hair girl with blonde hair and blue hair bow, glass eyes, earrings.

American School Boy (so-called): Bisque shoulder head, molded blonde hair (sometimes brown hair), glass eyes, closed mouth; kid or cloth body, good bisque or kid arms; nicely dressed; all in good condition.

12in (31cm) **$350**
Composition body,
9—10in (23—25cm) **400**

13in (33cm) bisque molded hair boy with glass eyes, all original.

German Bisque Portrait Dolls

BELOW LEFT: 13in (33cm) ***Uncle Sam***, incised "S 1", all original. *Wenham Museum Collection, Wenham, Massachusetts.*

ABOVE RIGHT: 4½in (12cm) old lady character doll, all original. *Carol Green Collection.*

13½in (34cm) character man with molded mustache, unmarked. *Gladyse Hills Hilsdorf Collection.*

Admiral Dewey: 1898. Perfect bisque head with portrait face, glass eyes, molded mustache, goatee; five-piece papier-mâché body; original uniform; all in good condition.

MARK: Sometimes "S" or "D" with a number.

8—9 in (20—23cm) **$ 350—400**
Historical Gentlemen,
15in (38cm) **2000****

Uncle Sam: Ca. 1900. Perfect bisque head portrait of old man with mohair wig and goatee, glass eyes; composition body; original clothes; all in good condition.

MARK: Usually "S" with a number.

12—15in (31—38cm) **$1600—1800****
8—9in (20—23cm) **350—400**
Old Rip,
8—9in (20—23cm) **350—400**

Old Lady: Ca. 1900. Perfect bisque head of old lady, character face, gray mohair wig, glass eyes, closed mouth; five-piece papier-mâché body; appropriate clothes; all in good condition. Unmarked.

4½in (12cm) **$400—450****
Hexe Witch,
8in (20cm) **500—600**

Man with mustache: Ca. 1910. Bisque portrait face with bald head with wig, glass eyes, heavy molded eyebrows, wrinkles, molded shaggy mustache, long nose; jointed composition body. Unmarked.

13½in (34cm) **$2500 up****

**Not enough price samples to compute a reliable range.

German Bisque
(Unmarked or Unidentified Marks)

Maker: Various German firms
Date: 1880—on
Material: Bisque head, composition, kid or cloth body
Size: Various
Mark: Some numbered, some "Germany," some both

Child Doll with closed mouth:
Ca. 1880—1890. Perfect bisque shoulder head, kid or cloth body, gusseted at hips and knees, good bisque hands; good wig; nicely dressed; all in good condition.

Kid or cloth body,
sometimes mold 639 or 698:

14—16in (36—41cm)	**$650—750***
19—21in (48—53cm)	**900—1100***
22—23in (56—58cm)	**1150—1250***

Composition body:

15—17in (38—43cm)	**1400—1500**
19—21in (48—53cm)	**1700—1800**
22—25in (56—64cm)	**1700—2000**

*Allow extra for swivel neck or unusual face.

13in (33cm) closed-mouth child with turned shoulder head, all original. *Emma Wedmore Collection.*

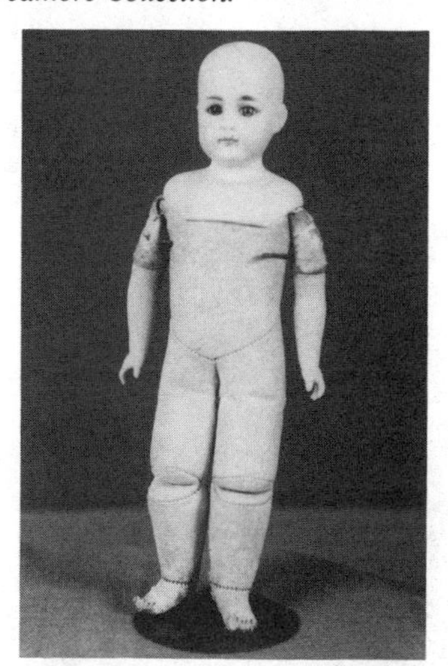

10in (25cm) closed-mouth child shoulder head, incised "50/1." *Joanna Ott Collection.*

17in (43cm) closed-mouth child, incised "11," swivel neck, kid body, all original. *Betty Harms Collection.*

German Bisque continued

Child Doll with open mouth: Late 1880s—1900. Perfect fine, pale bisque head, ball-jointed composition body or kid body with bisque lower arms; good wig, glass eyes, open mouth; dressed; all in good condition.

16—19in (41—48cm)	**$350—400***
21—24in (53—61cm)	**425—475***
28—30in (71—76cm)	**800—900***

*More for an unusual face.

Child Doll with open mouth: 1900—1940. Perfect bisque head, ball-jointed composition, kid or cloth body with bisque lower arms; good wig, glass sleep eyes, open mouth; pretty clothes; all in good condition.

11—13in (28—33cm)	**$175—225**
15—17in (38—43cm)	**250—300**
22—24in (56—61cm)	**350—400**
28—30in (71—76cm)	**500—600**

*Allow more for a doll with unusual face.

28in (71cm) shoulder head, incised "246," kid body. *Emma Wedmore Collection.*

16in (41cm) swivel neck, kid body, incised "51/7." *Carol Green Collection.*

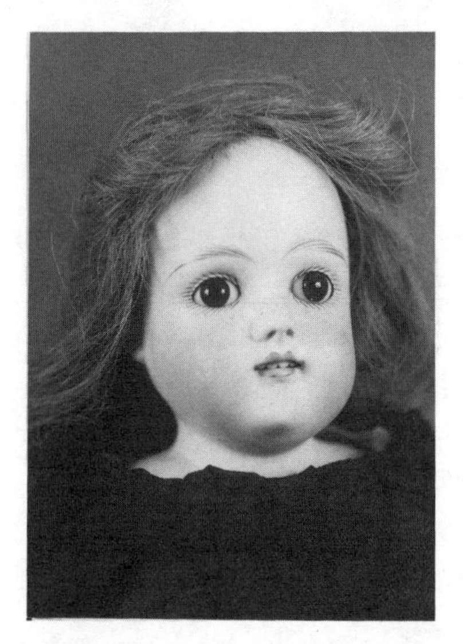

16in (41cm) shoulder head, kid body, incised "7." *Dr. Carole Stoessel Zvonar Collection.*

German Bisque continued

Name shoulder head child: 1890 to World War I. Perfect bisque shoulder head marked with doll's name, jointed kid or cloth body, bisque lower arms; good wig, glass eyes, open mouth; well dressed; all in good condition. Names include ***Rosebud, Lilly, Daisy, Alma, Mabel, Darling*** and ***Ruth.***

15—18in (38—46cm) **$200—250**
21—22in (53—56cm) **300—350**

Tiny child doll: Ca. 1900—1940. Perfect bisque socket head of good quality, five-piece composition body of good quality with molded and painted shoes and stockings; good wig, set or sleep eyes, open mouth; cute clothes; all in good condition.

5—7in (12—18cm) **$150—200**
8—10in (20—25cm) **175—225**
Fully jointed body,
7—8in (18—20cm) **250—300**
Closed mouth:
8in (20cm) **300—350**
4½—5½in (12—14cm) **200—225**

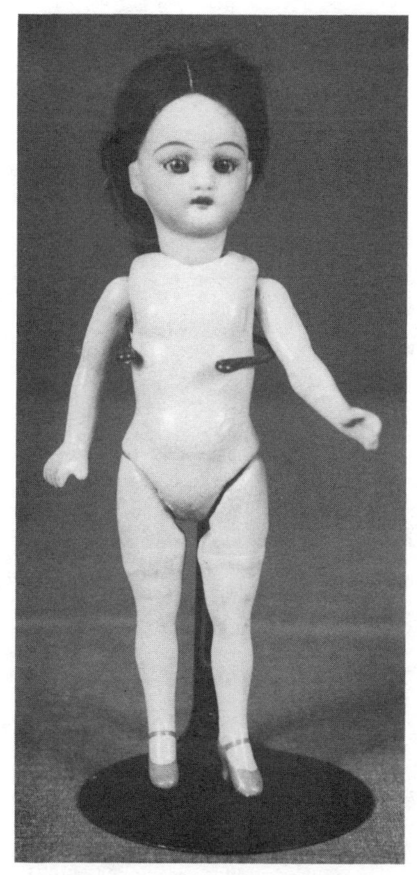

7in (18cm) tiny child doll with long white painted stockings. *H&J Foulke, Inc.*

5½in (14cm) tiny child doll, incised "13a," all original. *H&J Foulke, Inc.*

German Bisque continued

Character Baby: 1910—on. Perfect bisque head, good wig or solid dome with painted hair, sleep eyes, open mouth; composition bent-limb baby body; suitably dressed; all in good condition.

7½in (19cm) painted eyes	**$200—225**
13—15in (33—38cm)	**325—375***
18—20in (46—51cm)	**425—475***
22—24in (56—61cm)	**575—675***

* Allow more for open/closed mouth, closed mouth or unusual face.

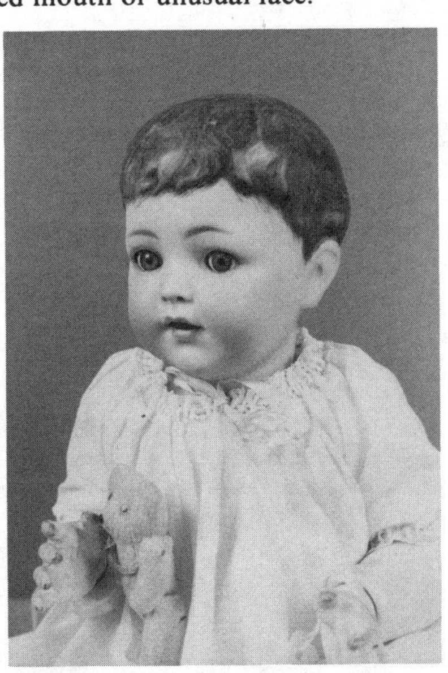

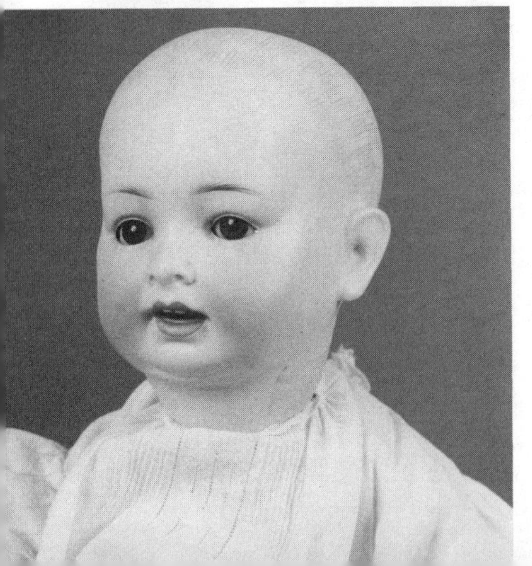

COUNTERCLOCKWISE:
16in (41cm) unmarked character baby with molded brown hair, pierced nose. *Dr. Carole Stoessel Zvonar Collection.*

21in (53cm) character baby, incised "100/10½," flirty eyes. *Dr. Carole Stoessel Zvonar Collection.*

17in (43cm) character baby, incised "21-7." *Dr. Carole Stoessel Zvonar Collection.*

German Bisque continued

Character Child: 1910—on. Bisque head with good wig or solid dome head with painted hair, sleep or painted eyes, open or closed mouth, expressive character face; jointed composition body; dressed; all in good condition.

15—18in (38—46cm)	**$1200 up***
#149, 18in (46cm)	**2600 up**
#163, 13in (33cm)	**950**
#134, 18in (46cm)	**3000 up**
#112, 128, 18—20in (46—51cm)	**3500 up**

*Depending upon individual face.

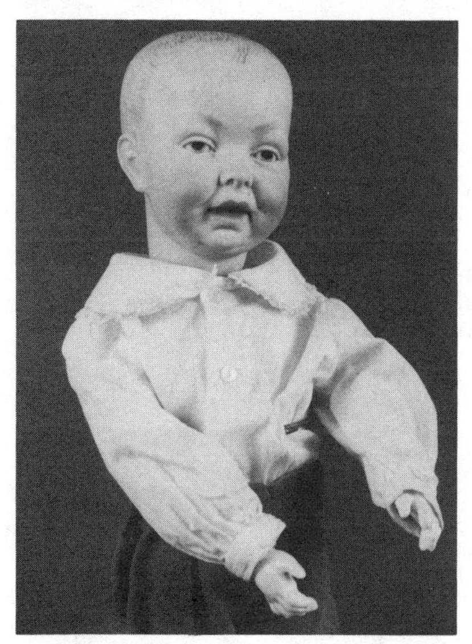

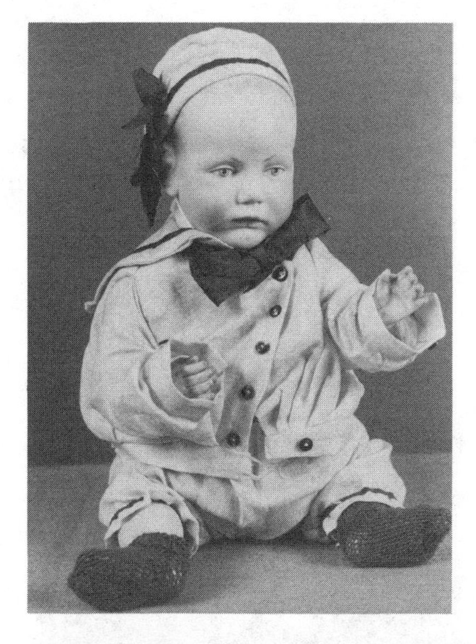

CLOCKWISE:
16in (41cm) character, incised "159-3." *Richard Wright Antiques.*

13in (33cm) unmarked character baby, rare face, all original. *Esther Schwartz Collection.*

18in (46cm) character child, incised "149." *Dr. Carole Stoessel Zvonar Collection.*

German Bisque "Dolly" Faces

Numerous companies produced the girl dolls with open mouths, sleep eyes, mohair wigs and ball-jointed composition or kid bodies between 1900—1930. These all run approximately the same price for a perfect good-quality bisque head and appropriate body with nice clothes. Do not pay as much for the very late bisques and the cheaply-made bodies.

Trade Names	**Makers**
My Girlie	G & S
My Sweetheart	MOA Welsch
Viola	P. Sch.
Princess	S & C
Duchess (A.M.)	E. U. Steiner
Dollar Princess	G. B.
Majestic	L H B
Darling	L H K
Pansy	Gebrüder Knoch
Beauty (A.M.)	Gebrüder Krauss
Columbia (A.M.)	

16—18in (41—46cm) **$275—300***
21—23in (53—58cm) **350—400***
27—28in (69—71cm) **450—550***

*More for an especially pretty face.

19in (48cm) shoulder head with dolly face, incised "27/118." *Emma Wedmore Collection.*

20in (51cm) dolly face, incised "K 10 C," plaster pate. *Dr. Carole Stoessel Zvonar Collection.*

German Bisque Infants

Date: 1924—on
Material: Bisque head, cloth body
(See also specific makers, such as Armand Marseille, Century Doll Co., and so on)

Marked Baby Phyllis: Baby Phyllis Doll Co., Brooklyn, N.Y., U.S.A. Heads by Armand Marseille. Perfect solid dome bisque head with painted hair, sleep eyes, closed mouth; cloth body with composition hands; appropriate clothes; all in good condition.

MARK: BABY PHYLLIS
Made in Germany
24014

Head circumference:
12—13in (31—33cm) **$450****

Marked Baby Gloria: Heads possibly by Armand Marseille. Perfect solid dome head with molded and painted hair, sleep eyes, smiling face with open mouth and two upper teeth, dimples; cloth mama doll body with composition limbs; appropriately dressed; all in good condition.

MARK: Baby Gloria
Germany

17—18in (43—46cm) long **$650—750****

Gerling Baby: Gerling Toy Co., New York, N.Y., U.S.A. Perfect solid dome bisque head with painted hair, glass sleep eyes, closed mouth, open nostrils; cloth body with composition hands; dressed; all in good condition.

MARK: "ARTHUR A. GERLING"

15—16in (38—41cm) long **$650—700****

Marked O.I.C. Baby: Perfect bisque solid dome head with screaming features, tiny glass eyes, wide open mouth with molded tongue; cloth body; dressed; all in good condition.

MARK:

"255
3
O.I.C."

13in (33cm) **$2000****

**Not enough price samples to compute a reliable range.

German Bisque Infants continued

Infant, unmarked or unidentified maker: Perfect bisque head with molded and painted hair, glass sleep eyes; cloth body, celluloid or composition hands; dressed; all in good condition.

10—12in (25—31cm) long	**$300—350***
15—18in (38—46cm) long	**500—600***

*More depending upon appeal and rarity of face.

Siegfried: Perfect bisque solid dome head with molded hair and flange neck, sleep eyes, closed mouth, side nose, pronounced philtrum; cloth body with composition hands; dressed; all in good condition.

MARK: Siegfried
made in Germany
9

Head circumference:
12—13in (31—33cm) **$1800—2000**

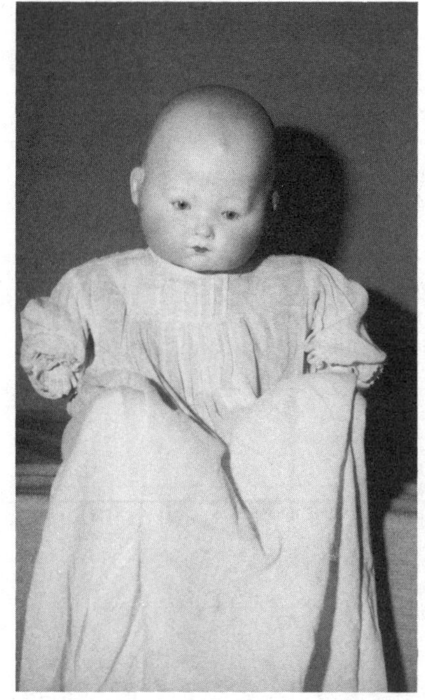

19in (48cm) long with 14½in (37cm) head circumference, ***Kiddiejoy*** 345/6 infant. *Dr. Carole Stoessel Zvonar Collection.*

12in (31cm) long H u B 500/2K baby with open mouth and spring tongue on composition body. *Dr. Carole Stoessel Zvonar Collection.*

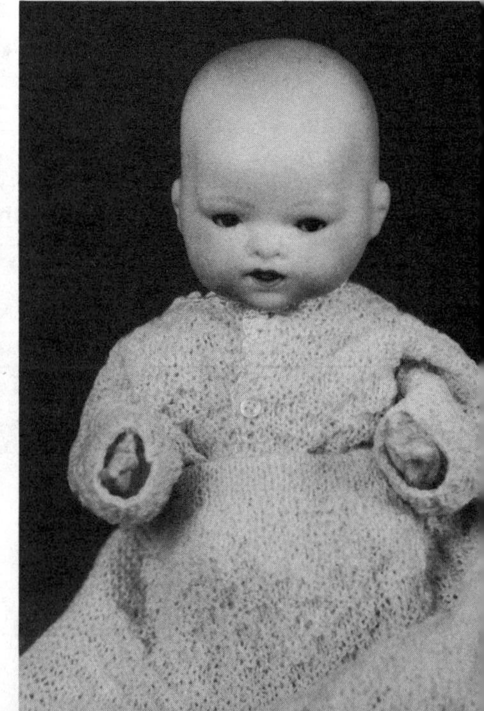

Gesland

Maker: Heads: François Gaultier, Paris, France.
Bodies: E., F. & A. Gesland, Paris, France

Date: Late 1860s—on

Material: Bisque head, stockinette stuffed body on wire frame, bisque or composition lower arms and legs

Size: Various

Mark: Heads: F. G

Gesland Bodied: Fashion Lady: bisque swivel head, good wig, paperweight eyes, closed mouth, pierced ears; stockinette body with bisque hands and legs; dressed; all in good condition.

18—23in (46—58cm) **$3200—3700**

Bébé-type bisque swivel head: Good wig, paperweight eyes, closed mouth, pierced ears; stockinette body with composition lower arms and legs; dressed; all in good condition.

21—24in (53—61cm) **$3600—4000***

*Good early face.

17in (43cm) Gesland fashion lady, all original.

14in (36cm) Gesland bébé with F. G. head.

Gladdie

Maker: Made in Germany for George Borgfeldt, New York, N.Y., U.S.A.
Date: 1929
Material: Ceramic head, cloth torso, composition arms and legs
Size: 17—22in (43—56cm)
Designer: Helen W. Jensen
Mark: [sic] *Gladdie*
Copyriht By
Helen W. Jensen

Marked Gladdie: Ceramic head, molded and painted hair, glass eyes, open/closed mouth with molded teeth, laughing face; cloth torso, composition arms and legs; dressed; all in good condition.

19in (48cm) **$ 850—950**

Bisque head,
13in (33cm) **2800****

**Not enough price samples to compute a reliable range.

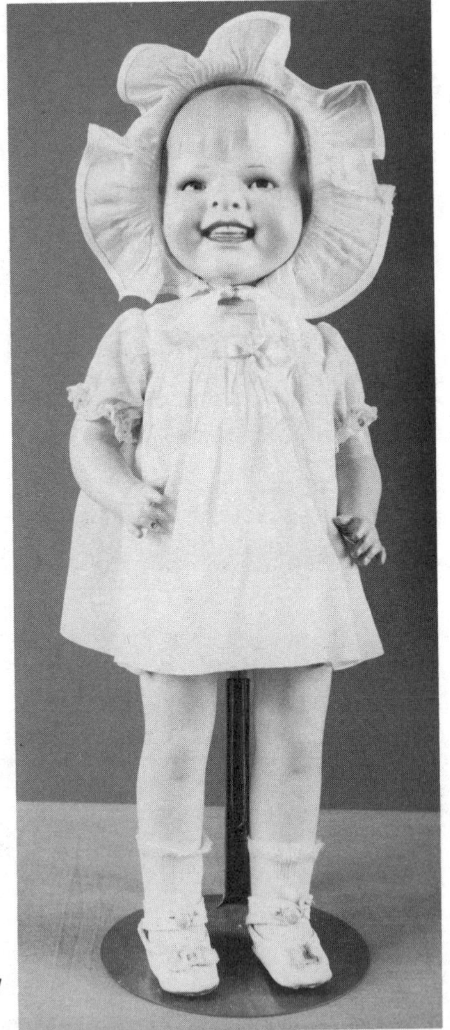

19in (48cm) ***Gladdie***, all original. *Pearl D. Morley Collection.*

Godey's Little Lady Dolls

Maker: Ruth Gibbs, Flemington, N.J., U.S.A.
Date: 1946
Material: China head and limbs, cloth body
Size: Most 7in (18cm); a few 12 or 13in (31 or 33cm)
Designer: Herbert Johnson
Mark: Paper label inside skirt "Godey's Little Lady Dolls;" "R. G." incised on back plate.

Ruth Gibbs Doll: China head with painted black, brown, blonde or auburn hair and features; pink cloth body with china limbs and painted slippers which often matched the hair color; original clothes, usually in an old-fashioned style.

7in (18cm)	**$50—55**
13in (33cm) undressed	**90—100**

7in (18cm) ***Lucky Penny Series*** of Godey's Little Lady Dolls. *H&J Foulke, Inc.*

Goebel

Maker: William Goebel, Thüringia, Germany
Date: 1879—on
Material: Bisque heads, composition bodies; also all-bisque
Size: Various
Mark: [mark] or [mark] or "B" + number; "Germany"

Goebel Child Doll: Ca. 1900. Perfect bisque socket head, good wig, sleep eyes, open mouth; composition jointed body; dressed; all in good condition.
16—18in (41—46cm) **$275—300**
21—23in (53—58cm) **350—400**

Goebel Character Doll: Ca. 1910. Perfect bisque head with molded hair in various styles, character face smiling or somber with painted features; papier-mâché five-piece body; all in excellent condition.
6½in (17cm) **$300—350**

Goebel Character Baby: Ca. 1910. Perfect bisque socket head, good wig, sleep eyes, open mouth with teeth; composition jointed baby body; dressed; all in good condition.
14—16in (36—41cm) **$350—400**
20—21in (51—53cm) **500—550**

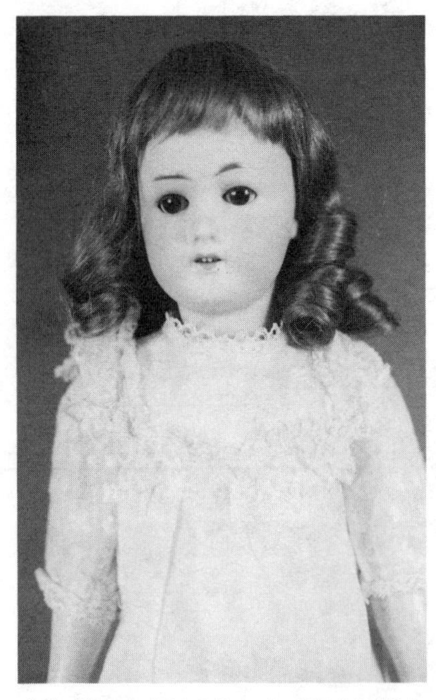

23in (58cm) child doll, incised "B 3." *H&J Foulke, Inc.*

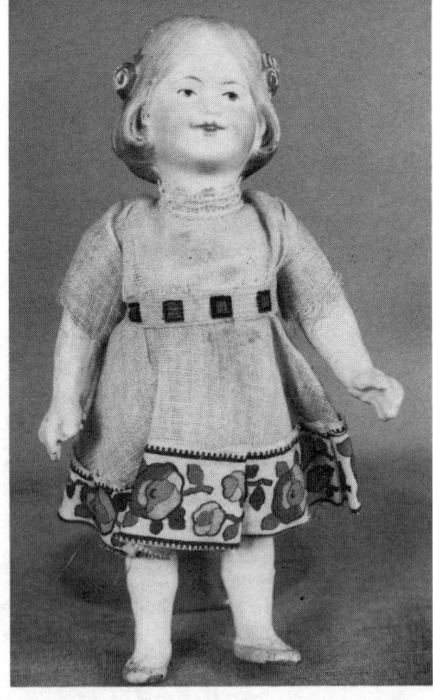

6½in (17cm) character girl with molded flowers in her hair. *H&J Foulke, Inc.*

Googly-Eyed Dolls

Maker: J. D. Kestner, Armand Marseille and other German and French firms
Date: Ca. 1911—on
Material: Bisque heads and composition or papier-mâché bodies or all-bisque
Size: Usually small
Mark: Various

All-Bisque Googly: Jointed at shoulders and hips, molded shoes and socks; mohair wig, glass eyes, impish mouth; undressed; in perfect condition.

4—5in (10—13cm) Glass eyes, stiff neck	**$ 450—500**
4—5in (10—13cm) Glass eyes, swivel neck	**600—650**
4—5in (10—13cm) Painted eyes, swivel neck	**375—425**
5in (13cm) Jointed elbows and knees	**1500—1650**

Painted eyes, composition body: Perfect bisque swivel head with molded hair, painted eyes to the side, impish mouth; composition body jointed at shoulders and hips with molded and painted shoes and socks; cute clothes; all in good condition. By A.M., Heubach, Goebel and others.

7—8in (18—20cm)	**$350—400**
10in (25cm)	**450—500**

10½in (27cm) P. M. 950 googly, jointed toddler body. *Richard Wright Antiques.*

4¾in (12cm) all-bisque Kestner googly, incised "111," jointed elbows and knees. *Jan Foulke Collection.*

Googly-Eyed Dolls continued

Glass eyes, composition body: Perfect bisque head, molded and painted socks and shoes; proper wig, sleep or set googly eyes look to side, impish mouth closed; original composition body jointed at neck, shoulders and hips; cute clothes; all in nice condition.

JDK 221:
12—13in (31—33cm) **$4000—4500**
15—16in (38—41cm) **4800—5200**

#165:
13—15in (33—38cm) **3500—4000**

AM #323 other similar models:
6½—7½in (17—19cm) **550—650**
9—10in (23—25cm) **800—850**

AM #253: Watermelon mouth,
6½—7½in (17—19cm) **650—750**

SFBJ #245:
8in (20cm) **1000—1200**
15in (38cm) **4500—5000**

K ★ R 131:
15—16in (38—41cm) **6500—7000**

AM #240:
11in (28cm) **1600—1800**

Heubach Einco:
14—16in (36—41cm) **6500—7500**

172, 173:
16in (41cm) **4500—5000**

7½in (19cm) Herm Steiner googly. *H&J Foulke, Inc.*

Very rare Heubach Köppelsdorf googlies. **Left doll:** 14in (36cm) from mold 318. **Right doll:** 12in (31cm) from mold 319. *Lesley Hurford Collection. Photograph courtesy of the owner.*

Googly-Eyed Dolls continued

Composition face: 1912—1914. Made by various companies in 9½—14in (24—36cm) sizes; marked with paper label on clothing. Called "Hug Me Kiddies" as well as other trade names. Round all-composition or composition mask face, wig, round glass eyes looking to the side, watermelon mouth; felt body; original clothes; all in good condition.

10in (25cm)	**$500—550**
12in (31cm)	**700—750**

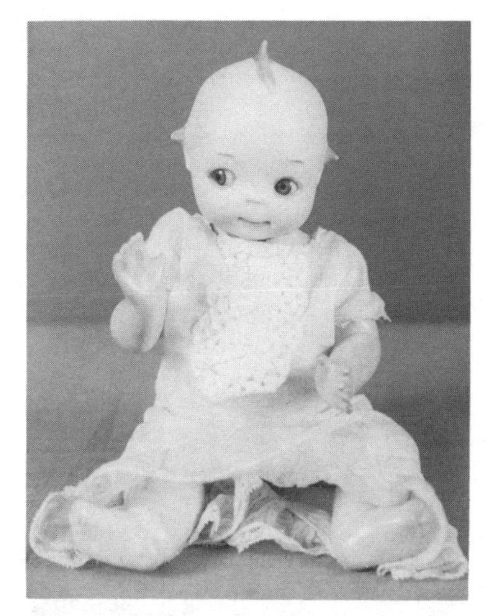

12in (31cm) 240 googly baby. *Richard Wright Antiques.*

10in (25cm) A. M. 253 googly toddler. *Richard Wright Antiques.*

9in (23cm) 173 flirty-eyed googly, toddler body. *Richard Wright Antiques.*

Googly-Eyed Dolls continued

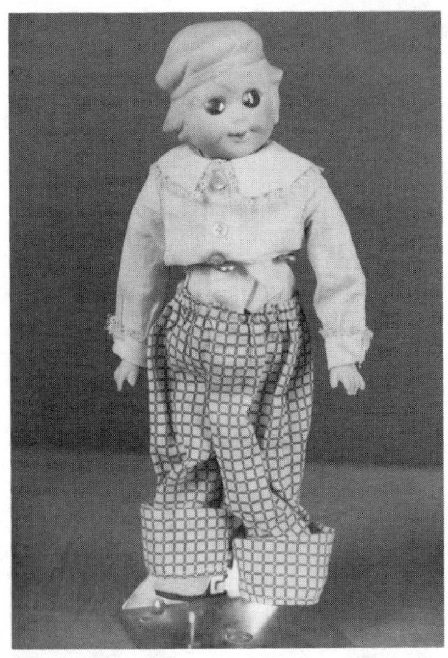

10in (25cm) boy with disc eyes, DRGM 954692. *Richard Wright Antiques.*

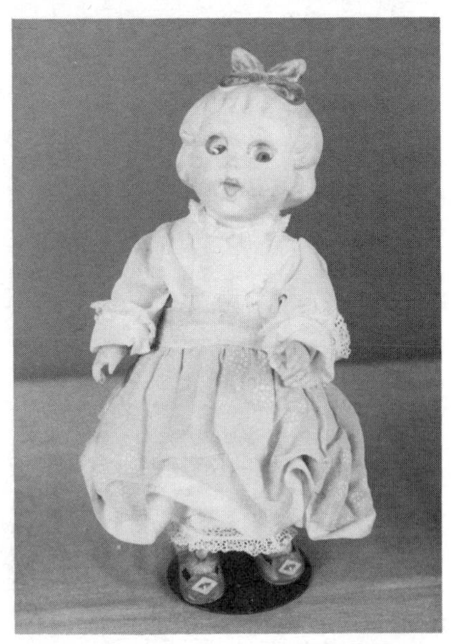

10in (25cm) girl with disc eyes, DRGM 954692//223/I. *Richard Wright Antiques.*

Disc Eyes: Bisque shoulder head, character face, molded hair with bow or cap, closed mouth; inset eyes have floating disc with transparent covering. Girl is mold 223.

MARK: "DRGM 954692."

10in (25cm) **$900—1100**

Googly with molded hat: Perfect bisque head with glass side-glancing eyes, watermelon mouth, molded hat; jointed composition body.

MARK:

"Dep
Elite"
(letters and numbers)

12—13in (31—33cm) **$2000—2200**

Googly with molded hat, incised "Dep// Elite//U.S. 1." *Esther Schwartz Collection.*

Greiner

Maker: Ludwig Greiner of Philadelphia, PA., U.S.A.
Date: 1858—1883
Material: Heads of papier-mâché, cloth bodies, homemade in most cases, but later some Lacmann bodies were used.
Size: Various, 13—over 35in (33—over 89cm)
Mark: Paper label on back shoulder:

GREINER'S
IMPROVED
PATENTHEADS
Pat. March 30TH '58

or

GREINER'S
PATENT DOLL HEADS
No 7
Pat. Mar. 30'58. Ext.'72

Greiner: Blonde or black molded hair, painted features; homemade cloth body, leather arms; nice old clothes; entire doll in good condition.

'58 label:
20—23in (51—58cm) **$ 900—1100***
28—30in (71—76cm) **1500—1700***
Glass eyes,
19—21in (48—53cm) **1500****
'72 label:
23—24in (58—61cm) **450—550**
30in (76cm) **650—750**

*Additional for mint condition.
**Not enough price samples to compute a reliable range.

LEFT:
26in (66cm) Greiner with '58 label. *Joanna Ott Collection.*

RIGHT:
Side view of the 26in (66cm) Greiner with '58 label. *Joanna Ott Collection.*

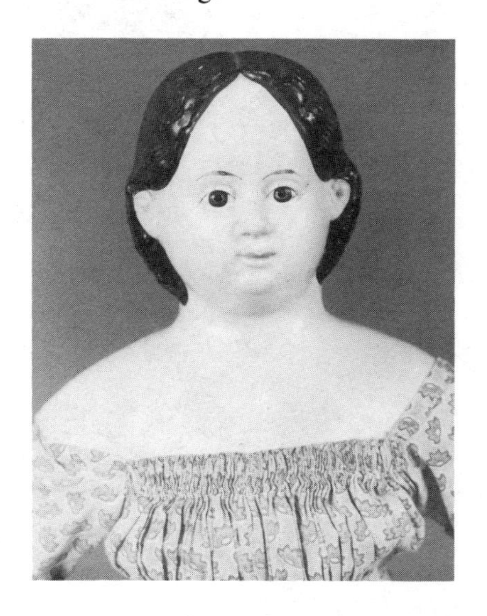

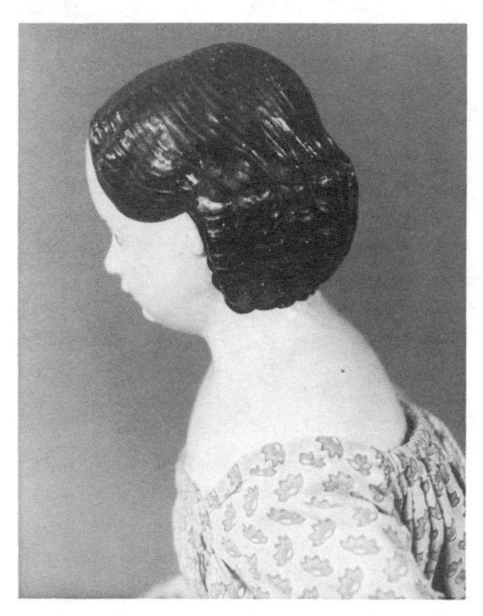

Heinrich Handwerck

Maker: Heinrich Handwerck of Waltershausen, Thüringia, Germany (Some heads by Simon & Halbig)

Date: 1876—on

Material: Bisque head, composition ball-jointed body

Size: Various

Mark: "Germany—Handwerck" sometimes with "S & H" and numbers such as 69, 79, 99, 109, 119 and others

Hch 6/0 H.

H HANDWERCK— Germany —

22in (56cm) Heinrich Handwerck 99 child, all original. *H&J Foulke, Inc.*

Marked Handwerck Child Doll: Ca. 1890—on. Perfect bisque socket head, original or good wig, sleep or set eyes, open mouth, pierced ears; ball-jointed body; dressed; entire doll in good condition.

17—19in (43—48cm)	$ **375—425**
21—23in (53—58cm)	**450—475**
24—26in (61—66cm)	**500—550**
28—30in (71—76cm)	**800—900**
32—33in (89—91cm)	**1100—1200**
35—36in (89—91cm)	**1500—1650**
39—42in (99—107cm)	**2500 up**

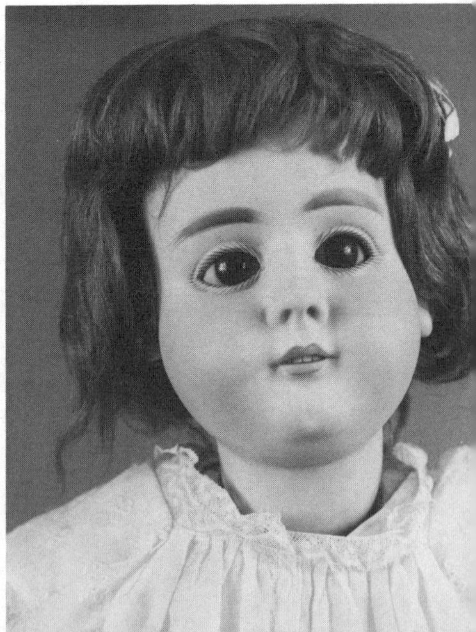

25in (64cm) Heinrich Handwerck 79. *Dr. Carole Stoessel Zvonar Collection.*

Max Handwerck

Maker: Max Handwerck of Waltershausen, Thüringia, Germany
Date: 1900—on
Material: Bisque socket head, ball-jointed composition body
Size: Various
Mark: Max HANDWERCK Germany

"Max Handwerck" with numbers and sometimes "Germany;" also "Bébé Elite."

Marked Max Handwerck Child Doll: Perfect bisque socket head, original or good wig, set or sleep eyes, open mouth, pierced ears; original ball-jointed body; well dressed; all in good condition.
20—24in (51—61cm) **$425—475**

Marked Bébé Elite Character: Perfect bisque socket head with sleep eyes, open mouth with upper teeth, smiling character face; bent-limb composition baby body; appropriate clothes; all in good condition.
16—18in (41—46cm) **$425—500**

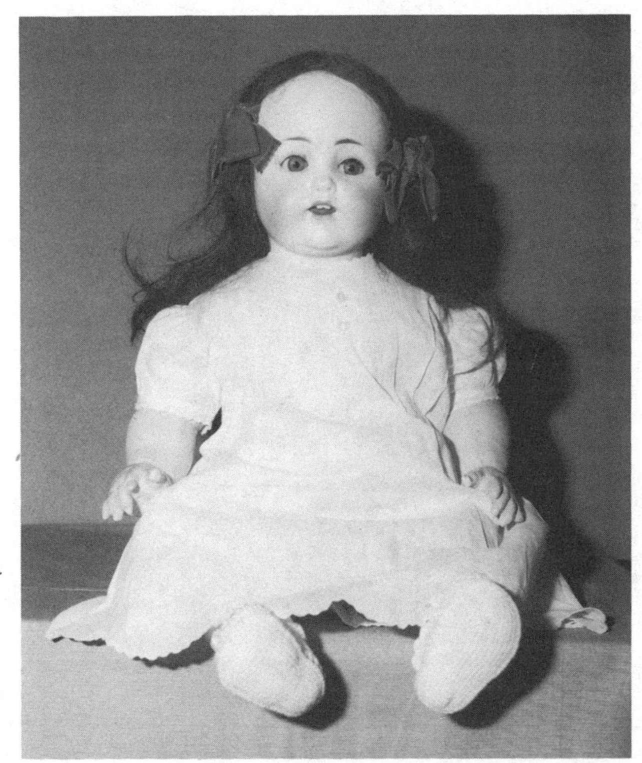

21in (53cm) ***Bébé Elite*** character baby, B 90/185 also with Goebel trademark. *Dr. Carole Stoessel Zvonar Collection.*

Hansi

Maker or Distributor: P. J. Gallais & Co., Paris, France
Date: 1917—1918
Material: Earthenware
Size: 7½in (19cm)
Designer: L'oncle Hansi
Mark: None on doll; paper wrist tag "Vive la France! Gretel;" on the other side "Hansi"

Yerri or Gretel: Earthenware head with painted hair and eyes, closed mouth; jointed five-piece earthenware body with painted shoes and socks; original Alsatian costume; all in good condition.
7½in (19cm) **$250**

7½in (19cm) ***Gretel***, all original. *H&J Foulke, Inc.*

Happifat

Maker: Registered by Borgfeldt in United States and Germany
Date: 1913—1921
Material: All-composition, all-bisque or composition head and hands with stuffed body
Size: All-bisque 3½—4½in (9—11cm); composition about 10in (25cm)
Designer: Kate Jordan
Mark: © on German all-bisque

Happifat: All-bisque with jointed arms, painted features, molded clothes.
4—4½in (10—12cm):

German	**$225—250**
Nippon	**125—150**
Baby Happifat, 4in (10cm)	**300**
Composition head and hands, cloth body, 10in (25cm)	**450****

**Not enough price samples to compute a reliable range.

4½in (12cm) ***Happifat*** girl.

4in (10cm) ***Happifat*** baby with molded underwear. *H&J Foulke, Inc.*

HEbee-SHEbee

Maker: Edward Imeson Horsman Co. (EIH), New York, N.Y., U.S.A. (All-bisque made in Germany)
Date: 1925
Material: Composition, some all-bisque
Size: Various
Designer: Charles H. Twelvetrees
Mark: All-bisque: Sticker on foot or torso, "Germany" on skirt bottom

---

HEbee-SHEbee: Jointed at shoulders and hips; painted eyes; molded white chemise and real ties in molded shoes; all in fair condition. Blue shoes indicate a ***HEbee***; pink ones a ***SHEbee***.

All-bisque (some are not hip jointed and do not have holes for shoelaces),	
4—5in (10—13cm):	
German	**$450—500**
Nippon	**200—225**
Japan	**50—60**
7in (18cm) German	**900—950**
Composition,	
11in (28cm)	**350—400****

**Not enough price samples to compute a reliable range.

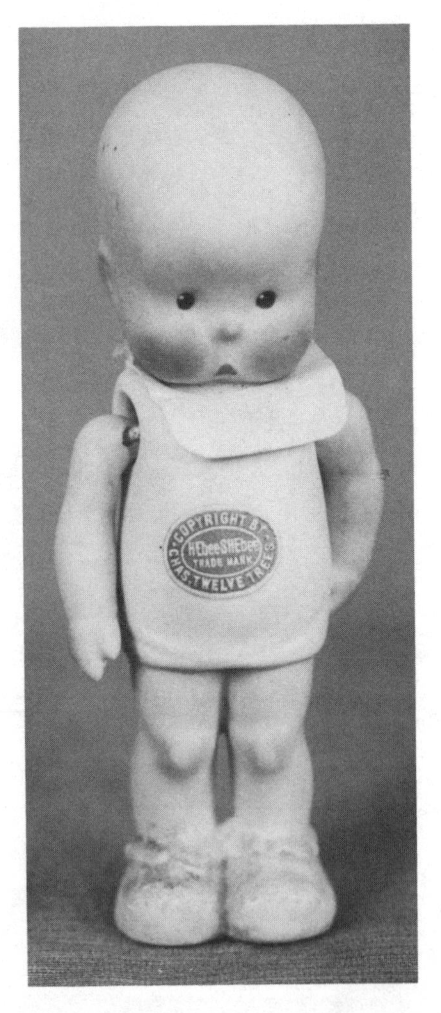

4¼in (11cm) ***HEbee-SHEbee*** with pink booties, original label and bib. *Jan Foulke Collection.*

Hedwig Dolls

Maker: Clothes: Hedwig, Philadelphia, PA., U.S.A.; Dolls: unknown
Date: Ca. 1940s
Material: All-composition
Size: 14in (36cm)
Designer: Marguerite de Angeli (dolls are based on characters from her books)
Mark: None on doll; wrist tag only: "Hedwig Dolls
Registered Authorized
from the books of
Marguerite de Angeli"
(shows line drawing of four dolls)

De Angeli/Hedwig Doll: All-composition, jointed at neck, shoulders and hips; mohair wig, sleep or painted eyes; original clothes; all in very good condition.
Elin from *Elin's Amerika*, Swedish costume
Hannah from *Thee Hannah,* Quaker costume
Lydia from *Henner's Lydia,* Pennsylvania Dutch
Suzanne from *Petite Suzanne,* French Canadian
14in (36cm) **$175—225**

14in (36cm) ***Lydia***, all original.

Mme. Hendren

Maker: Averill Manufacturing Co., New York, N.Y., U.S.A.
Date: 1915—on
Material: Composition heads, cloth and composition bodies
Size: Various
Designer: Many by Georgene Averill
Mark: Cloth tag attached to clothes

Tagged Mme. Hendren Character: Ca. 1915—on. Composition character face, usually with painted features, molded hair or wig (sometimes yarn); hard-stuffed cloth body with composition hands; original clothes often of felt, included Dutch children, Indians, Sailors, Cowboys, Blacks; all in good condition.
10—14in (25—36cm) **$95—110**

Marked Mama Dolls: Ca. 1920—on. Composition shoulder head, lower arms and legs, cloth torso with cry box; mohair wig or molded hair, sleep eyes, open mouth with teeth or closed mouth; appropriately dressed; all in good condition. Names such as ***Baby Hendren, Baby Georgene***, and others.
20in (51cm) **$125—150**
24in (61cm) **150—175**

Dolly Reckord: 1922. Composition shoulder head, lower arms and legs, cloth torso with record player; nice human hair wig, sleep eyes, open mouth with upper teeth; appropriate clothes; all in good condition.
26in (66cm) **$425—475**

Snookums: 1927. Composition shoulder head, molded and painted hair with hole for one tuft of hair, painted eyes, smiling face with open/closed mouth; composition yoke and arms, cloth body and legs; dressed; all in good condition. From the comic strip "The Newlyweds" by George McManus.
14in (36cm) **$250—300**

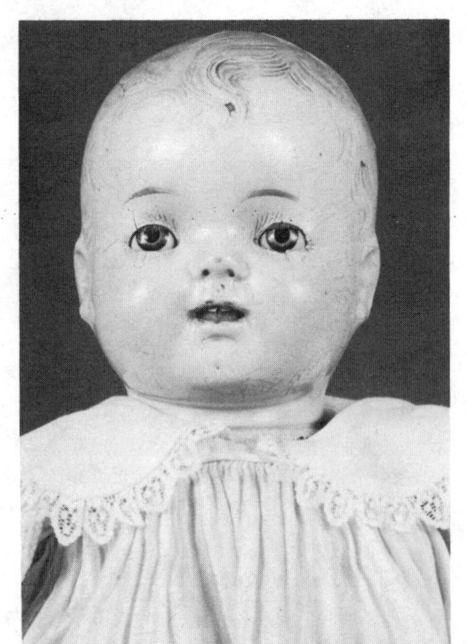

21in (53cm) ***Baby Hendren***, replaced dress. *Betty Harms Collection.*

OPPOSITE PAGE: 24in (61cm) DEP on Jumeau body. *Betty Harms Collection.*

Mme. Hendren continued on page 193

16in (41cm) Alexander ***Elise***, all original. *Virginia Ann Heyerdahl Collection.*

BELOW LEFT: 21in (53cm) Alexander ***Cissy***, all original. *H&J Foulke, Inc.*

BELOW: 15in (38cm) Freundlich soldier, all original. *H&J Foulke, Inc.*

21in (53cm) Ideal ***Deanna Durbin***, all original. *H&J Foulke, Inc.*

OPPOSITE PAGE: 12in (31cm) Oriental papier-mâché baby, all original. *H&J Foulke, Inc.*

15in (38cm) German celluloid-type boy, all original. *H&J Foulke, Inc.*

LEFT: 15in (38cm) Russian cloth lady, all original. *H&J Foulke, Inc.*

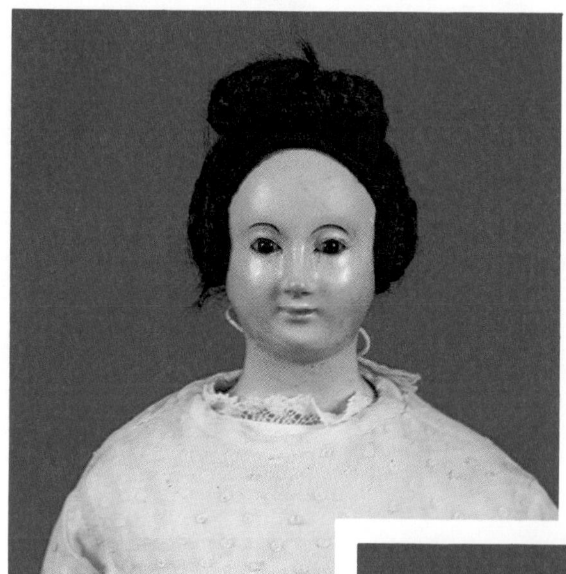

17in (43cm) French-type papier-mâché.

PAGE 184: 13in (33cm) Steiner ***Le Parisiene***. *Betty Harms Collection.*

OPPOSITE PAGE: 28in (71cm) S & H 1039 brown bisque. *Betty Harms Collection.*

13in (33cm) molded hair papier-mâché.

22in (56cm) K★R 117, all original. *Carole Stoessel Zvonar Collection.*

PAGE 185: 19in (48cm) ***Tete Jumeau***, all original. *Betty Harms Collection.*

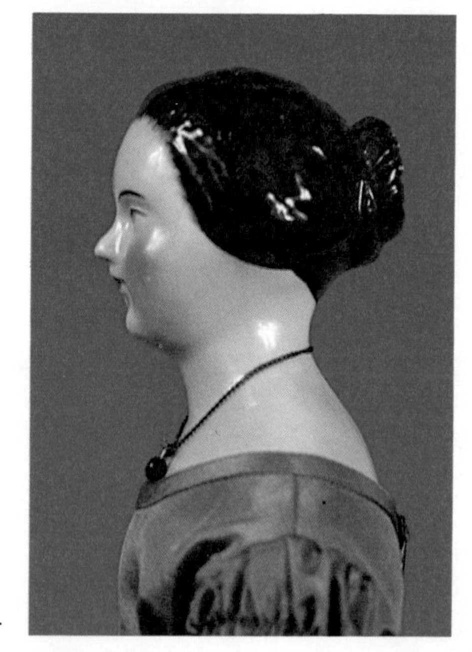

China head with molded bun.

22in (56cm) India Rubber Comb shoulder head, all original.

14in (36cm) Effanbee ***Suzanne***, all original. *H&J Foulke, Inc.*

BELOW: 12in (46cm) Maude Tousey Fangel ***Sweets***, all original. *Jan Foulke Collection.*

OPPOSITE PAGE: 18in (46cm) all-composition toddler, all original. *H&J Foulke, Inc.*

17in (43cm) Rohmer fashion lady.

OPPOSITE PAGE: 20in (51cm) china head boy with brown eyes.

12in (31cm) W. D., all original. *Betty Harms Collection.*

Mme. Hendren continued from page 176

Sunny Boy and Girl: Ca. 1929. Marked on head. Celluloid head with glass eyes; stuffed body with composition arms and legs; original clothes; all in good condition.
15in (38cm) **$150—200****

**Not enough price samples to compute a reliable range.

Body Twists: 1928. All-composition, jointed at neck, shoulders, hips, at waist with a large round ball joint; molded and painted hair, painted eyes, closed mouth; dressed; all in good condition. Advertised as ***Dimmie*** and ***Jimmie***.
14½in (37cm) **$275**

26in (66cm) ***Dolly Reckord***. *Betty Harms Collection.*

Whistling Doll: 1925—1929. Composition head with molded hair, side-glancing eyes, mouth pursed to whistle through round opening; composition arms, cloth torso; legs are coiled spring bellows covered with cloth; when head is pushed down or feet are pushed up, the doll whistles. Original or appropriate clothes; all in good condition.

MARK: None

Original Cardboard Tag:

"I whistle when you dance me on
one foot and then the other.
Patented Feb. 2, 1926
Genuine Madame Hendren Doll."

14—15in (36—38cm)
Sailor, Cowboy, Cop or
Boy ("Dan") **$125—150**

14—15in (36—38cm)
black "Rufus" or
"Dolly Dingle" **150**

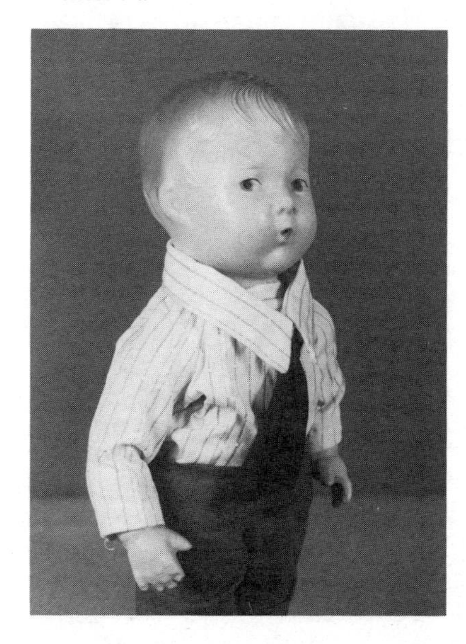

14in (36cm) ***Whistling Dan***, replaced clothes. *H&J Foulke, Inc.*

OPPOSITE PAGE: 17in (43cm) S & H 908. *Carol Green Collection.*

Gebrüder Heubach

Maker: Gebrüder Heubach of Licht and Sonneberg, Thüringia, Germany (porcelain factory)
Date: 1820—on
Material: Bisque head, kid, cloth or jointed composition body or composition bent-limb body
Size: Various
Mark:

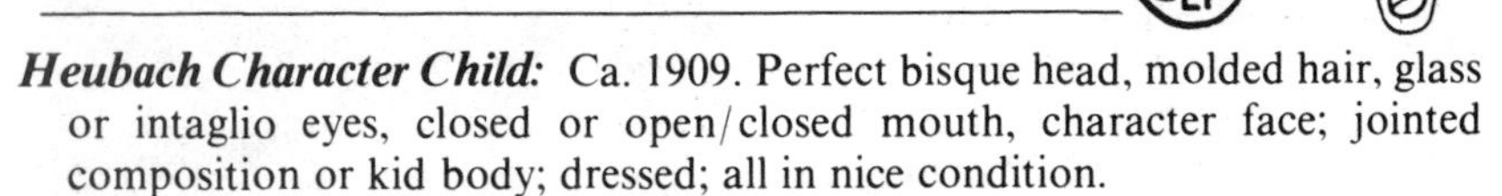

Heubach Character Child: Ca. 1909. Perfect bisque head, molded hair, glass or intaglio eyes, closed or open/closed mouth, character face; jointed composition or kid body; dressed; all in nice condition.

#5730 Santa child, JCB,
20—22in (51—56cm) **$2500—2600**
#8192 open mouth child:
8—9in (20—23cm)
five-piece body **325—350**
14in (36cm) JCB **500—550**
#6969, 6970, 7246, 8017, 7407, pouty child, JCB:
12—13in (31—33cm) **1600—1800**
17—18in (43—46cm) **2500—2600**
#7604 laughing child, intaglio eyes, composition body,
13—14in (33—36cm) **425—500**
#7644 shoulder head, laughing child,
14—15in (36—38cm) **400—425**
#5636 laughing child, glass eyes, JCB,
12—14in (31—36cm) **1200—1300**
#7788 Coquette, JCB, 11in (28cm) **550—650**
#7850 Coquette, shoulder head,
12in (31cm) **450—550**
#7877, 7977, Baby Stuart:
11—12in (28—31cm) **1000**
Glass eyes, removable bonnet,
12in (31cm) **1650**
#8774 Whistling Jim,
13in (33cm) **950—1050**
#5777 Dolly Dimple, JCB,
24in (61cm) **2500—3000**
#5730 smiling shoulder head,
22in (56cm) **1400—1500**
#7622 pouty with molded hair, JCB,
16in (41cm) **900—1000**
#10633, 10586 open mouth child, JCB,
25in (64cm) **800—850**
#10532, 7711 open mouth child, JCB,
12—14in (31—36cm) **450—550**
#6896 pouty, JCB,
19in (48cm) **750**
#8191 grinning, JCB,
12in (31cm) **750—850**
#8413 grinning, JCB,
13in (33cm) **600—650**

Gebrüder Heubach 7616 shoulder head character. *Alice Pat Young Collection.*

Gebrüder Heubach continued

Position Babies	**250 up**
All-bisque girl with bows or hair band, 7in (18cm)	**750**
Bunny Boy or ***Girl***, 5½in (14cm)	**250—375**
All-bisque boy or girl, 4in (10cm)	**225**
Chin-Chin character, 4in (10cm)	**225**
Action figures:	
6in (15cm)	**225—275**
4in (10cm)	**150**
#7926 lady, 15—17in (38—43cm)	**2500—3000**

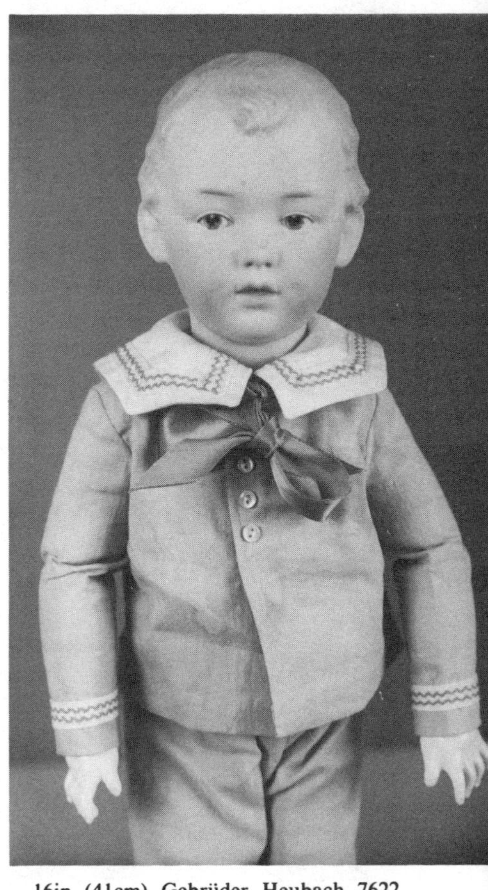

16in (41cm) Gebrüder Heubach 7622 character. *Richard Wright Antiques.*

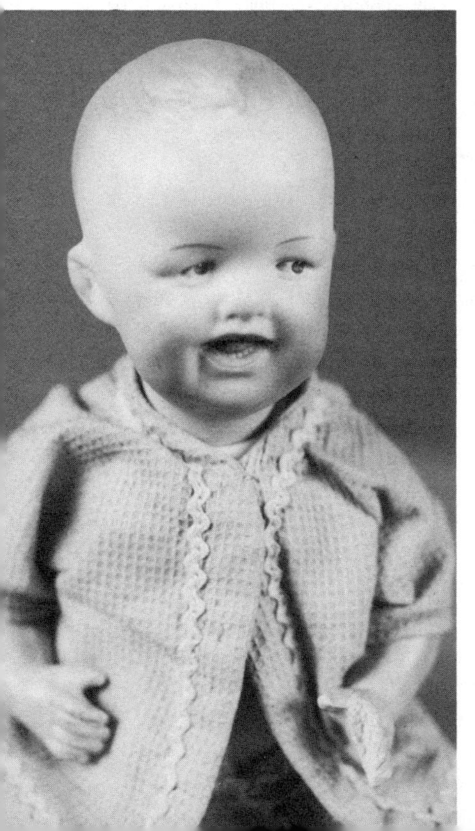

10in (25cm) Gebrüder Heubach 8191 character.

Gebrüder Heubach continued

27in (69cm) Gebrüder Heubach 6969 character. *Richard Wright Antiques.*

8½in (22cm) Gebrüder Heubach 8192 child. *H&J Foulke, Inc.*

12in (31cm) smiling Gebrüder Heubach character 5636. *Betty Harms Collection.*

Gebrüder Heubach continued

23in (58cm) Gebrüder Heubach 5689 character. *Betty Harms Collection.*

20in (51cm) Gebrüder Heubach 10633 shoulder head child with ***Dainty Dorothy*** label. *Emma Wedmore Collection.*

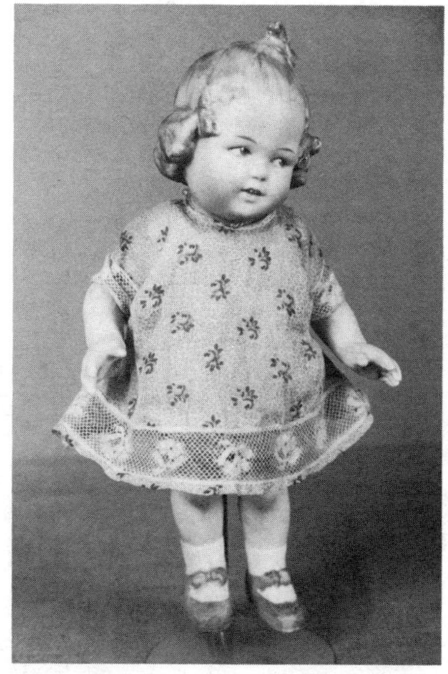

7in (18cm) all-bisque Gebrüder Heubach girl, all original. *Esther Schwartz Collection.*

Gebrüder Heubach continued

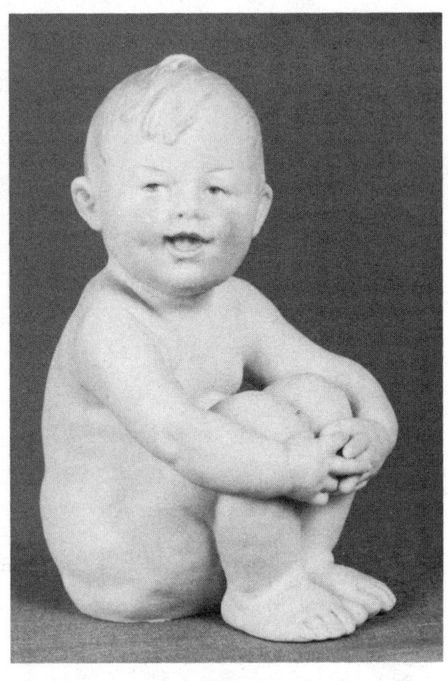

LEFT:
5in (13cm) Gebrüder Heubach pair, incised "10470." *Richard Wright Antiques.*

RIGHT:
Gebrüder Heubach all-bisque piano baby. *H&J Foulke, Inc.*

Heubach Infants: Ca. 1910. Perfect bisque head, molded hair or good wig, intaglio eyes, open or closed mouth, character face; composition bent-limb body; dressed; all in nice condition.

Pouty Babies #7602 and others:

6in (15cm)	**$200**
8—10in (20—25cm)	**300—350**
12—15in (31—38cm)	**400—500**

Shoulder head on kid body,

12—14in (31—36cm)	**300—400**

10in (25cm) Gebrüder Heubach pouty baby. *H&J Foulke, Inc.*

Heubach Köppelsdorf

Maker: Ernst Heubach of Köppelsdorf, Thüringia, Germany (porcelain factory)
Date: 1887—on
Material: Bisque head, kid, cloth or composition bodies
Size: Various

Mark: Heubach-Köppelsdorf
250 - 15/o [a]
Germany

Heubach Child Doll: Ca. 1887—on. Perfect bisque head, good wig, sleep eyes, open mouth; kid, cloth or jointed composition body; dressed; all in good condition.

Kid or cloth body, often mold 275:

13—14in (33—36cm)	**$150—175**
20—22in (51—56cm)	**300—325**

Composition body, often mold 250:

8—9in (20—23cm)	**125**
14—16in (36—41cm)	**250—275**
21—23in (53—58cm)	**350—375**
30in (76cm)	**550—650**

Character Baby: 1910—on. Often mold numbers 300, 320 and 342. Perfect bisque head, good wig, sleep eyes, open mouth (sometimes also wobbly tongue and pierced nostrils); composition bent-limb baby or toddler body; dressed; all in good condition.

9—11in (23—28cm)	**$275—300**
14—15in (36—38cm)	**400—425**
20—22in (51—56cm)	**525—575**
24in (61cm)	**650**

Toddler:

14—15in (36—38cm)	**525—575**
25in (64cm)	**750—850**

Character Children: 1910—on. Perfect bisque shoulder head with molded hair in various styles, some with hair bows, painted eyes, open/closed mouth; cloth body with composition lower arms.

#262 and others,

12in (31cm)	**$375—425****

**Not enough price samples to compute a reliable range.

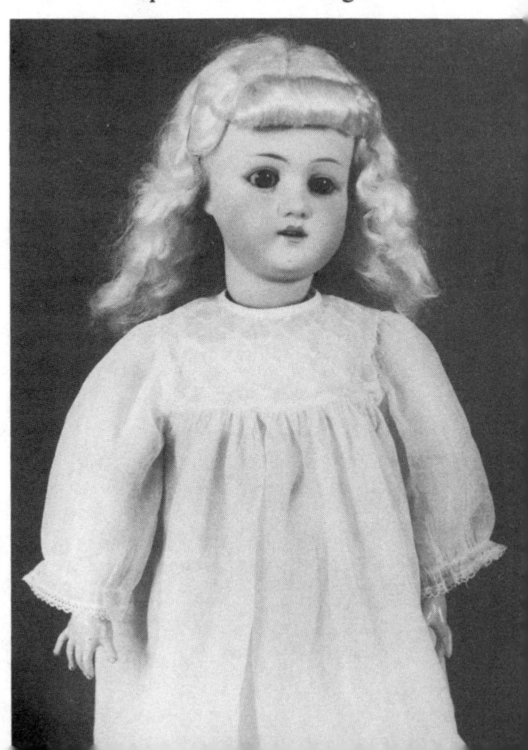

23in (58cm) Heubach Köppelsdorf 250 child. *H&J Foulke, Inc.*

Heubach Köppelsdorf continued

Infant: Ca. 1925. Perfect bisque head, molded and painted hair, sleep eyes, closed mouth; cloth body, composition or celluloid hands, appropriate clothes; all in good condition.

#349, 10—12in (25—31cm) **$400—425****

#338, 12—14in (31—36cm) **650****

#340, 15—16in (38—41cm) **750****

**Not enough price samples to compute a reliable range.

Gypsy: Ca. late 1920s. Tan bisque head, matching toddler body; mohair wig, sleep eyes, open mouth with teeth, brass earrings; appropriate costume; all in good condition.

#452 12in (31cm) **$375—425****

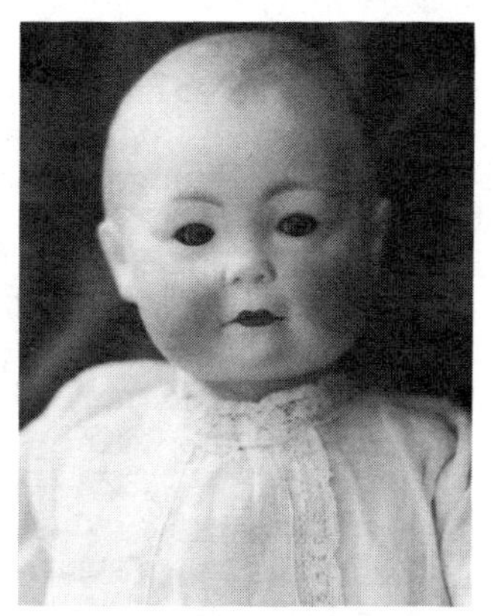

15½in (30cm) long Heubach Köppelsdorf 340 infant. *Mimi Hiscox Collection.*

15in (38cm) Heubach Köppelsdorf 342 character baby. *H&J Foulke, Inc.*

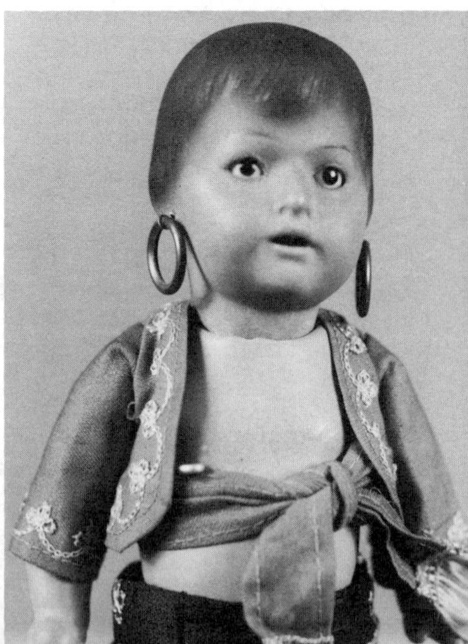

9in (23cm) Heubach Köppelsdorf 452 ***Gypsy***, all original.

Holz-Masse
(Composition)

Maker: Cuno & Otto Dressel, Sonneburg, Thüringia, Germany
Date: 1875—on
Material: Composition head, arms and legs, cloth body
Size: Various
Mark:

Marked Holz-Masse: Composition shoulder head, molded hair or mohair wig, glass or painted eyes, sometimes pierced ears; cloth body with composition arms and legs with molded boots; old clothes; all in good condition.

Molded hair:

18—20in (46—51cm)	**$275—300**
23—25in (58—64cm)	**325—350**

Wigged:

16—18in (41—46cm)	**300—350**

26in (66cm) Holz-Masse lady doll, all original. *Dr. Carole Stoessel Zvonar Collection.*

Horsman

Maker: E. I. Horsman Co., New York, N.Y., U.S.A.
Date: 1901—on

Billiken: 1909. Compositoin head with peak of hair at top of head, slanted slits for eyes, watermelon mouth; velvet or plush body; in good condition only.
MARK: Cloth label on body; "Billiken" on right foot
12in (31cm) **$300—325**

12in (31cm) ***Billiken*** with label. *Betty Harms Collection.*

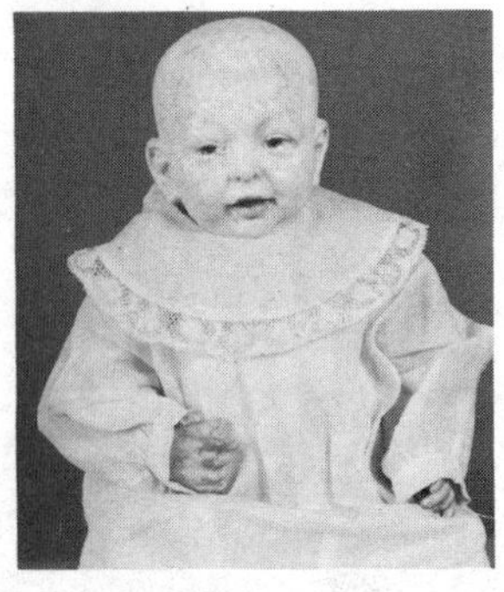

Baby Bumps-type doll, all-composition. *Betty Harms Collection.*

Baby Bumps: 1910. Composition head with molded hair and painted features; stuffed cloth body. Head looks like Kämmer & Reinhardt's "Baby" mold number 100.
MARK: None
10—12in (25—31cm) **$135-165**
Black, 10in (25cm) **165**

Can't Break 'Em Characters: Ca. 1910. Heads and hands of "Can't Break 'Em" composition, hard stuffed cloth bodies with swivel joints at shoulders and hips; molded hair, painted eyes, character faces; appropriate clothes; all in good condition.
MARK: "E.I.H.1911"
12in (31cm) **$110—135**

Early Babies: Ca. 1915. Head of strong composition, hard stuffed cloth body, composition hands; good wig, glass eyes; appropriate clothes, all in good condition.
MARK: "E.I.H. 1915"
12—14in (31—36cm) **$100—125**

Gene Carr Character: 1916. Composition head with molded and painted hair, eyes painted open or closed, wide smiling mouth with teeth; cloth body with composition hands; original or appropriate clothes; all in good condition. Names such as: ***Snowball*** (Black Boy); ***Mike*** and ***Jane*** (eyes open); ***Blink*** and ***Skinney*** (eyes closed). Designed by Bernard Lipfert from Gene Carr's cartoon characters.
MARK: None
13—14in (33—36cm) **$200—250**

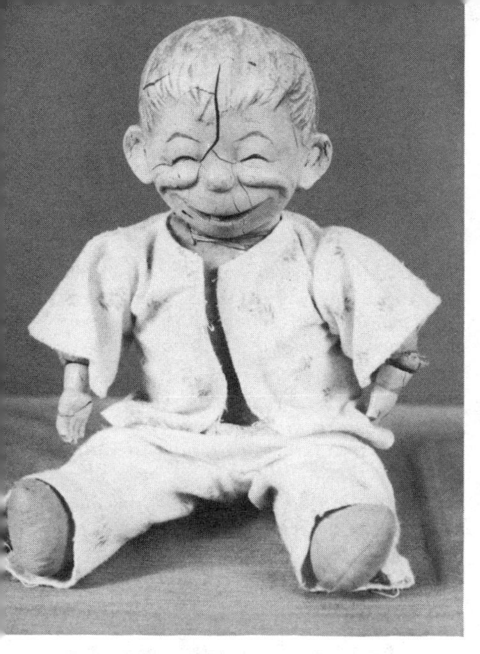

Above Left: 13in (33cm) ***Mike.*** *Betty Harms Collection.*

Above Right: 14½in (37cm) mama doll, all original. *Miriam Blankman Collection.*

Below: 14in (36cm) ***Jackie Coogan.*** *Betty Harms Collection.*

Rosebud: 1920s. Composition swivel head, mohair wig, tin sleep eyes, open mouth with teeth, smiling face with dimples; cloth torso, composition arms and legs; original clothes; all in good condition. Various sizes.

MARK: "ROSEBUD"

18—22in (46—56cm) **$150—200**

Mama Dolls: Ca. 1920—1940. Composition head, cloth body, composition arms and lower legs; mohair wig or molded hair, sleep eyes; original clothes; all in very good condition.

MARK: "E. I. H. Co." or "HORSMAN"

16—18in (41—46cm) **$95—110**
22—24in (56—61cm) **125—135**

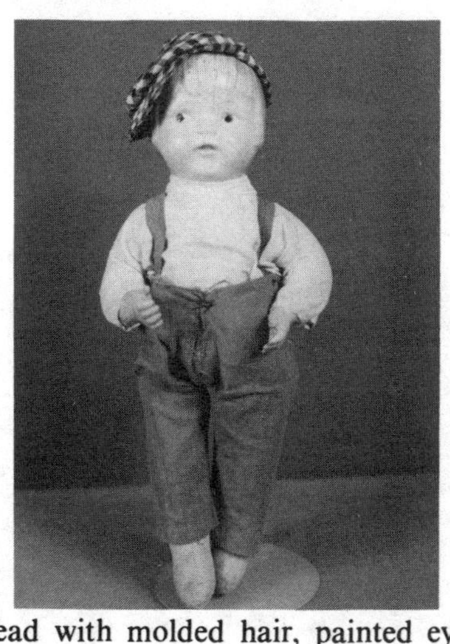

Jackie Coogan: 1921. Composition head with molded hair, painted eyes, closed mouth; cloth torso with composition hands; appropriate clothes; all in good condition.

MARK: "E. I. H. Co. 19 © 21"

14in (36cm) **$400—450****

**Not enough price samples to compute a reliable range

Above Left: 12in (31cm) bisque head ***Tynie Baby***, all original with label. *Jimmy and Faye Rodolfos Collection.*

Above Right: Close-up of the label for 12in (31cm) ***Tynie Baby*** which reads: "HORSMAN//Tynie Baby//TRADE MARK." *Jimmy and Faye Rodolfos Collection.*

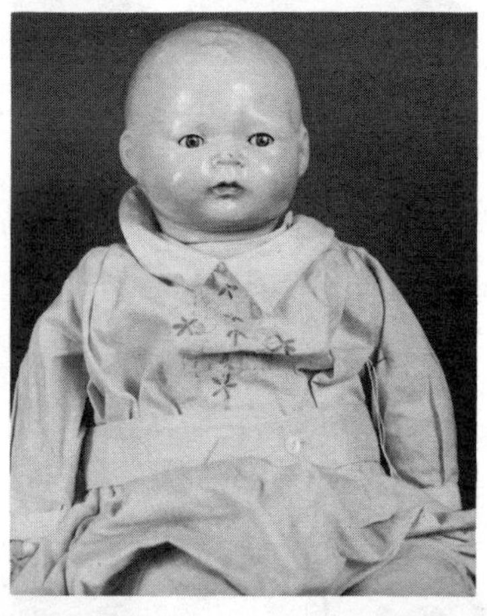

Left: 24in (61cm) composition ***Tynie Baby*** replaced clothes. *Betty Harms Collection.*

Marked Tynie Baby: 1924. Solid dome infant head with sleep eyes, closed mouth, slightly frowning face; cloth body with composition arms; appropriate clothes; all in good condition. Designed by Bernard Lipfert. © 1924

MARK: E.I. Horsman Inc. Made in Germany

Bisque head,

14in (36cm) **$650—750**

Composition head,

13in (33cm) **225**

All-bisque with swivel neck, glass eyes, wigged or solid dome head, 9in (23cm) **1100****

**Not enough price samples to compute a reliable range.

Ella Cinders: 1925. Composition head with molded hair, painted eyes; cloth body with composition arms and lower legs; original clothes; all in fair condition. From the comic strip by Bill Conselman and Charlie Plumb, for the Metropolitan Newspaper Service.

MARK: "1925 © MNS"

18in (46cm) **$500**

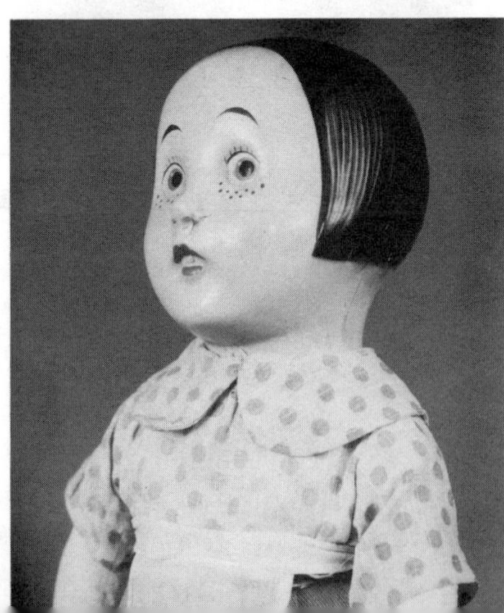

18in (46cm) **Ella Cinders,** all original. *H&J Foulke, Inc.*

Horsman continued

Baby Dimples: 1928. Composition head with molded and painted hair, tin sleep eyes, open mouth, smiling face; soft cloth body with composition arms and legs; original or appropriate old clothes; all in good condition. Various sizes.

MARK: "©
E. I. H. CO. INC."

16—18in (41—46cm) **$150—175**
22—24in (56—61cm) **200—225**

Child Dolls: Ca. 1930s and 1940s. All-composition with swivel neck, shoulders and hips; mohair wig, sleep eyes; original clothes; all in good condition.

MARK: "HORSMAN"

14—15in (36—38cm) **$100—125**
Toddlers, 16in (41cm) **125—150**

Jeanie: Ca. 1937. All-composition with swivel neck, shoulders, and hips; molded and painted hair with peak on top, sleep eyes, closed mouth; appropriate old clothes; all in good condition.

MARK: "JEANIE
HORSMAN"

14in (36cm) **$110—135**

Below Left: 17in (43cm) ***Baby Dimples***, replaced clothes. *Betty Harms Collection.*

Below Right: 17in (43cm) all-composition toddler, all original. *H&J Foulke, Inc.*

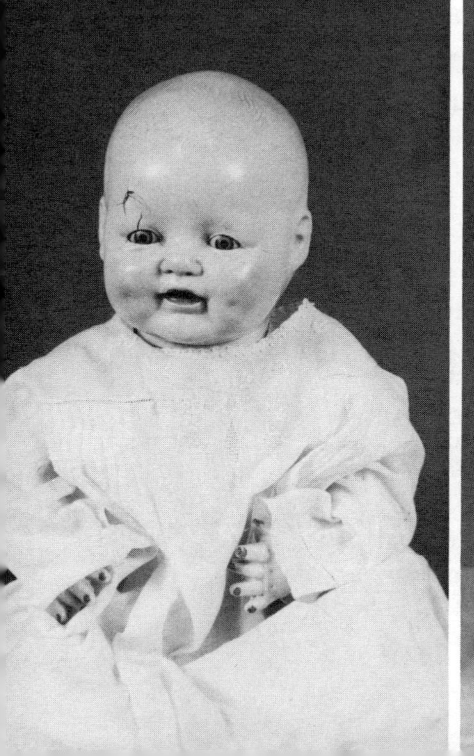

Mary Hoyer

Maker: The Mary Hoyer Doll Mfg. Co., Reading, PA., U.S.A.
Date: Ca. 1925—on
Material: First all-composition, later all-hard plastic
Size: 14 and 18in (36 and 46cm)
Mark: Embossed on torso: "The Mary Hoyer Doll" or in a circle: "ORIGINAL Mary Hoyer Doll"

Marked Mary Hoyer: Material as above; swivel neck; jointed shoulders and hips, original wig, sleep eyes with eyelashes, closed mouth; all in good condition. Original tagged factory clothes or garments made at home from Mary Hoyer patterns.

Composition, 14in (36cm)	**$225—250**
Hard plastic, 14in (36cm)	**225—250**

14in (36cm) Mary Hoyer, all original.
Virginia Ann Heyerdahl Collection.

14in (36cm) Mary Hoyer, all original.
Virginia Ann Heyerdahl Collection.

A. Hülss

Maker: Adolf Hülss of Waltershausen, Thüringia, Germany; heads by Simon & Halbig

Date: 1915—1925

Material: Bisque socket heads, composition bodies (later heads of painted bisque)

Size: Various

Mark:

SIMON & HALBIG

Marked Hülss Character Baby: 1909—on. Mold number 156. Perfect bisque head with good wig, sleep eyes, open mouth with teeth and tongue, smiling face; composition bent-limb body; nicely dressed; all in good condition.

16—18in (41—46cm) **$500—600***

Jointed composition toddler body,

15—16in (38—41cm) **650—700***

22in (56cm) **850—900***

*Allow extra for flirty eyes.

21in (53cm) Hülss character toddler with flirty eyes. *H&J Foulke, Inc.*

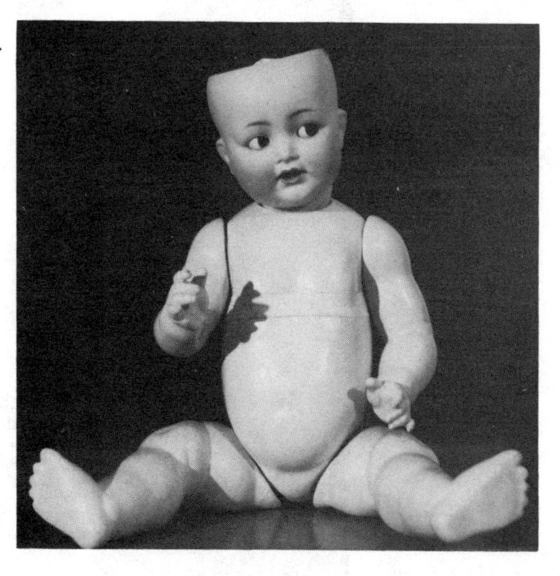

Huret

Maker: Maison Huret, Paris, France
Date: 1850—on
Material: China or bisque heads; kid or wood jointed bodies, sometimes with pewter hands and feet
Size: Various
Mark: "Huret" or "Maison Huret" stamped on body

Marked Huret Doll: China or bisque shoulder head, good wig, painted or glass eyes, closed mouth; kid or wood jointed body; beautifully dressed; all in good condition.
16—20in (41—51cm) **$4000—4500 up**

17in (43cm) Huret-type china shoulder head with glass eyes.

Ideal

Maker: Ideal Novelty and Toy Co., Brooklyn, N.Y., U.S.A.
Date: 1907—on
Mark: Various, usually including "IDEAL"

Uneeda Kid: 1914—1919. Composition head with molded brown hair, blue painted eyes, closed mouth; cloth body with composition arms and legs with molded black boots; original bloomer suit, yellow slicker and rain hat; carrying a box of Uneeda Biscuits; all in good condition, showing some wear.

16in (41cm)	**$200—225**
Molded hat	**250**

Shirley Temple: 1935. For detailed information see pages 335, 336 and 337.

Betsy Wetsy: 1937—on. Composition head with molded hair, sleep eyes; soft rubber body jointed at neck, shoulders and hips; drinks, wets; appropriate clothes; all in good condition. This doll went through many changes including hard plastic head on rubber body, later vinyl body, later completely vinyl. Various sizes.
MARK: "IDEAL"

12—14in (31—36cm)
rubber body **$85—95**

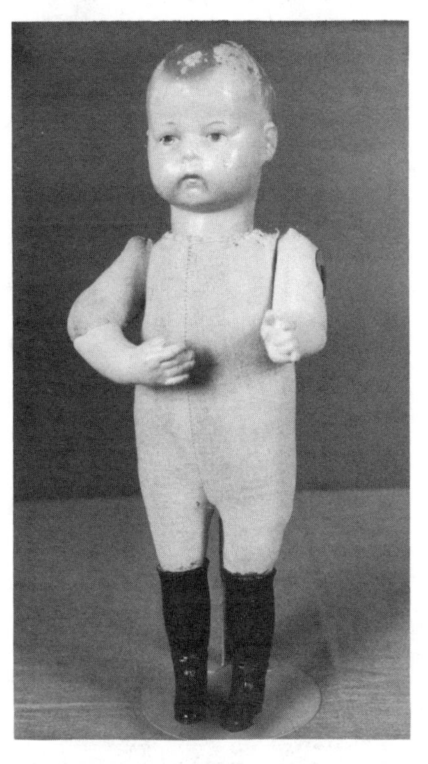

16in (41cm) ***Uneeda Kid.*** *Joanna Ott Collection.*

Baby Snooks (Fanny Brice): 1938. Head, torso, hands and feet of composition, arms and legs made of flexible metal cable; molded hair, smiling mouth; original clothes; all in good condition.
MARK: On head: "IDEAL"
Round paper tag:
"FLEXY — an Ideal Doll
Fanny Brice's Baby Snooks"

12in (31cm) **$225—250**

Mortimer Snerd: 1938—1939. Head, hands and feet of composition, arms and legs of flexible metal cable, torso of wire mesh; in original clothes; all in good condition.
MARK: Head embossed:
"Ideal Doll"

13in (33cm) **$225—250**

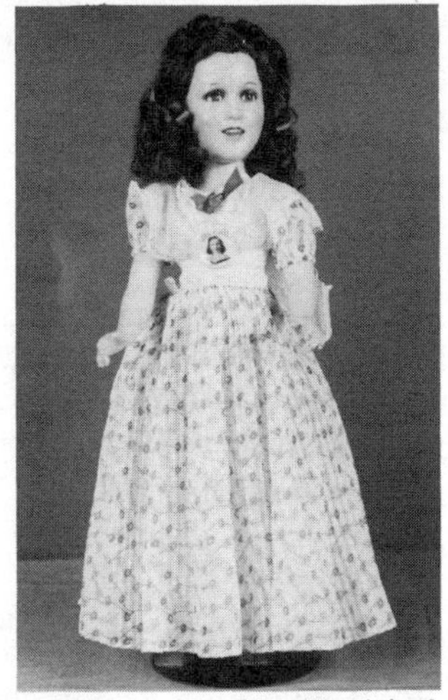

21in(53cm) ***Deanna Durbin,*** all original.
H&J Foulke, Inc.

9in (23cm) ***Jiminy Cricket,*** all original.

Deanna Durbin: 1938. All-composition, jointed at neck, shoulders and hips; original human hair or mohair wig, sleep eyes, smiling mouth with teeth; original clothing; all in good condition. Various sizes.

MARK: Metal button with picture: "DEANNA DURBIN, IDEAL DOLL, U.S.A."

14in (36cm) **$300—350**
20—21in (51—53cm) **500**

Snow White: 1939. All-composition, jointed at neck, shoulders, and hips; black mohair wig, lashed sleep eyes, open mouth; original dress with velvet bodice and cape, and rayon skirt with figures of seven dwarfs; in good condition. 11in (28cm), 13in (33cm) and 18in (46cm) sizes.

MARK: On body:
"SHIRLEY TEMPLE/18"
On dress:
"An Ideal Doll"

11—13in (28—33cm) **$400 up****
18in (46cm) **350 up****

Judy Garland as Dorothy of the Wizard of Oz: 1939. All-composition, jointed at neck, shoulders and hips; dark human hair wig, dark sleep eyes, open mouth with teeth; original dress; all in good condition.

MARK: On head and body: "IDEAL DOLL"

16in (41cm) **$900—1000****

Composition and wood segmented characters: 1940. Molded composition heads with painted features, wood segmented bodies. Label on front torso gives name of character.

Pinocchio, 10½in (27cm) **$200—225**
King-Little, 14in (36cm) n) **175—200**
Jiminy Cricket, 9in (23cm) **175—200**

**Not enough price samples to compute a reliable range.

Magic Skin Baby: 1940. Composition head with molded hair (later babies had hard plastic heads), sleep eyes, closed mouth; stuffed latex rubber body, jointed shoulders and hips; appropriate clothes; all in good condition. Various sizes.

MARK: On head: "IDEAL"

15in (38cm) **$65—75**

Flexy Dolls: Ca. 1942. Head, hands and feet of composition, arms and legs of flexible metal cable, torso of wire mesh; in original clothes; all in good condition.

MARK: On head: "Ideal Doll"

12in (31cm) **$150—175**

The original box for the 14in (36cm) ***Magic Skin Baby.*** *H&J Foulke, Inc.*

14in (36cm) ***Magic Skin Baby,*** all original, boxed. *H&J Foulke, Inc.*

14in (36cm) ***Toni,*** all original. *H&J Foulke, Inc.*

Toni and P-90 and P-91 Family: 1948—on. Series of girl dolls. Most were completely of hard plastic with jointed neck, shoulders and hips, nylon wig, sleep eyes, closed mouth; original clothes; all in excellent condition. Various sizes, but most are 14in (36cm).

MARK: On head: "IDEAL DOLL" On body: "IDEAL DOLL
P-90
Made in USA"

Toni, 14—15in (36—38cm)	**$100—110**
21in (53cm)	**150**
Mary Hartline, 14in (36cm)	**110—125**
Betsy McCall, vinyl head, 14in (36cm)	**125—135**
Harriet Hubbard Ayer, vinyl head, 14in (36cm)	**110—125**
Miss Curity, 14in (36cm)	**110—125**
Sara Ann, 14in (36cm)	**110—125**

Ideal continued

Saucy Walker: 1951. All-hard plastic, jointed at neck, shoulders and hips with walking mechanism; synthetic wig, flirty eyes, open mouth with tongue and teeth; original clothes; all in good condition. Various sizes, usually 19—23in (49—58cm).

MARK: "IDEAL DOLL"

19—22in (48—56cm) **$85—110**

Miss Revlon: 1955. Vinyl head with rooted hair, sleep eyes, closed mouth, earrings; hard plastic body with jointed waist and knees, high-heeled feet, vinyl arms with polished nails; original clothes; all in good condition.

MARK: On head and body:

"IDEAL DOLL"

Miss Revlon, 17—19in (43—48cm) **$75—100**

Little Miss Revlon, 10½in (27cm) **50—60**

Peter and Patty Playpal: 1960. Vinyl heads with rooted hair, sleep eyes; hard vinyl body, jointed at shoulders and hips; appropriate clothes; all in excellent condition.

MARK: Peter:

"IDEAL TOY CORP.
BE—35—38"

Patty:

"IDEAL DOLL
G-35"

35—36in (89—91cm) **$175—225**

14in (36cm) ***Sara Ann,*** all original. *H&J Foulke, Inc.*

14in (36cm) ***Betsy McCall,*** all original. *H&J Foulke, Inc.*

Ideal continued

10½in (27cm) ***Little Miss Revlon***, all original. *H&J Foulke, Inc.*

Italian Bisque

Maker: Ceramica Furga of Canneto sull'Oglio, Mantua, Italy; and possibly others
Date: Ca. 1910—on for those shown here
Material: Bisque head, composition body sometimes with cardboard torso
Size: Various
Mark: "Furga Canneto & Oglio" —— Italy —— or I/6

Marked Italian Bisque Doll: Perfect bisque dolly-face head with suitable wig, painted eyebrows and eyelashes, glass eyes, closed or open mouth with teeth; composition body (some quite crude); dressed; all in good condition.
Closed mouth, 7—8in (18—20cm) **$175—225****
Open mouth, 14—16in (36—41cm) **275—325****

**Not enough price samples to compute a reliable range.

7in (18cm) girl incised "Italy," five-piece composition body. *H&J Foulke, Inc.*

Italian Hard Plastic

Maker: Bonomi, Ottolini, Ratti, Furga, and other Italian firms
Date: Later 1940s and 1950s
Material: Heavy hard plastic, sometimes painted, or plastic coated papier-mâché
Size: Various
Mark: Usually a wrist tag; company name on head

Italian Hard Plastic: Heavy, fine quality material jointed at shoulders and hips; human hair wig, sleep eyes, sometimes flirty, often a character face; original clothes; all in excellent condition.

15—17in (38—43cm) **$80—95**
19—22in (48—56cm) **100—125**

17in (18cm) girl by Ratti. *H&J Foulke, Inc.*

Japanese Bisque Caucasian Dolls

Maker: Various Japanese firms; heads were imported by New York importers, such as Morimura Brothers, Yamato Importing Co., and others.
Date: 1915—on
Material: Bisque head, composition body
Size: Various
Mark: Morimura Brothers
Various other marks with Japan or Nippon, such as J. W., F. Y., and others

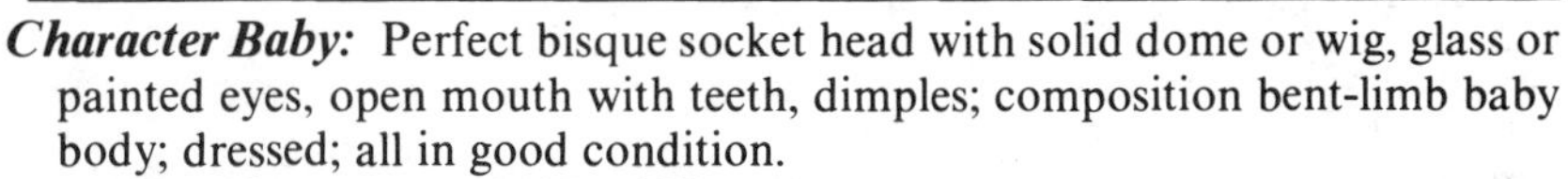

Character Baby: Perfect bisque socket head with solid dome or wig, glass or painted eyes, open mouth with teeth, dimples; composition bent-limb baby body; dressed; all in good condition.

Size	Price
9in (23cm)	**$125—135**
12—15in (31—38cm)	**175—225**
20—22in (51—56cm)	**375—400**

Child Doll: Perfect bisque head, mohair wig, glass sleep eyes, open mouth; jointed composition or kid body; dressed; all in good condition.

Size	Price
16—19in (41—48cm)	**$225—275**
24—25in (61—64cm)	**325—375**

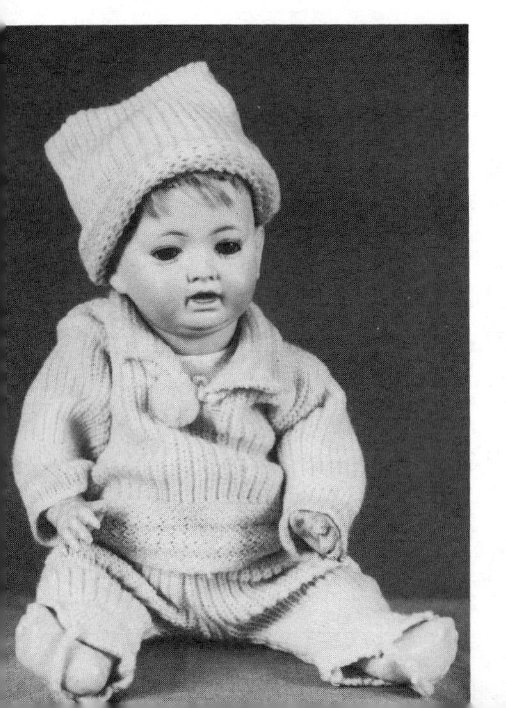

14in (36cm) character baby by Morimura Brothers. *H&J Foulke, Inc.*

Eduardo Juan

Maker: Eduardo Juan, Austria
Date: Ca. 1900—on
Material: Bisque head, jointed composition body
Mark:

"1904
Eduardo Juan
Made in Austria"

Eduardo Juan Doll: Perfect bisque head, good wig, sleep eyes, open mouth with teeth, chin dimple; jointed composition body; appropriate clothes; all in good condition.

26in (66cm) **$500—600****

**Not enough price samples to compute a reliable range.

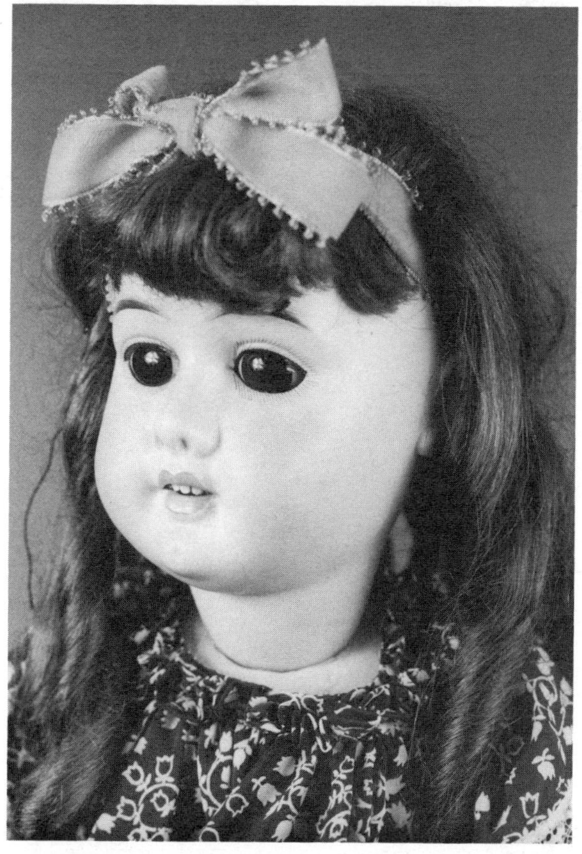

26in (66cm) Eduardo Juan doll. *Dr. Carole Stoessel Zvonar Collection.*

Jullien

Maker: Jullien, Jeune of Paris, France
Date: 1875—1904 when joined with S.F.B.J.
Material: Bisque head, composition and wood body
Size: Various
Mark: "JULLIEN" with size number

JULLIEN
1

Marked Jullien Bébé: Bisque head, lovely wig, paperweight eyes, closed mouth, pierced ears; jointed wood and composition body, pretty old clothes; all in good condition.

18—20in (46—51cm)	**$3000—3200**
24—26in (61—66cm)	**3600—3800**
Open mouth, 22—24in (56—61cm)	**2000—2400**

24in (61cm) Jullien, walking body. *H&J Foulke, Inc.*

Jumeau

Maker: Maison Jumeau, Paris, France
Date: 1842—on
Material: Bisque head, kid or composition body
Size: Various
Mark: Only body stamped in blue after (1878):
Various head marks (see individual dolls listed below).

JUMEAU
MEDAILLE D'OR
PARIS

Fashion Lady: Late 1860s—on. Usually marked with number only on head, blue stamp on body. Perfect bisque swivel head on shoulder plate, good wig, paperweight eyes, closed mouth, pierced ears; all-kid body or kid with bisque lower arms and legs; appropriate clothes; all in good condition.

12—13in (31—33cm) **$1600—1800**
16—18in (41—46cm) **2500—2800**
22—24in (56—61cm) **3300—3800**

20in (51cm) Jumeau fashion lady, kid body. *Betty Harms Collection.*

Long-Face Triste Bébé: Ca. 1870s. Usually marked with number only on head, blue stamp on body. Perfect bisque socket head with beautiful wig, blown glass eyes, closed mouth, applied pierced ears; jointed composition body with straight wrists; lovely clothes; all in good condition.

20in (51cm) **$10,000**
26—29in (66—74cm) **12,000 up**

Early Almond-eyed Bébé (so-called Portrait Jumeau): Ca. 1870s. Usually marked with size number only on head with skin or other good wig; unusually large paperweight eyes, closed mouth, pierced ears; jointed composition body with straight wrists; nicely dressed; all in good condition.

12—14in (31—36cm) **$4000—4500**
17—19in (43—48cm) **5000—5500**

20in (51cm) long-face (***Triste***) Jumeau. *Betty Harms Collection.*

Jumeau continued

16in (41cm) early almond-eyed Jumeau (so-called Portrait Jumeau). *Richard Wright Antiques.*

17in (43cm) Tête Jumeau child. *Pearl D. Morley Collection.*

15in (38cm) E. J. bébé.

E. J. Bébé: Ca. 1880. Head incised as below, blue stamp on body. Perfect bisque socket head with good wig, paperweight eyes, closed mouth, pierced ears; jointed composition body with straight wrists; lovely clothes; all in good condition.

MARK: On head: DÉPOSÉ E. 7 J.

14—17in (36—43cm) **$4800—5300***

19—22in (48—56cm) **5600—6300***

26—27in (66—69cm) **7500—8500***

*Early face. EJA slightly higher. Tête-style face slightly lower.

Jumeau continued

Incised Jumeau Déposé Bébé: Ca. 1880. Head incised as below, blue stamp on body. Perfect bisque socket head with good wig, paperweight eyes, closed mouth, pierced ears; jointed composition body with straight wrists; lovely clothes; all in good condition.

MARK: Incised on head:

"JUMEAU
DEPOSE"

19—22in (48—56cm) **$4000—4500**

Tête Jumeau Bébé: 1879—1899, then through S.F.B.J. Red stamp on head as indicated below, blue stamp or "Bébé Jumeau" oval sticker on body. Perfect bisque head, original or good French wig, beautiful stationary eyes, closed mouth, pierced ears; jointed composition body with jointed or straight wrists; original or lovely clothes; all in good condition.

MARK:

DÉPOSÉ
TETE JUMEAU
B^TE SGDG
6

12—13in (31—33cm)	**$2000—2100***
14—16in (36—41cm)	**2200—2500***
18—20in (46—51cm)	**2600—3000***
21—23in (53—58cm	**3100—3300***
25—27in (64—69cm)	**3500—4000***
31—33in (79—84cm)	**5000—6000***

Composition lady body, 20in (51cm) **5000**

Open mouth:

14—16in (36—41cm)	**1400—1600**
20—22in (51—56cm)	**2000—2200**
24—25in (61—64cm)	**2400—2500**
32—34in(81—86cm)	**3200—3400**

*Allow more for an especially fine example.

28in (72cm) Tête Jumeau child with open mouth. *Betty Harms Collection.*

Jumeau continued

Two-Faced Jumeau: Perfect bisque head with two different faces, one smiling and one crying, covered by a lacy hood with a knob at the very top to rotate the faces; paperweight eyes, open/closed mouths; jointed composition body; appropriately dressed; all in good condition.
$8000**

Jumeau Composition Head: Ca. 1895. Papier-mâché socket head, good wig, paperweight eyes, open mouth; jointed composition and wood body; nicely dressed; all in good condition.
24in (61cm) **$900—950****

1907 Jumeau Child: Ca. 1900. Sometimes red-stamped "Tete Jumeau". Perfect bisque head, good quality wig, set or sleep eyes, open mouth, pierced ears; jointed composition body; nicely dressed; all in good condition.

18—20in (46—51cm)	**$1600—1800**
23—24in (58—61cm)	**2000—2200**
31in (79cm)	**2800—3000**

Jumeau Great Ladies: Ca. 1930s. Perfect bisque socket head with adult features, fancy mohair wig, fixed eyes, closed mouth; five-piece composition body with painted black slippers, metal stand attached to foot; a series of ladies dressed in fancy costumes; all original; in excellent condition.
MARK: "221" on head
10—11in (25—28cm) **$475—550**

Princess Elizabeth Jumeau: 1938 through S.F.B.J. Perfect bisque socket head highly colored, good wig, glass flirty eyes, closed mouth; jointed composition body; dressed; all in good condition.
MARK:

UNIS FRANCE
71 149
306
JUMEAU
1938
PARIS

19in (48cm) **$1000—1200**

**Not enough price samples to compute a reliable range.

24in (61cm) Jumeau with composition head. *Betty Harms Collection.*

Jumeau continued

23in (58cm) 1907 Jumeau, all original.
Betty Harms Collection.

K & K

Maker: K & K Toy Co., New York, N.Y., U.S.A.
Date: 1915—1925
Material: Bisque head, cloth and composition body
Size: Various
Mark: Used mold numbers 45, 56 and 60

Germany
K & K
60
Thuringia

K & K Character Child: Perfect bisque shoulder head, mohair wig, sleep eyes, open mouth with teeth; cloth body with composition arms and legs; appropriate clothes; all in good condition.

18—20in (46—51cm) **$350—400**
Composition head, 18—20in (46—51cm) **100—125****
**Not enough price samples to compute a reliable range.

Mama doll with composition shoulder head by K & K Toy Co., replaced dress. *Betty Harms Collection.*

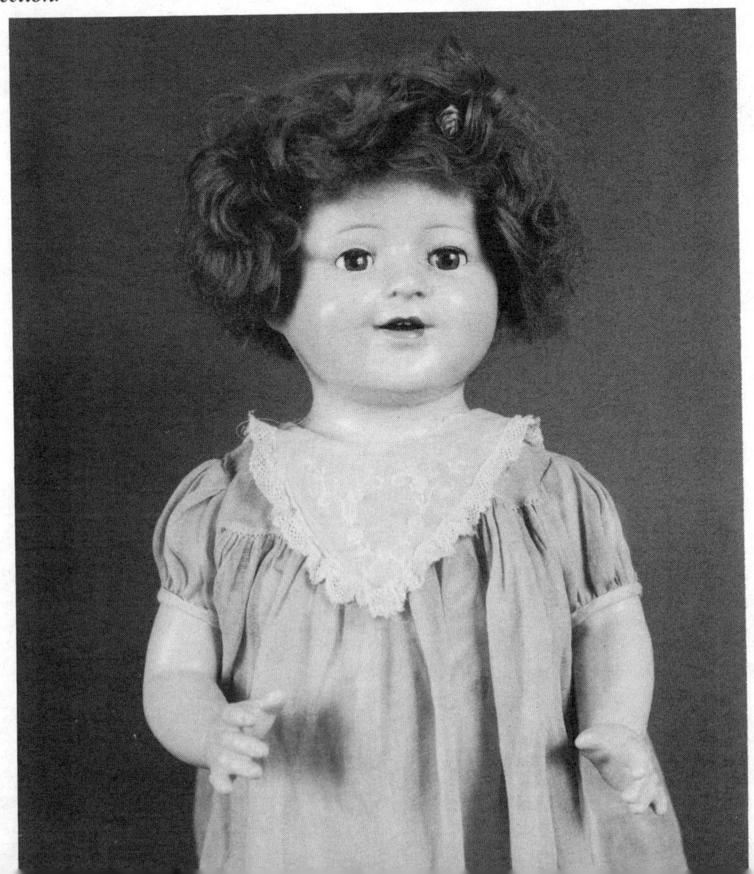

Kamkins

Maker: Louise R. Kampes Studios, Atlantic City, N.J., U.S.A.
Date: Ca. 1920
Material: Molded mask face, cloth stuffed torso and limbs
Size: About 16—19in (41—48cm)
Mark: Red paper heart on left side of chest:
Also sometimes stamped with black on foot or back of head:

KAMKINS
A DOLLY MADE TO LOVE
PATENTED BY L.R. KAMPES
ATLANTIC CITY, N.J.

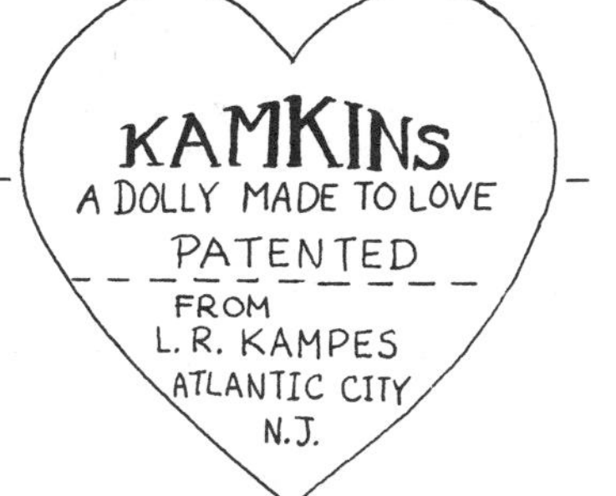

Marked Kamkins: Molded mask face with painted features, wig; cloth body and limbs; dressed; all in good condition.
19—20in (48—51cm) **$800—900**

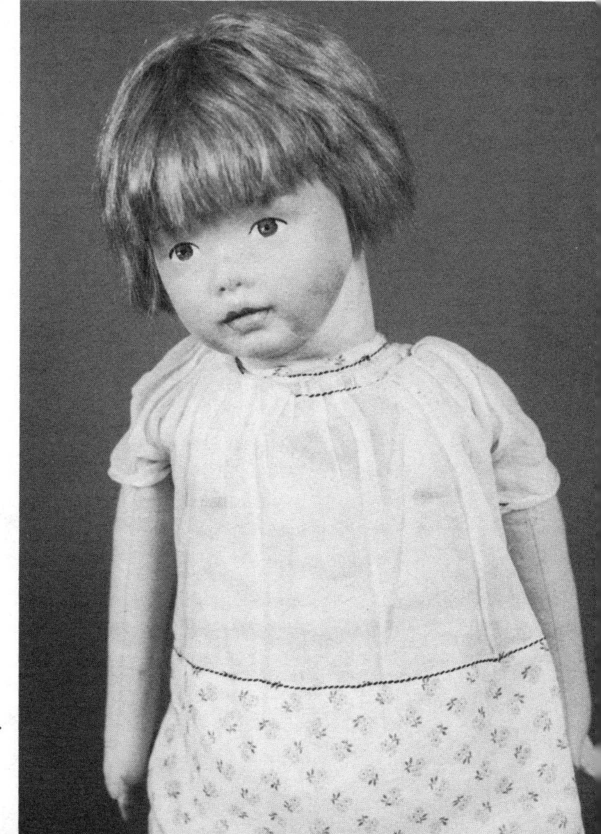

19in (48cm) ***Kamkins***, all original.
Betty Harms Collection.

Kämmer & Reinhardt

Maker: Kämmer & Reinhardt of Waltershausen, Thüringia, Germany
Heads often by Simon & Halbig

Date: 1886—on

Material: Bisque socket head, composition body, later papier-mâché, rubber or celluloid heads, composition bodies

Size: 5½ to 42in (14 to 107cm)

Mark: In 1895 began using "K(star)R," sometimes with "S & H," often "Germany." Mold number for bisque socket head begins with a 1; for papier-mâché, 9; for celluloid, 7.
Size number is height in centimeters.

K & R
SIMON & HALBIG
116/A
50

Child Doll: 1895—1930s. Often mold number 403. Perfect bisque head, original or good wig, sleep eyes, open mouth, pierced ears; dressed; ball-jointed composition body; all in good condition.

14—16in (36—41cm)	**$ 400—450**
19—21in (48—53cm)	**550—600**
23—25in (58—64cm)	**650—750**
28—29in (71—74cm)	**850—950**
32—33in (81—84cm)	**1300—1500**
35—36in (89—91cm)	**1700—1800**
39—42in (99—107cm)	**2500 up**
Walker, 25in (64cm)	**750**

K ★ R 191 child. *H&J Foulke, Inc.*

11in (28cm) K ★ R child, jointed composition body. *H&J Foulke, Inc.*

Kämmer & Reinhardt continued

Tiny Child Doll: Perfect bisque head, mohair wig, sleep eyes, open mouth; five-piece composition body with molded and painted shoes and socks.

6—7in (15—18cm)	**$250—275**
8—9in (20—23cm)	**275—325**
Walker, 6—7in (15—18cm)	**350—375**

34in (86cm) K ★ R child. *Dr. Carole Stoessel Zvonar Collection.*

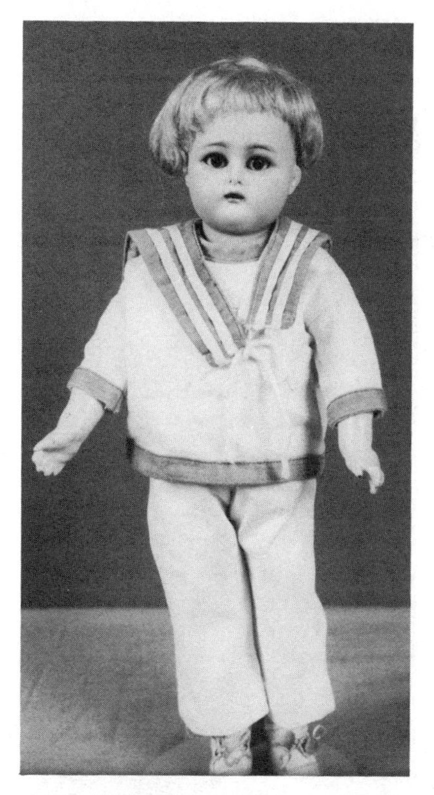

13½in (34cm) K ★ R child, all original. *Emma Wedmore Collection.*

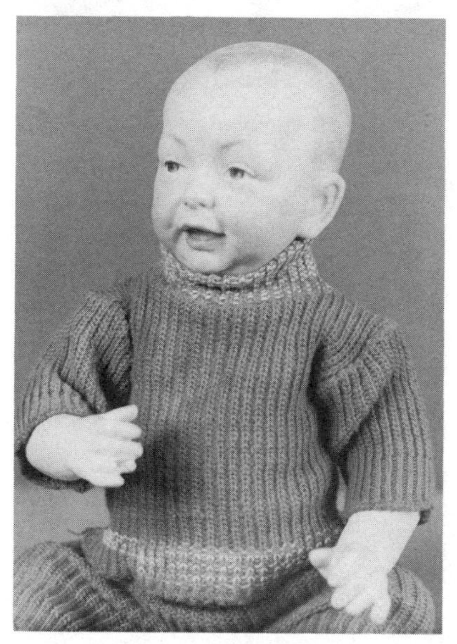

14in (36cm) K ★ R ***Baby***, brown painted eyes. *Richard Wright Antiques.*

Kämmer & Reinhardt continued

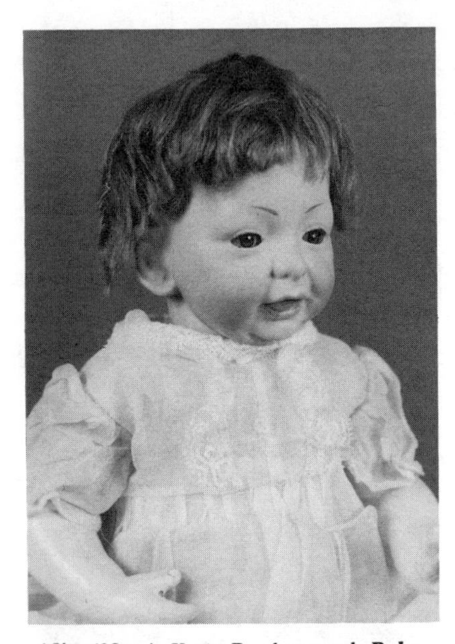

15in (38cm) K ★ R glass-eyed **Baby**. *Richard Wright Antiques.*

Baby #100 (so-called Kaiser Baby): 1909. Perfect bisque solid-dome head, original composition bent-limb body; intaglio eyes, open/closed mouth; dressed; all in good condition.

14in (36cm)	**$ 575—600**
16—18in (41—46cm)	**650—750**
20in (51cm)	**900**
Glass eyes (unmarked):	
15in (38cm)	**1700**
12in (31cm)	**1400**

7in (18cm) K★R 101 character girl, all original. *Lorna Lieberman Collection.*

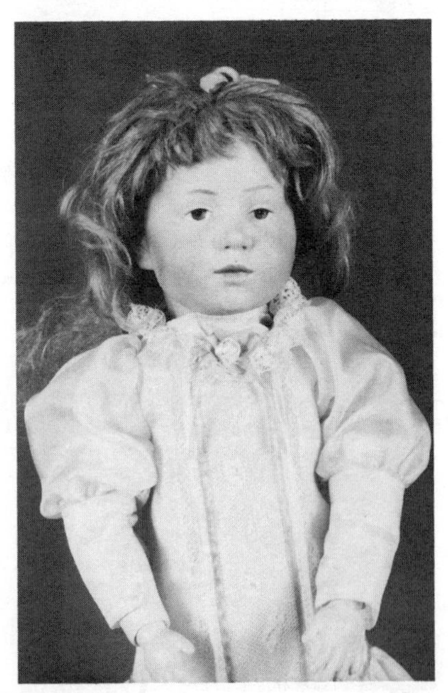

17½in (46cm) K★R 101 character child. *Carol Green Collection.*

Kämmer & Reinhardt continued

Character Children: 1910—on. Perfect bisque socket head, good wig, painted or glass eyes, closed mouth; composition ball-jointed body; nicely dressed; all in good condition.

#101:

7in (18cm) five-piece body	**$ 950**
7—8in (18—20cm) JCB	**1100**
13—15in (33—38cm)	**1750—2150**
17—18in (43—46cm)	**2300—2500**
Glass eyes, 16in (41cm)	**4000****

#102:

12in (31cm)	**8500****

#103, 104:

18—20in (46—51cm)	**15,000****

#107:

15in (38cm)	**6000****

#114:

7in (18cm) five-piece body	**1100**
7—8in (18—20cm)	**1200—1300**
13—15in (33—38cm)	**2200—2700**
19in (48cm)	**3800—4000**
Glass eyes, 25in (64cm)	**6700**

#109:

17—19in (43—48cm)	**6000—7000****
Glass eyes, 22in (56cm)	**15,000****

#112, 112x:

14in (36cm)	**5000—6000****
Glass eyes, 16in (41cm)	**8000****

#115, 115A:

Baby, 13in (33cm)	**2000**
23in (58cm)	**4200**
Toddler, 15—18in (38—46cm)	**3500—3800**

**Not enough price samples to compute a reliable range.

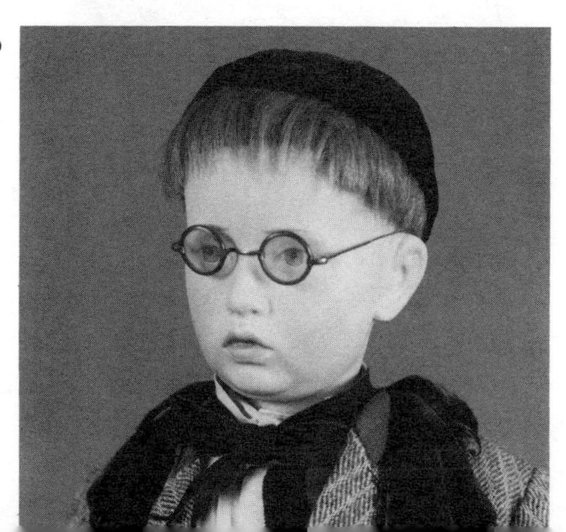

22in (56cm) K★R 107 character boy. *Richard Wright Antiques.*

Kämmer & Reinhardt continued

#116, 116A, open/closed mouth:	
Baby, 16—19in (41—48cm)	**2000—2100**
Toddler, 18in (46cm)	**2400**
23in (58cm)	**3000**
#116A, open mouth:	
Baby, 18in (46cm)	**1600**
Toddler, 13in (33cm)	**1650**
#117, 117A:	
8½in (22cm) five-piece body	**1400**
15—17in (38—43cm)	**3500**
20—21in (51—53cm)	**4200**
27—28in (69—71cm)	**5500—6500**
#117, open mouth:	
26in (66cm)	**3000—3500**
34in (86cm)	**4500**
#117x, open mouth:	
15in (38cm)	**1500—1600**
#117n, flirty eyes:	
18in (46cm)	**1100—1300**
25in (64cm)	**1600—1700**
31—34in (79—86cm)	**2200—2400**
#123, 124	**8000—10,000****
#127:	
Baby, 12in (31cm)	**700—750**
18—21in (46—53cm)	**900—1100**
Child or Toddler, 13in (33cm)	**900—1000**

**Not enough price samples to compute a reliable range.

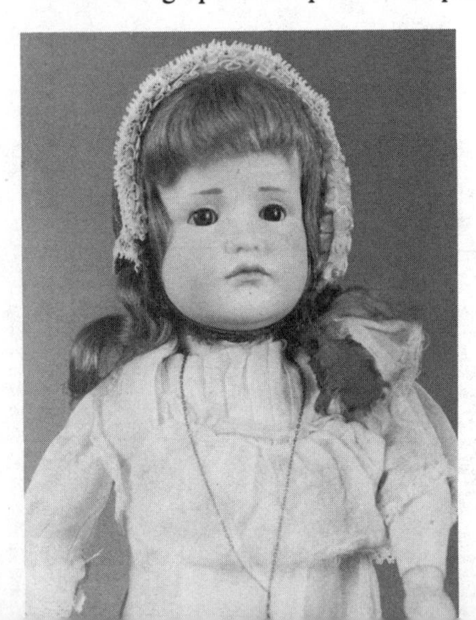

OPPOSITE PAGE: CLOCKWISE:
9in (23cm) K★R 109 character child, all original. *Zelda H. Cushner Collection.*

19in (48cm) K★R 114 character girl with painted eyes. *Carol Green Collection.*

15in (38cm) K★R 115/A character toddler. *Carol Green Collection.*

16½in (42cm) K★R 116/A character toddler. *Carol Green Collection.*

17in (43cm) K★R 114 character child with glass eyes. *Richard Wright Antiques.*

Kämmer & Reinhardt continued

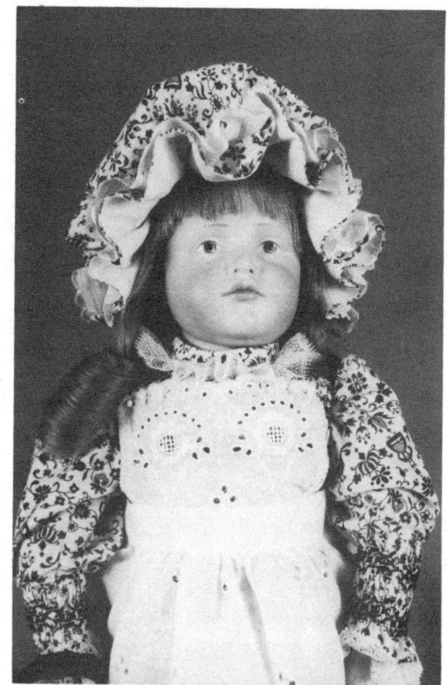

Kämmer & Reinhardt continued

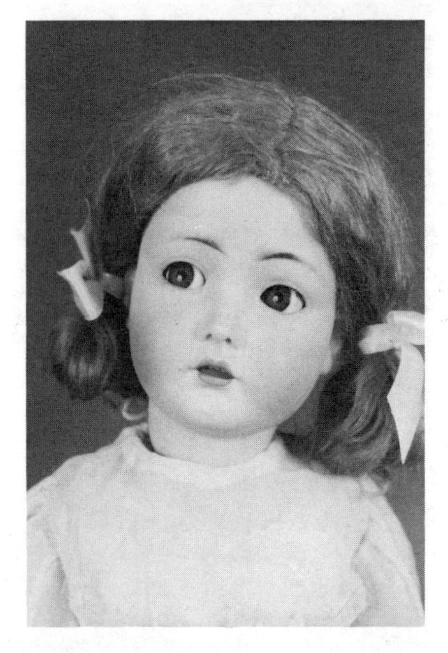

26in (66cm) K★R 117n character child with flirty eyes. *Anna May Case Collection.*

23in (58cm) K★R 117 character child. *Dr. Carole Stoessel Zvonar Collection.*

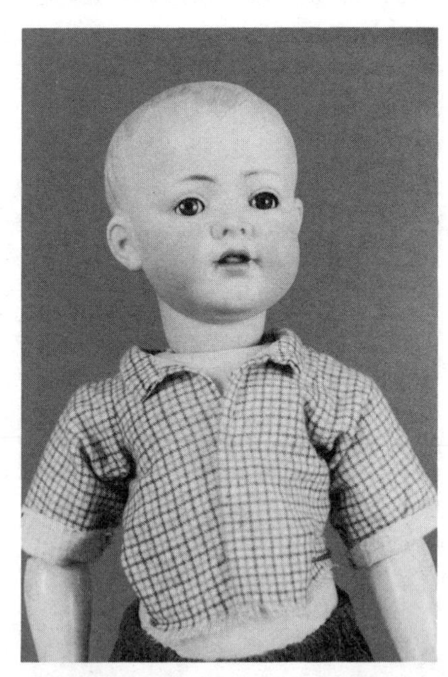

19in (48cm) K★R 127 toddler. *Richard Wright Antiques.*

Kämmer & Reinhardt continued

Character Babies or Toddlers: 1909—on. Usually mold number 126, less often mold numbers 121, 122 and 128. Perfect bisque head, original or good wig, sleep eyes, open mouth; composition bent-limb or jointed toddler body; nicely dressed; may have voice box or spring tongue; all in good condition.

#126, #22, #26 Baby:

10—12in (25—31cm)	**$ 375—425**
15—17in (38—43cm)	**500—550***
20—22in (51—56cm)	**650—750***
24—25in (61—64cm)	**800—850***
30—33in (76—84cm)	**1800—2000**

#126 Toddler:

6—7in (15—18cm)	**350**
12—15in (31—38cm)	**575—650***
20—21in (51—53cm)	**850—900***
35in (89cm)	**3500**

#126 Child:

39in (99cm)	**3000**

#121, 122, 128 Baby:

11—12in (28—31cm)	**375—475**
16—18in (41—46cm)	**750—850**
23—24in (58—61cm)	**1000—1200**

#121, 122 Toddler:

16in (41cm)	**850**
27in (69cm)	**1650**

#118A Baby:

18in (46cm)	**1250****

#135 Baby:

18in (46cm)	**1250****

*Allow $50 extra for flirty eyes.
**Not enough price samples to compute a reliable range.

11in (28cm) K★R 126 character baby, all original.
H&J Foulke, Inc.

Kämmer & Reinhardt continued

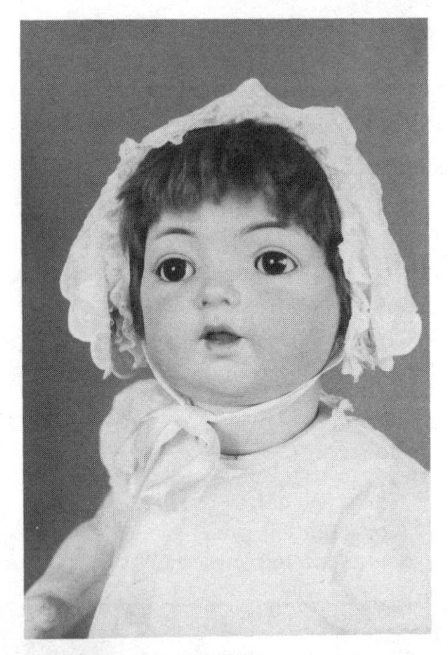

25in (64cm) K★R 121 character baby, all original. *Anna May Case Collection.*

16½in (42cm) K★R 123 ***Max*** comic character googly. *Ralph's Antique Doll Museum.*

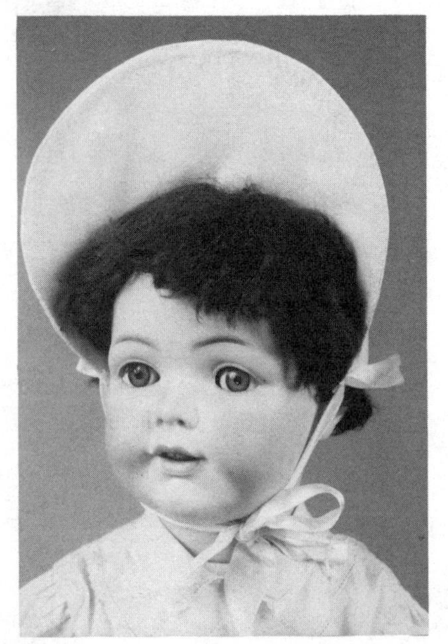

26in (66cm) K★R 22 character baby with tremble tongue. *Dr. Carole Stoessel Zvonar Collection.*

Infant: 1924—on. Perfect bisque head, molded and painted hair, glass eyes, open mouth; pink cloth body, composition hands; nicely dressed; all in good condition.

14in (36cm) **$1000****

**Not enough price samples to compute a reliable range.

Kestner

Maker: J. D. Kestner, Jr., Waltershausen, Thüringia, Germany
Date: 1805—on
Material: Bisque heads, kid or composition bodies, bodies on tiny dolls are jointed at the knee, but not the elbow
Size: Various
Mark: Socket Head — Numbers such as "171," "146," "164," "192" (pierced ears), "195" (see Mark A)
Shoulder Head — Numbers such as "154," "159" (see Mark A)
Both — "A5," "B6," "C7" and "Made in Germany"
Composition Body — See Mark B
Kid Body — Sometimes Mark C

Mark A:
made in
D Germany. 8.
162.

Mark B:
Excelsior
DRP. No. 70686
Germany

Mark C:
J.D.K.
Germany

Child doll, closed mouth, marked with size number only: Ca. 1880. Perfect bisque head, plaster dome, good wig, paperweight or sleep eyes, closed mouth; composition ball-jointed body with straight wrists; well dressed; all in good condition.

169, 128X:

15—17in (38—43cm)	**$1600—1900**
24—25in (61—64cm)	**2300—2400**
28—29in (71—74cm)	**2600—2850**

XI and pouty:

16—17in (41—43cm)	**1950—2150**
20—22in (51—56cm)	**2300—2400**
25—27in (64—69cm)	**3000**

16in (41cm) closed-mouth child, ball-jointed body. *Betty Harms Collection.*

Kestner continued

15in (38cm) closed-mouth child, ball-jointed body. *H&J Foulke, Inc.*

Closed-mouth shoulder head doll: Ca. 1880. Same as child doll on page 235 but on kid or cloth body with bisque arms, plaster dome; head is usually slightly turned.

14—16in (36—41cm)	**$750—850**
19—21in (48—53cm)	**1000—1200**
22—24in (56—61cm)	**1250—1450**

Bisque shoulder head on jointed kid body: Late 1880s to late 1930s. Mold numbers such as 154, 147, 148, 149, 166, 195 and heads with letter sizing only. Plaster dome, good wig, sleep eyes, open mouth; dressed; all in good condition.

16—18in (41—46cm)	**$375—425**
22—24in (56—61cm)	**500—550**
28—29in (71—74cm)	**700—800**

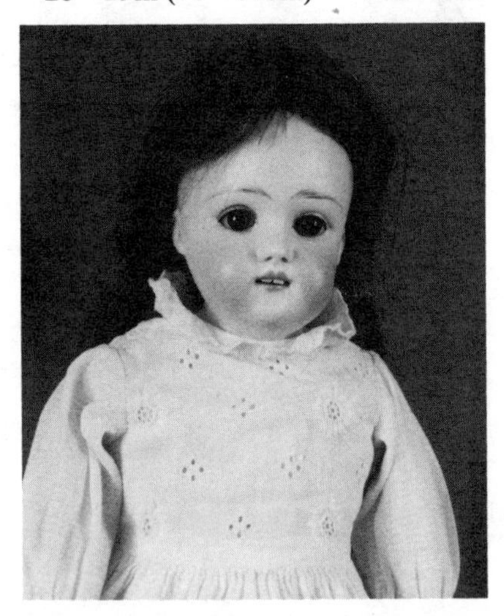

18½in (47cm) shoulder head with two square upper teeth, kid body. *H&J Foulke, Inc.*

16in (41cm) closed-mouth child incised "XI," swivel neck, kid body. *Betty Harms Collection.*

Kestner continued

Child doll, open mouth: Late 1880s to late 1930s. Mold numbers such as 129, 142, 144, 146, 152, 156, 160, 164, 167, 168, 174, 196, 214. Bisque socket head on ball-jointed body; plaster dome, good wig, sleep eyes, open mouth; dressed; all in good condition.

MARK: made in D Germany. 8. 162.

13—15in (33—38cm)	$ **400—450**
17—19in (43—48cm)	**475**
21—23in (53—58cm)	**500—550**
24—26in (61—66cm)	**600—650**
28—30in (71—76cm)	**800—900**
34—36in (86—91cm)	**1400—1600**
42in (107cm)	**2500 up**

#155:

7—9in (18—23cm)	**350—400**

#192:

21—23in (53—58cm)	**700—750**

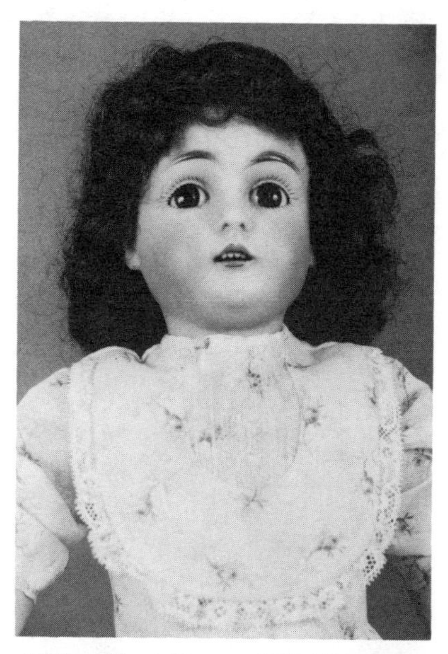

18½in (47cm) Kestner 167 child. *H&J Foulke, Inc.*

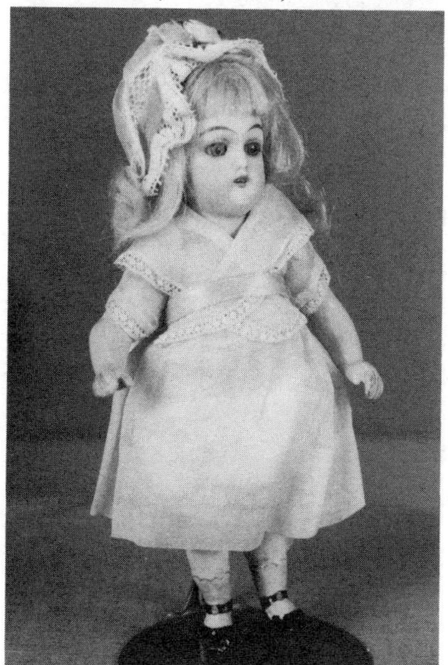

6½in (17cm) 189 child, jointed knees. *H&J Foulke, Inc.*

27in (69cm) 171 Kestner child. *H&J Foulke, Inc.*

Kestner continued

24in (61cm) J.D.K. 214 child. *Emma Wedmore Collection.*

13in (33cm) Kestner 196 child with real eyebrows. *Emma Wedmore Collection.*

20in (51cm) Kestner 149 child. *Mary Lou Rubright Collection.*

Kestner continued

Character Child: 1910—on. Mold numbers such as 183, 185 and others. Perfect bisque head character face, plaster pate, wig, painted or glass eyes, closed or open/closed mouth; good jointed composition body; dressed; all in good condition.

#143:
7—8in (18—20cm) **$ 400**
12—13in (31—33cm) **525—625**
20—21in (51—53cm) **850—950**

#178-190, 212:
Painted Eyes:
11—12in (28—31cm) **1600—1700**
18in (46cm) **3000**
Glass Eyes:
11—12in (28—31cm) **2000—2200**
15in (38cm) **2800**
18in (46cm) **3500**
12in (31cm) boxed set, one body, four heads **6000—6500**

#241:
21—22in (53—56cm) **3000—3500**

#249:
20in (51cm) **900—1000**

#260 Toddler:
8in (20cm) **400—425**
12—14in (31—36cm) **600—650**
18—20in (46—51cm) **750—850**

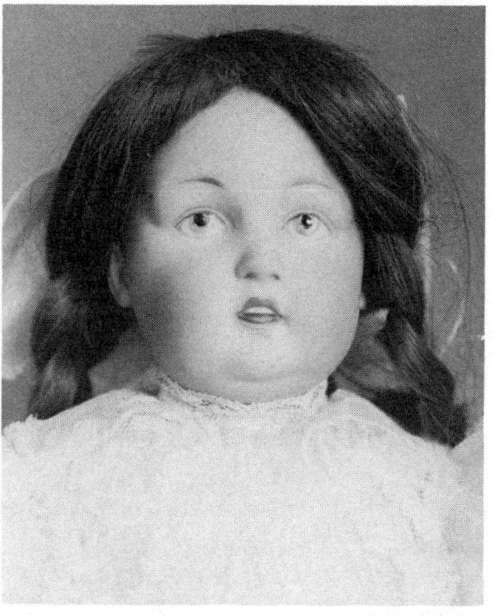

18in (46cm) Kestner 180 character child, painted eyes. *Richard Wright Antiques.*

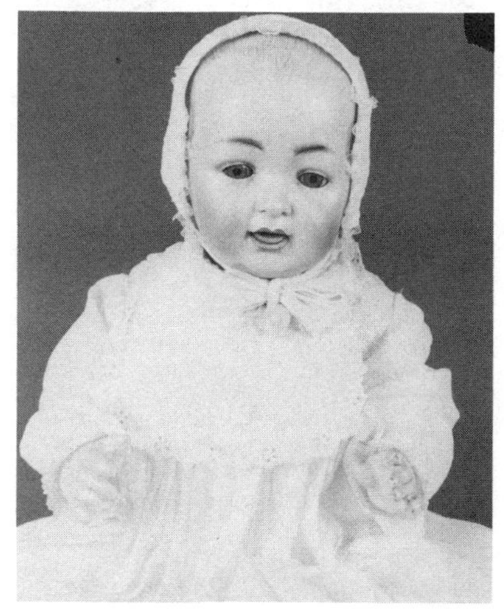

22in (56cm) 151 character baby, attributed to Kestner. *H&J Foulke, Inc.*

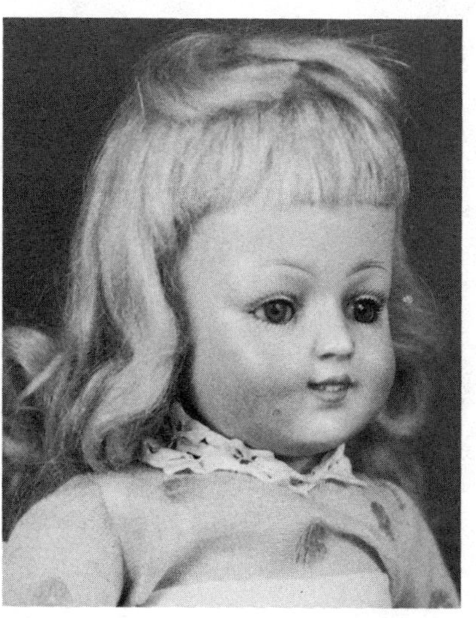

11½in (29cm) Kestner 185 character child with glass eyes. *Edna Black Collection.*

Kestner continued

Character Baby: 1910—on. Mold numbers such as 245, 237, 211, 257, 226. Perfect bisque head, molded and/or painted hair or good wig, sleep or set eyes, open mouth; bent-limb body; well dressed; nice condition.

MARK: made in
F. Germany. 10
211
J.D.K.

Hilda 245, 237 and solid dome:
12—14in (31—36cm) **$1900—2300**
16—18in (41—46cm) **2600—2800**
20—22in (51—56cm) **3200**

#211, 226, JDK (solid dome):
12—13in (31—33cm) **400—450**
18—20in (46—51cm) **650—750**
24—25in (61—64cm) **1100—1150**

#247:
16—18in (41—46cm) **1000—1200**

#257:
12—14in (31—36cm) **475—525**
18—20in (46—51cm) **650—750**

Solid dome, fat-faced:
16—18in (41—46cm) **750—850****
24in (61cm) **1600****

#234, 235, 238:
16in (41cm) **550—650****

#150, 151, 152, 142 (attributed):
10—12in (25—31cm) **375—400**
16—18in (41—46cm) **550—600***
23—24in (58—61cm) **750—850***

*Slightly less for 152.
**Not enough price samples to compute a reliable range.

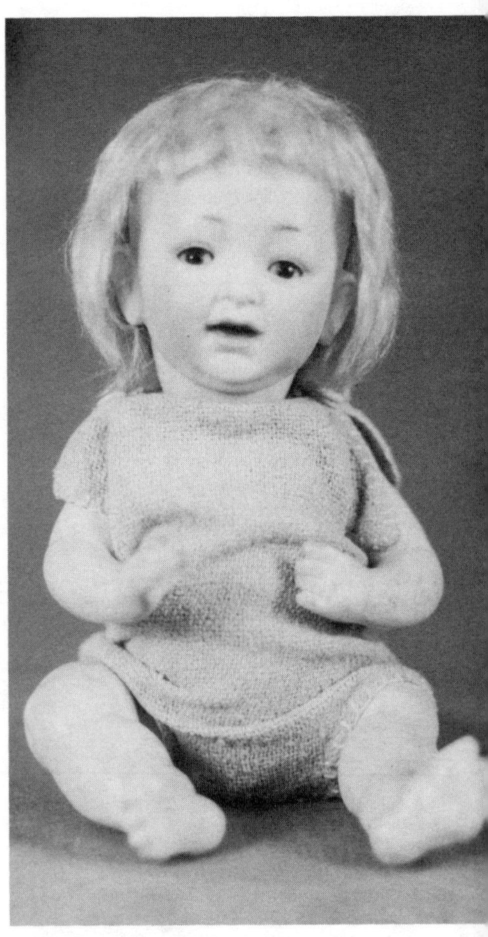

11½in (29cm) JDK 211 character baby.
H&J Foulke, Inc.

Kestner continued

17in (43cm) 152 character baby, attributed to Kestner. *H&J Foulke, Inc.*

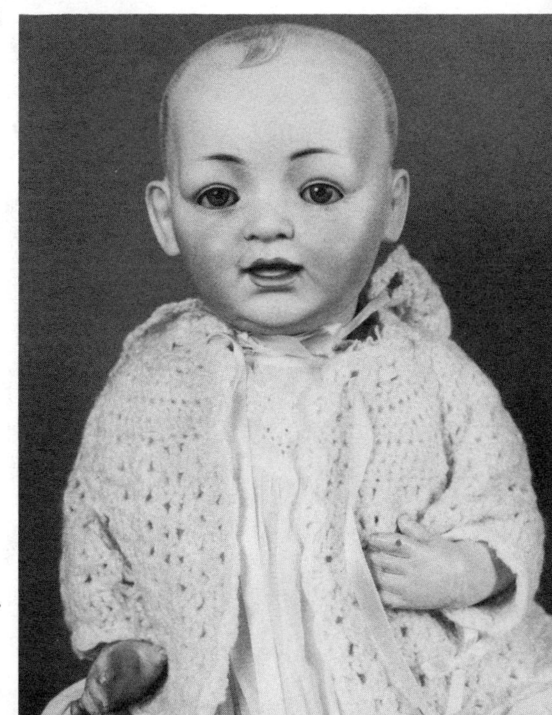

18in (46cm) JDK character baby. *Esther Schwartz Collection.*

Kestner continued

23in (58cm) 143 character child. *Esther Schwartz Collection.*

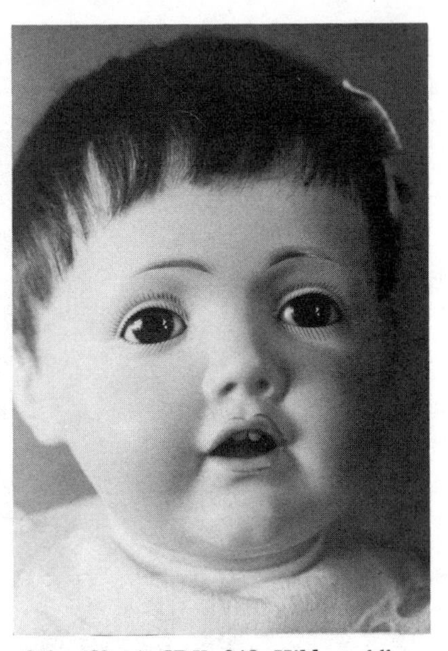

21in (53cm) JDK 245 ***Hilda*** toddler. *Mary Lou Rubright Collection.*

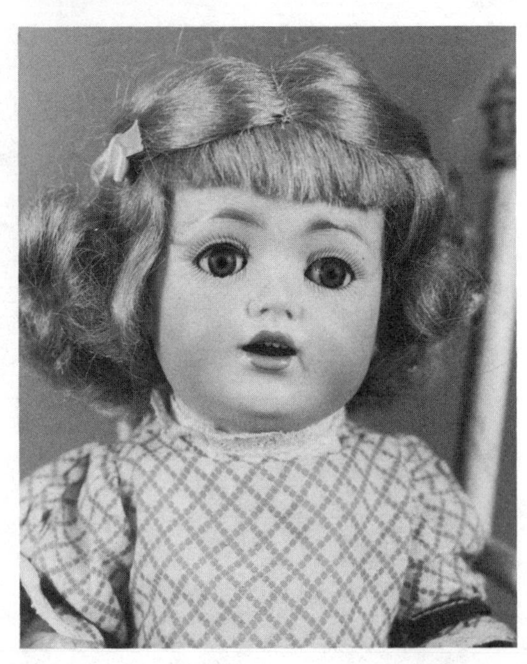

12½in (32cm) JDK 260 character. *Ruth Noden Collection.*

Kestner continued

Gibson Girl: Ca. 1910. Sometimes mold number 172; sometimes marked "Gibson Girl" on body. Perfect bisque shoulder head with good wig, glass eyes, *closed* mouth, up-lifted chin; kid body with bisque lower arms; beautifully dressed; all in good condition.

10—12in (25—31cm) **$1200—1400**
20in (51cm) **3200—3700**

Lady Doll: Mold number 162. Perfect bisque socket head, plaster dome, wig in Gibson Girl style, sleep eyes, open mouth with upper teeth; jointed composition body with molded breasts, nipped-in waist, slender arms and legs; appropriate lady clothes; all in good condition.

16—18in (41—46cm) **$850—950**

10in (25cm) Kestner 172 ***Gibson Girl***. *Ruth Noden Collection.*

20in (51cm) Kestner 162 lady doll. *Emma Wedmore Collection.*

Kewpie

Maker: Various
Date: 1913—on
Size: 2in (5.1cm) up
Designer: Rose O'Neill, U.S.A. U.S. Agent: George Borgfeldt & Co., New York, N.Y., U.S.A.
Mark: Red and gold paper heart or shield on chest and round label on back

All-Bisque: Made by J. D. Kestner and other German firms. Often have imperfections in making. Sometimes signed on foot "O'Neill." Standing, legs together, arms jointed, blue wings, painted features, eyes to side.

2—2½in (5—6cm)	**$ 85—95**
4—5in (10—13cm)	**100—125**
6in (15cm)	**150**
7in (18cm)	**200—250**
8—9in (20—23cm)	**350—400**
Jointed hips, 4in (10cm)	**400—450**
Black Hottentot, 5in (13cm)	**350**
Button hole	**165**
Pincushion, 2—3in (5—8cm)	**250—300**
Action Kewpies (sometimes stamped ©):	
Thinker, 6in (15cm)	**375—400**
Kewpie with cat, 3½in (9cm)	**350**
Confederate Soldier, 3½in (9cm)	**275—300**
Kewpie holding pen, 3in (8cm)	**350**
Lying on stomach, 4in (10cm)	**350**
Gardener, Sweeper, Soldier, Farmer, 4in (10cm)	**400**
Kewpie with rabbit, 2in (5cm)	**250**
Doodledog:	
3in (8cm)	**600**
1½in (4cm)	**350**
Huggers, 3½in (9cm)	**150—175**
Guitar player, 3½in (9cm)	**300**
Traveler, 3½in (9cm)	**300**
Governor, 3½in (9cm)	**350**
Kewpie with teddy, 4in (10cm)	**600**
Kewpie with turkey, 2in (5cm)	**350**
Kewpie and ***Doodledog*** on bench, 3½in (9cm)	**1400**
Perfume bottle, 3½in (9cm)	**450**
Kewpie with rose, 2in (5cm)	**250**
Kewpie with outhouse, 2½in (6cm)	**825**
Kewpie with umbrella and ***Doodledog***, 3½in (9cm)	**750**
Kewpie with Prussian helmet, 6in (15cm)	**450**

Kewpie continued

7in (18cm) all-bisque ***Kewpie*** with label.
H&J Foulke, Inc.

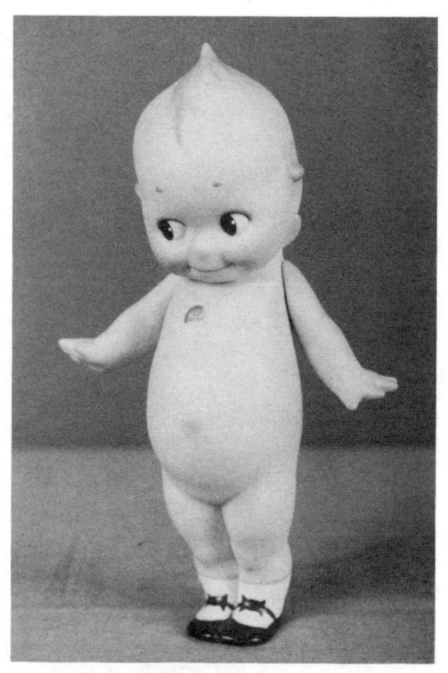

11in (28cm) ***Kewpie*** with painted shoes and socks. *Richard Wright Antiques.*

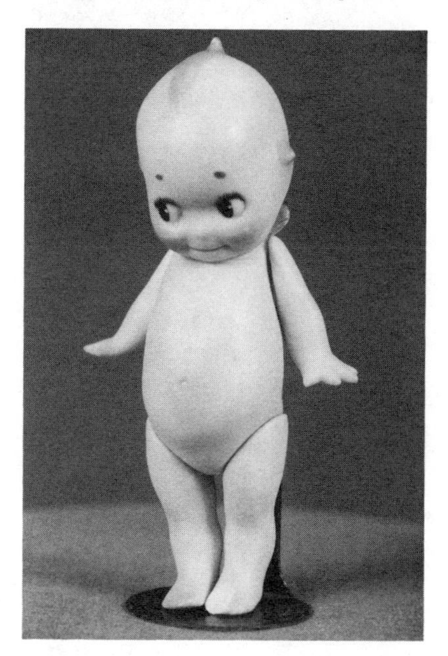

5½in (14cm) ***Kewpie*** with jointed hips.
H&J Foulke, Inc.

Kewpie continued

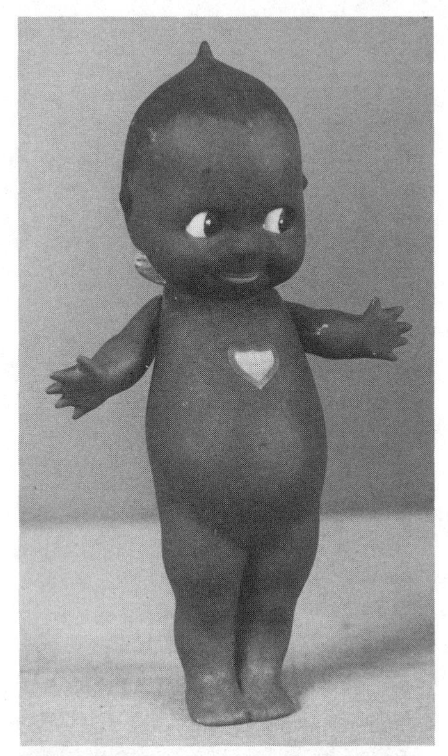

9in (23cm) ***Kewpie Hottentot***, with original label. *Richard Wright Antiques.*

5in (13cm) action ***Kewpie Huggers***. *H&J Foulke, Inc.*

3in (8cm) ***Kewpie Doodledog***, signed Rose O'Neill. *Richard Wright Antiques.*

Kewpie continued

Bisque head on chubby jointed toddler body, glass eyes: Made by J. D. Kestner.

MARK:

"Ges. gesch.
O'Neill J.D.K."

12in (31cm) **$3500—4500****

Bisque head on cloth body, painted eyes:

12in (31cm)	**$1500—1800****
Glass eyes (mold 1377)	**2000****

Celluloid: Made by Karl Standfuss, Deuben near Dresden, Saxony, Germany. Straight standing, arms jointed, blue wings; very good condition.

2in (5cm)	**$ 25—30**
5in (13cm)	**50**
8in (20cm)	**100—110**
Black, 2½in (6cm)	**60**

All-Composition: Made by Cameo Doll Co., Rex Doll Co., and Mutual Doll Co., all of New York, N.Y., U.S.A. All-composition, jointed at shoulders, some at neck and hips.

8in (20cm)	**$100**
11—13in (28—33cm)	**150**
Black	**225—250**
Talcum container, 7in (18cm)	**150—175**

**Not enough price samples to compute a reliable range.

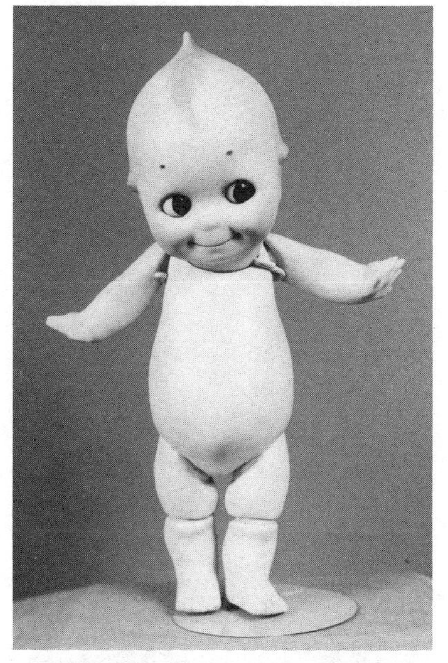

14in (36cm) JDK O'Neill ***Kewpie***, jointed composition body. *Betty Harms Collection.*

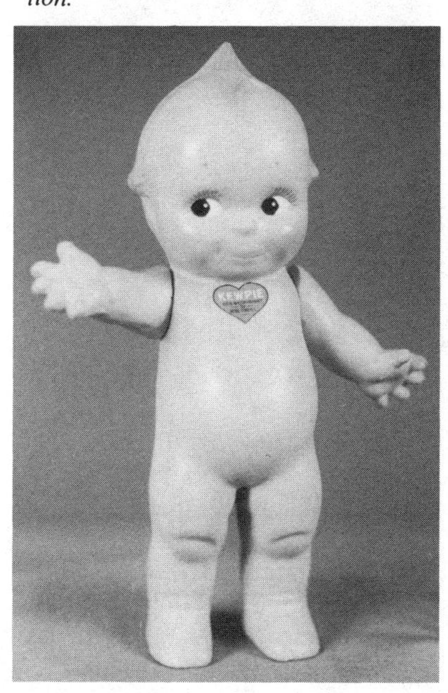

12in (31cm) all-composition ***Kewpie*** with heart label. *H&J Foulke, Inc.*

Kewpie continued

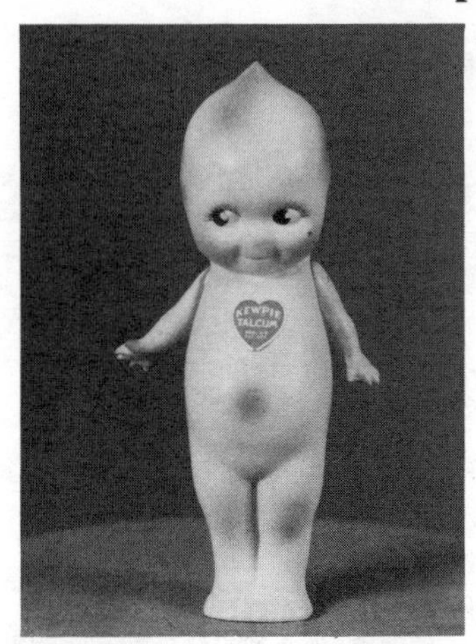

7in (18cm) ***Kewpie*** talcum powder container. *H&J Foulke, Inc.*

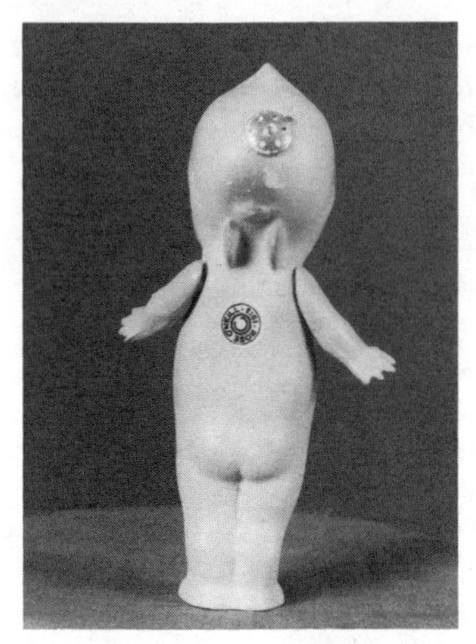

The back of the 7in (18cm) ***Kewpie*** talcum powder container. *H&J Foulke, Inc.*

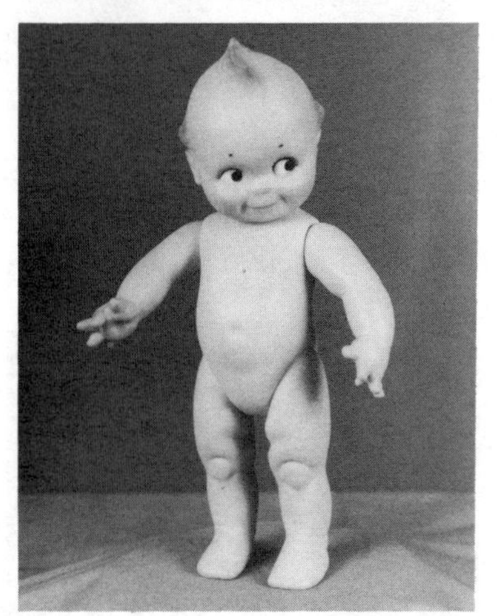

12in (31cm) vinyl ***Kewpie***. *H&J Foulke, Inc.*

All-Cloth: Made by Richard G. Kreuger, Inc., New York, N.Y., U.S.A. Patent number 1785800. Mask face with fat-shaped cloth body, including tiny wings and peak on head. Cloth label sewn in side seam.

10—12in (25—31cm) **$100—125**

Hard Plastic: Ca. 1950s.

Standing ***Kewpie***, one piece with jointed arms, 8in (20cm) **$ 50—60**

Fully jointed with sleep eyes, all original clothes, 13in (33cm) **250****

**Not enough price samples to compute a reliable range.

Vinyl: Ca. 1960s made by Cameo Doll Co.

Ragsy Kewpie, molded suit and cap, 8in (20cm) **$ 40**

10in (25cm), jointed arms **40**

12in (31cm), fully jointed **75**

27in (69cm), mint-in-box **200—225**

18in (46cm) ***Kewpie*** baby, hinged body **150—175**

Kley & Hahn

Maker: Kley & Hahn of Ohrdruf, Thüringia, Germany
Date: 1895—on
Material: Bisque head, composition body
Size: Various
Mark:

K&H
Germany

K H
Walküre

Child Doll: Mold #250 or Walküre mark. Perfect bisque head, wig, glass eyes, open mouth; jointed composition child body; fully dressed; all in good condition.

18—20in (46—51cm)	**$ 375—425**
24—26in (61—66cm)	**500—550**
32—33in (81—84cm)	**1100—1200**

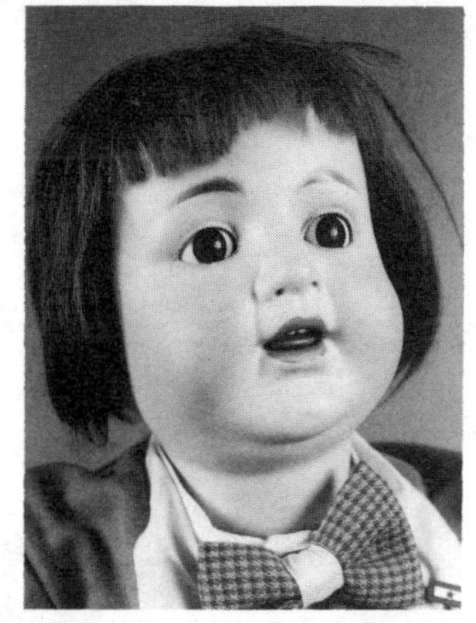

29in (74cm) K & H 680 character with pierced nose. *Dr. Carole Stoessel Zvonar Collection.*

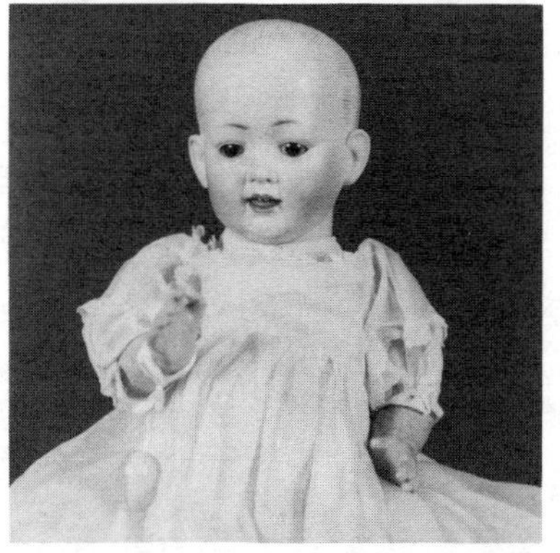

17in (43cm) K & H 158 character baby. *H&J Foulke, Inc.*

Character Baby: Perfect bisque head with molded hair or good wig, sleep or painted eyes, open or closed mouth; bent-limb baby body; nicely dressed; all in good condition.

#167, 176, 525, 531:

13—14in (33—36cm)	**$450—475**
18—20in (46—51cm)	**550—650**
24—25in (61—64cm)	**800—850**

#680, 568:

18—20in (46—51cm)	**850—900***

*Allow more for toddler or child body.

Character Child: Perfect bisque head, wig, glass or painted eyes, closed mouth; jointed composition child or toddler body; fully dressed; all in good condition.

#520, 526, 546, 536, 549:
19—21in (48—53cm) **$3500—4200**

#154:
Open mouth, 19in (48cm) **900—1000**
Closed mouth, 16—17in (41—43cm) **2200**

#157:
16—17in (41—43cm) **1800—2000**

20in (51cm) K & H 549 character child with glass eyes. *Pearl D. Morley Collection.*

Kling

Maker: Kling & Co., Ohrdruf, Thüringia, Germany (porcelain factory)
Date: 1836-on
Material: Bisque or china shoulder head, cloth body, bisque lower limbs; bisque socket head, composition body, all-bisque.
Size: Various
Mark: (K in bell) and numbers such as "189-9."

China shoulder head: Ca. 1880. Black- or blonde-haired china head with bangs, sometimes with a pink tint; cloth body with china limbs or kid body; dressed; all in good condition.

18—20in (46—51cm)	**$325—375**
22—24in (56—61cm)	**400—425**

Bisque shoulder head: Ca. 1880. Molded hair, painted eyes, closed mouth; cloth body with bisque lower limbs; dressed; all in good condition.

12—15in (31—38cm)	**$200—250**
22—24in (56—61cm)	**425—475**

Marked Kling all-bisque child: Jointed shoulders and hips; wig, glass eyes, closed mouth; molded footwear.
MARK: Kling bell and/or "36-10n"

4in (10cm)	**$135—165**

Bisque shoulder head: Ca. 1890. Mohair or human hair wig, glass sleep eyes, open mouth; kid or cloth body with bisque lower arms; dressed; all in good condition.

16—18in (41—46cm)	**$375—400****
23—24in (58—61cm)	**450—500****

**Not enough price samples to compute a reliable range.

22in (56cm) china shoulder head incised with "K" in bell, mold #189. *Dr. Carole Stoessel Zvonar Collection.*

Kling continued

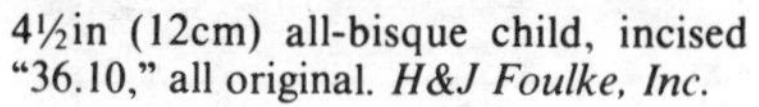

4½in (12cm) all-bisque child, incised "36.10," all original. *H&J Foulke, Inc.*

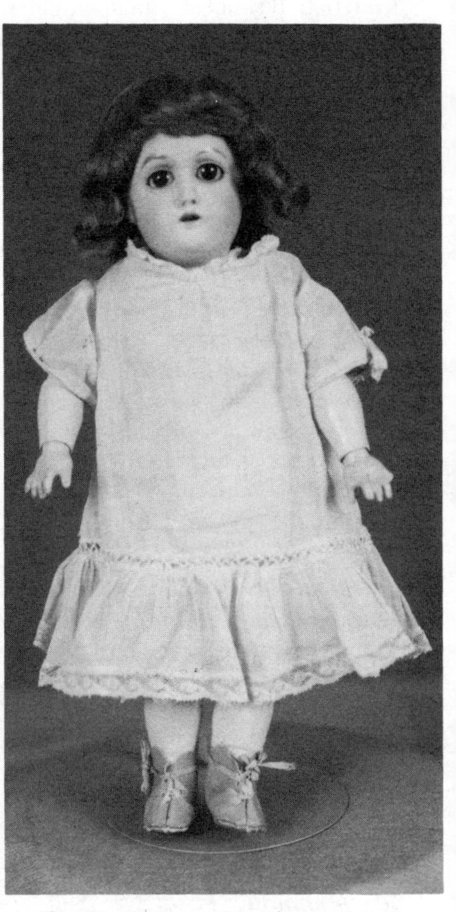

13in (33cm) Kling child socket head mold number 372.3 with "K" in bell on jointed composition body. *Dr. Carole Stoessel Zvonar Collection.*

Bisque socket head: Ca. 1890s. On ball-jointed composition body; good wig, sleep eyes, open mouth; nice clothes; all in good condition.

18—21in (46—53cm) **$400—450****

**Not enough price samples to compute a reliable range.

König & Wernicke

Maker: König & Wernicke, Waltershausen, Thüringia, Germany
Date: 1912—on
Material: Bisque heads, composition bodies or all-composition
Size: Various
Mark: "K & W" sometimes with mold number 1070; "Made in Germany" (with size number).
Sometimes heads with mold numbers "98" and "99" are found on marked "K & W" bodies.
Body Mark:

K & W Character: Bisque head with good wig, sleep eyes, open mouth; composition baby or toddler body; appropriate clothes; all in good condition.

15in (38cm)	**$450***
21—22in (53—56cm)	**550—650***

*Allow extra for toddler body and flirty eyes.

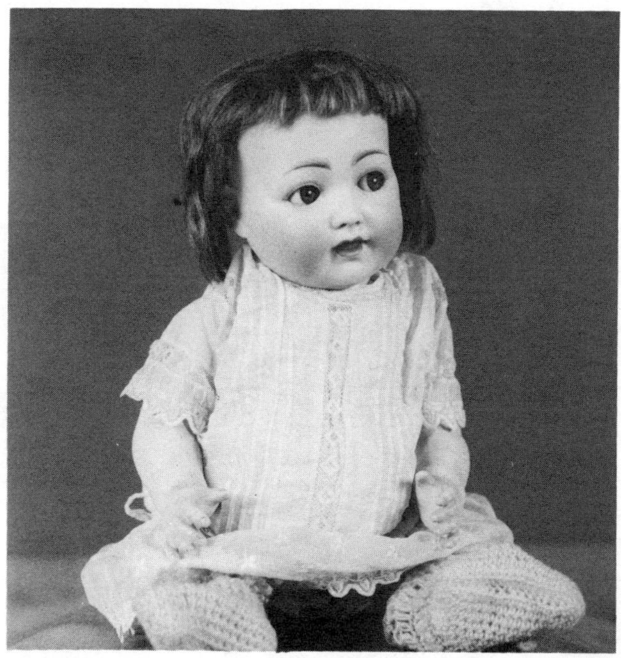

14in (36cm) 98/6 character baby on marked "K & W" body. *H&J Foulke, Inc.*

Käthe Kruse

Maker: Käthe Kruse, Berlin, Germany
Date: 1910—on
Material: Molded muslin head (hand-painted), jointed cloth body, later of hard plastic material.
Size: Various
Mark: On cloth: "Käthe Kruse" on sole of foot, sometimes also "Germany" and a number
Hard plastic on back: Turtle mark and "Käthe Kruse"

Käthe Kruse 81971 — Made in Germany

Cloth Käthe Kruse: Molded muslin head, hand-painted; jointed at shoulders and hips.

Doll I (1910—1929), painted hair, wide hips, 16—17in (41—43cm):

Mint, all original	**$1100—1400**
Good condition, suitably dressed	**700—750**

Doll IH (after 1929), wigged:

Mint, all original	**1000—1200**
Good condition, suitably dressed	**650—700**
Doll II (1922) "Schlenkerchen" Smiling Baby, 13in (33cm)	**800—900**
Doll V (1925) Babies "***Traumerchen***" (closed eyes) and "***Du Mein***" (open eyes), 19½—23½in (50—60cm)	**1800—2000**

Doll VIII (1929) wigged "German Child" 20½in (52cm):

Mint, all original	**1000—1200**
Good condition, suitably dressed	**650—700**
U. S. Zone Germany (1945—1951), 14in (36cm)	**550**

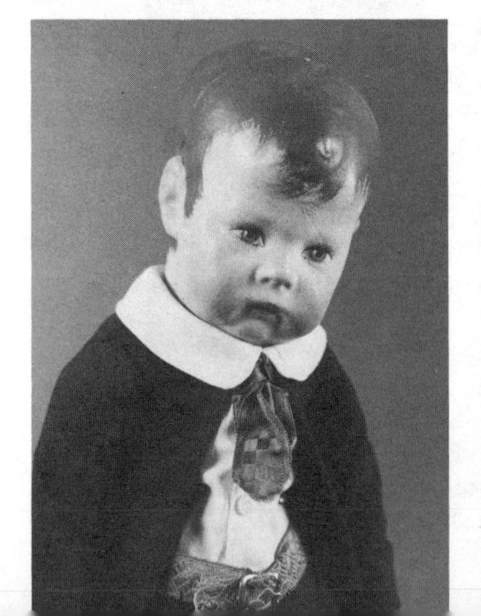

16in (41cm) Käthe Kruse boy, ***Doll I,*** all original. *Pearl D. Morley Collection.*

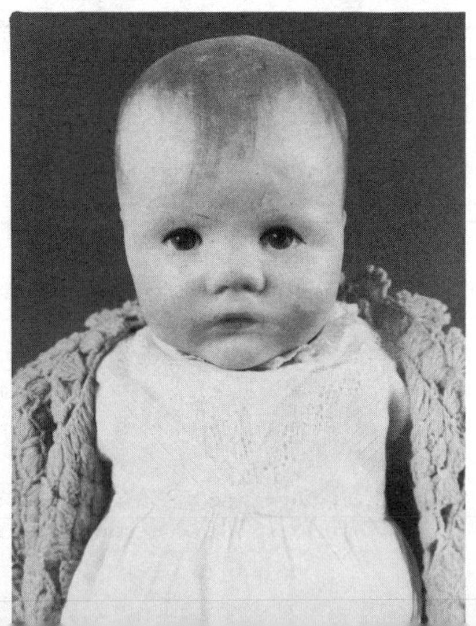

20in (51cm) Käthe Kruse baby, ***Doll V, Du Mein.***

Käthe Kruse continued

All-Hard Plastic Käthe Kruse: Wig or molded hair and sleep or painted eyes; jointed neck, shoulders and hips; original clothes; all in excellent condition. Turtle mark. (1955—1961).

16in (41cm)	**$325—375**

Hard Plastic Head: Ca. 1950s—on. Hard plastic head with lovely wig, painted eyes; pink muslin body; original clothes; all in excellent condition.

10in (25cm)	**$250**
14in (36cm)	**400**

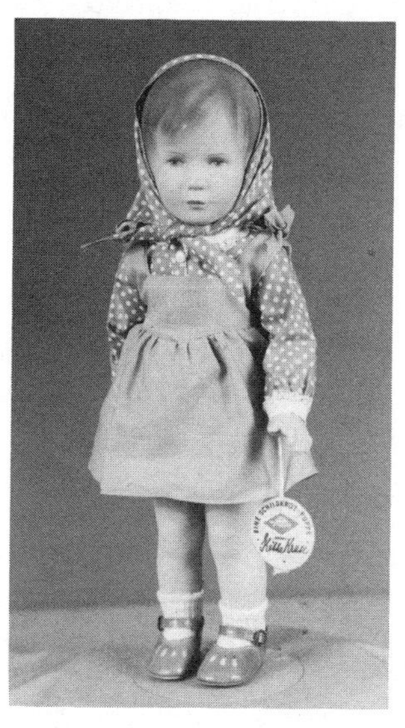

16in (41cm) hard plastic Käthe Kruse child, rare form with molded hair. *H&J Foulke, Inc.*

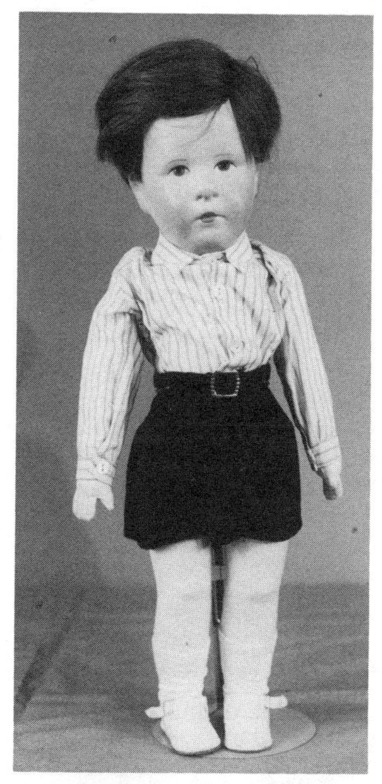

17in (43cm) Käthe Kruse, ***Doll VIII,*** U. S. Zone Germany. *H&J Foulke, Inc.*

Käthe Kruse with hard plastic head, soft cloth body. *H&J Foulke, Inc.*

Gebrüder Kuhnlenz

Maker: Gebrüder Kuhnlenz, Kronach, Bavaria
Date: 1884—1919
Material: Bisque head, composition body
Size: Various
Mark: " G.K. "
with numbers

41.28	56.18	44.15
41.29	56.30	44.16
41.32		44.17
		44.20
		44.35

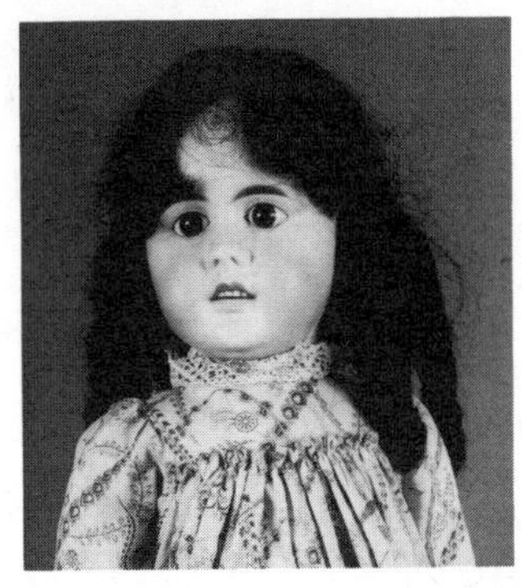

23in (58cm) 41.32 child with molded upper teeth. *Carol Green Collection.*

G. K. doll with closed mouth: Ca. 1890. Perfect bisque socket head, inset glass eyes, closed mouth, round cheeks; jointed composition body; dressed; all in good condition.
Mold *#32,* 16—20in (41—51cm) **$850—1150**
Mold *#38*, kid body, shoulder head, 20—23in (51—58cm) **750—850**

G. K. child doll: Ca. 1890—on. Perfect bisque socket head with distinctive face, almost a character look, long cheeks, sleep eyes, open mouth, molded teeth; jointed composition body; dressed; all in good condition.
Mold *#41*, 19—22in (48—56cm) **$550—650**

G. K. Tiny Doll: Perfect bisque socket head, wig, stationary glass eyes, open mouth with molded teeth; five-piece composition body with molded shoes and socks; all in good condition.
8—8½in (20—22cm) **$125—150**

8in (20cm) G. K. child with Belton-type head, closed mouth. *H&J Foulke, Inc.*

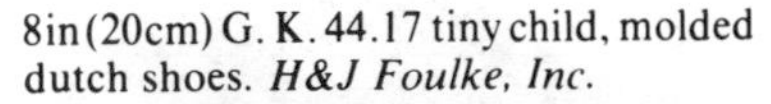

8in (20cm) G. K. 44.17 tiny child, molded dutch shoes. *H&J Foulke, Inc.*

Lanternier

Maker: A Lanternier & Cie. of Limoges, France
Date: 1855—on
Material: Bisque head, papier-mâché body
Size: Various
Mark: Anchor with "Limoges A. L.—France" or "Fabrication Française A.L. & Cie. Limoges", sometimes "Cherie", "Favorite", "La Georgienne", "Lorraine"

LIMOGES
A L

FABRICATION
FRANÇAISE
AL & Cie
LIMOGES
A 1

Marked Lanternier Child: Ca. 1915. Perfect bisque head, good or original wig, large stationary eyes, open mouth, pierced ears; papier-mâché jointed body; pretty clothes; all in good condition.

16—18in (41—46cm)	**$625—675***
22—23in (56—58cm)	**750—850***
28in (71cm)	**1150—1250***

*Depending greatly on how pretty the doll is.

Marked Toto: Ca. 1915. Perfect bisque smiling character face, good wig, glass eyes, open/closed mouth with molded teeth, pierced ears; jointed French composition body; dressed; marked "Toto, AL & C, Limoges," all in good condition.

18in (46cm)	**$850—900**

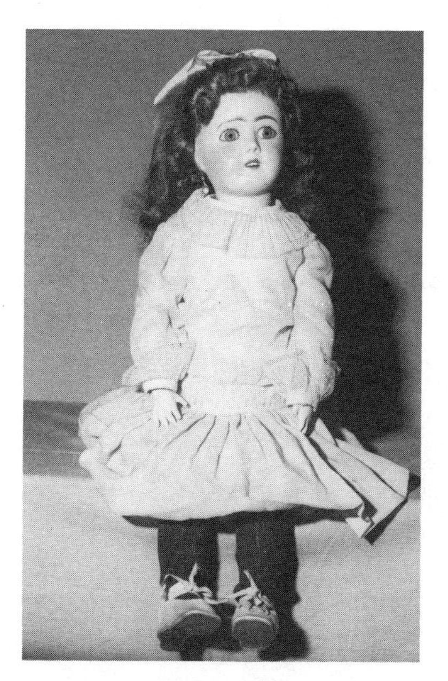

21in (53cm) Limoges child. *Dr. Carole Stoessel Zvonar Collection.*

Lenci

Maker: Enrico & Elenadi Scavini, Turin, Italy
Date: 1920—on
Material: Pressed felt head with painted features, jointed felt bodies
Size: 5—45in (13—114cm)
Mark: "LENCI" on cloth and various paper tags; sometimes stamped on bottom of foot

Lenci: All-felt (sometimes cloth torso) with swivel head, jointed shoulders and hips; painted features, eyes usually side-glancing; original clothes, often of felt or organdy; in excellent condition.

Miniatures and Mascottes:

8—9in (20—23cm) Regionals	**$ 175—200**
Children or unusual costumes	**200—250 up**

Children #300, 109, 149, 159, 111:

13in (33cm)	**650 up**
16—18in (41—46cm)	**850 up**
20—22in (51—56cm)	**1200 up**
"Lucia" face, 14in (36cm)	**400 up**
Ladies and long-limbed novelty dolls, 24—28in (61—71cm)	**1000 up**
Glass eyes, 20in (51cm)	**2350**
Celluloid-type, 6in (15cm)	**40**

Collector's Note: Mint examples of rare dolls will bring higher prices. To bring the prices quoted, Lenci dolls must be clean and have good color. Faded and dirty dolls bring only about one-third to one-half these prices.

9in (23cm) Mascotte with felt hair. *H&J Foulke, Inc.*

Lenci continued

9in (23cm) Lenci in regional costume. *H&J Foulke, Inc.*

19in (48cm) Lenci ***Benedetta,*** all original. *Beth Foulke Collection.*

17in (43cm) Lenci child 178G, all original. *Beth Foulke Collection.*

19in (48cm) Lenci 1500 pouty, all original. *Beth Foulke Collection.*

Lenci continued

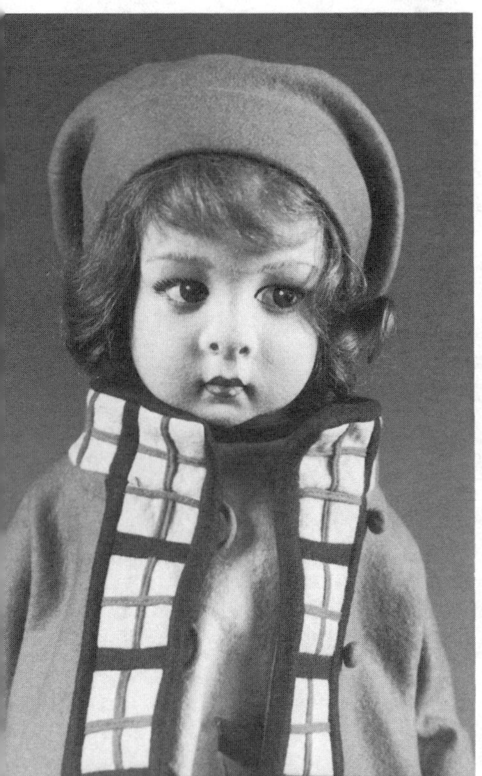

18in (46cm) pouty girl, all original. *Pearl D. Morley Collection.*

17in (43cm) Lenci 300 boy, all original.

Lenci continued

17in (43cm) Lenci 300 boy as ***Sardinian Soldier,*** all original.

14in (36cm) Lenci ***Lucia,*** all original. *Beth Foulke Collection.*

Lenci-Type

Maker: Various Italian, French and English firms such as Marguerin, Alma, and others.
Date: 1920—1940
Material: Felt and cloth
Size: 6in (15cm) up
Mark: Various paper labels, if any

Felt or Cloth Doll: Mohair wig, painted features; original clothes or costume.
Child dolls,
16—18in (41—46cm) up to **$350** depending upon quality and rarity.
Foreign costume, 7½—8½in (19—22cm) **$25—35**

12in (31cm) Italian ***Eros*** regional doll, all original. *H&J Foulke, Inc.*

12in (31cm) Italian ***Maois*** regional doll, all original. *H&J Foulke, Inc.*

Liberty of London

Maker: Liberty & Co. of London, England
Date: 1906—on
Material: All-fabric
Size: Various
Mark: Cloth label or paper tag "Liberty of London"

British Coronation Dolls: 1939. All-cloth with painted and needle-sculpted faces; original clothes; excellent condition.
The Royal Family and Coronation Participants:
5½—9½in (14—24cm) **$70-80**
Other English Historical and Ceremonial Characters: All-cloth with painted and needle-sculpted faces, original clothes; excellent condition.
9in (23cm) **75-85**

Liberty of London ***Queen Elizabeth II*** in coronation robes. *H&J Foulke, Inc.*

Limbach

Maker: Limbach Porzellanfabrik, Limbach, Thüringia, Germany (porcelain factory)
Date: Factory started in 1772
Material: Bisque head, composition body; all bisque
Size: Various
Mark: Sometimes with "Wally"

Limbach Child Doll: Ca. 1890. Perfect bisque head, good wig, glass eyes, open mouth with teeth; composition jointed body; dressed; all in good condition.

15—18in (38—46cm) **$325—375**
23—24in (58—61cm) **425—475**

Limbach Character Baby: Ca. 1910. Bisque head with molded hair, glass or painted eyes, open/closed mouth; composition baby body; dressed; all in good condition.

Mold #8682, 15in (38cm) **$900—1000****

**Not enough price samples to compute a reliable range.

All-Bisque Child: Ca. 1900. Child all of bisque (sometimes pink bisque) with wire jointed shoulders and hips; molded hair (often with a blue molded bow) or bald head with mohair wig, painted eyes, closed mouth; white stockings, blue garters, brown slippers or strap shoes.

MARK: P.23
GERMANY

3—4in (8—10cm) **$45—55**
Glass eyes, 8in (20cm) **225—250**

All-Bisque Baby: Ca. 1910. Baby with painted hair and facial features; wire jointed shoulders and hips, bent arms and legs; bare feet.

MARK: Clover and number

4in (10cm) **$50—60**
Swivel neck, 6in (15cm) **150**

7in (18cm) all-bisque Limbach baby P.2/1 with clover. *Dr. Carole Stoessel Zvonar Collection.*

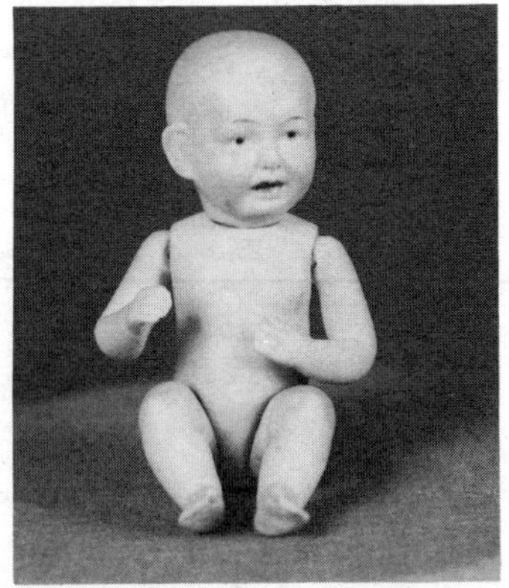

6in (15cm) all-bisque Limbach baby with swivel neck and molded loop. *Dr. Carole Stoessel Zvonar Collection.*

Albert Marque

Maker: Unknown, possibly artist produced
Date: 1916
Material: Bisque head, jointed composition body with bisque lower arms
Size: 21—22in (53—56cm) one size only
Designer: Albert Marque, French sculptor
Mark: A Marque

---

*A. **Marque Doll:*** Bisque head with wistful character face, mohair wig, paperweight eyes, closed mouth; jointed composition body of special design with bisque lower arms and hands, fixed wrists; appropriate clothes (some original ones from Paris designer Margaines-Lacroix).
21—22in (53—56cm) **$35,000—38,000**

Signed A. Marque doll. *Elizabeth McIntyre.*

Armand Marseille
(A.M.)

Maker: Armand Marseille of Köppelsdorf, Thüringia, Germany (porcelain factory)
Date: 1865—on
Material: Bisque socket and shoulder head, composition, cloth or kid body
Size: Various
Mark: Armand Marseille
Germany
990
A 9/0 M

Child Doll: Ca. 1890—on. Mold numbers such as 390, 1894, 370, 3200, also sometimes horseshoe mark. Perfect bisque head, nice wig, set or sleep eyes, open mouth; composition ball-jointed body or jointed kid body with bisque lower arms; pretty clothes; all in good condition.

#390, (larger sizes marked only "A M" with size number):

5—6in (13—15cm) five-piece body	**$ 125**
8—9in (20—23cm) five-piece body	**125**
11—13in (28—33cm)	**175—225**
15—17in (38—43cm)	**250—300**
19—20in (48—51cm)	**325—350**
22—24in (56—61cm)	**350—400**
28—30in (71—76cm)	**500—600**
32—33in (81—84cm)	**800—900**
35—36in (89—91cm)	**1300—1400**
40—42in (102—107cm)	**2000**

#1894, composition body:

15—16in (38—41cm)	**350—400**
19—20in (48—51cm)	**425—475**
23—24in (58—61cm)	**500—525**

#370, 3200, 1894, kid body:

16—18in (41—46cm)	**225—250**
22—24in (56—61cm)	**300—325**

Florodora:

15—17in (38—43cm)	**250—300**
22—24in (56—61cm)	**375—425**

Queen Louise:

23—25in (58—64cm)	**425—475**
32—33in (81—84cm)	**800—900**

21in (53cm) A.M. ***Florodora***. *H&J Foulke, Inc.*

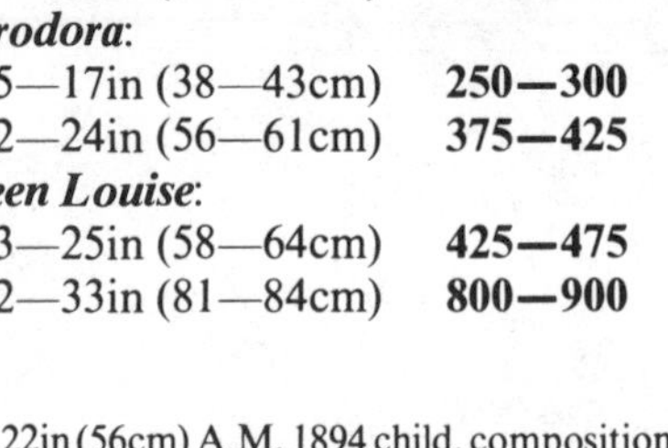

22in (56cm) A.M. 1894 child, composition body. *H&J Foulke, Inc.*

Armand Marseille (A.M.) continued

7½in (19cm) A.M. 390, five-piece composition body. *H&J Foulke, Inc.*

12in (31cm) A.M. 1894 shoulder head child. *H&J Foulke, Inc.*

Character Baby: 1910—on. Mold numbers such as 990, 992, 985, 971, 996, and others. Bisque head, good wig, sleep eyes, open mouth some with teeth; composition bent-limb body; suitably dressed; all in nice condition.

Mold #990, 985, 971, 996, 1330, 326 (solid dome), 327, 329 and other common numbers:

13—15in (33—38cm) **$350—375***
18—19in (46—48cm) **425—475***
22—24in (56—61cm) **575—675***

#233:

13—15in (33—38cm) **425—475**

#518:

16—18in (41—46cm) **450—550**

#560A:

13—15in (33—38cm) **425—475***
18—19in (46—48cm) **550—650***

#580, 590 (open/closed mouth):

16—18in (40—46cm) **1250—1350***

#590 (open mouth):

15—17in (38—43cm) **850—950**

#248 (open/closed mouth):

12—14in (31—36cm) **1200—1300***

#248 (open mouth):

12—14in (31—36cm) **600—800**

*Allow extra for toddler body.

26in (66cm) A.M. 390 child. *H&J Foulke, Inc.*

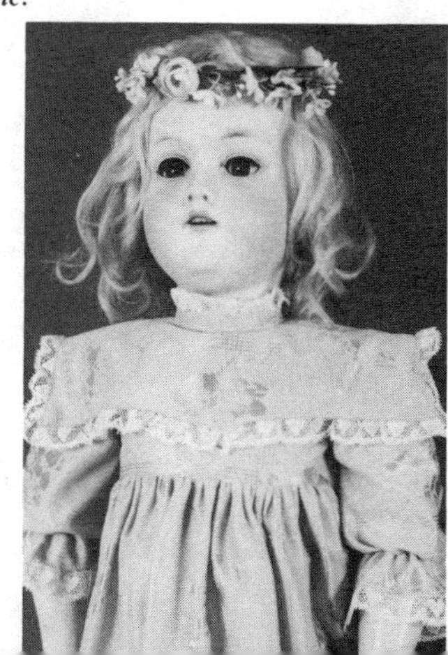

Armand Marseille (A.M.) continued

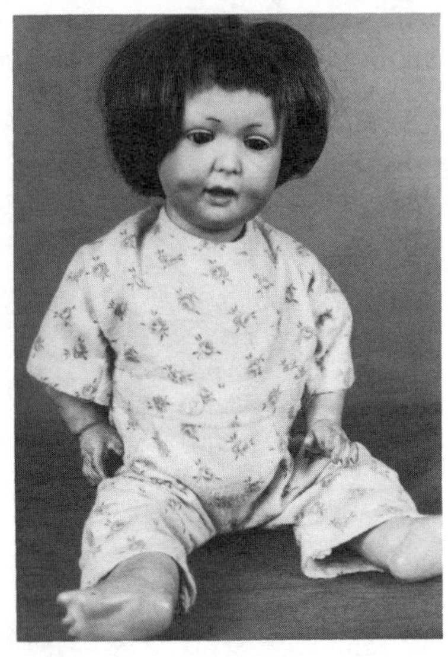

A.M. 580 character baby. *Esther Schwartz Collection.*

Character Children: 1910—on. Mold numbers such as 500, 550, 590, 600, and others. Bisque head, molded hair or wig, glass or painted eyes, open or closed mouth; composition body; dressed; all in good condition.

#500, 600:

15in (38cm) **$ 450—550**

#550:

16—18in (41—46cm) **2500—2700**

#230, Fany (molded hair):

14—15in (36—38cm) **5500—6000**

#231 Fany (wigged):

12—14in (31—36cm) **4200—4600**

#400:

15in (38cm) **2800****

**Not enough price samples to compute a reliable range.

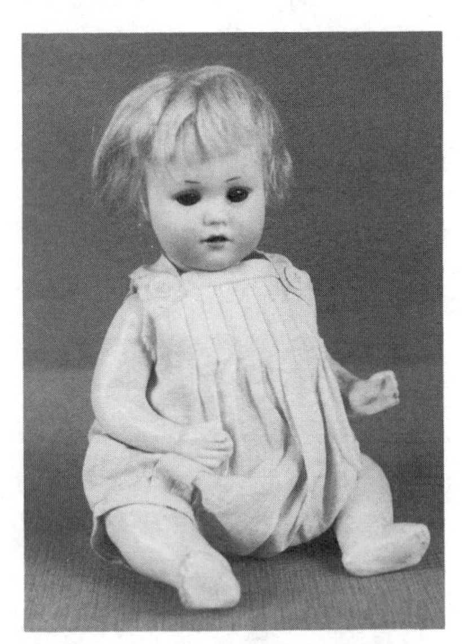

Small A.M. 248/ G.B. 251 character baby. *Jimmy and Faye Rodolfos Collection.*

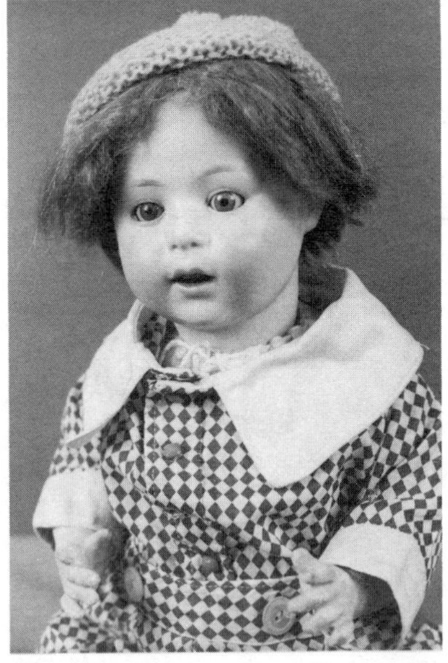

17in (43cm) A.M. 233 character baby, open mouth. *Dr. Carole Stoessel Zvonar Collection.*

Armand Marseille (A.M.) continued

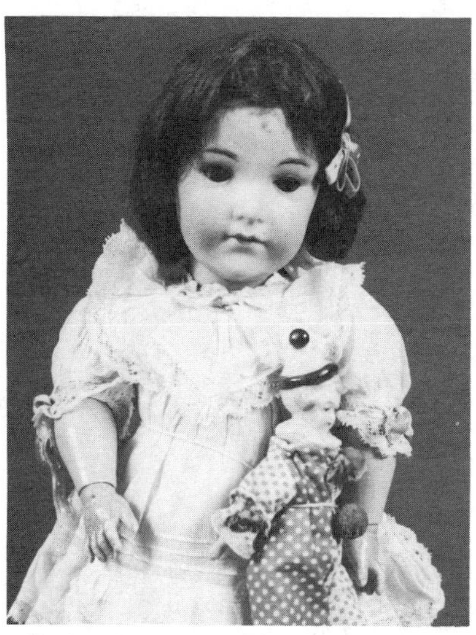

12½in (32cm) A.M. 400 character child, jointed composition body.

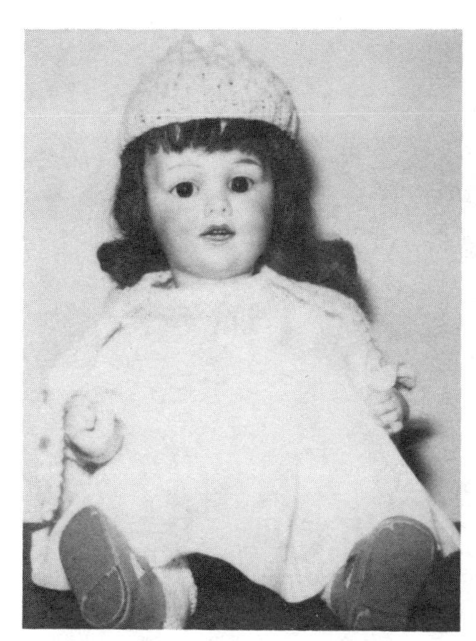

11½in (29cm) A.M. 410 toddler with retractable teeth; when she sleeps her lower teeth are replaced by a tongue. *Edna Black Collection. Photograph courtesy of the owner.*

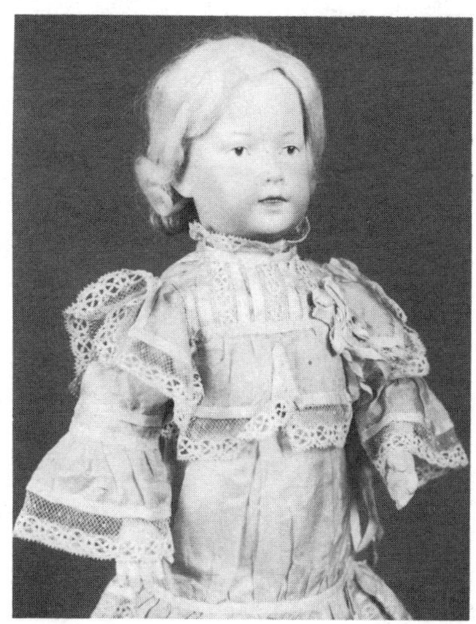

16in (41cm) A.M. character girl with intaglio eyes. *Richard Wright Collection.*

Armand Marseille (A.M.) continued

16in (41cm) A.M. 267//G.B. 329 character baby. *Joanna Ott Collection.*

11in (28cm) A.M. 256 character child for Maar. *Joanna Ott Collection.*

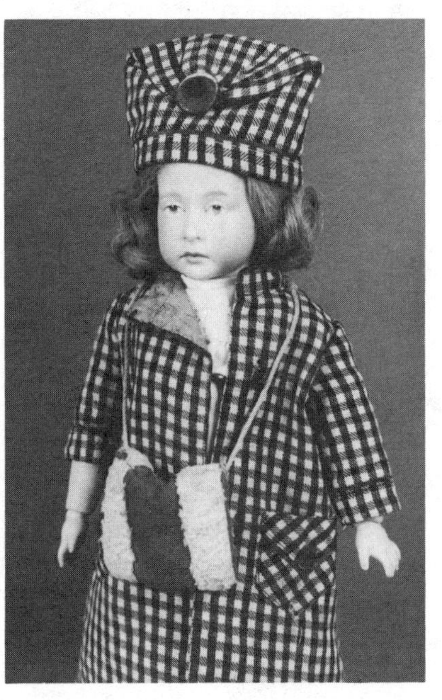

17in (43cm) A.M. character girl with intaglio eyes. *Richard Wright Collection.*

Armand Marseille (A.M.) continued

Marked Just Me Character: Ca. 1925. Perfect bisque socket head, curly wig, glass eyes to side, closed mouth; composition body; dressed; all in good condition. Some of these dolls, particularly the painted bisque ones, were used by Vogue Doll Company in the 1930s and will be found with original Vogue labeled clothes.

MARK:

Just ME
Registered
Germany
A 310/5/0 M

9in (23cm)	**$1050—1150**
Painted bisque:	
7—8in (18cm)	**450—500**
10in (25cm)	**600—650**

Lady: 1910—1930. Bisque head with mature face, mohair wig, sleep eyes, open or closed mouth; composition lady body with molded bust, long slender arms and legs; appropriate clothes; all in good condition.

#401 and ***400***,

14in (36cm)

open mouth	**$ 750—800**
closed mouth	**1200—1400**

8in (20cm) A.M. ***Just Me*** character. *Betty Harms Collection.*

14in (36cm) A.M. 400 lady, painted bisque, closed mouth. *Alice Mahoney Collection.*

Armand Marseille (A.M.) continued

Infant: 1924—on. Mold numbers 351 (open mouth) or 341 (closed mouth). Solid-dome bisque head with molded and/or painted hair, sleep eyes; composition body or hard-stuffed jointed cloth body or soft-stuffed cloth body; dressed; all in good condition.

#351, 341, Kiddiejoy and Our Pet:

Head circumference:

8—10in (20—25cm)	**$250—300**
13—14in (33—36cm)	**400—450**

#352

15—17in long (38—43cm)	**450—550**

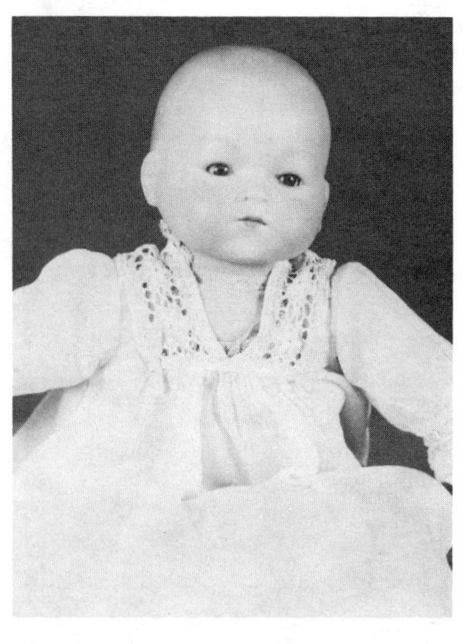

14in (36cm) A.M. 341 infant. *H&J Foulke, Inc.*

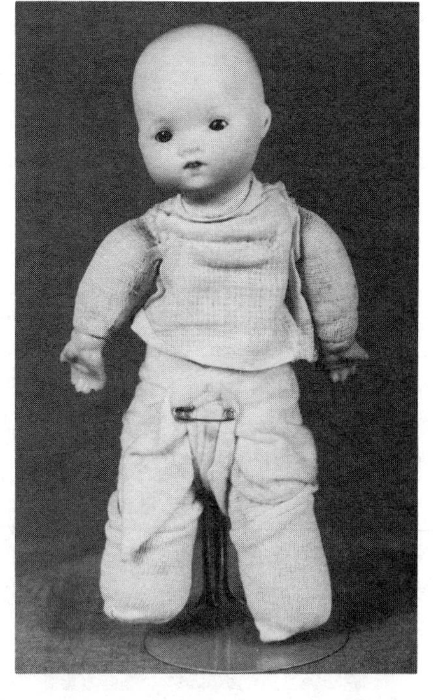

8½in (22cm) A.M. 342 infant, open/closed mouth with molded teeth, cloth body. *H&J Foulke, Inc.*

Mascotte

Maker: May Freres Cie, 1890—1897; Jules Nicholas Steiner, 1898—on. Paris, France
Date: 1890—1902
Material: Bisque head, composition and wood jointed body
Size: Various
Mark:

"BÉBÉ MASCOTTE
PARIS"

Bébé Mascotte: Bisque socket head, good wig, closed mouth, paperweight eyes, pierced ears; jointed composition and wood body; appropriate clothes; all in good condition.
20—24in (51—61cm) **$3300—3800**

25in (64cm) ***Bébé Mascotte***. *Ruth Noden Collection.*

Metal Dolls

Maker: Various U.S. companies
Date: Ca. 1914—on
Material: All-metal body
Size: Various
Mark: Various

Metal Child: All-metal, body fully jointed at neck, shoulders, elbows, wrists, hips, knees and ankles; sleep eyes, open/closed mouth with painted teeth; dressed; all in good condition.
16—18in (41—46cm) **$225—250****

**Not enough price samples to compute a reliable range.

Metal Baby: All-metal (with bent limbs) jointed at shoulders and hips with metal springs; molded and painted hair and facial features, painted or sleep eyes, closed or open mouth; appropriate clothes; all in good condition.
10—12in (25—31cm) **$65—85**

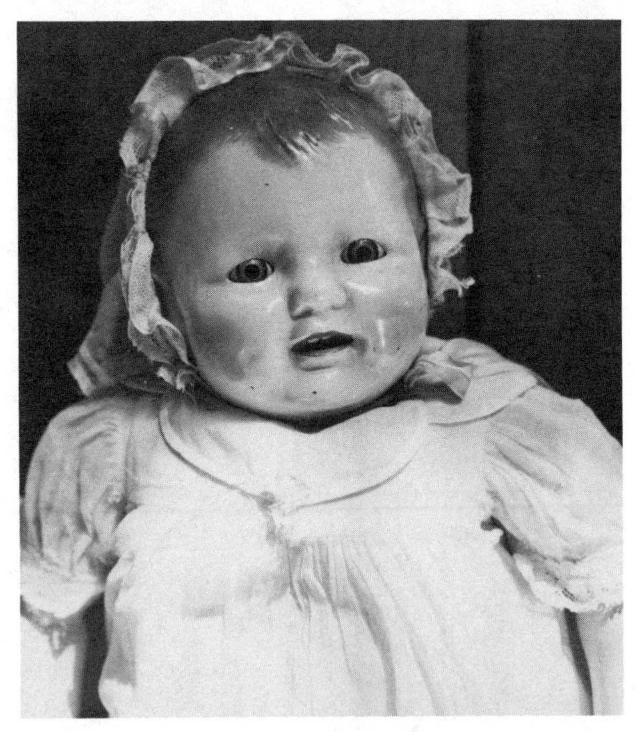

Large metal head baby. *Louise Ceglia.*

Metal Heads

Maker: Buschow & Beck, Germany (Minerva); Karl Standfuss, Germany (Juno); Alfred Heller, Germany (Diana)
Date: Ca. 1888—on
Material: Metal shoulder head, kid or cloth body
Size: Various
Mark:

Marked Metal Head: Metal shoulder head on cloth or kid body, bisque or composition hands; dressed; good condition, not repainted.

With molded hair, painted eyes, 12—14in (31—36cm)	**$ 75—85**
With molded hair, glass eyes, 16—18in (41—46cm)	**100—115**
With wig and glass eyes, 16—18in (41—46cm)	**125—150**

18in (46cm) and 22in (56cm) Minerva tin head dolls with painted eyes and commercial cloth bodies; 17in (43cm) Minerva tin head with wig and glass eyes; 12in (31cm) brass head with glass eyes and Kidolene body. *Joanna Ott Collection.*

Metal, Swiss

Maker: A. Bucherer, Amriswil, Switzerland
Date: 1921
Material: Composition head, hands and feet, metal ball-jointed body
Size: 8in (20cm) average
Mark:

"MADE IN
SWITZERLAND
PATENTS
APPLIED FOR"

Bucherer Doll: Composition character head often with molded hat; metal ball-jointed body; original clothes, often felt; all in good condition.
Comic characters: Mutt, Jeff, Maggie, Jiggs, and others. **$250 up**
Regular People: lady, man, fireman, and others. **125—150**

7—8in (18—20cm) ***Mutt*** and ***Jeff*** Comic Characters. *Howard Foulke Collection.*

Missionary Ragbabies

Maker: Julia Beecher, Elmira, N.Y., U.S.A.
Date: 1893—1910
Material: All-cloth
Size: 16—23in (41—58cm)
Designer: Julia Jones Beecher
Mark: None

Beecher Baby: Handmade stuffed stockinette doll with looped wool hair, painted eyes and mouth, needle-sculpted face; appropriately dressed; all in good condition.
20in (51cm) **$850****

**Not enough price samples to compute a reliable range.

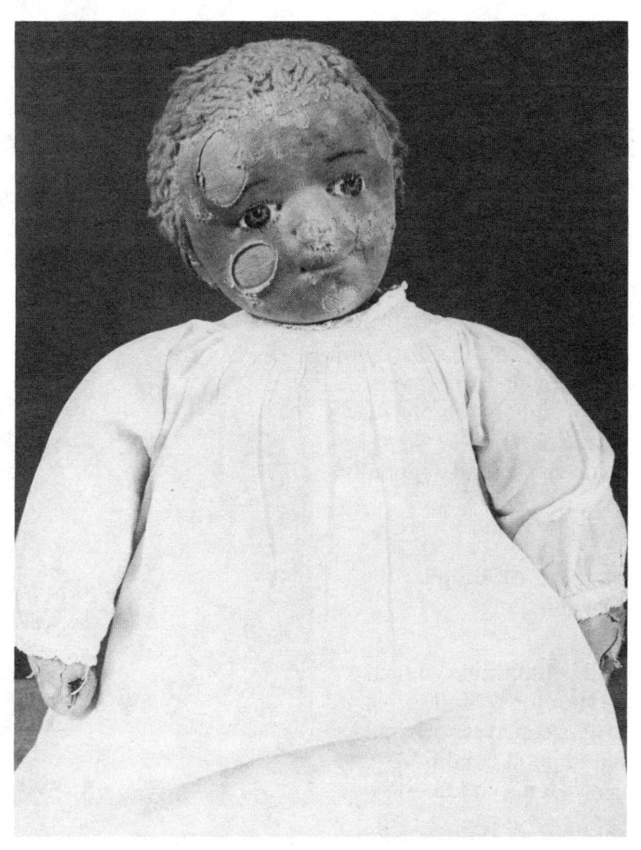

23in (58cm) Beecher ***Missionary Ragbaby***.

Molly-'es

Maker: International Doll Co., Philadelphia, PA., U.S.A.
Date: 1920s—on
Material: All-cloth or all-composition, later hard plastic and vinyl
Size: Various
Clothes Designer: Mollye Goldman*
Mark: Usually a paper tag, dolls unmarked except for vinyl

Babies: All-composition, jointed at neck, shoulders and hips; molded hair or wigs, sleep eyes; beautiful original outfits; all in good condition.
12—15in (31—38cm) **$85—110**

Internationals: All-cloth with mask faces, mohair wigs (sometimes yarn), painted features; variety of costumes, all original clothes; in excellent condition with wrist tag.
13in (33cm) **$55—65**
Mint-in-box **75**

Sabu: All brown composition; very elaborate costume based on the character in *The Thief of Baghdad;* original clothes; all in good condition.
15in (38cm) **$375—400****

**Not enough price samples to compute a reliable range.

Toddlers: All-composition, jointed at neck, shoulders and hips; mohair wig, sleep eyes; original clothes; all in good condition.
14—16in (36—41cm) **$125—150**

*She bought undressed dolls from various manufacturers.

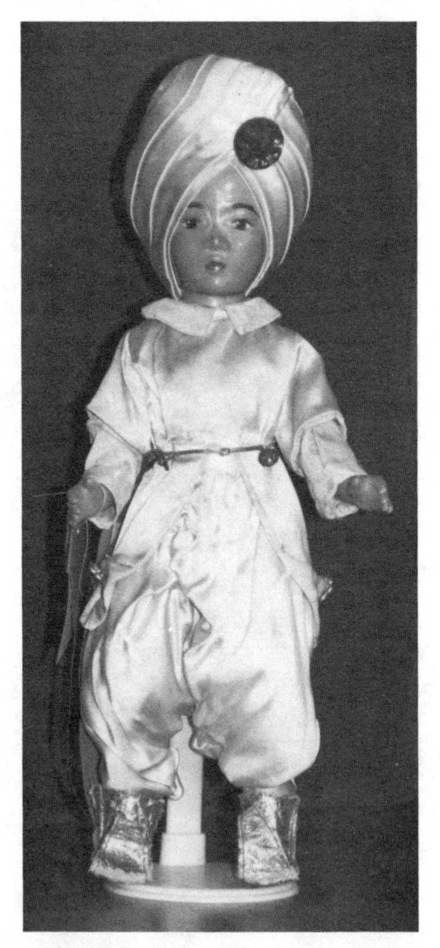

15in (38cm) ***Sabu***, all original. *Paula Ryscik Collection.*

Mon Cherie

Maker: Possibly L. Prieur, Paris, France
Date: Ca. 1900
Material: Bisque head, jointed composition body
Mark:

"LP Paris
Mon Cherie"

Mon Cherie child: Perfect bisque head, good wig, stationary glass eyes, open mouth with molded teeth, pierced ears; jointed composition body; appropriate clothes all in good condition.
24—26in (61—66cm) **$850—950****

**Not enough price samples to compute a reliable range.

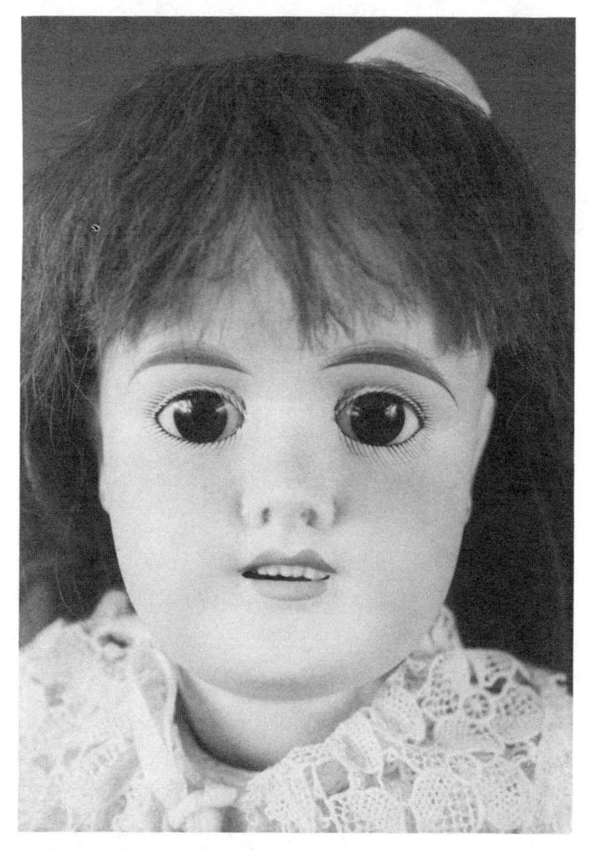

26in (66cm) ***Mon Cherie***. *Dr. Carole Stoessel Zvonar Collection.*

Monica

Maker: Monica Doll Studios, Hollywood, CA., U.S.A.
Date: 1941—1951
Material: All-composition
Size: 15in (38cm), 17in (43cm), 20in (51cm), 22in (56cm), 24in (61cm); later 11in (28cm)
Mark: None

Monica: Composition swivel head, human hair rooted in scalp, painted eyes with eye shadow, closed mouth; composition body with adult-type legs and arms, fingers with painted nails; dressed; in good condition (nearly all have crazing on faces).
$275—325

15in (38cm) ***Monica***, all original with wrist tag. *H&J Foulke, Inc.*

Motschmann

Maker: Ch. Motschmann, Sonneberg, Thüringia, Germany
Date: 1857—1860s
Material: Papier-mâché, composition and cloth
Size: 8in (20cm) to about 28in (71cm)
Mark: On cloth upper leg:

Marked or Unmarked Motschmann-type Baby: Wax-over-composition head with painted hair or wig, glass eyes, closed mouth or open with bamboo teeth; composition lower torso, arms and legs jointed at ankles and wrists, cloth midsection and upper arms and legs called floating joints; dressed; wear acceptable, fair condition.

15—17in (38—43cm) **$375—425**
22—24in (56—61cm) **$525—575**

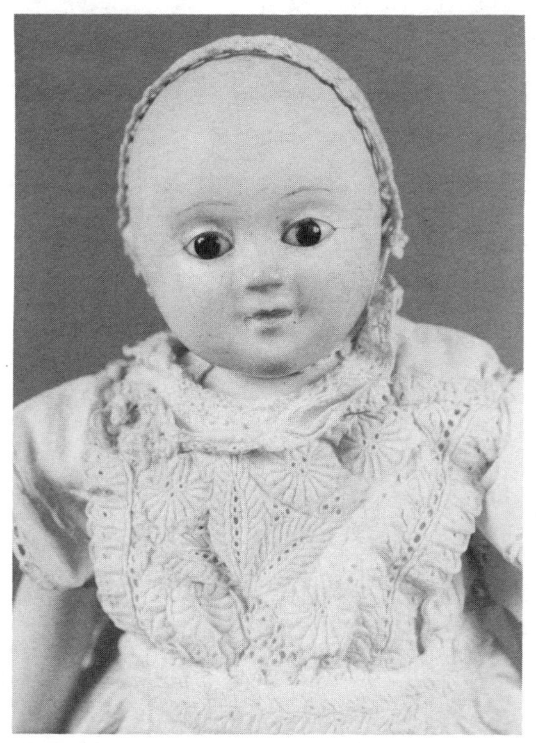

Motschmann baby, all original. *Dr. Carole Stoessel Zvonar Collection.*

Munich Art Dolls

Maker: Marion Kaulitz
Date: 1908—1912
Material: All-composition, fully-jointed bodies
Size: Various
Designer: Paul Vogelsanger, and others
Mark: Sometimes signed on doll's neck

Munich Art Doll: Molded composition character heads, with hand-painted features; fully-jointed composition bodies; dressed; all in good condition.

18—19in (46—48cm)

All original	**$1500**
Appropriate clothes	**1200—1500**

17in (43cm) Munich Art Doll. *Nancy Schwartz Blaisure Collection.*

Nancy Ann Storybook

Maker: Nancy Ann Storybook Dolls Co., South San Francisco, CA., U.S.A.
Date: Mid 1930s
Material: Painted bisque, later plastic
Size: About 5½in (14cm)
Mark: Painted Bisque:

"Story
Book
Doll
U.S.A."

Hard Plastic:

"STORYBOOK
DOLLS
U.S.A.
TRADEMARK
REG."

Also a wrist tag identifying particular model

Marked Storybook Doll: Painted bisque, mohair wig, painted eyes; one-piece body, head and legs, jointed arms; original clothes; excellent condition.

Painted Bisque **$40 up**
Hard Plastic **35 up**
Bent-limb baby:
Painted bisque **50—60**
Hard plastic **40—50**

Hard plastic Nancy Ann Storybook doll, all original. *H&J Foulke, Inc.*

Black hard plastic Nancy Ann Storybook doll, all original. *H&J Foulke, Inc.*

Oriental Dolls

Japanese Traditional Girl Doll: 1850—on. Papier-mâché swivel head on shoulder plate, hips, lower legs and feet (early ones have jointed wrists and ankles); cloth midsection, cloth (floating) upper arms and legs; hair wig, dark glass eyes, pierced ears and nostrils; original or appropriate clothes; all in good condition.

Ca. 1890 12—15in (31—38cm) **$125—150**
Ca. 1930—1940s 12—15in (31—38cm) **50—75**

Japanese Traditional Baby Doll: Ca. 1920—on. Papier-mâché with bent arms and legs; hair wig, dark glass eyes; original or appropriate clothes; all in good condition.

7—8in (18—20cm) **$40—45**
11—12in (28—31cm) **75—85**

Japanese Baby with Bisque Head: Ca. 1926—on. White bisque head, sleep eyes, closed mouth; five-piece papier-mâché body; original clothes; excellent condition.

6—7in (15—18cm) **$45—55**

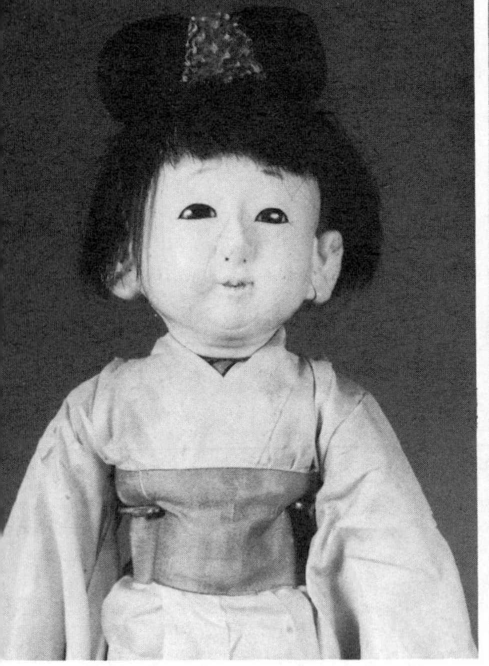

18in (46cm) traditional Japanese girl doll, ca. 1900. *H&J Foulke, Inc.*

9½in (24cm) traditional Japanese baby, ca. 1920, all original. *H&J Foulke, Inc.*

Oriental Dolls continued

Oriental Bisque Dolls: Ca. 1900-on. Made by German firms such as Simon & Halbig, Armand Marseille, J. D. Kestner, and others. Bisque head tinted yellow; matching ball-jointed or baby body.

S&H 1329 girl,
14—16in (36—41cm) **$1800—2000**

A.M. 353 baby,
11—12in (28—31cm) **900—1100**

J.D.K. 243 baby,
14in (36cm) **2800—3000**

S&H 1099, 1129, and 1199 girl,
14—16in (36—41cm) **2200—2400**

#220,
15—17in (38—43cm) **2500—3000**

A.M. girl, 9in (23cm) **600—650**

#164, 17in (43cm) **1900—2100**

JDK molded hair baby,
17in (43cm) **3200****

**Not enough price samples to compute a reliable range.

Baby Butterfly: 1911—1913. Made by E. I. Horsman. Composition head and hands, cloth body; painted black hair, painted features.

13in (33cm) **$150****

**Not enough price samples to compute a reliable range.

Oriental Composition Dolls: Ca. 1930. Unknown maker. All-composition baby, jointed at shoulders and hips; painted facial features; sometimes with black yarn hair, original costume of colorful taffeta with braid trim; feet painted black or white for shoes.

10—12in (25—31cm) **$75—85**

7in (18cm) Japanese baby with white bisque head. *H&J Foulke, Inc.*

14in (36cm) JDK 243 Oriental baby, original shirt and label. *Mary Lou Rubright Collection.*

17in (43cm) S & H 1199 Oriental girl. *Mary Lou Rubright Collection.*

Oriental Dolls continued

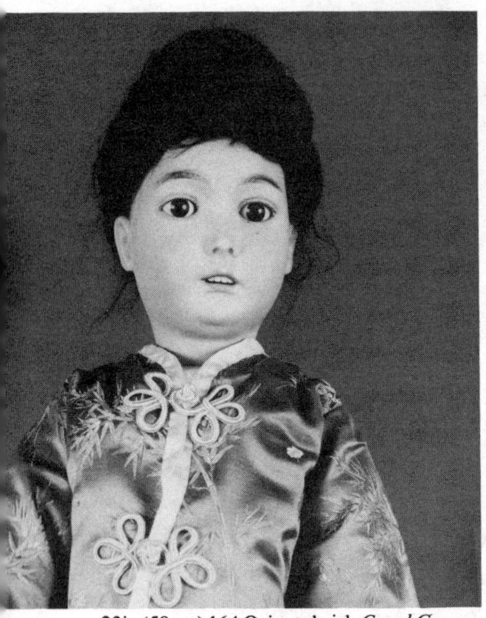

23in (58cm) 164 Oriental girl. *Carol Green Collection.*

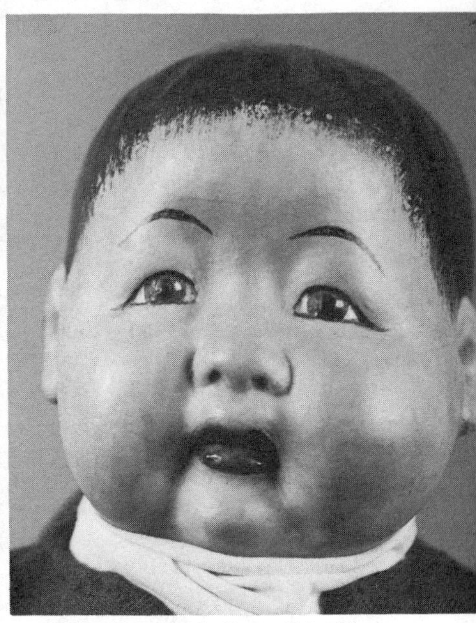

13in (33cm) ***Baby Butterfly*** by Horsman.

10in (25cm) composition Oriental baby, all original. *H&J Foulke, Inc.*

Orsini

Maker: Unknown, but all-bisque dolls were possibly made by J. D. Kestner
Date: 1916—on
Material: Bisque head with cloth and/or composition body or all-bisque
Size: Various
Designer: Jeanne Orsini
Mark: Character heads: Copr. By J. I. Orsini Germany

All-bisque:
J10 © 1920
J10 © 1919

All-Bisque Character: Jointed at shoulders and hips; wig, sleep eyes, character face; painted shoes and stockings over the knee; paper label on front: "ViVi", "MiMi", "DiDi" and "ZiZi"

MiMi or DiDi: 5in (13cm) **$1150—1250**
7in (18cm) **1400—1500**

Kiddiejoy Character Baby: Bisque head with molded hair, glass eyes, open mouth with tongue, smiling face; cloth body; dressed and in excellent condition.

MARK: "Kiddiejoy J10 © 1926."

14in (36cm) **1000—1250**

Painted Bisque Character Baby: Painted bisque head with molded hair or wig, flirty eyes, eye shadow on top eyelid, painted lower eyelashes, open mouth with two upper teeth and tongue, rosy cheeks, smiling face; composition baby body; appropriate clothes. Mold number 1440 or 1430 with wig, 1429 with molded hair.

14in (36cm) **$1500—1800****

**Not enough price samples to compute a reliable range.

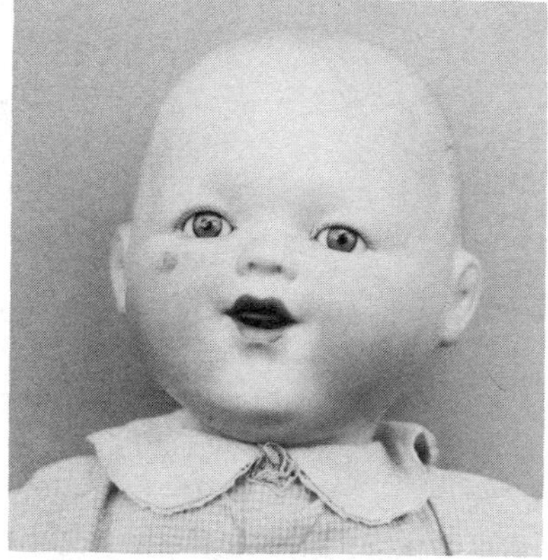

14in (36cm) Orsini ***Kiddiejoy*** baby. *Richard Wright Antiques.*

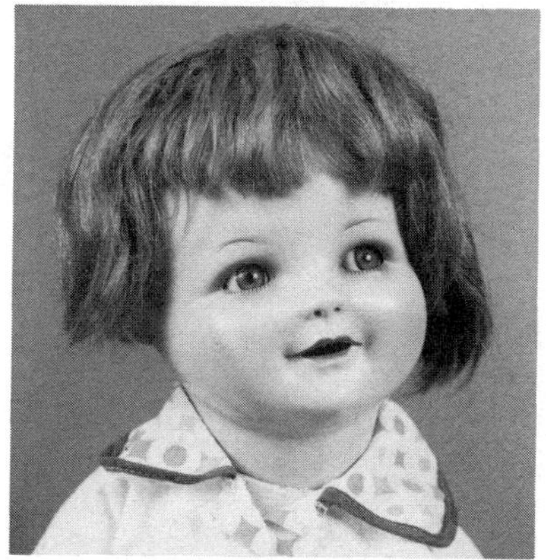

14in (36cm) painted bisque head incised ***1440*** with flirty eyes. *Dr. Carole Stoessel Zvonar Collection.*

P. D.

Maker: Probably Petit & Dumontier, Paris, France
Date: 1878—1890
Material: Bisque head, composition body
Size: Various
Mark: "P. D." with size number

P. D. Bébé: Bisque head with good wig, paperweight eyes, closed mouth, pierced ears; jointed composition body (some have metal hands); appropriate clothes; all in good condition.
18—22in (46—56cm) **$3500—4000****
**Not enough price samples to compute a reliable range.

27in (69cm) P. D. with metal hands. *Betty Harms Collection.*

Painted Bisque

Maker: Various German firms
Date: Ca. 1930
Material: Layer of flesh-colored paint over bisque not fired in, all painted bisque or painted bisque head and composition or cloth body.

Painted Bisque Tinies: All-bisque jointed at shoulders and hips; molded hair, painted features; molded and painted shoes and socks; dressed or undressed.

Child, 4in (10cm) **$25—30**
6in (15cm) **45**
Baby, 4in (10cm) **30—35**

Painted Bisque Character Baby or Toddler: Smiling character face with wig, sleep eyes, open mouth with teeth; composition body; dressed; all in good condition.

Toddler, 16in (41cm) **$200—250**

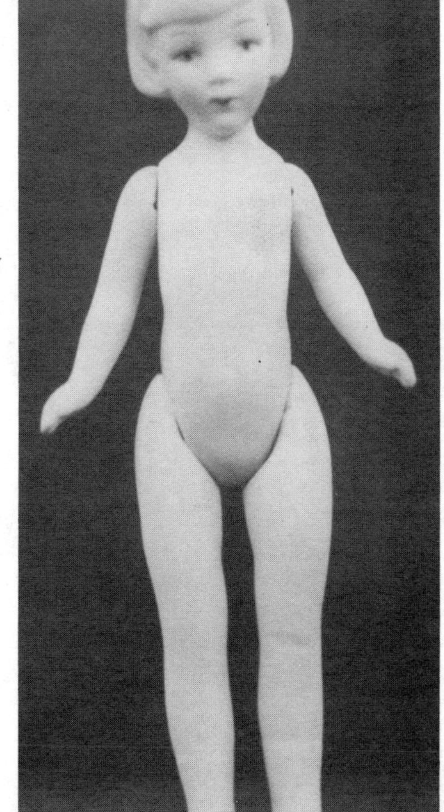

7in (18cm) painted bisque girl. *H&J Foulke, Inc.*

Papier-mâché
(French-Type)

Maker: Unknown
Date: Ca. 1825—1860
Material: Papier-mâché shoulder head, pink kid body
Size: Various
Mark: None

French-type Papier-mâché: Shoulder head with painted black pate, brush marks around face, nailed on wig (often missing), set-in glass eyes, open mouth with bamboo teeth, pierced nose; pink kid body with stiff arms and legs; appropriate old clothes; all in good condition, showing some wear.
18—22in (46—56cm) **$900—1100**

17in (43cm) French-type papier-mâché, kid body.

15in (38cm) French-type papier-mâché with pink kid body, human hair wig.

18in (46cm) French-type papier-mâché lady with bamboo teeth, glass eyes and real hair.

Papier-mâché
(German)

Maker: Various firms
Date: Ca. 1820s—on
Material: Papier-mâché shoulder head, cloth body, sometimes leather arms or kid body with wood limbs
Size: Various
Mark: Usually unmarked; some marked

A.W.
Ser:a/3

Papier-mâché Shoulder Head: Ca. 1820s to 1850s. Unretouched shoulder head, molded hair, painted eyes; cloth body; original or appropriate old clothing; entire doll in good condition.

23—25in (58—64cm) **$750—850**

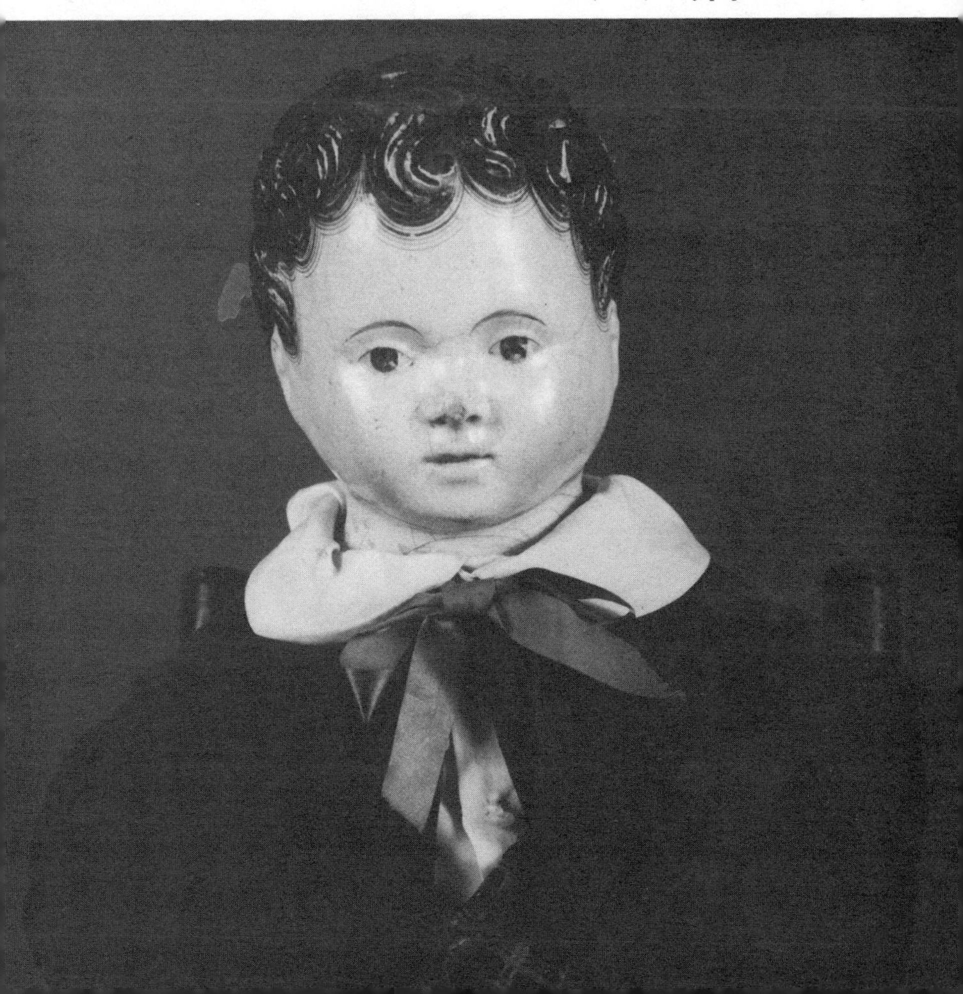

32in (81cm) early papier-mâché boy.

Papier-Mâché (German) continued

German Papier-mâché: Ca. 1880—1910. Shoulder head with molded and painted black or blonde hair, painted eyes, closed mouth; cloth body sometimes with leather arms; old or appropriate clothes; all in good condition, showing some wear.

14—16in (36—41cm)	**$175—200**
22—24in (56—61cm)	**225—275**
With wig and glass eyes, 22—24in (56—61cm)	**300—350**

German Papier-mâché: Ca. 1920—on. Papier-mâché head and hands or arms, hard stuffed cloth body; good hair wig, painted eyes, original child clothes; all in good condition.

8in (20cm)	**$50—60**
12in (31cm)	**80—90**

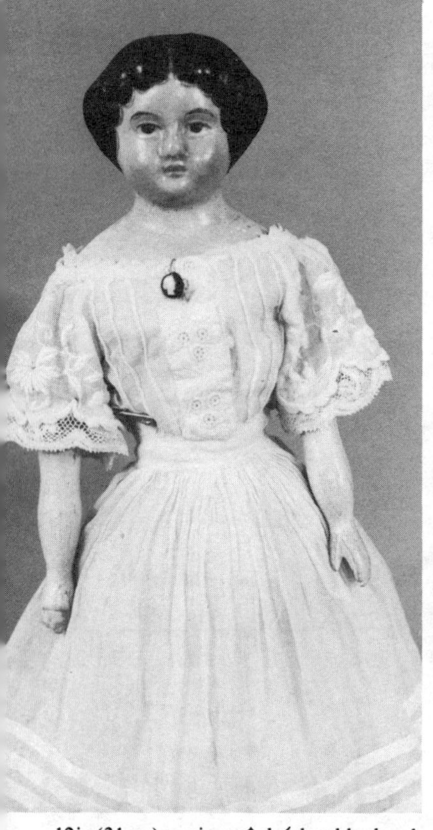

12in (31cm) papier-mâché shoulder head, cloth body, wooden limbs, all original. *H&J Foulke, Inc.*

8in (20cm) papier-mâché pair, all original.

Papier-mâché

(Molded hair, so-called milliners' models)

Maker: Unknown German firms
Date: Ca. 1820s into the 1860s
Material: Papier-mâché shoulder heads, stiff slender kid bodies, wooden extremities
Size: Various
Mark: None

Molded Hair Papier-mâché: Unretouched shoulder head, various molded hairdos, eyes blue, black or brown, painted features; original kid body, wooden arms and legs; original or very old handmade clothing; entire doll in fair condition.

6in (15cm)	**$275—300***
9—10in (23—25cm)	**325—350***
14—15in (36—38cm)	**450***
22—23in (56—58cm)	**750***
Fully wigged model or partially molded with real curls framing face, 10—12in (25—31cm)	**900—1000****
Rare molded hat and snood, 17½in (45cm)	**1500—1650****
Males, 18—22in (46—56cm)	**850—950****

*Depending upon condition and rarity of hairdo.
**Not enough price samples to compute a reliable range.

13in (33cm) lady with fancy hairdo, all original.

9in (23cm) lady with short molded hair. *Joanna Ott Collection.*

Papier-Mâché (Molded Hair) continued

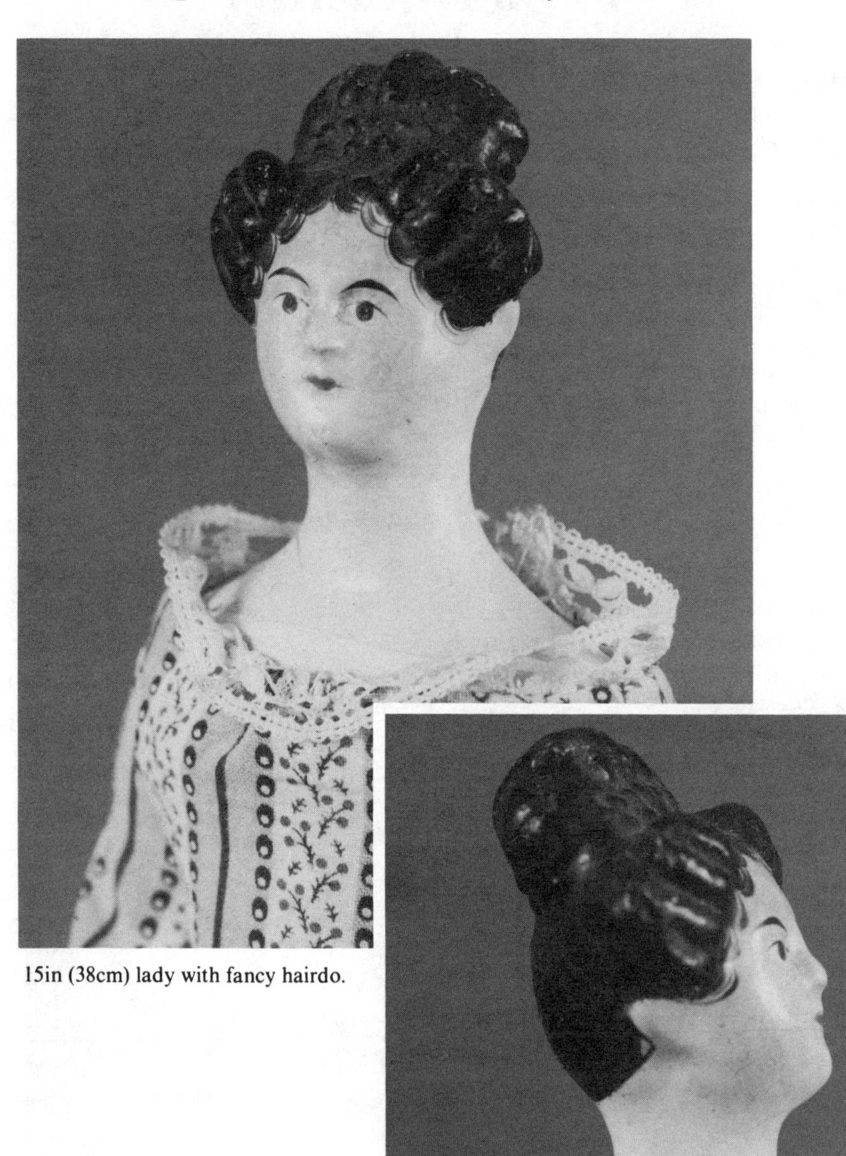

15in (38cm) lady with fancy hairdo.

Side view of 15in (38cm) lady with fancy hairdo.

Parian-Type
(Untinted Bisque)

Maker: Various German firms
Date: Ca. 1860s through 1870s
Material: Untinted bisque shoulder head, cloth or kid body, leather, wood, china or combination extremities
Size: Various
Mark: None

Unmarked Parian: Pale or untinted shoulder head, sometimes with molded blouse, beautifully molded hairdo, (may have ribbons, beads, comb or other decoration), painted eyes, closed mouth; cloth body; lovely clothes; entire doll in fine condition.

16—17in (41—43cm)	**$400—450**
22—23in (56—58cm)	**600—650**
Very fancy hairdo and/or elaborately decorated blouse	**700 up**
Very fancy with glass eyes	**1250 up**
Common, plain style, 15—17in (38—43cm)	**250—300**

10½in (25cm) lady with pink lustre snood.

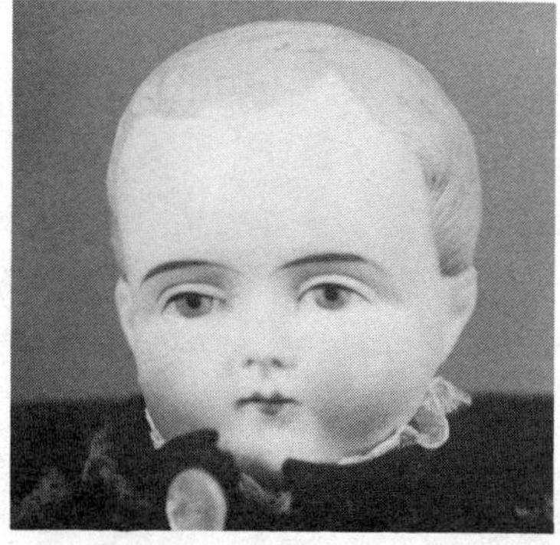

18in (46cm) boy, turned shoulder head. *Joanna Ott Collection.*

18in (46cm) lady with molded and applied flowers in her hair. *H&J Foulke, Inc.*

Parian-Type continued

5in (13cm) parian head, unusual hairdo with fancy braids and curls.

Paris Bébé

Maker: Danel & Cie., Paris, France, (later possibly Jumeau)
Date: 1889—1895
Material: Bisque socket head, jointed composition body
Size: Various
Mark: On head: TÊTE DÉPOSÉ
PARIS BEBE
On body:
PARIS-BEBE
Bréveté

Marked Paris Bébé: Bisque socket head, good wig, paperweight eyes, closed mouth; pierced ears; composition jointed body; dressed; all in good condition.

24—27in (61—69cm) **$3600—4000**

18in (46cm) rare black ***Paris Bébé***. *Zona Wickham Collection.*

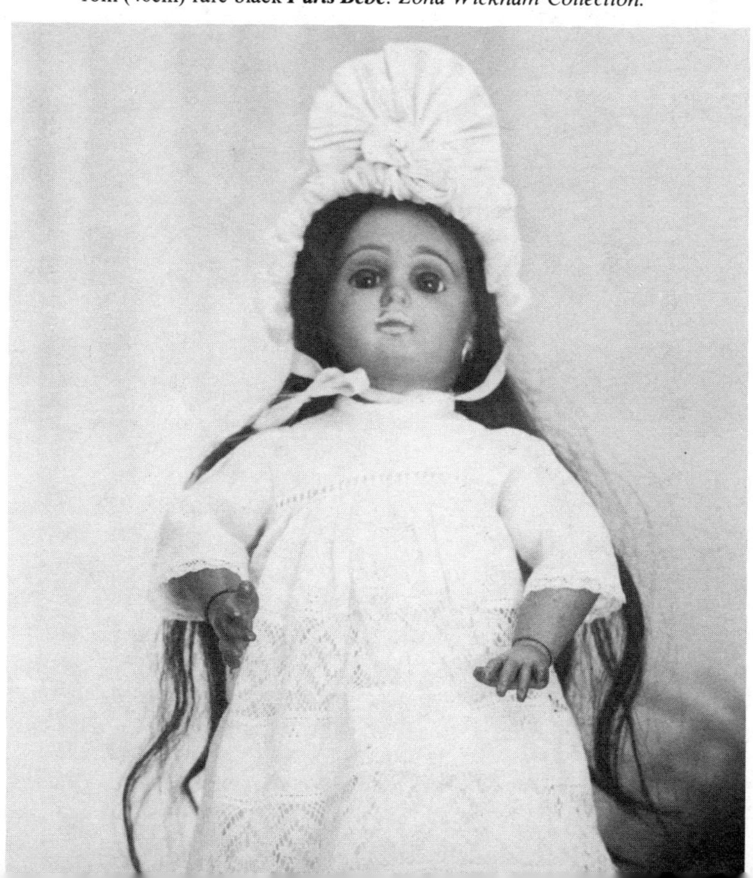

Parsons-Jackson

Maker: Parsons-Jackson Co. of Cleveland, OH., U.S.A.
Date: 1910—1919
Material: Biskoline (similar to celluloid), jointed with steel springs
Size: Various
Marks: Embossed figure of small stork on back of head and/or on back or shoulders sometimes with "TRADEMARK
PARSONS—JACKSON. CO.
CLEVELAND, OHIO"
On head: On body: TRADEMARK

Marked Parsons-Jackson Baby: Socket head and bent-limb baby body of Biskoline; molded-painted hair, painted eyes; spring joint construction; nicely dressed; all in good condition.

12in (31cm) **$125—150**

Toddler with molded shoes & socks, 14in (36cm) **200**

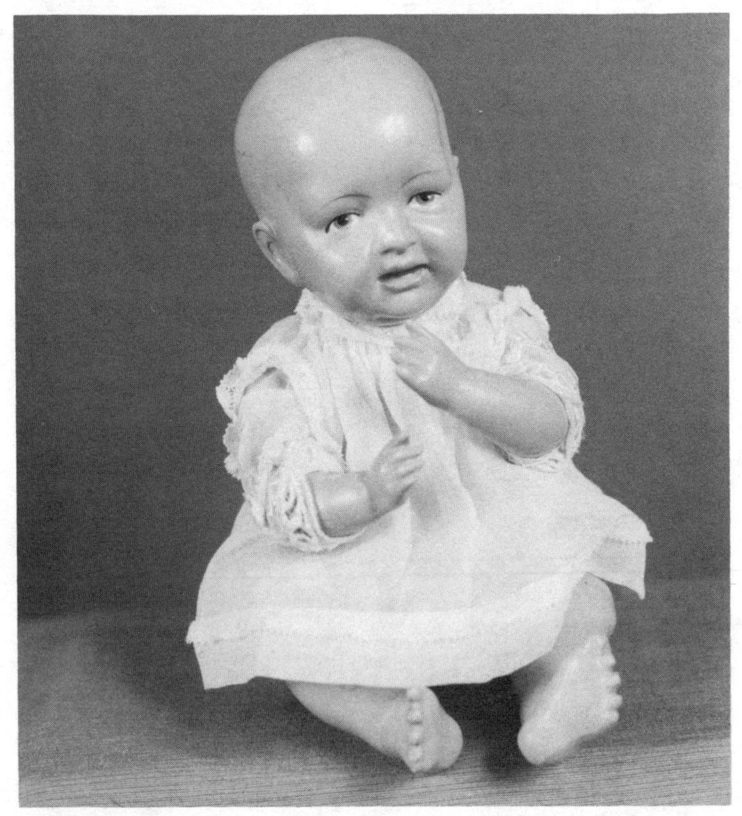

11in (28cm) Parsons-Jackson baby. *Betty Harms Collection.*

Peg-Wooden or Dutch Dolls

Maker: Craftsmen of the Grödner Tal, Austria, and Sonneberg, Thüringia, Germany
Date: Late 18th—20th century
Material: All-wood, ball-jointed (larger ones) or pegged
Size: Various
Mark: None

Early to Mid 19th Century: Delicately carved head, varnished, carved and painted hair and features, sometimes with a yellow tuck comb in hair, painted spit curls, sometimes earrings; mortise and tenon peg joints; old clothes; all in good condition.

3—4in (8—10cm)	**$300—400**
7—8in (18—20cm)	**600—700**
10—12in (25—31cm)	**800—900**

Late 19th Century: Wooden head with painted hair, carving not so elaborate as previously, sometimes earrings, spit curls; dressed; all in good condition.

8—10in (20—25cm)	**150—175**
12in (31cm)	**175—200**
Early 20th century:	**50—75**

10in (25cm) peg-wooden doll with carved side curls, all original. *H&J Foulke, Inc.*

Dora Petzold

Maker: Dora Petzold, Berlin, Germany
Date: 1920—on
Material: Composition or cloth head, cloth body
Size: Various
Mark: "DORA PETZOLD
Registered
Trade Mark
Doll
Germany"

Dora Petzold Doll: Molded composition or cloth head with closed mouth, hair wig, pensive character face, painted features; cloth body sometimes with especially long arms and legs; dressed; all in good condition. Many unmarked.

20—24in (51—61cm) **$700—800**

28in (71cm) Dora Petzold doll. *H&J Foulke, Inc.*

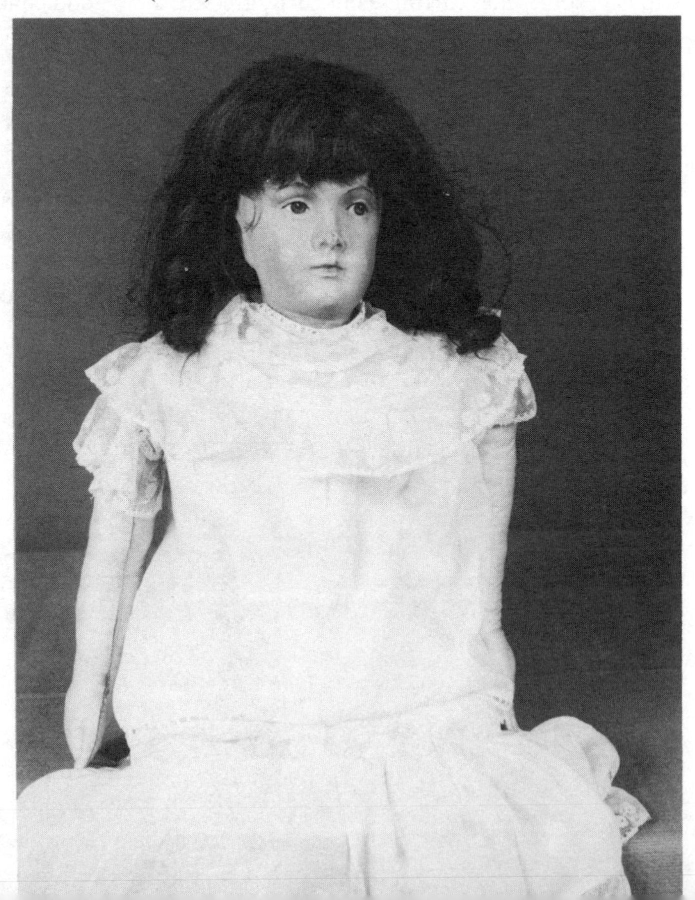

Phénix Bébé

Maker: Henri Alexandre, Paris, France; Torrel; Jules Steiner; Jules Mettais
Date: 1889—1900
Material: Bisque head, jointed composition body (sometimes one-piece arms and legs)
Size: Various
Designer: Henri Alexandre
Mark:

PHÉNIX
★ 95

Marked Bébé Phénix: 1889—1900. Perfect bisque head, French jointed body, sometimes with one-piece arms and legs; lovely old wig, bulbous set eyes, closed mouth, pierced ears; well dressed; all in good condition.

14—16in (36—41cm)	**$2400—2500**
22—24in (56—61cm)	**3000—3100**
Open mouth, 20—22in (51—56cm)	**2000—2100**

21in (53cm) ***Phénix Bébé*** incised "Modele ★ 92." *Betty Harms Collection.*

Philadelphia Baby

Maker: J. B. Sheppard & Co., Philadelphia, PA., U.S.A.
Date: Ca. 1900
Material: All-cloth
Size: 18—22in (46—56cm)
Mark: None

Philadelphia Baby: All-cloth with treated shoulder-type head, lower arms and legs; painted hair, well-molded facial features, ears; stocking body; fair condition only, showing much wear.
21in (53cm) **$1000—1200**

20in (51cm) ***Philadelphia Baby.***

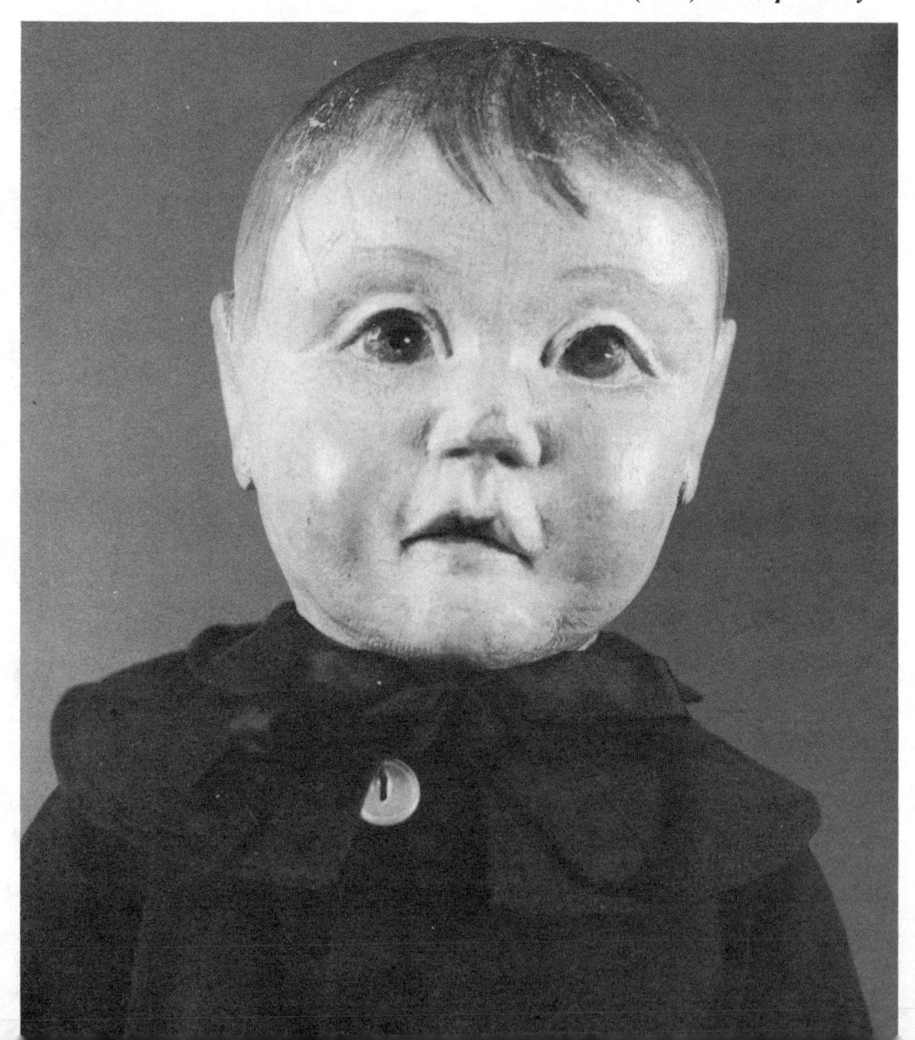

Piano Baby

Maker: Gebrüder Heubach, Kestner and other makers
Date: 1880—on
Material: All-bisque
Size: Usually under 12in (31cm), some larger
Mark: Many unsigned; some with maker's particular mark

Piano Baby: All-bisque immobile with molded clothes and painted features; made in various sitting and lying positions. Heubach quality.

3—4in (8—10cm)	**$110—135**
7—8in (18—20cm)	**275—325**
11—12in (28—31cm)	**450—500**
4in (10cm) wigged	**200—250**

*More depending upon uniqueness.

11½in (29cm) Heubach piano baby. *Betty Harms Collection.*

5in (13cm) kneeling child with real hair wig. *H&J Foulke, Inc.*

Pincushion Dolls*

Maker: Various German firms
Date: 1900—on
Material: China
Size: Up to about 7in (18cm)
Mark: "Germany" and numbers

Pincushions: China half figures with molded hair and painted features; usually with molded clothes, hats, lovely modeling and painting.

Ordinary, arms close	**$25**
Arms extending but hands coming back to figure	**35 up**
Hands extended	**75 up**
Bisque child, glass eyes, 2in (5cm)	**165**

*Also called half-dolls.

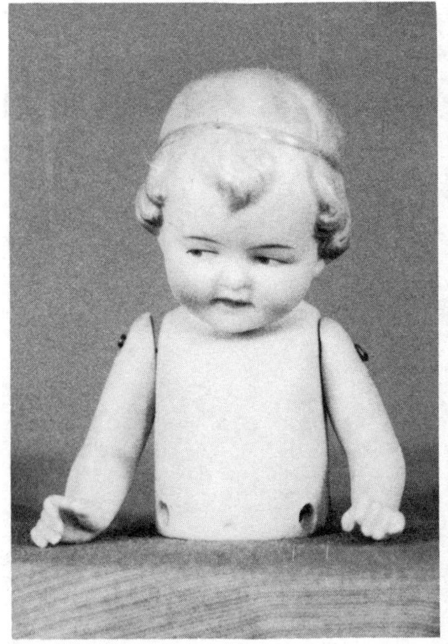

Child pincushion with jointed arms, possibly by Goebel. *H&J Foulke, Inc.*

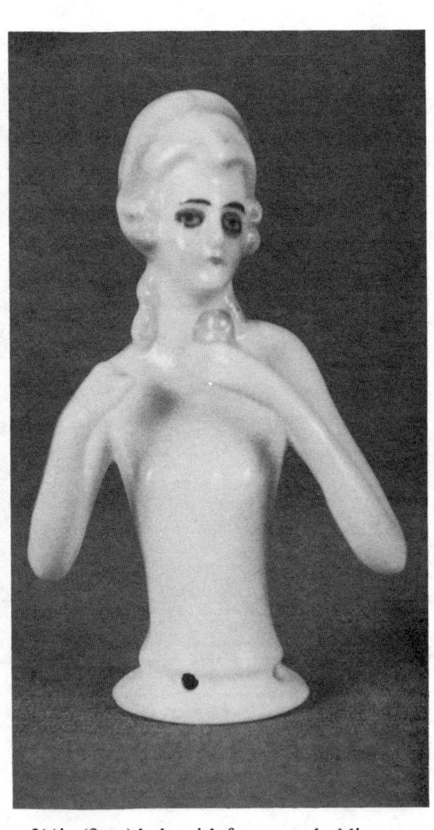

3½in (9cm) lady with free arms holding a rose. *H&J Foulke, Inc.*

2¼in (6cm) lady by Dressel & Kister. *H&J Foulke, Inc.*

4in (10cm) lady incised ***1523 Germany.*** *H&J Foulke, Inc.*

Lady with bald head, incised ***Sp 1120,*** replaced wig. *H&J Foulke, Inc.*

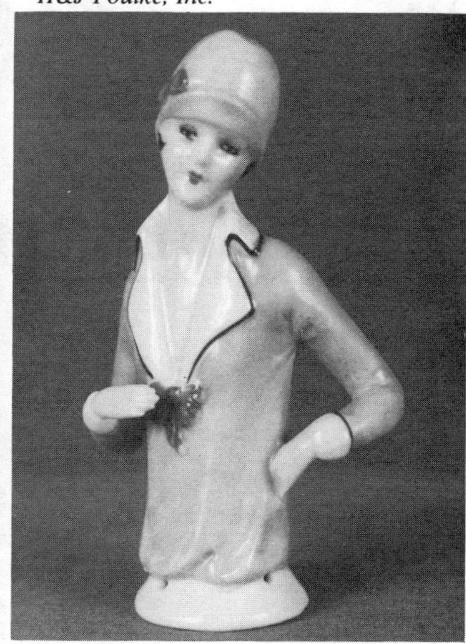

4½in (12cm) flapper lady. *H&J Foulke, Inc.*

Poir

Maker: Eugenie Poir, Paris, France; also Gre-Poir (French doll makers)
Date: 1920s
Material: All-cloth, felt face and limbs or all-felt
Size: Various
Mark: None on doll; paper label on clothes

Poir Child: All-fabric movable arms and legs; mohair wig; painted facial features; original clothes, all in good condition.
16—19in (41—48cm) **$250—300**

Close-up showing the cardboard tag on the 17in (43cm) Eugenie Poir ***Bimba***.

17in (43cm) Eugenie Poir ***Bimba,*** all original with cardboard tag. *H&J Foulke, Inc.*

Pre-Greiner
(So-called)

Maker: Unknown and various
Date: First half of 1880s
Material: Papier-mâché shoulder head, stuffed cloth body, mostly homemade, wood, leather or cloth extremities
Size: Various
Mark: None

Unmarked Pre-Greiner: Papier-mâché shoulder head; molded and painted black hair, pupil-less black glass eyes; cloth stuffed body, leather extremities; dressed in good old or original clothes; all in good condition.

18—20in (46—51cm)	**$ 650—750**
26—29in (66—74cm)	**1100—1300**
Painted eyes, 23—25in (58—64cm)	**750—850**

35in (89cm) so-called Pre-Greiner doll with glass eyes.

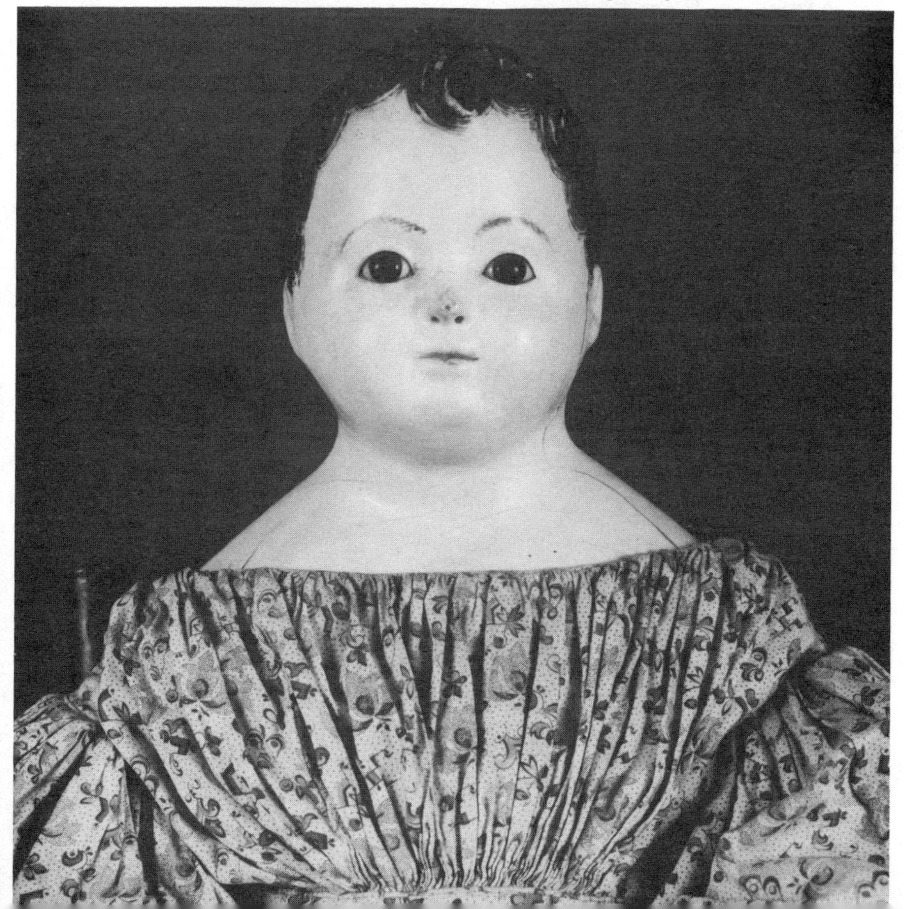

Presbyterian Rag Doll

Maker: Various Presbyterian Ladies' Circles
Date: Ca. 1900—on
Material: All-cloth
Size: About 17in (43cm)
Mark: None

Early Presbyterian Rag Doll: All-cloth with flat hand-painted features and hair; appropriate clothes; all in fair condition showing wear.
17in (43cm) **$600—800****
**Not enough price samples to compute a reliable range.

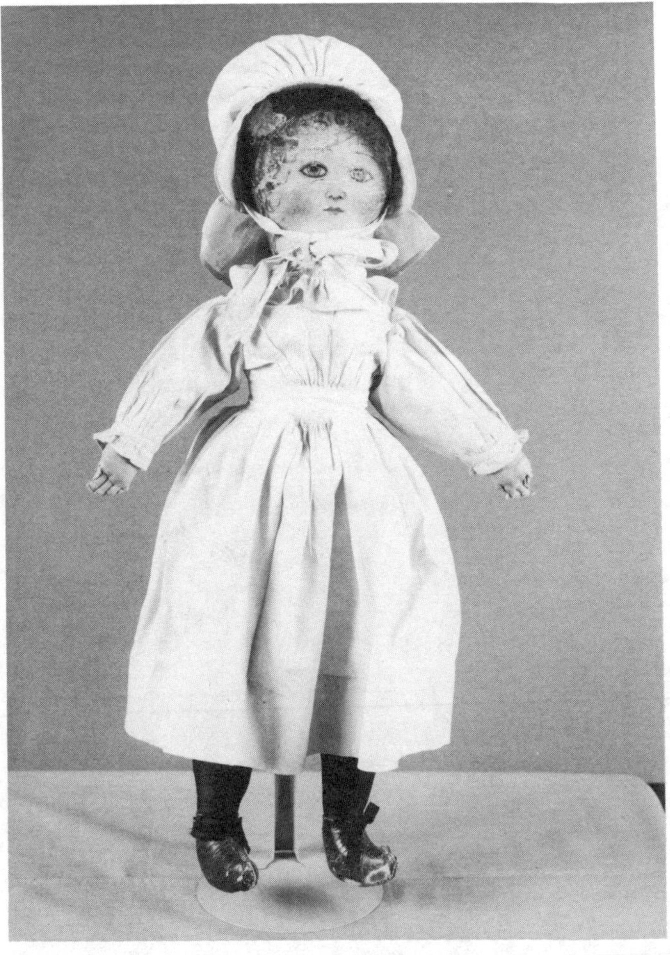

17in (43cm) Presbyterian rag doll, all original. *Pearl D. Morley Collection.*

Queen Anne-Type

Maker: English Craftsmen
Date: Late 17th—mid 19th century
Material: All-wood or wooden head and torso with leather or cloth limbs
Size: Various
Mark: None

18th Century: Carved wooden face, flax or hair wig, pupil-less glass eyes (sometimes painted), dotted eyebrows and eyelashes; jointed wooden body; old clothes, all in good condition.
14—15in (36—38cm) **$5000 up**
18—20in (46—51cm) **6000—1000 up**
Late 18th Century: Wooden head, gessoed, dotted eyelashes and eyebrows, glass eyes (later sometimes blue); pointed torso; old clothes; all in good condition.
15—16in (38—41cm) **3300—3500**
20in (51cm) **4000—4200**

19in (48cm) Queen Anne-type doll with one-piece rolled cloth arms, glass eyes.

8½in (22cm) Queen Anne-type doll with painted eyes.

Rabery & Delphieu

Maker: Rabery & Delphieu of Paris, France
Date: 1856 (founded)—1899—then with S. F. B. J.
Material: Bisque head, composition body
Size: Various
Mark: "R. D." (from 1890)
On back of head: R 5/0 D
Body mark: BÉBÉ RABERY S^{c}
(Please note last two lines illegible)

Marked R. D. Bébé: Ca. 1880s. Bisque head, lovely wig, paperweight eyes, closed mouth; jointed composition body; beautifully dressed; entire doll in nice condition.

20—21in (51—53cm) **$2500—2600***
28in (71cm) **3000—3200***
Open mouth,
18—20in (46—51cm) **1600—1700***

*Allow more for a lovely face.

19in (48cm) R. D. bébé.

Raggedy Ann and Andy

Maker: Various
Date: 1915 to present
Material: All-cloth
Size: 4½—39in (12—99cm)
Creator: Johnny B. Gruelle
Mark: As indicated below

Early Raggedy Ann and Andy: All-cloth with movable arms and legs; brown yarn hair, button eyes, painted features; legs or striped fabric for hose and black for shoes; original clothes; all in fair condition.
MARK: "PATENTED SEPT. 7, 1915"
(black stamp on front torso)
16in (41cm) **$300—325**

Molly-'es Raggedy Ann and Andy: 1935—1938, manufactured by Molly-'es Doll Outfitters. Same as above, but with red hair and printed features; original clothes; all in good condition.
MARK:
"Raggedy Ann and Raggedy Andy Dolls
Manufactured by Molly'es Doll Outfitters"
(printed writing in black on front torso)
16in (41cm) **$100—125**

Georgene Raggedy Ann and Andy: 1938-1963, manufactured by Georgene Novelties. Same as above, but with red hair and printed features; original clothes; all in good condition.
MARK: Cloth label sewn in side seam of body.
15—18in (38—46cm) **$40—50**

Knickerbocker Toy Co. Raggedy Ann and Andy: 1963 to 1982.
12in (31cm) **$10—12**
36in (91cm) **50—75**

Applause Raggedy Ann and Andy, embroidered features. Available in toy stores.

Raleigh

Maker: Jessie McCutcheon Raleigh, Chicago, IL., U.S.A.
Date: 1916—1920
Material: All-composition or composition heads and cloth bodies
Size: Various
Designer: Jessie McCutcheon Raleigh
Mark: None

Raleigh Doll: Composition head, molded hair or wig, sleep or painted eyes; composition or cloth body; appropriate clothes; all in good condition.
13in (33cm) **$240—265**
18in (46cm) **325—375**

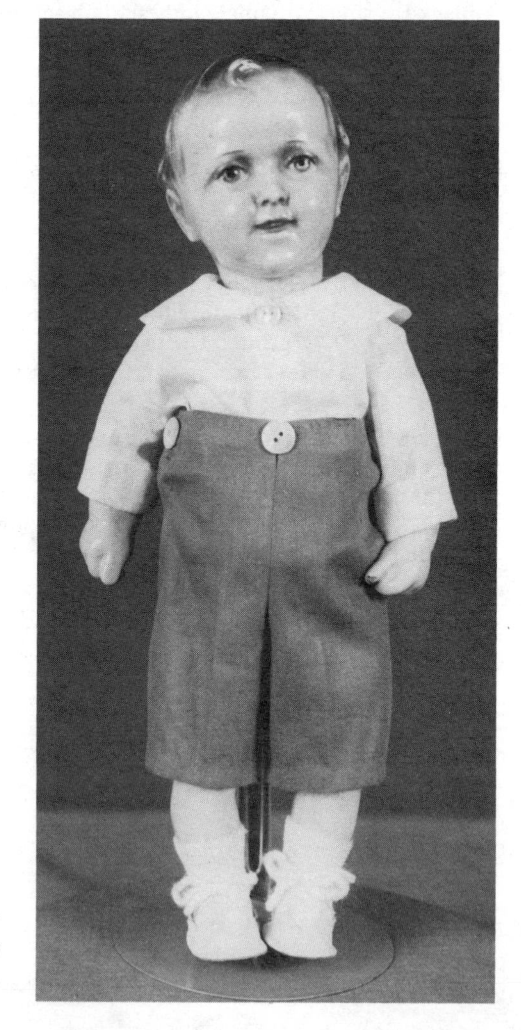

Raleigh ***Sonnie***, redressed in a copy of original outfit. *Joanna Ott Collection.*

Rawhide Dolls

Maker: Darrow Manufacturing Co., Bristol, CT., U.S.A.
Date: 1866—77
Material: Rawhide leather shoulder head; cloth body with leather arms
Size: 14—18in (36—46cm)
Mark: Paper label on front torso:

Darrow Rawhide Doll: Leather shoulder head with molded and painted black hair and painted features; cloth body with leather arms; appropriately dressed; only in fair condition as most have little paint left.
17in (43cm) **$300—400**

16in (41cm) Darrow rawhide doll.

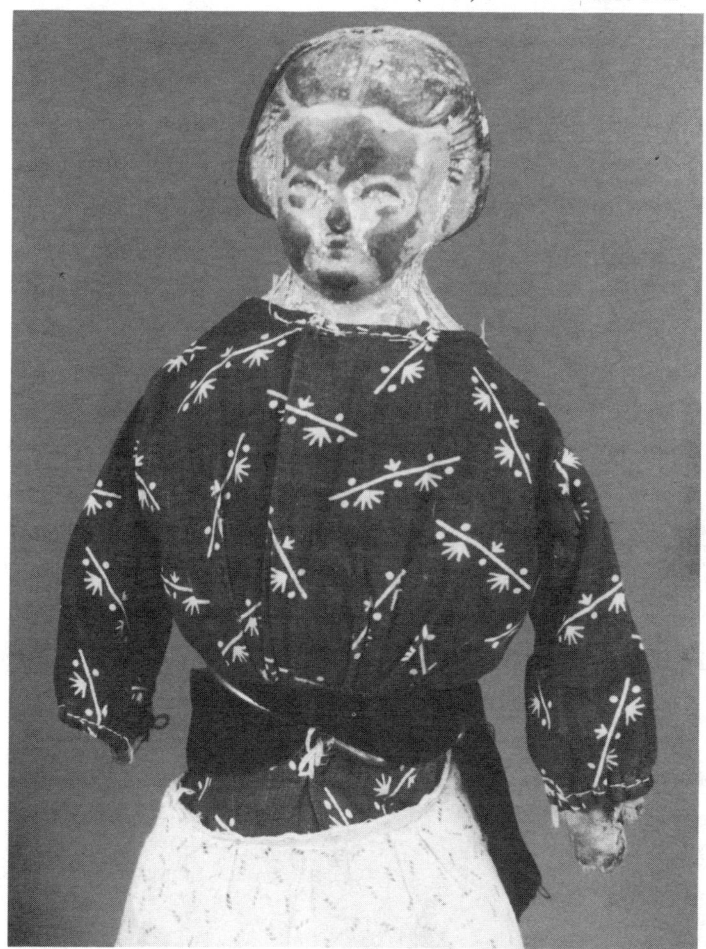

Raynal

Maker: Raynal, France
Date: 1925
Material: Felt and cloth, sometimes celluloid hands
Size: 17—18in (43—46cm)
Mark: "Raynal" on necklace or shoe soles

Raynal Doll: Molded felt mask face with mohair wig, beautifully painted eyes, closed lips, rosy cheeks; stuffed cloth body (may have celluloid hands); original clothes often of felt; all in good condition.
17—18in (43—46cm) **$250—300**

17—18in (43—46cm) Raynal girl with pink cloth body and celluloid hands; "Raynal" on necklace and shoes. *Kathy George Collection. Photograph by Jim George.*

Recknagel

Maker: Th. Recknagel of Alexandrienthal, Thüringia, Germany
Date: 1886—on
Material: Bisque head, composition or wood-jointed body
Size: Various, usually smaller
Mark: "R.A." with numbers, sometimes "Germany"

R. A. Child: Ca. 1890s-World War I. Perfect marked bisque head, jointed composition or wooden body; good wig, set or sleep eyes, open mouth; some dolls with molded painted shoes and socks; all in good condition.

8—10in (20—25cm)	**$125—150**
14in (36cm)	**175—200**

R. A. Character Baby: 1909-World War I. Perfect bisque socket head; composition bent-limb baby or straight-leg curved-arm toddler body; sleep or set eyes; nicely dressed; all in good condition.

9—11in (23—28cm)	**$175—225**
Bonnet Baby with painted eyes, 8—9in (20—23cm)	**450—475**
Pouty with glass eyes, closed mouth, composition body, 7in (18cm)	**200—225**

23in (58cm) child doll by R. A. *Emma Wedmore Collection.*

7in (18cm) R. A. pouty baby. *H&J Foulke, Inc.*

Otto Reinecke

Maker: Otto Reinecke, Porzellanfabrik Moschendorf, Hof-Moschendorf, Bavaria, Germany, (porcelain factory)
Date: 1878—on
Material: Bisque head, bent-limb composition body
Size: Various
Mark: "P M" also PM

and numbers such as "23" and "914," also "Germany."
On back of head: "Trebor"

PM
914.
Germany
1

Marked Reinecke Baby: Ca. 1910. Perfect bisque socket head, good wig, sleep eyes, open mouth; five-piece composition bent-limb baby body; dressed, all in nice condition.

10—12in (25—31cm)	**$275—300**
18—19in (46—48cm)	**425—475**
24—25in (61—64cm)	**575—675**

Marked "Trebor" Child: Bisque socket head, wig, sleep eyes, open mouth; jointed composition body; appropriate clothes; all in good condition.

17—19in (43—48cm) **$375—425****

**Not enough price samples to compute a reliable range.

23in (58cm) P. M. 23 toddler. *Dr. Carole Stoessel Zvonar Collection.*

Revalo

Maker: Gebrüder Ohlhaver, Thüringia, Germany (some heads made by Gebrüder Heubach)
Date: 1918—on
Material: Bisque socket head, ball-jointed composition body
Size: Various
Mark:

Revalo
Germany
3

Character Baby or Toddler: Perfect bisque socket head, good wig, sleep eyes, hair eyelashes, painted lower eyelashes, open mouth; ball-jointed toddler or baby bent-limb body; dressed; all in good condition.
16—18in (41—46cm) Toddler **$650—700**

Character Doll: Bisque head with molded hair, painted eyes, open/closed mouth; composition body; dressed; all in good condition.
Coquette, 10—12in (25—31cm) **$550—650**

Child Doll: Bisque socket head, good wig, sleep eyes, hair eyelashes, painted lower eyelashes, open mouth; ball-jointed composition body; dressed; all in good condition.
17—18in (43—46cm) **$450—475**
20—22in (51—56cm) **525—550**

23in (58cm) Revalo child.

Grace Corry Rockwell

Maker: Unknown
Date: 1920s
Material: Bisque head, cloth and composition body
Size: About 20in (51cm)
Mark:

Copr. by
Grace C. Rockwell
Germany

Grace Corry Child: Composition smiling face, molded hair, sometimes with wig, painted eyes, closed mouth; cloth and composition body; appropriate clothes; all in good condition. Some dolls with tagged Madame Hendren clothing have heads by Grace Corry. See *3rd Blue Book of Dolls & Values*™, page 153.
14in (36cm) **$375—400**

Grace Corry Rockwell Child: Bisque head with molded hair or wig, sleep eyes, closed mouth; cloth and composition body; appropriate clothes; all in good condition.
20in (51cm) **$3200****

**Not enough price samples to compute a reliable range.

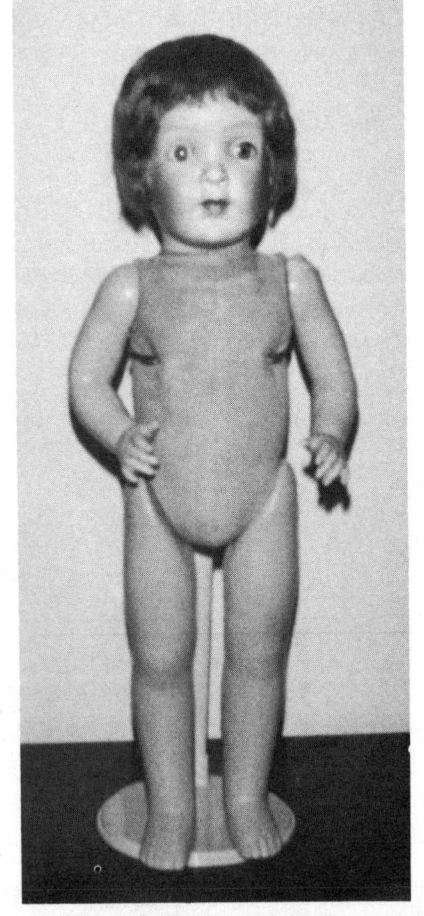

20in (51cm) Grace Corry Rockwell child.
Pearl Church Collection.

Rohmer Fashion

Maker: Mademoiselle Marie Rohmer, Paris, France
Date: 1866—1880
Material: China or bisque shoulder head, jointed kid body
Size: Various
Mark:

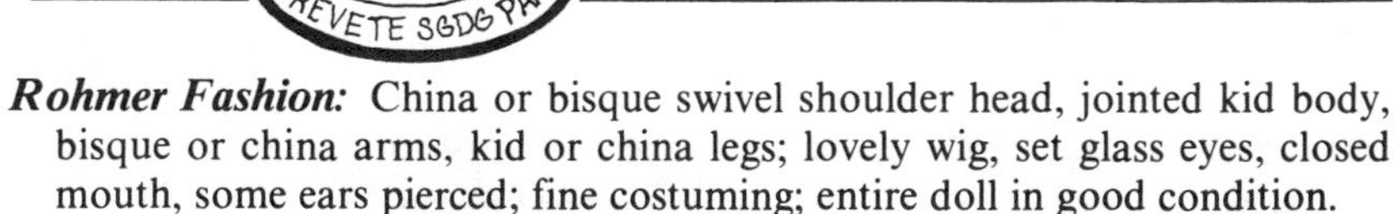

Rohmer Fashion: China or bisque swivel shoulder head, jointed kid body, bisque or china arms, kid or china legs; lovely wig, set glass eyes, closed mouth, some ears pierced; fine costuming; entire doll in good condition.
16—20in (41—51cm) **$4000—4500 up**

17in (43cm) Rohmer fashion lady, bisque shoulder head with painted eyes.

Rollinson Doll

Maker: Utley Doll Co., Holyoke, MA., U.S.A.
Date: 1916—1919
Material: All-cloth
Size: 14—28in (36—71cm)
Designer: Gertrude F. Rollinson
Mark: Stamp in shape of a diamond with a doll in center, around border "Rollinson Doll Holyoke, Mass."

Marked Rollinson doll: All molded cloth with painted head and limbs; painted hair or human hair wig, painted features (sometimes teeth also); dressed; all in good condition.
18in (46cm) **$650****

**Not enough price samples to compute a reliable range.

Large Rollinson doll, missing wig. *H&J Foulke, Inc.*

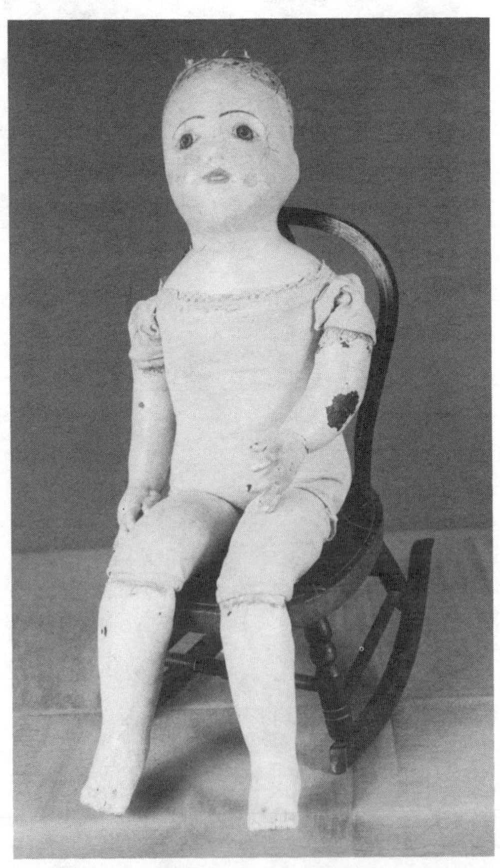

Rubber Head Dolls

Maker: Goodyear Rubber Co., New Haven, CT., U.S.A.; New York Rubber Co., B. F. Lee, India Rubber Comb Co., and others, all of New York, N.Y., U.S.A.
Date: 1851—on
Material: Rubber head, cloth body
Size: Various
Mark: Various depending upon company, but most are not marked

---

Rubber Head Doll: Rubber shoulder head with molded hair and painted features; cloth body, sometimes with leather arms; appropriate clothes; usually found in poor condition as the paint chips easily and the hardened rubber is often misshapen.

Plain hairdo, good condition:

14in (36cm)	**$400—425**
18in (46cm)	**500—550**

Fancy hairdo with molded braid and flowers, excellent condition,

18in (46cm)	**1300****

**Not enough price samples to compute a reliable range.

22in (56cm) I. R. Comb rubber head doll, blonde molded hair with blue hair bow, all original.

S & Co.

Maker: S & Co.
Date: Ca. 1910—on
Material: Bisque socket head, composition baby body
Size: Various
Mark: Stamped in green: GESCHUTZ S & Co GERMANY

Incised Lori: Perfect bisque solid dome head, painted hair, sleep eyes, closed mouth; composition baby body with bent limbs; dressed; all in good condition.

12—15in (31—38cm) **$1200—1500**
19—22in (48—56cm) **2400—2600**

Mold #232
(open-mouth ***Lori***):
13—14in (33—36cm) **900—1000****
21—24in (53—61cm) **1400—1600****

DIP,
(wig, glass eyes, closed mouth):
15—18in (38—46cm) **950—1250**

DV,
(molded hair, glass eyes, open/closed mouth):
13—14in (33—36cm) **900—950**

DI,
(molded hair, intaglio eyes, open/closed mouth):
13—14in (33—36cm) **800—850**

**Not enough price samples to compute a reliable range.

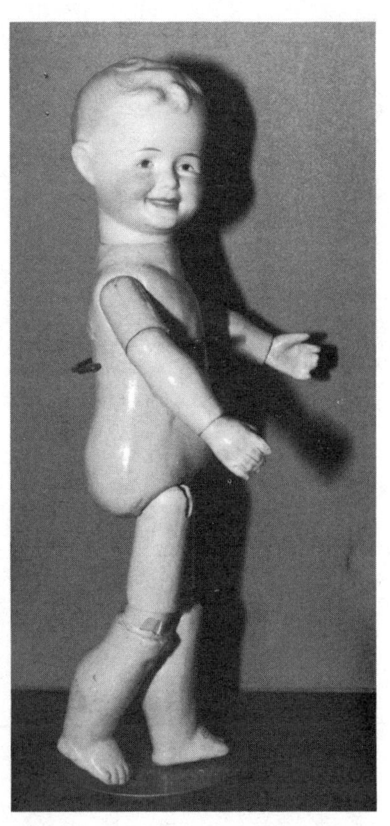

10in (25cm) character boy incised "BO." *Lynn Murray Collection. Photograph courtesy of the owner.*

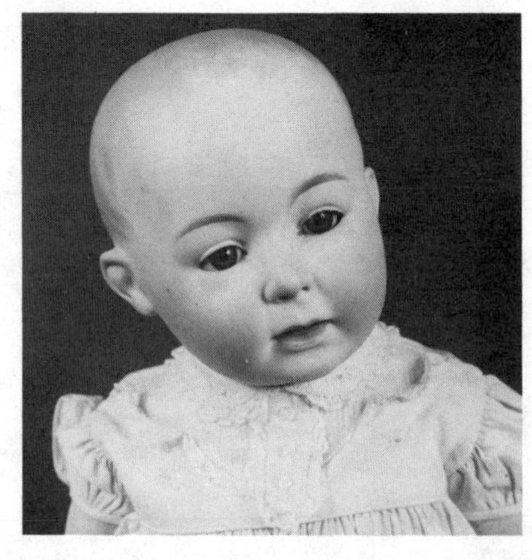

Lori baby.

S & Q

Maker: Possibly Schuetzmeister & Quendt, Boilstadt, Thüringia, Germany
Date: 1893—on
Material: Bisque head, composition body
Size: Various
Distributor: John Bing Co., New York, N.Y., U.S.A.
Mark:

301

Germany

S & Q Character Baby: Ca. 1910. Mold number 201. Perfect bisque head with mohair wig, sleep eyes, open mouth with tongue and teeth, slightly smiling; composition baby body; nicely dressed; all in good condition.

16—17in (41—43cm) **$400—450**
22—24in (56—61cm) **650—700**

S & Q Child Doll: Ca. 1900. Mold number 301. Perfect bisque head with mohair wig, sleep eyes, open mouth with teeth; jointed composition body; nicely dressed.

22—24in (56—61cm) **$350—400**

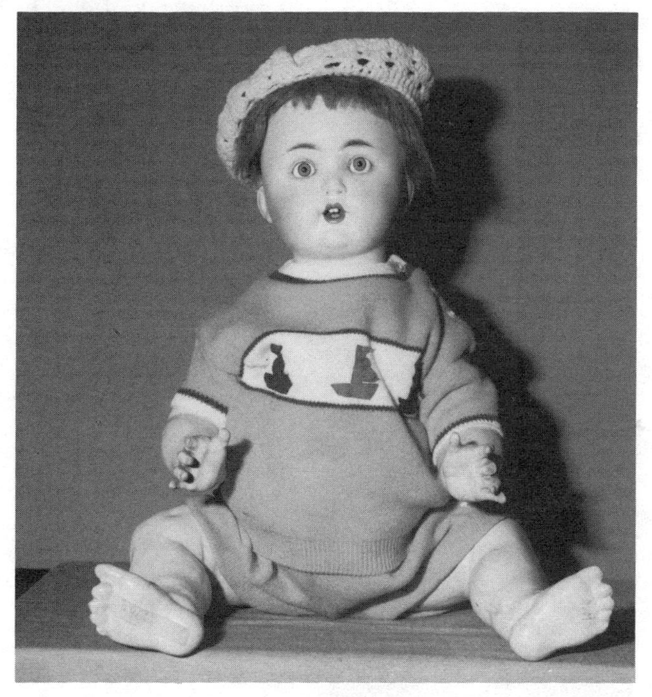

24in (61cm) S & Q 201 character baby. *India Stoessel Collection.*

S.F.B.J.

Maker: Société Française de Fabrication de Bébés & Jouets, Paris, France
Date: 1899—
Material: Bisque head, composition body
Mark:

17in (43cm) S.F.B.J. Jumeau mold child.
H&J Foulke, Inc.

Child Doll: 1899—on. Perfect bisque head, good French wig, sleep eyes, open mouth, pierced ears; jointed composition body; nicely dressed; all in good condition.

Jumeau-type (no mold number):
16—18in (41—46cm) **$900—1100**
21—23in (53—58cm) **1250—1500**
26—27in (66—69cm) **1900—2000**

#301:
15—16in (38—41cm) **625—675**
20—22in (51—56cm) **825—875**
25—27in (64—69cm) **1000—1200**
31—32in (79—81cm) **1500—1700**

#60:
17—18in (43—46cm) **600—650**
24—25in (61—64cm) **750—800**

Walking & Kiss-Throwing: 1905-on. Perfect bisque head, composition body with straight legs, walking mechanism at top, hand raises to throw a kiss, head moves from side to side, eyes flirt; good wig, glass eyes, open mouth, pierced ears; nicely dressed; all in working order.
22—24in (56—61cm) **$1550—1650**

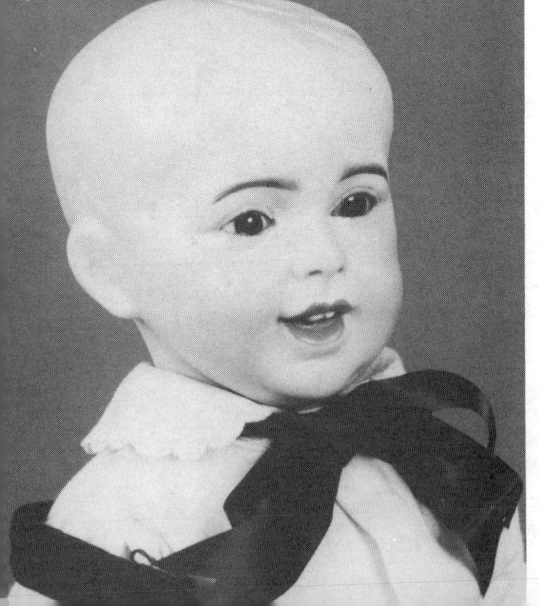
20½in (52cm) S.F.B.J. 235 character child.
Richard Wright Antiques.

S.F.B.J. continued

Character Dolls: 1910—on. Perfect bisque head, wig, molded, sometimes flocked hair on mold numbers 237, 226, 227 and 235, sleep eyes, composition body; nicely dressed; all in good condition.

#226, 235:
15—17in (38—43cm) **$1650—1850**

#227, 237:
17—19in (43—48cm) **1900—2200**

#236:
Baby, 17—18in (43—46cm) **1400—1500**
Toddler:
12in (31cm) **1300—1400**
18—20in (46—51cm) **1800—1900**
27—28in (69—71cm) **2500—2700**

#238:
Child:
15—16in (38—41cm) **2400—2600**
21—22in (53—56cm) **3500—3600**

#247:
Toddler:
16—18in (41—46cm) **2200—2400**
27in (69cm) **3100—3200**

251:
Baby, 8—9in (20—23cm) **750—850**
Toddler:
21—22in (53—56cm) **1800—1900**
14—15in (36—38cm) **1150—1250**

#252:
Baby, 10—12in (25—31cm) **2100—2200**
Toddler:
12in (31cm) **3500—3600**
24in (61cm) **8000**

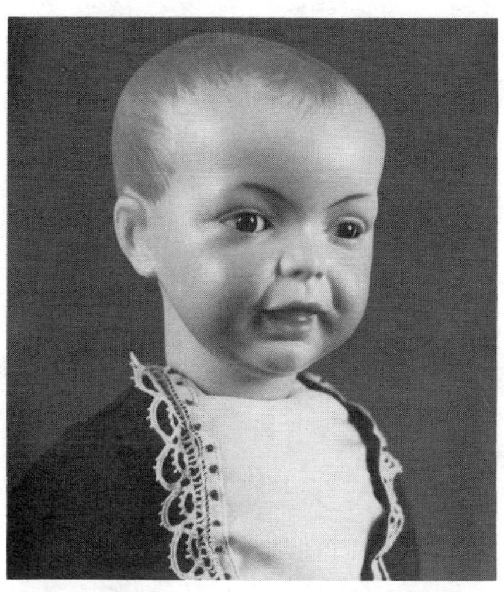

16in (41cm) S.F.B.J. 226 character toddler.

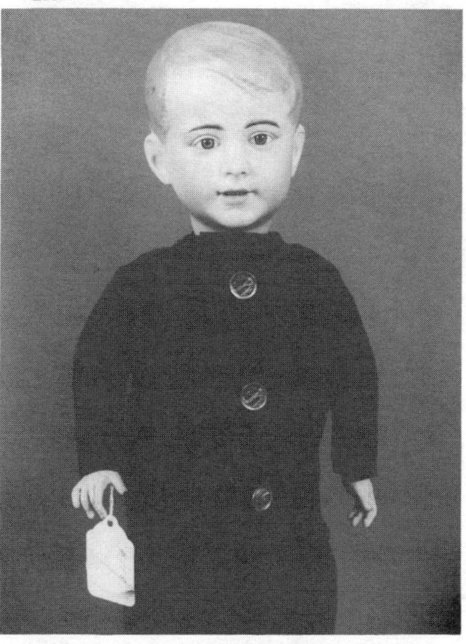

19in (48cm) S.F.B.J. 237 character boy. *Richard Wright Antiques.*

S.F.B.J. continued

11in (28cm) S.F.B.J. 251 toddler.

16in (41cm) S.F.B.J. 252 pouty toddler.
Richard Wright Antiques.

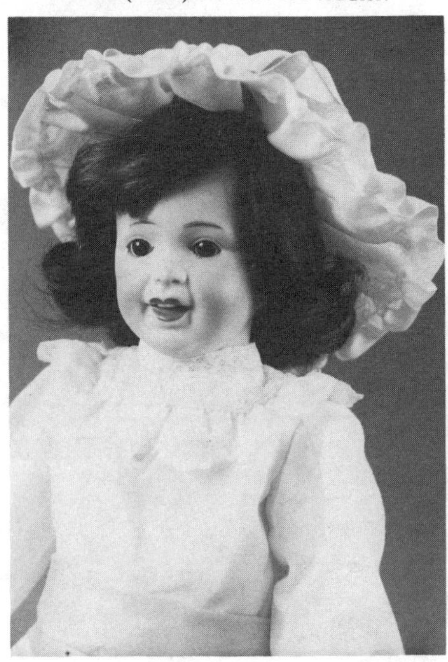

13½in (34cm) S.F.B.J. 236 toddler.

24in (61cm) S.F.B.J. 247 character.
Richard Wright Collection.

Bruno Schmidt

Maker: Bruno Schmidt of Waltershausen, Thüringia, Germany
Date: 1900—on
Material: Bisque head, composition body
Size: Various
Mark:

2096-4

Marked B. S. W. Character Baby: Ca. 1910. Perfect bisque head, good wig, sleep eyes, open mouth; composition bent-limb baby body; dressed; all in good condition.
15—18in (38—46cm) **$450—550**
Toddler, 15in (38cm) **650**

21in (53cm) B. S. W. character girl.

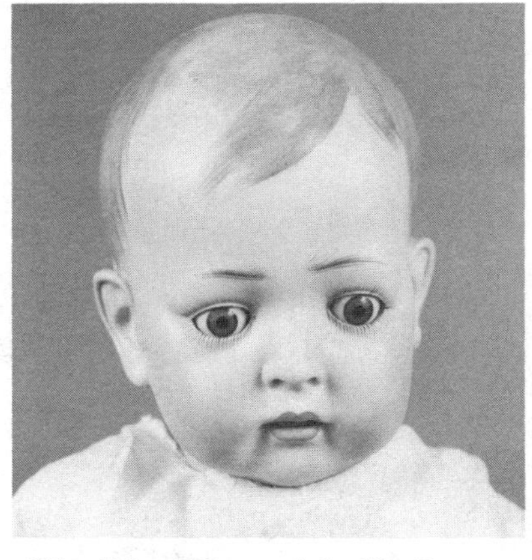

22in (56cm) Bruno Schmidt ***Tommy Tucker*** baby, open mouth. *Dr. Carole Stoessel Zvonar Collection.*

Marked B. S. W. Child Doll: Bisque head, good wig, sleep eyes, open mouth; jointed composition child body; dressed; all in good condition.
20—22in (51—56cm) **$425—475**
30in (76cm) **850—950**

Marked B. S. W. Character Dolls: Bisque socket head, glass eyes; jointed composition body; dressed; all in good condition.
#2048 or ***2096, Tommy Tucker***, molded hair, open mouth, 22—24in (56—61cm) **$1100—1300**
#2097 Toddler, 18—20in (46—51cm) **800—1000**
#2033, Wendy, closed mouth, glass eyes, 18in (46cm) **5000 up****
**Not enough price samples to compute a reliable range.

Franz Schmidt

Maker: Franz Schmidt & Co. of Georgenthal near Waltershausen, Thüringia, Germany
Date: 1890—on
Material: Bisque socket head, jointed bent-limb or toddler body of composition
Size: Various
Mark:
1295
F. S. & Co.
Made in
Germany
30

Marked F. Schmidt Doll: Ca. 1910. Perfect bisque character head, good wig, sleep eyes, open mouth, may have open nostrils; jointed bent-limb body; suitably dressed; all in good condition.

#1272:

15—17in (38—43cm)	**$475—525**
24in (61cm)	**750—850**

#1295, 1296:

15—17in (38—43cm)	**425—475**
19—21in (48—53cm)	**575—625**

#1262:

19in (48cm)	**3000 up****

**Not enough price samples to compute a reliable range.

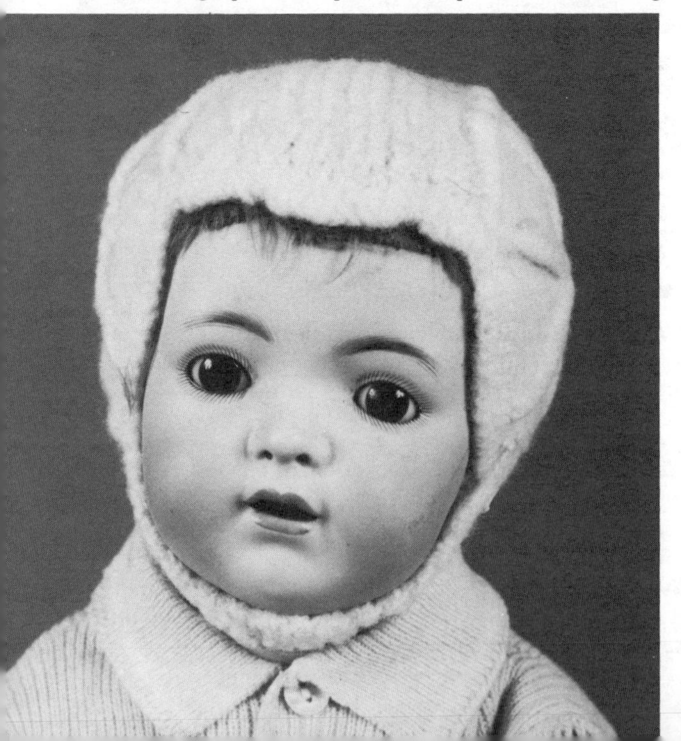

19in (48cm) F.S. &. Co. 1295 character baby, pierced nostrils. *Dr. Carole Stoessel Zvonar Collection.*

Schmitt

Maker: Schmitt & Fils, Paris, France
Date: 1863—1891
Material: Bisque socket head, composition jointed body
Size: Various
Mark: On both head and body:

Marked Schmitt Bébé: Ca. 1879. Perfect bisque socket head with skin or good wig, large paperweight eyes, closed mouth, pierced ears; Schmitt-jointed composition body; appropriate clothes; all in good condition.

18—19in (46—48cm) **$5500 up**
28in (71cm) **12,000****
**Not enough price samples to compute a reliable range.

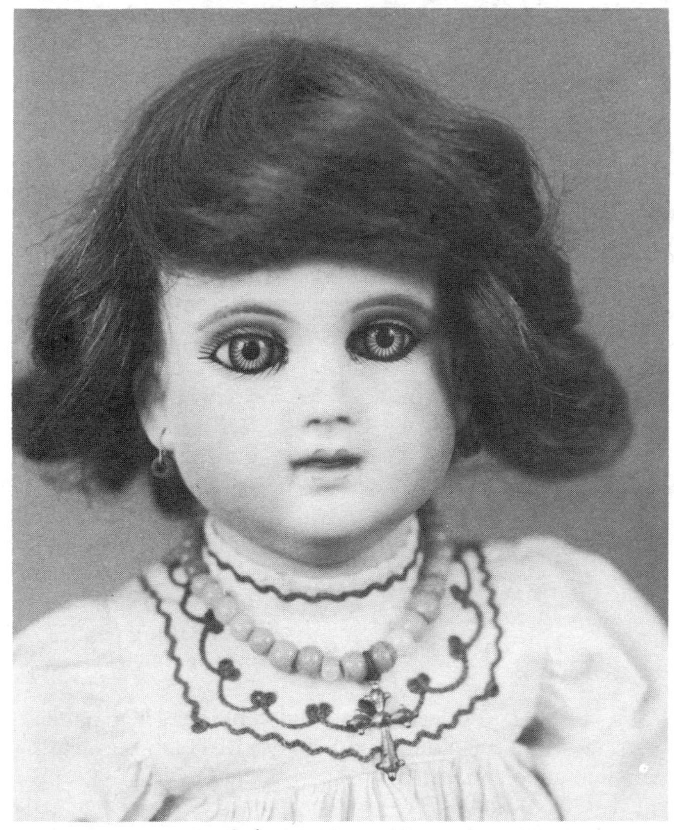

14in (48cm) Schmitt bébé with shield mark. *Ruth Noden Collection.*

Schoenau & Hoffmeister

Maker: Schoenau & Hoffmeister of Burggrub, Bavaria, Germany
Date: 1901—on
Material: Bisque head, composition body
Size: Various
Mark: "Porzellanfabrik Burggrub" or 

and numbers such as 169, 769. Also "Hanna" or "Burggrub/Baby"

Child Doll: 1901—on. Mold numbers such as 1909, 5500, 5800, 5700. Perfect bisque head; original or good wig, sleep eyes, open mouth; ball-jointed body; original or good clothes; all in nice condition.

15—17in (38—43cm) **$275—300***
21—24in (53—61cm) **375—450***
28—30in (71—76cm) **600—700***
*Allow more for an especially wide-eyed doll.

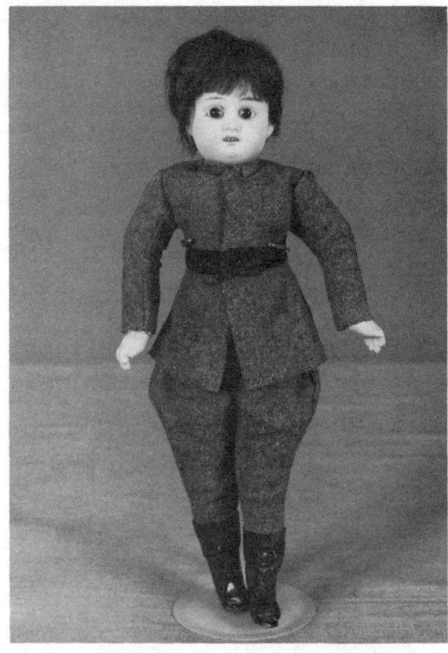

11in (28cm) S PB H 1909 child. *H&J Foulke, Inc.*

Character Baby: 1910—on. Mold numbers 169, 769, "Burggrub Baby" or "Porzellanfabrik Burggrub." Perfect bisque socket head, good wig, sleep eyes, open mouth; composition bent-limb baby body; all in good condition.

15—16in (38—41cm) **$375—400***
24—25in (61—63cm) **575—675***
Hanna:
24in (61cm) **800—900***
*Allow more for toddler.

Princess Elizabeth: Ca. 1930. Perfect bisque head with good wig, glass sleep eyes, smiling mouth with teeth; chubby five-piece composition body; appropriate clothes; all in good condition.
MARK: "Porzellanfabrik Burggrub/Princess Elizabeth."

17in (43cm) **$2200—2300**
21in (53cm) **2800—3000**

Pouty Baby: Ca. 1925. Perfect bisque solid dome head with painted hair, tiny sleep eyes, closed pouty mouth; cloth body with composition arms and legs; dressed; all in good condition.

12—14in (31—36cm) **$700—750****
**Not enough price samples to compute a reliable range.

Das Lachencle Baby by Porzellanfabrik Burggrub, 1930-4// Made in Germany// D.R.G.M. *Richard Wright Antiques.*

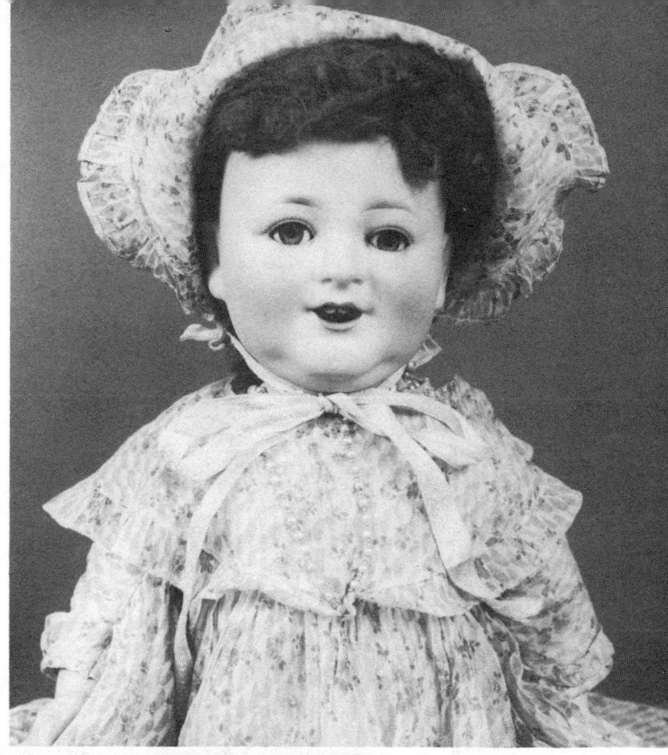

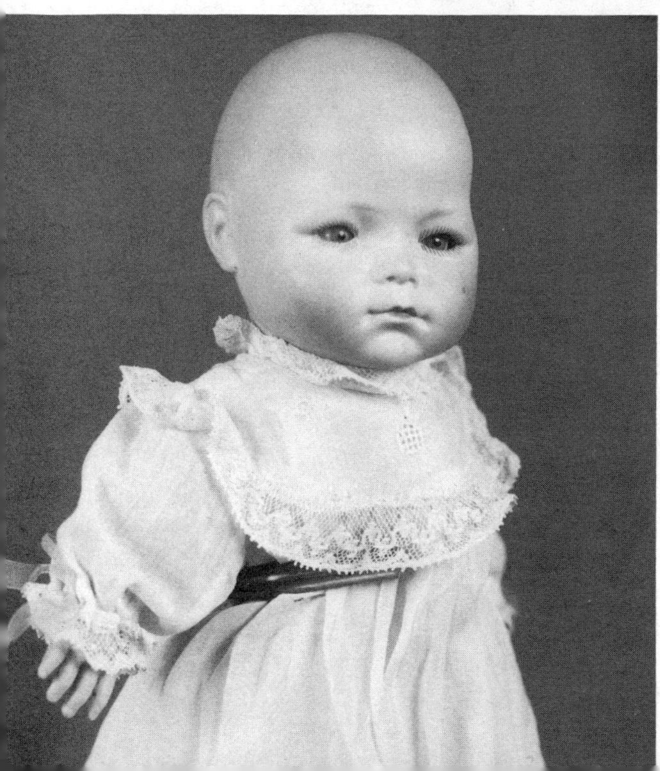

13in (33cm) S PB H pouty baby. *Jimmy and Faye Rodolfos Collection.*

Schoenhut

Maker: Albert Schoenhut & Co., Philadephia, PA., U.S.A.
Date: 1872—on
Material: Wood, spring-jointed, holes in bottom of feet to fit metal stand
Size: Various models 11—21in (28—53cm)
Designer: Early: Adolph Graziana and Mr. Leslie
Later: Harry E. Schoenhut
Mark: Paper label:

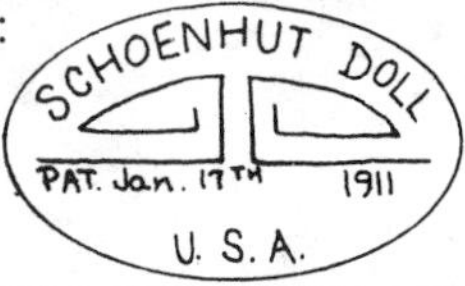

Incised: SCHOENHUT DOLL
PAT. JAN. 17, '11, U.S.A.
& FOREIGN COUNTRIES

Character: 1911—1930. Wooden head and spring-jointed wooden body, marked head and/or body; original or appropriate wig, brown or blue intaglio eyes, open/closed mouth with painted teeth or closed mouth; original or suitable clothing; nothing repainted.

16—19in (41—48cm):

Excellent condition	**$1000—1200***
Good condition, some wear	**600—700***

*More depending upon rarity of face.

14½in (37cm) pouty girl, all original. *Esther Schwartz Collection.*

Character with carved hair: Ca. 1911—1930. Wooden head with carved hair, comb marks, possibly a ribbon or bow, intaglio eyes, mouth usually closed; spring-jointed wooden body; original or suitable clothes.

14—16in (36—41cm):

Excellent condition	**$1300—1500**
Good, some wear	**900—1000**
Molded cap,	**1800****

**Not enough price samples to compute a reliable range.

Baby Face: Ca. 1913—1930. Wooden head and fully-jointed toddler or bent-limb baby body, marked head and/or body; painted hair or mohair wig, painted eyes, open mouth; suitably dressed; nothing repainted; all in good condition.

MARK: H.E. SCHOENHUT © 1913

Baby body, 15in (38cm)	**$550—650**
Toddler, 15in (38cm)	**600—650**

Schoenhut continued

Dolly Face: Ca. 1915—1930. Wooden head and spring-jointed wooden body; original or appropriate mohair wig, decal eyes, open/closed mouth with painted teeth; original or suitable clothes; all in good condition.

14—16in (36—41cm) **$400—425**
21in (53cm) **500—550**

Walker: Ca. 1919—1930. All-wood with "baby face," mohair wig, painted eyes; curved arms, straight legs with "walker" joint at hip; original or appropriate clothes; all in good condition. No holes in bottom of feet.

11—13in (28—33cm) **$500—600**

Sleep Eyes: Ca. 1920—1930. Used with "baby face" or "dolly face" heads. Mouths on this type were open with teeth or barely open with carved teeth. Excellent condition.

17—19in (43—48cm) **$750—850**

Schoenhut Soft Body Mamma Doll: Ca. 1925. Wood socket head fitting into a papier-mâché yoke attached to a cloth body with wooden hands and cry box; original mohair wig, painted eyes, closed mouth; original or appropriate clothes; all in excellent condition.

15—17in (38—43cm) **$750—800**

MARK: H.E. SCHOENHUT © 1913

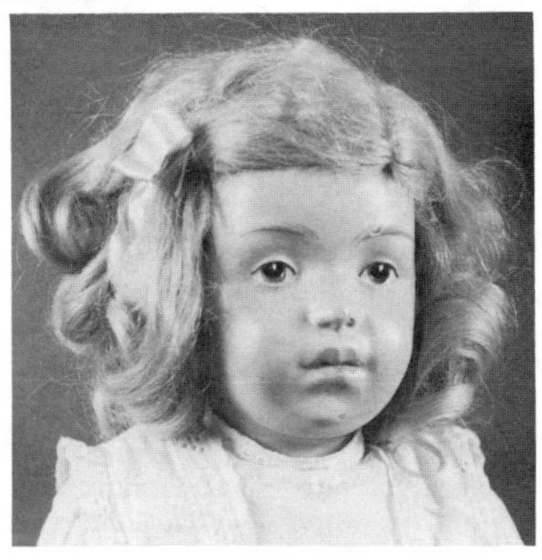

16in (41cm) pouty girl with very full lips. *Pearl D. Morley Collection.*

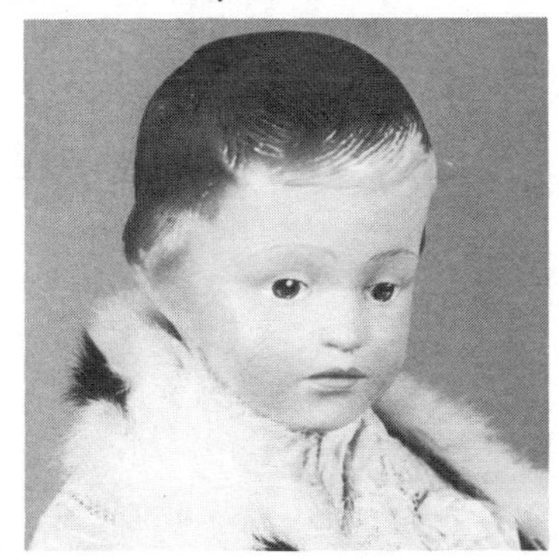

Schoenhut child with carved hair could be used as girl or boy. *Esther Schwartz Collection.*

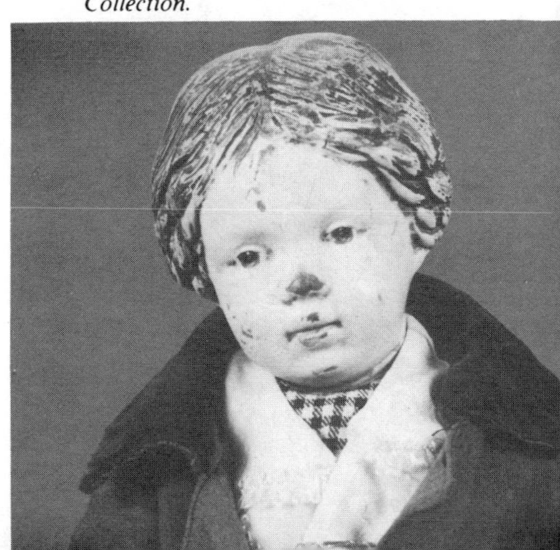

16in (41cm) girl with carved hair and bow. *Betty Harms Collection.*

Schoenhut continued

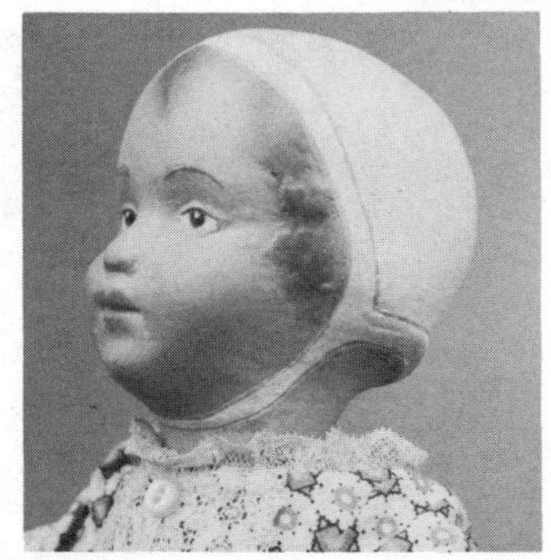

15in (38cm) rare Schoenhut with carved bonnet, repainted. *Richard Wright Antiques.*

15in (38cm) Schoenhut child with sleep eyes. *Betty Harms Collection.*

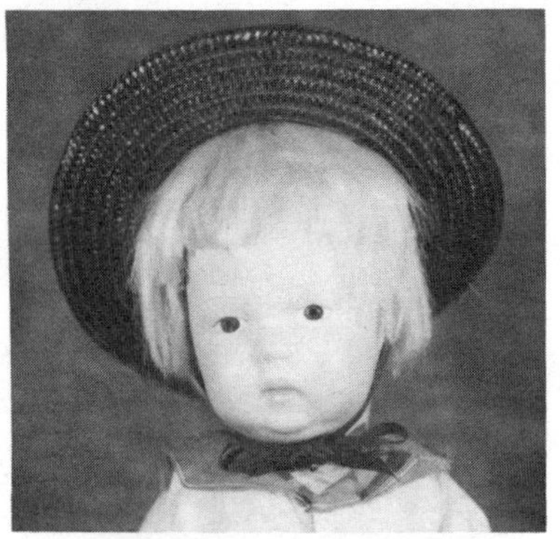

14in (36cm) Schoenhut with baby face. *Roberts Collection.*

15in (38cm) ***Soft Body Mamma Doll*** completely original. *Miriam Blankman Collection.*

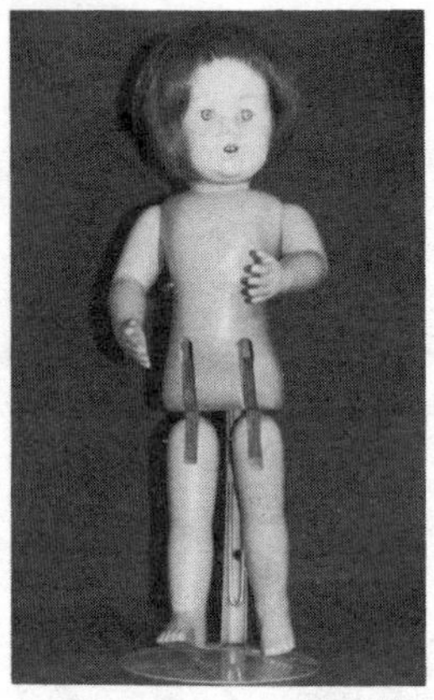

Schoenhut walking child with open mouth and teeth. *Paula Ryscik Collection.*

Shirley Temple

Maker: Ideal Toy Corp., New York, N.Y., U.S.A.
Date: 1934 to present
Size: 7½—36in (19—91cm)
Designer: Bernard Lipfert
Mark: See individual doll listings below. (Ideal used marked Shirley Temple bodies for other dolls).

All-Composition Child: 1934 through late 1930s. Marked head and body, jointed composition body; all original including wig and clothes; entire doll in very good condition. Came in sizes 11—27in (28—69cm)

MARK: On body:

SHIRLEY TEMPLE
13

On head:

13
SHIRLEY TEMPLE

11in (28cm)	**$600**
13in (33cm)	**475—500***
18in (46cm)	**500—550***
22in (56cm)	**600—650***
25in (64cm)	**750***
27in (69cm)	**850—950***
Button	**75**

On cloth label:

Genuine
SHIRLEY TEMPLE
DOLL
REGISTERED U.S. PAT OFF
IDEAL NOVELTY & TOY CO
MADE IN USA

*Allow more for a mint-in-box doll or one with unusual dress.

27in (69cm) composition ***Shirley Temple*** with flirty eyes, all original. *H&J Foulke, Inc.*

15in (38cm) composition ***Shirley Temple,*** all original. *H&J Foulke, Inc.*

Shirley Temple continued

Unusual Japanese-made Shirley with molded hair: From late 1930s. All-composition.

7½in (19cm) **$175—225****

Baby: 1934 through late 1930s. Composition swivel head with molded hair or blonde mohair wig, sleep eyes, open smiling mouth, dimples; cloth body, composition arms and legs; appropriate clothes; all in good condition. Came in six sizes, 16—25in (41—64cm).

MARK: "Shirley Temple" on head

16—18in (41—46cm) **$550—650***

Hawaiian Shirley: Brown composition with black yarn hair, painted eyes; original grass skirt and ornaments; all in good condition.

18in (46cm) **$600****

**Not enough price samples to compute a reliable range.

*Allow more for mint condition.

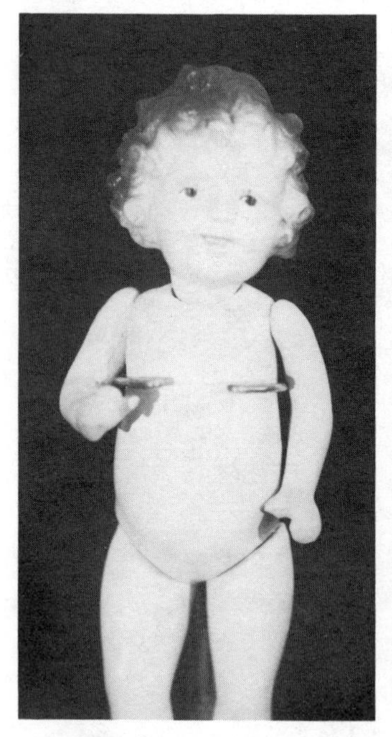

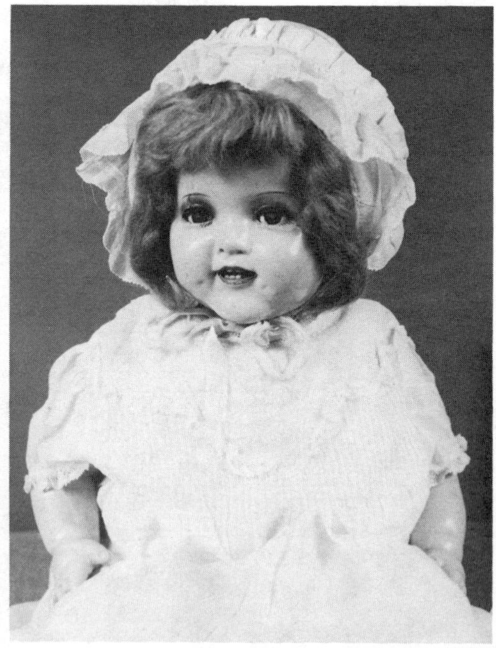

LEFT:
7½in (19cm) Japanese-made composition ***Shirley Temple*** . *H&J Foulke, Inc.*

RIGHT:
21in (53cm) ***Shirley Temple*** baby, replaced dress. *Betty Harms Collection.*

Shirley Temple continued

Vinyl and Plastic: 1957. Vinyl and plastic, rooted hair, sleep eyes; jointed at shoulders and hips; original clothes; all in excellent condition. Came in sizes 12in (31cm), 15in (38cm), 17in (43cm), 19in (48cm) and 36in (91cm)

MARK: "Ideal Doll ST—12"
(number denotes size)

12in (31cm)	**$ 125—150**
15in (38cm)	**225**
17in (43cm)	**250—300**
19in (48cm)	**350**
36in (91cm)	**1100—1400**

Vinyl and Plastic: 1973. Vinyl and plastic, rooted hair, painted eyes, smiling mouth; jointed shoulders and hips; original clothes; all in mint condition.

16in (41cm) size only	**$65—75**
Boxed	**90—110**

19in (48cm) vinyl ***Shirley Temple,*** 1957, all original. *H&J Foulke, Inc.*

17in (43cm) vinyl ***Shirley Temple,*** 1957, all original. *H&J Foulke, Inc.*

Simon & Halbig

Maker: Simon & Halbig of Gräfenhain, Thüringia, Germany (porcelain factory)
Date: 1870s—on
Material: Bisque head, kid (sometimes cloth) or composition body
Size: Various
Mark:

S 13 H
949

1079-2
DEP
S H
Germany

28in (71cm) S 15 H//949 child with bald head, very pale bisque. *Esther Schwartz Collection.*

Child doll with closed mouth: Ca. 1880s. Mold numbers such as 719, 939, 949, and others. Perfect bisque socket head on ball-jointed wood and composition body; good wig, glass set or sleep eyes, closed mouth, pierced ears; dressed; all in good condition.

#719, 939, 949:
15—16in (38—41cm) **$1550—1750**
21—23in (53—58cm) **2200—2500**
28in (71cm) **3000**

#905, 908:
11—12in (28—31cm) **1150—1250****
18—20in (46—51cm) **2500****

#950 on kid body:
9—10in (23—25cm) **400—450**
18in (46cm) **1150—1250**

#939, 949 kid body:
20—21in (51—53cm) **1300—1500**

**Not enough price samples to compute a reliable range.

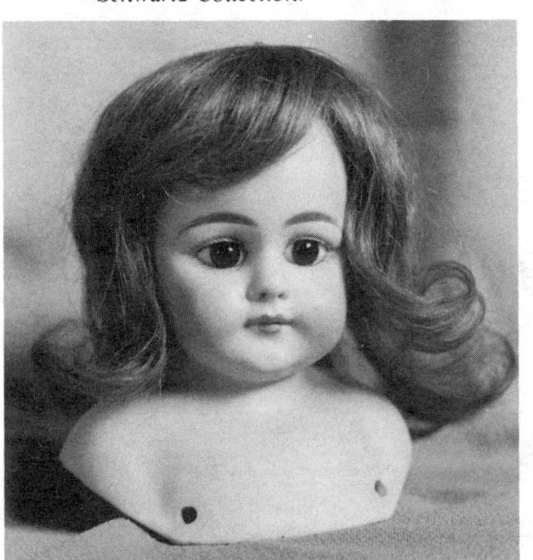

S & H 740 shoulder head. *Marceil Drake Collection. Photograph courtesy of owner.*

Child doll with open mouth and composition body: Ca. 1889 to 1930s. Perfect bisque head, good wig, sleep eyes, open mouth, pierced ears; original ball-jointed composition body; very pretty clothes; all in nice condition.

#719, 939, 949:

14—15in (36—38cm) **$575—675**
18—20in (46—51cm) **850—950**
23—24in (58—61cm) **1250—1350**
30—31in (76—79cm) **2100—2300**

#1079, 550, 1039, 540, 1078, 1009:

12—14in (31—36cm) **350—400**
17—19in (43—48cm) **400—450**
22—24in (56—61cm) **500—600**
28—30in (71—76cm) **850—950**
32—33in (81—84cm) **1100—1200**
35—36in (89—91cm) **1500—1600**
39—42in (99—107cm) **2500+**

#1249, Santa:

16—17in (41—43cm) **725—775**
25—27in (64—69cm) **1000—1200**
35—36in (89—91cm) **2000**

#1039 key-wind walking body:

16—18in (41—46cm) **1000—1200**

#1039 walking, kissing:

20—22in (51—56cm) **800—900**

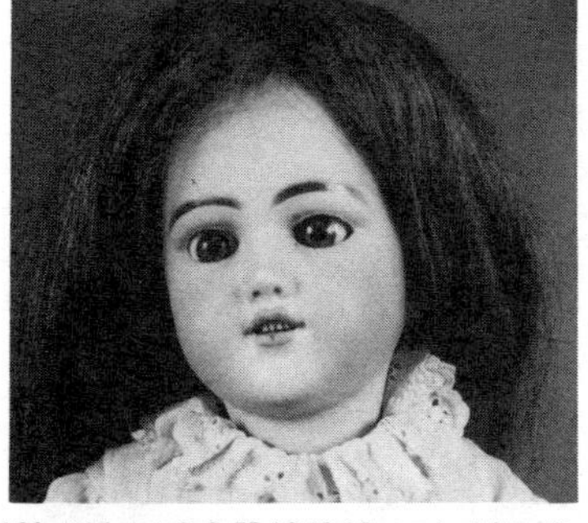

18in (46cm) S & H 1249 (***Santa***) child. *Dr. Carole Stoessel Zvonar Collection.*

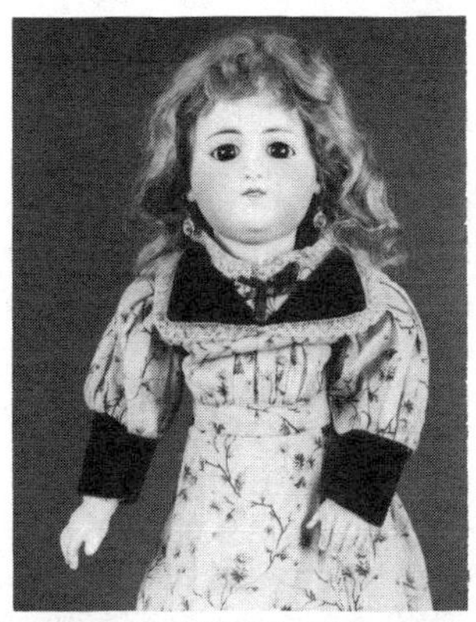

17in (43cm) S & H 908 child, all original. *Carol Green Collection.*

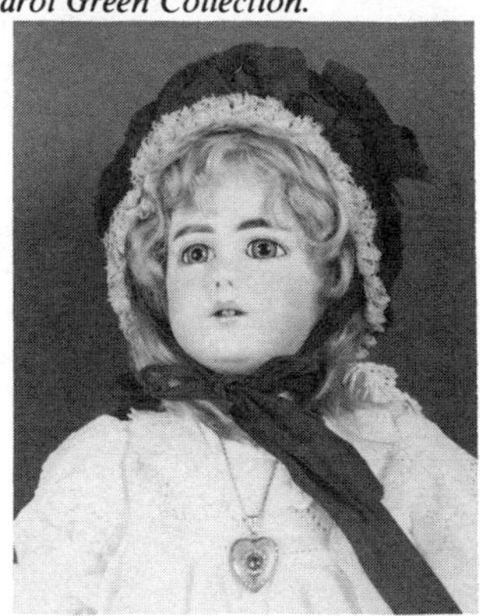

27in (69cm) S & H 939 child, two rows of teeth. *Betty Harms Collection.*

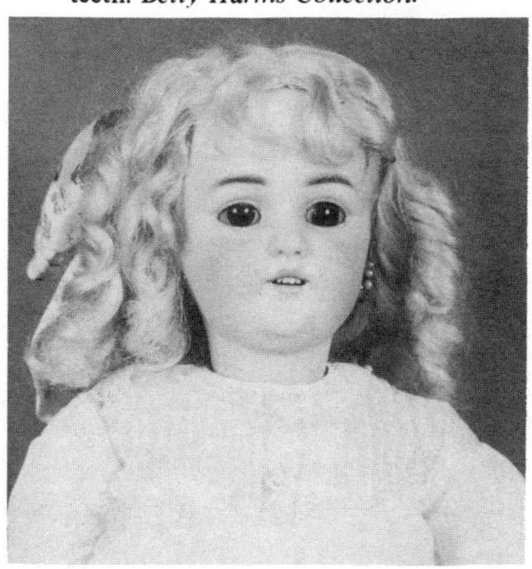

24in (61cm) S & H 1079 child. *Jane Young Collection.*

Child doll with open mouth and kid body: Ca. 1889 to 1930s. Mold numbers such as 1010, 1040, 1080, 1250, and others. Shoulder head with stationary neck, sleep eyes, open mouth, pierced ears; kid body, bisque arms, cloth lower legs; well costumed; all in good condition.

#1040, 1080, 1010:
17—19in (43—48cm) **$400—450**
22—24in (56—61cm) **500—600**
29in (74cm) **800—850**

#1009 fashion-type body:
20—22in (51—56cm) **600—700**

#1250, 1260:
16—18in (41—46cm) **425—475**
24in (61cm) **700**

11in (28cm) S & H 1039 with flirty eyes. *H&J Foulke, Inc.*

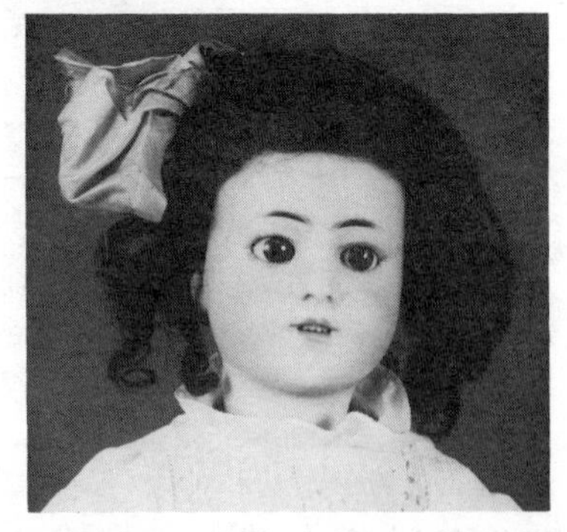

24in (61cm) S & H 550 child. *H&J Foulke, Inc.*

Tiny Child doll: Ca. 1889 to 1930s. Usually mold number 1079 or 1078. Perfect bisque head, nice wig, sleep eyes, open mouth; composition body with molded shoes and socks; appropriate clothes; all in good condition.
7—8in (18—20cm) **$225—250**
Fully jointed:
8in (20cm) **350**
10in (25cm) **400**

So-called Little Women type: Ca. 1900. Mold number 1160. Shoulder head with fancy mohair wig, glass set eyes, closed mouth; cloth body with bisque limbs, molded boots; dressed; all in good condition.
5½—7in (14—18cm) **$300—350**
10—11in (25—28cm) **375—450**

17in (43cm) S & H 1250 child on kid body. *Dr. Carole Stoessel Zvonar Collection.*

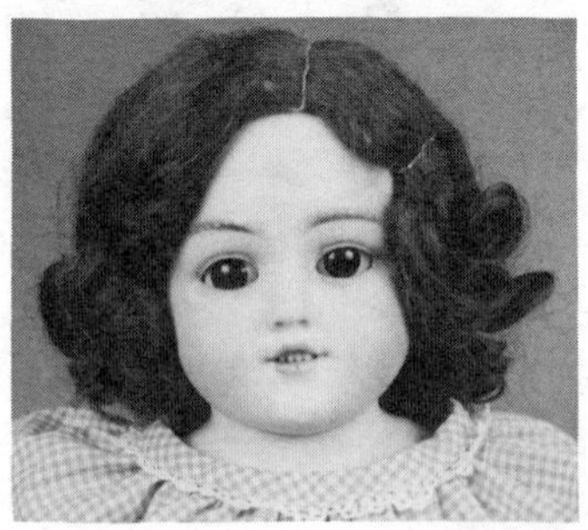

10in (25cm) S & H 1160 so-called ***Little Women.*** *Betty McSpadden Collection.*

Simon & Halbig continued

Character Child: Ca. 1910. Perfect bisque socket head with wig or molded hair, painted or glass eyes, open or closed mouth, character face; jointed composition body; dressed; all in good condition.

#120:	
20—22in (51—56cm)	**$2000—2500****
#150:	
18—20in (46—51cm)	**8000 up****
#151:	
16in (41cm)	**5000****
#153:	
16in (41cm)	**5000 up****
#1279:	
14—16in (36—41cm)	**900—1000**
24in (61cm)	**2000—2200**
30in (76cm)	**3000**
#1299:	
16—18in (41—46cm)	**800—900**
23in (58cm)	**1400**
#1388:	
27in (69cm) lady with flirty eyes	**14,000****
#1478:	
14in (36cm)	**3000 up****
IV:	
18in (46cm)	**6000 up****

**Not enough price samples to compute a reliable range.

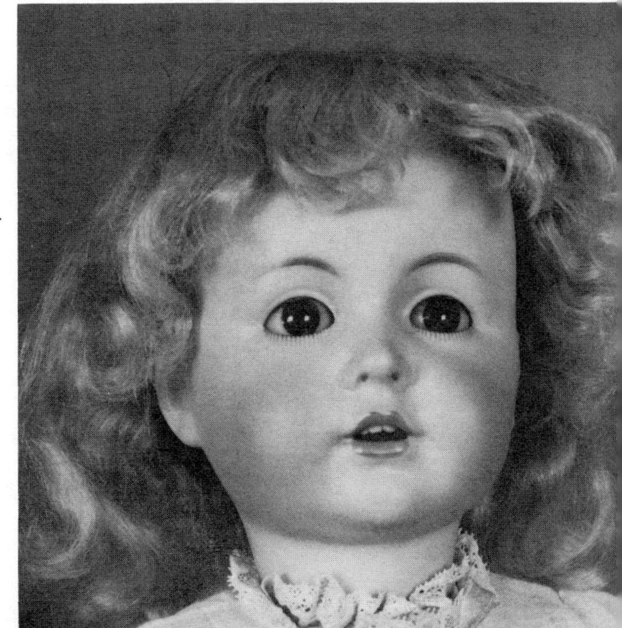

21in (53cm) S & H 120 character girl. *Roberts Collection.*

Simon & Halbig continued

Character Baby: Ca. 1909 to 1930s. Perfect bisque head, molded hair or wig, sleep or painted eyes, open or open/closed mouth; composition bent-limb baby or toddler body; nicely dressed; all in good condition.

#1294 Baby:
15—17in (38—43cm) **$ 500—550**
24—25in (61—64cm) **800—850**
Clockwork,
25in (64cm) **1800—2000****

#1428:
Baby, 12in (31cm) **850—950**
Toddler,
11—12in (28—31cm) **1250—1350**

#1488:
Baby, 18in (46cm) **2000—2200****
Toddler,
18—20in (46—51cm) **3500—3800****

#1498:
Baby, 18in (46cm) **2000—2200****
Toddler,
18—20in (46—51cm) **3500—3800****

Lady doll: Ca. 1910. Mold number 1159. Perfect bisque socket head, good wig, sleep eyes, open mouth, pierced ears; lady body, molded bust, slim arms and legs; elegantly dressed; all in good condition.

#1159:
14in (36cm) **$800—850**
20—22in (51—56cm) **1650—1950**
27—28in (69—71cm) **2400—2500**

Tin eyelids,
20in (51cm) **2500****

Lady doll: Ca. 1910. With closed mouth. Perfect bisque head with good wig, set glass eyes; composition lady body, molded bust, slim arms and legs; nicely dressed; all in good condition.

#1469, 14—15in (36—38cm) **$1200—1400****
#1303, 15in (38cm) **4000 up****

**Not enough price samples to compute a reliable range.

9in (23cm) S & H 1078 flapper, all original. *Mary Lou Rubright Collection.*

Simon & Halbig continued

23in (58cm) unmarked character S & H 1388. *Dr. Carole Stoessel Zvonar Collection.*

17in (43cm) S & H 151 character child. *Carol Green Collection.*

24½in (62cm) S & H 150 character. *Mary Lou Rubright Collection.*

19in (48cm) S & H 1299 character girl, eyes permanently set to side. *Ann Lessey Collection.*

Simon & Halbig continued

19in (48cm) S & H 1279 character girl. *Mary Lou Rubright Collection.*

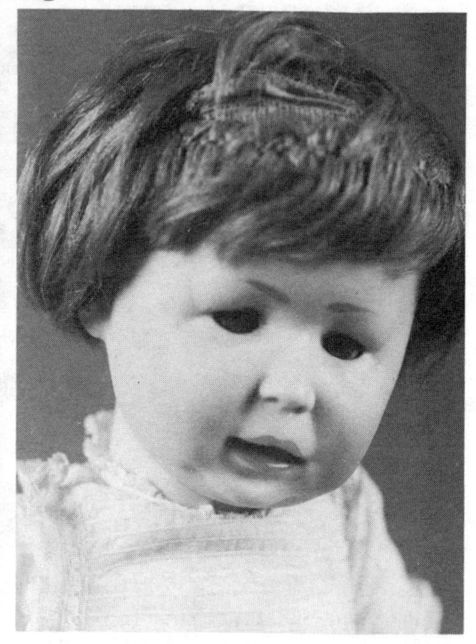

15in (38cm) 1428 baby.

22in (56cm) S & H 1294 toddler. *Dr. Carole Stoessel Zvonar Collection.*

20in (51cm) S & H 1159 with jointed lady body. *C. C. Collection.*

Simonne

Maker: F. Simonne, Paris, France
Date: 1848—1878?
Material: Bisque head, kid or composition body
Size: Various
Mark: Sticker or stamped on body:

Simonne Lady Doll: Late 1860s—on. Perfect bisque turning head on shoulder plate, wig, paperweight eyes, closed mouth, pierced ears; kid body, bisque arms; dressed; all in good condition.
17—18in (43—46cm) **$2500—3000**

Simonne Bébé: 1870s. Perfect bisque head, composition and wood jointed body; wig, paperweight eyes, closed mouth, pierced ears; dressed; all in good condition. Rare.
15—16in (38—41cm) **$4500****
**Not enough price samples to compute a reliable range.

24in (61cm) child with Simonne label on body. *Crandall Collection.*

Snow Babies

Maker: Various German firms
Date: Ca. 1890 until World War II
Material: All-bisque
Size: 1—3in (3—8cm) usually
Mark: Sometimes "Germany"

Snow Babies: All-bisque with snow suits and caps of pebbly-textured bisque; painted features; various standing, lying or sitting positions.

1½in (4cm)	**$30** and up depending upon action
1½in (4cm) snow bear	**30**
1½in (4cm) snowman	**65**
3in (8cm) baby riding snow bear	**150**
2½in (6cm) tumbling snow baby	**95**
2in (5cm) musical snow baby	**40**
2in (5cm) baby on sled	**65**
3in (8cm) baby on sled	**125**
2in (5cm) reindeer pulling snow baby	**150**

2½in (6cm) snow baby sledding. *H&J Foulke, Inc.*

Pair of 2in (5cm) early snow babies. *H&J Foulke, Inc.*

Steiff

Maker: Fraulein Margarete Steiff, Würtemberg, Germany
Date: 1894—on
Material: Felt, plush or velvet
Size: Various
Mark: Metal button in ear

Steiff Doll: Felt, plush or velvet, jointed; seam down middle of face, button eyes, painted features; original clothes; most are character dolls, many have large shoes to enable them to stand; all in good condition.

10—12in (25—31cm) **$500—600**
Characters, 15—21in (38—53cm) **850 up***

*Depending upon rarity.

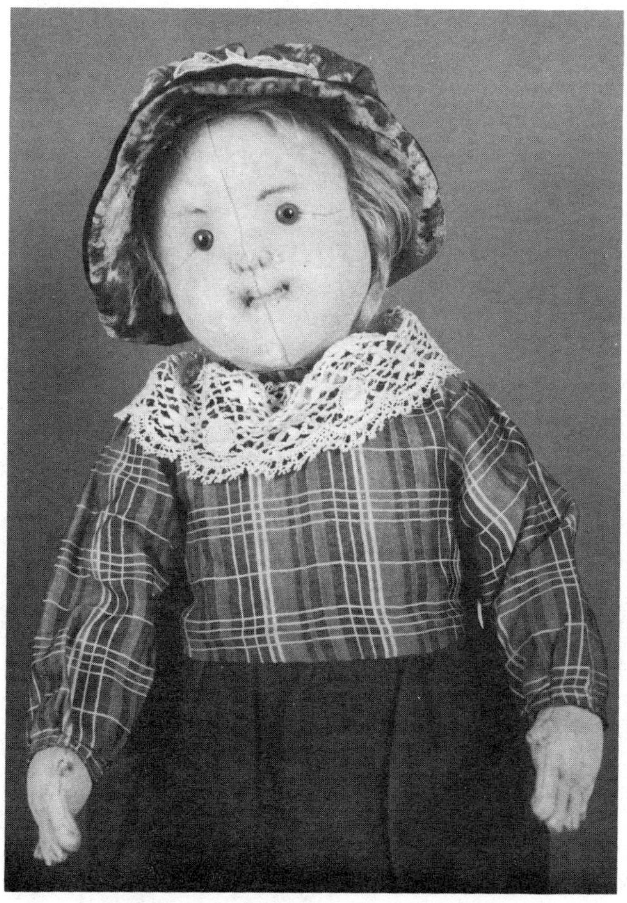

19in (48cm) Steiff lady. *Betty Harms Collection.*

Herm Steiner

Maker: Hermann Steiner of Sonneberg, Thüringia, Germany
Date: 1921—on
Material: Bisque head, cloth or composition body
Size: Various, usually small
Mark:

15
HSt
Germany
240

Herm Steiner
HSt
Germany

Herm Steiner Child: Perfect bisque head, wig, sleep eyes, open mouth; jointed composition body; dressed; in good condition.

7—8in (18—20cm) **$125—150**
12in (31cm) **165—185**

Herm Steiner Infant: Perfect bisque head, molded hair, sleep eyes, closed mouth; cloth body; dressed; in good condition.

Head circumference:
8in (20cm) **$200***
10—11in (25—28cm) **250—275***
*Allow more for open mouth.

Herm Steiner Character Baby: Ca. 1910. Perfect bisque socket head, good wig, sleep eyes, open mouth with teeth; composition jointed baby body; dressed; all in good condition.

10—12in (25—31cm) **$200—250**

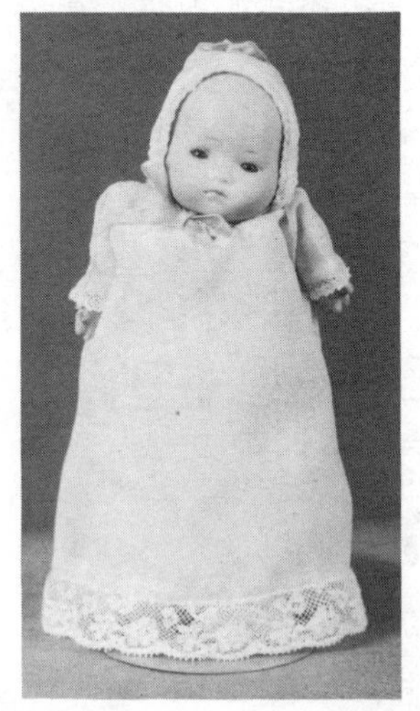

8in (20cm) Herm Steiner infant. *H&J Foulke, Inc.*

8½in (22cm) Herm Steiner character baby. *Joanna Ott Collection.*

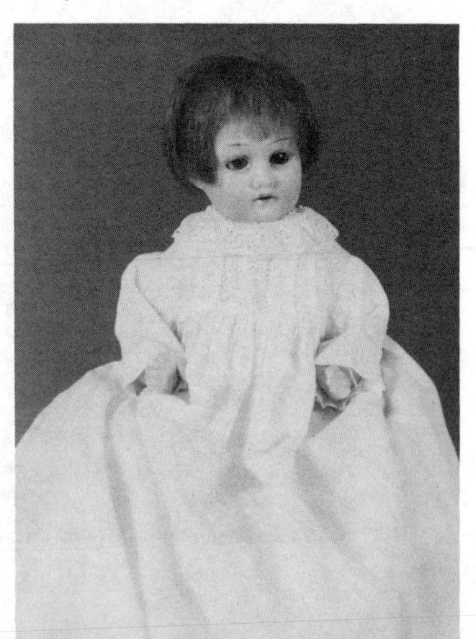

Jules Steiner

Maker: Jules Nicholas Steiner and Successors, Paris, France
Date: 1855—1908
Material: Bisque head, jointed papier-mâché body
Size: Various
Mark: Various as shown below

Marked Bourgoin Steiner Bébé: Ca. late 1870s. Perfect bisque socket head, cardboard pate, appropriate wig, bulgy paperweight eyes with tinting on upper eyelids, closed mouth, round face, pierced ears with tinted tips; jointed composition body; dressed; all in good condition. Sometimes with wire-operated sleep eyes.

MARK: (incised)

STE A O

(red script)

J Steiner. Bte S.g. Dg. J Bourgoin Sr

16—18in (41—46cm) **$3600—3800**
22—24in (56—61cm) **4200—4400**

18in (46cm) Jules Steiner "A" series with wire eyes. *Betty Harms Collection.*

Jules Steiner continued

Round face with open mouth: Ca. 1870s. Perfect very pale bisque socket head, appropriate wig, bulgy paperweight eyes, open mouth with pointed teeth, round face, pierced ears; jointed composition body; dressed; all in good condition.

MARK: None, but sometimes body has a label

Two rows of teeth, 18—20in (46—51cm) **$2500—2700**

Kicking, crying bébé, mechanical key-wind body with composition arms and lower legs, 20—22in (51—56cm) **1900—2100**

Motschmann-type body with bisque shoulders, hips and lower arms and legs, 18—21in (46—53cm) **3600—4000**

17in (43cm) Jules Steiner "C" series with open mouth and two rows of teeth. *Betty Harms Collection.*

"C" Series Bébé: Ca. 1880. Perfect bisque socket head, cardboard pate, appropriate wig, sleep eyes with wire mechanism, closed mouth, full cheeks, pierced ears; jointed composition body; dressed; all in good condition.

MARK: (incised)

STE C 4 (red stamp)

J. STEINER B. S.G. D.G.

16—18in (41—46cm) **$3500—3800**

22—23in (56—58cm) **4000—4500**

Le Petit Parisien Bébé: Ca. 1889. Perfect bisque socket head, cardboard pate, appropriate wig, paperweight eyes, closed mouth, pierced ears; jointed composition body; dressed; all in good condition.

MARK: Stamp on head or body:

"Le Petit Parisien
BEBE STEINER
MEDAILLE d'OR
PARIS 1889"

or paper label of doll carrying flag

16—18in (41—46cm) **$2800—3200**

24—25in (61—64cm) **4200—4500**

"A" Series Bébé: Ca. 1885. Perfect bisque socket head, cardboard pate, appropriate wig, paperweight eyes, closed mouth, pierced ears; jointed composition body; dressed; all in good condition.

MARK: (incised)

J. STEINER
B^TE S.G.D.G.
PARIS
F^IRE A 15

12—13in (31—33cm)	**$2300—2600**
20—22in (51—56cm)	**3400—3800**
With bisque hands, 22in (56cm)	**5500**

Bébé Le Parisien: Ca. 1892. Perfect bisque socket head, cardboard pate, appropriate wig, paperweight eyes, closed or open mouth, pierced ears; jointed composition body; dressed; all in good condition.

MARK: head (incised):

"A-19
PARIS"

(red stamp):

"LE PARISIEN"

body (purple stamp):

"BEBE 'LE PARISIEN'
MEDAILLE D'OR
PARIS"

Closed mouth:
20—22in (51—56cm) **$3400—3600**
27—28in (69—71cm) **5000—5500**

Open mouth:
20—21in (51—53cm) **2200—2400**

23in (58cm) Jules Steiner "A" series, all original. *Betty Harms Collection.*

13in (33cm) Jules Steiner "A-5" ***Le Parisien,*** all original. *Betty Harms Collection.*

Superior

Maker: Probably A. Fleishmann and Cramer; Müller and Strassburger; and G. Liedel, all from Sonneberg area of Germany
Date: 1850s—1890s
Material: Composition head, cloth body, cloth or kid extremities
Size: Various
Mark: Label "M & S SUPERIOR 2015" or "G. L. 2015 SUPERIOR PERFECTLY HARMLESS" or "M & S SUPERIOR 4515," later ones also marked "Germany"

Superior Doll: Label on back of shoulder head; papier-mâché shoulder head; black or blonde molded painted hair, brown or blue painted eyes; original cloth body, old kid arms and boots; quaint old clothing; all in nice condition.
16—18in (41—46cm) **$225—250**
22—24in (56—61cm) **300—325**

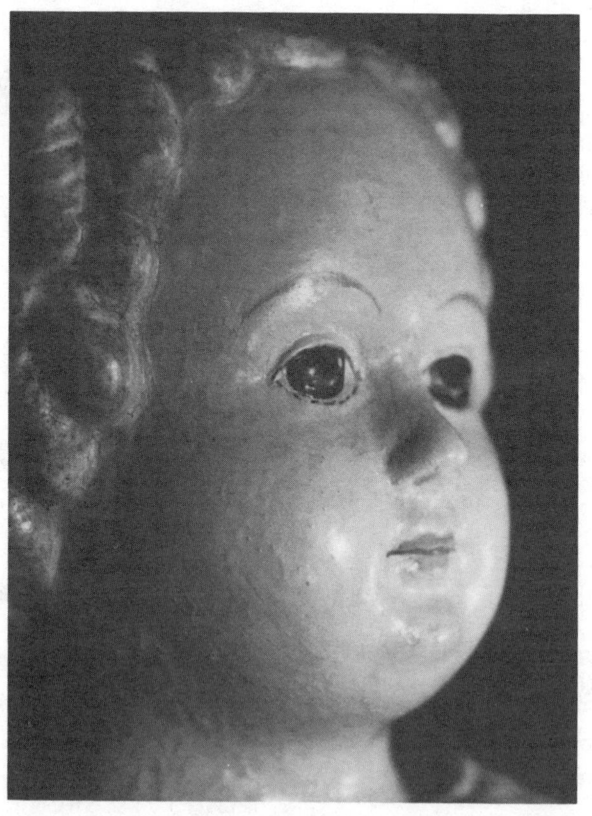

28in (71cm) Superior-type doll, blonde molded hair. *H&J Foulke, Inc.*

Tanagra

Maker: Albert Levy, Paris, France; also a Paris company with a factory at Montreuil-sous-Bois
Date: 1917-1925
Material: Bisque head, jointed composition and wood body
Size: Various
Mark: "Tanagra Perle
DEPOSE"

Marked Tanagra Child: Bisque socket head with good wig, sleep eyes, open mouth with teeth; ball-jointed composition body; dressed; all in good condition.
22—24in (56—61cm) **$850—950****

**Not enough price samples to compute a reliable range.

24in (61cm) ***Tanagra Perle***. *Dr. Carole Stoessel Zvonar Collection.*

Teddy Bear Dolls

Maker: Various firms
Date: 1907—on
Material: Plush jointed body, doll head of bisque, celluloid, or composition
Size: Usually 10—18in (25—46cm)

Teddy Bear Doll: Doll head on a teddy bear body stuffed and jointed at neck with swivel joints at shoulders and hips, plush cap with ears; all in good condition.

Bisque head, 13—14in (33—36cm)	**$350—400***
Celluloid head, 12in (31cm)	**125—150**

*Allow more for a character face.

Teddy bear doll with bisque head. *Betty Harms Collection.*

16in (41cm) teddy bear doll with celluloid face. *Betty Harms Collection.*

Terri Lee

Maker: TERRI LEE Sales Corp., V. Gradwohl, Pres., U.S.A.
Date: 1946-Lincoln, NE; then Apple Valley, CA. from 1951-Ca. 1962
Material: First dolls, rubbery plastic composition; later, hard plastic
Size: 16in (41cm) and 10in (25cm)
Mark: embossed across shoulders

First dolls: "TERRI LEE PAT. PENDING" raised letters

Later dolls: "TERRI LEE"

16in (41cm) ***Terri Lee***, Pat. Pending, red hair, all original. *H&J Foulke, Inc.*

Terri Lee Child Doll: Original wig, painted eyes; jointed at neck, shoulders and hips; all original clothing and accessories; very good condition.

16in (41cm):

Early model	**$175—200**
Hard plastic	**125—150**
Black	**300—350**
Jerri Lee, 16in (41cm)	**175**
Tiny Terri Lee, inset eyes, 10in (25cm)	**110—125**
Tiny Jerri Lee, inset eyes, 10in (25cm)	**165**
Connie Lynn	**250—300**
Linda Baby	**135—150**
Gene Autry	**450 up****

**Not enough price samples to compute a reliable range.

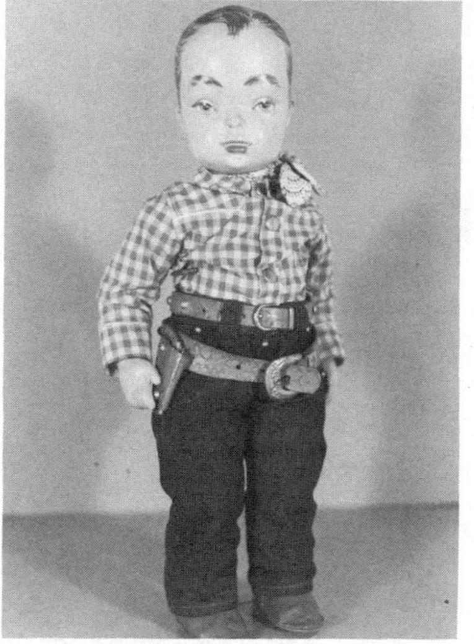

16in (41cm) ***Gene Autry***, with tagged original clothes. *Kathy George Collection. Photograph by Jim George.*

Unis

Maker: Société Française de Fabrication de Bébés et Jouets. (S. F. B. J.) of Paris and Montruil-sous-Bois, France
Date: 1922—on
Material: Bisque head, composition body
Size: 5in (13cm) up
Mark:

UNIS
71 · FRANCE · 149
301

Unis Child Doll: Perfect bisque head, papier-mâché body or wood and composition jointed body; good wig, sleep eyes, open mouth; pretty clothes; all in nice condition.

***#301 or 60*:**

14—16in (36—41cm)	**$450—500**
21—23in (53—58cm)	**600—700**

Costume Doll: Mold 301 or 60. Perfect bisque head, mohair wig, glass eyes (painted eyes on tiny dolls), open or closed mouth; five-piece papier-mâché body; original costume; all in good condition.

5—7in (13—18cm)	**$150—175**
11—13in (28—33cm)	**250—275**
7—10in (18—25cm), fully-jointed	**275—325**
11—13in (28—33cm) darked skinned	**250—300**

14½in (37cm) Unis 60 child, all original with wrist tag. *H&J Foulke, Inc.*

Verlingue

Maker: J. Verlingue of Boulogne-sur-Mer, France
Date: 1914—1921
Material: Bisque head, composition body
Size: Various
Mark:

Marked J. V. Child: Perfect bisque head, good wig, glass eyes, open mouth; jointed papier-mâché body; nicely dressed.
15—16in (38—41cm) **$450—475**
20—22in (51—56cm) **575—675**

Verlingue All-bisque Doll: Head with wig, swivel neck, sleep eyes, closed mouth; jointed shoulders and hips; long painted hose, garters, black boots; undressed; mediocre quality.
7in (18cm) **$250—275**

19in (48cm) ***Petite Francaise Liane*** child.
Dr. Carole Stoessel Zvonar Collection.

Vogue-Ginny

Maker: Vogue Dolls, Inc.
Date: 1937—on
Material: 1937—1948 composition, 1948—1962 hard plastic
Size: 7—8in (18—20cm)
Creator: Jennie Graves
Clothes Designer: Virginia Graves Carlson
Clothes Label: "Vogue," "Vogue Dolls," or

VOGUE DOLLS, INC. MEDFORD, MASS. USA ® REG U.S. PAT OFF

All-composition Toddles: Jointed neck, shoulders and hips; molded hair or mohair wig, painted eyes looking to side; original clothes; all in good condition.

MARK: "VOGUE" on head
"DOLL CO." on back
"TODDLES" stamped on sole of shoe

7—8in (18—20cm) **$150—200***

*Allow extra for special outfits.

Hard Plastic Ginny: All-hard plastic, jointed at neck, shoulders and hips (some have jointed knees and some walk); nice wig, sleep eyes (early ones have painted eyes, later dolls have molded eyelashes); original clothes; all in good condition.

MARK: On strung dolls:
"VOGUE DOLLS"
On walking dolls:
"GINNY//VOGUE DOLLS"

7—8in (18—20cm):

Painted eyes, 1948—1949	**$175—225***
Painted eyelashes, strung, 1950—1953	**175—200***
Caracul wig	**250—300**
Painted eyelashes, walks, 1954	**150—175***
Molded eyelashes, walks, 1955—1957	**125—150***
Molded eyelashes, walks, jointed knees, 1957—1962	**100—125***

*Allow extra for special outfits.

7½in (19cm) ***Toddles***, all original. *H&J Foulke, Inc.*

Vogue-Ginny continued

Hard Plastic Ginny Baby: Bent limbs, jointed at neck, shoulders and hips; caracul wig, painted or sleep eyes; original clothes; all in good condition.
8in (20cm) **$250**

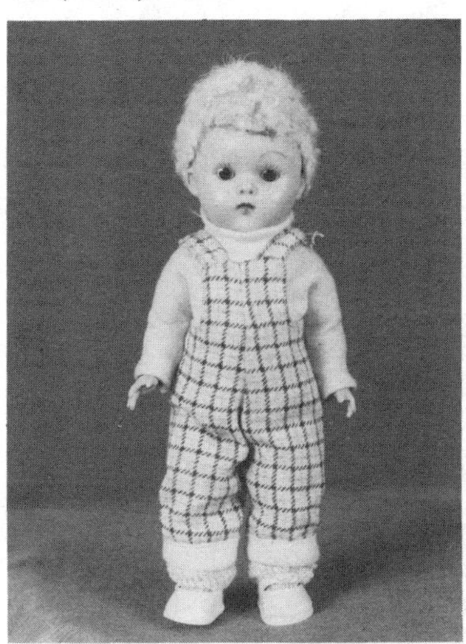

8in (20cm) ***Ginny*** with caracul wig, tagged clothes. *H&J Foulke, Inc.*

8in (20cm) ***Ginny***, all original from 1952 Kindergarten Series. *Beth Foulke Collection.*

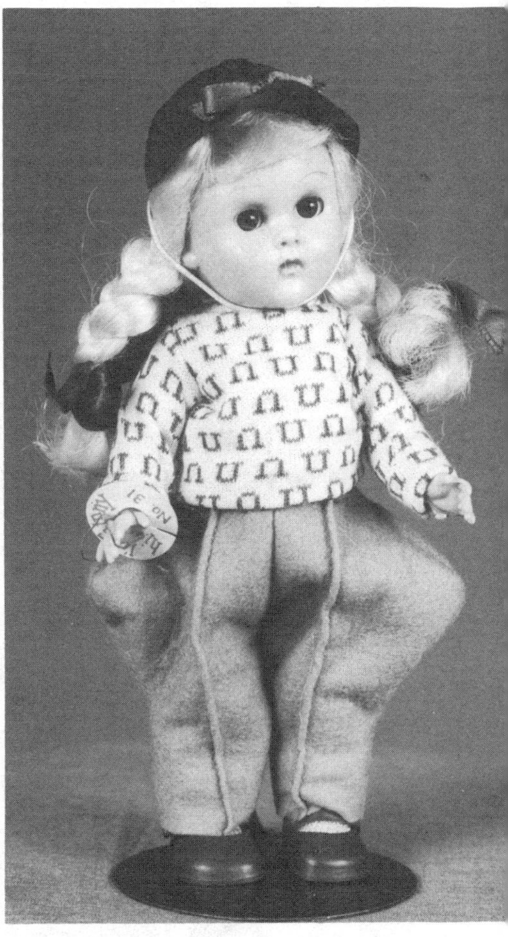

8in (20cm) ***Ginny*** with molded lashes, all original. *H&J Foulke, Inc.*

W.D.

Maker: Unknown French maker
Date: Ca. 1890
Material: Bisque head, jointed composition and wood body
Mark: "W.D."

W. D. Bébé: Perfect bisque head, good wig, stationary eyes, closed mouth, pierced ears; jointed composition and wood body; pretty clothes; all in good condition.

12in (31cm) **$1600–1800****

**Not enough price samples to compute a reliable range.

12in (31cm) W. D. with French label, all original. *Betty Harms Collection.*

WPA

Maker: Various artists under the sponsorship of the Works Projects Administration
Date: 1935—1943
Material: All-cloth
Size: 22in (56cm)
Mark: Usually a number and location, such as "#7040, Milwaukee, Wis."

WPA Cloth Doll: Stockinette head doll with yarn hair, molded face, painted features; cloth body; appropriate clothes; all in very good condition. Marked as above.

22in (56cm) **$400—500****

**Not enough price samples to compute a reliable range.

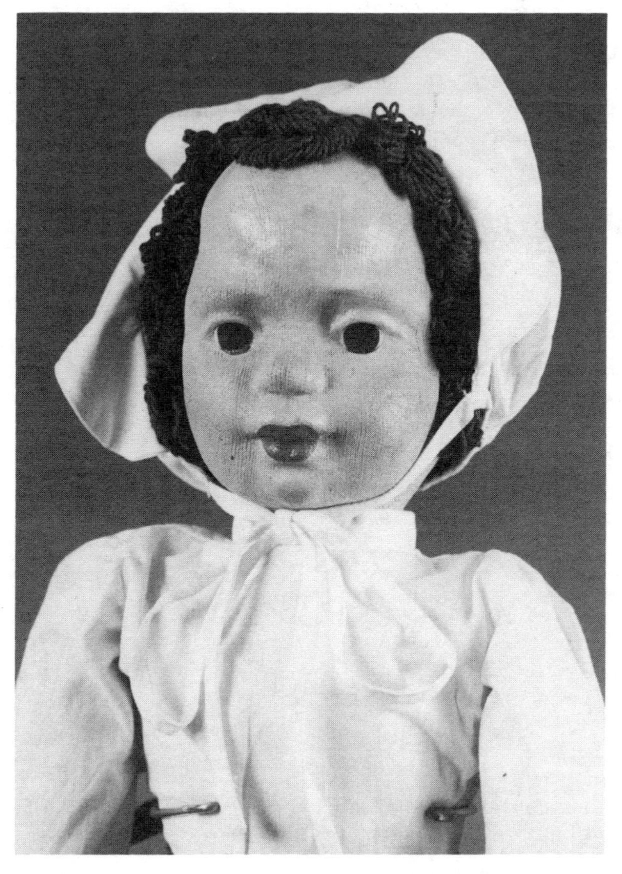

22in (56cm) WPA doll #7040, Milwaukee, Wis. *Pearl D. Morley Collection.*

WSK

Maker: Wiesenthal, Schindel & Kallenberg, Waltershausen, Thüringia, Germany (Heads made for them by porcelain factories including Simon & Halbig.)

Date: 1858—on

Material: Bisque heads, composition bodies, all-bisque dolls

Mark: Character baby: WSK 541 Child doll: SIMON & HALBIG WSK 4½

Marked Child Doll: Ca. 1890—on. Perfect bisque head with good wig, sleep eyes, stroked eyebrows, open mouth, pierced ears; ball-jointed composition body; appropriate clothes; all in good condition.

22—24in (56—61cm) **$450—475**

Marked Character Baby: Ca. 1910. Perfect bisque head with solid dome, painted hair, painted eyes, smiling open/closed mouth; composition bent-limb body; appropriate clothes; all in good condition. Mold 541.

14—15in (36—38cm) **$400—450**

24in (61cm) child doll from "My Dearie" line distributed in the United States by George Borgfeldt, 1908 to 1922. *Dr. Carole Stoessel Zvonar Collection.*

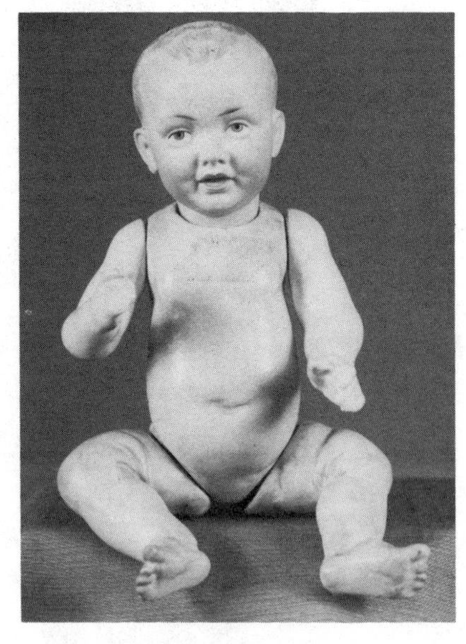

12in (31cm) character baby from mold 541. *Dr. Carole Stoessel Zvonar Collection.*

Wagner & Zetzsche

Maker: Wagner & Zetzsche, Ilmenau, Thüringia, Germany. Bisque heads by porcelain factories including Gebrüder Heubach

Date: 1875—on

Material: Bisque head, cloth, kid, or composition body, celluloid-type heads

---

Closed-mouth Child: Ca. 1880s. Perfect turned bisque shoulder head with solid dome (mold 639) or open crown (mold 698), sometimes with plaster dome, mohair wig, paperweight eyes (a few with sleep eyes), flat eyebrows, closed mouth, small ears; kid or cloth body with bisque hands; appropriate clothes; all in good condition.

MARK: Blue paper body label with "W Z" initials entwined in fancy scroll.

14—16in (36—41cm) **$750—850**
19—21in (48—53cm) **1000—1200**
22—24in (56—61cm) **1250—1450**

Character Baby: Ca. 1910. Perfect bisque socket head, wig, sleep eyes, smiling open mouth with upper teeth; bent-limb composition baby body; dressed; all in good condition. Mold #10586 made by Gebrüder Heubach.

MARK:

10586
W u Z
Y.
Germany
HEU BACH

16—18in (41—46cm) **$500—550**

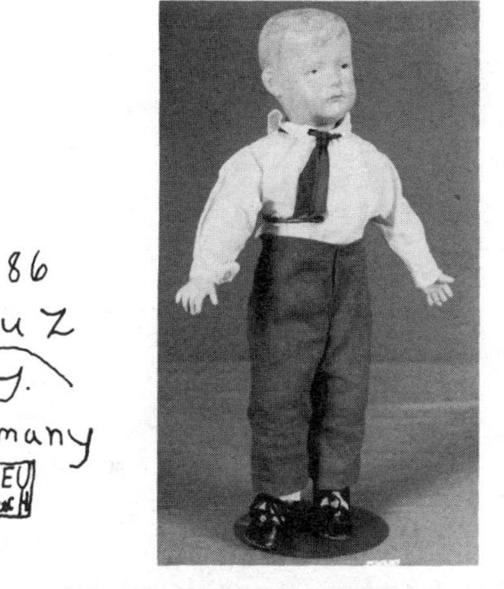

14in (36cm) ***Harald.*** *H&J Foulke, Inc.*

Harald: 1915. Celluloid-type head with molded hair, painted eyes, closed mouth, pouty expression; jointed oilcloth body with jointed composition arms; appropriately dressed, head in fair condition, body in good condition.

MARK: "Harald
W.Z."

14in (36cm) **$150—200**

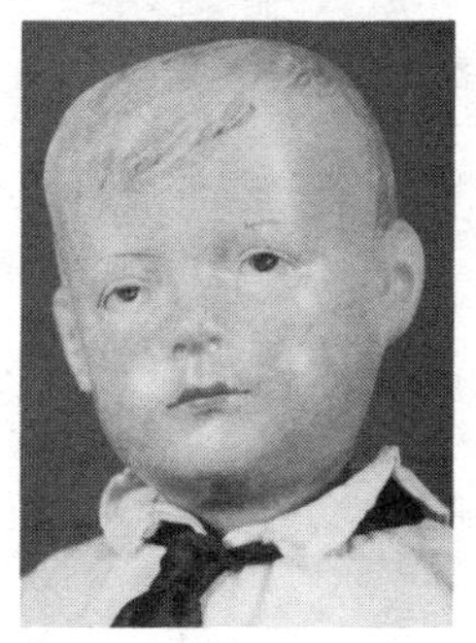

Close-up of 14in (36cm) ***Harald.*** *H&J Foulke, Inc.*

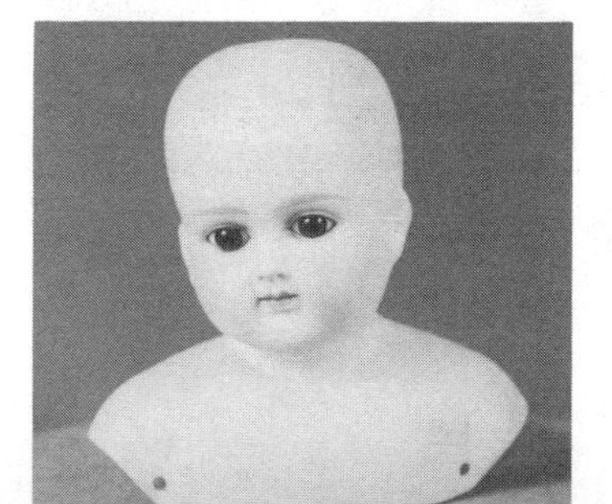

Solid dome bisque head #639, stationary eyes, closed mouth, used by W & Z. *H&J Foulke, Inc.*

Izannah Walker

Maker: Izannah Walker, Central Falls, R.I., U.S.A.
Date: 1873, but probably made as early as 1840s
Material: All-cloth
Size: 15—30in (38—76cm)
Mark: Later dolls are marked: " Patented Nov. 4th 1873 "

Izannah Walker Doll: Stockinette, pressed head, features and hair painted with oils, applied ears, treated limbs; muslin body; appropriate clothes; in fair condition.

18—20in (46—51cm) **$3500 up**
Good condition, **8000—11,500**

17in (43cm) Izannah Walker doll. *Pearl D. Morley Collection.*

Side view of 17in (43cm) Izannah Walker Doll. *Pearl D. Morley Collection.*

Wax Doll, Poured

Maker: Various firms in England, such as Montanari, Pierotti, and Lucy Peck
Date: Mid 19th century through the early 1900s
Material: Wax head, arms and legs, cloth body
Size: Various
Mark: Sometimes stamped on body with maker or store

Poured Wax Child: Head, lower arms and legs of wax; cloth body; set-in hair, glass eyes; original clothes or very well dressed; all in good condition.
14—16in (36—41cm) **$900—1000**
20—22in (51—56cm) **1150—1250**

22in (56cm) poured wax, all original. *Pearl D. Morley Collection.*

Wax Over Composition

Maker: Numerous firms in England, Germany or France
Date: During the 1800s
Material: Wax over shoulder head of some type of composition or papier-mâché, cloth body, wax over composition or wooden limbs
Size: Various
Mark: None

English Slit-head Wax: Ca. 1830—1860. Wax over shoulder head, not rewaxed; human hair wig, glass eyes (may open and close by a wire), faintly smiling; original cloth body with leather arms; original or suitable old clothing; all in good condition.
18—20in (46—51cm) **$400—450**
26—28in (66—71cm) **500—600**

Molded Hair Doll: Ca. 1850—on. Wax over shoulder head, not rewaxed; molded hair sometimes with bow, glass sleep or set eyes; original cloth body; wax over or wooden extremities with molded boots; nice old clothes; all in good condition.
21—25in (53—64cm) **$400—450**
Pumpkin head with molded pompadour and hair band, 15—18in (38—46cm) **250—275**

Wax Doll With Wig: Ca. mid 19th century into early 20th century. Wax over shoulder head, not rewaxed; blonde or brown human hair or mohair wig, blue, brown or black glass eyes, sleep or set, open or closed mouth; original cloth body, any combination of extremities mentioned above, also arms may be made of china; original clothing or suitably dressed; entire doll in nice condition.
17—19in (43—48cm) **$300—350**
23—26in (58—66cm) **400—450**

Bonnet Wax Doll: Ca. 1860 to 1880. Wax over shoulder head, with molded bonnet; molded hair may have some mohair or human hair attached, blue, brown or black set eyes; original cloth body and wooden extremities; nice old clothes; all in good condition.
12—14in (31—36cm) **$300—400**

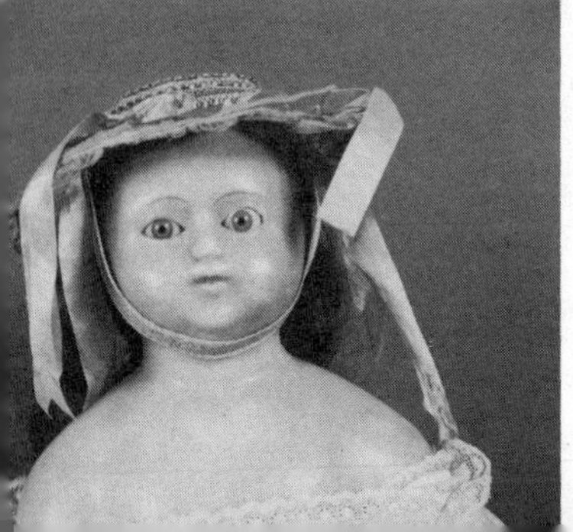

Left: 24in (61cm) wax over, English slit-head style, all original. *Betty Harms Collection.*

Right: 23in (58cm) wax over with blonde molded curly hair and blue hair band with molded bow. *Joanna Ott Collection.*

Norah Wellings

Maker: Victoria Toy Works, Wellington, Shropshire, England, for Norah Wellings
Date: 1926—Ca. 1960
Material: Fabric: Felt, velvet and velour, and other material, stuffed
Size: Various
Designer: Norah Wellings
Mark: On tag on foot: "Made in England by Norah Wellings"

Wellings Doll: All-fabric, stitch-jointed shoulders and hips; molded fabric face (also of papier-mâché, sometimes stockinette covered), painted features; all in excellent condition. Most commonly found are sailors, Canadian Mounties, Scots and Black Islanders.

Characters:

8in (20cm)	**$40—50**
11—12in (28—31cm)	**65—75**
14in (36cm)	**90—100**
15—18in (39—46cm)	**150—175**

Children:

Painted eyes, 16—18in (41—46cm)	**300—400**
Glass eyes, 16—18in (41—46cm)	**400—500**

11in (28cm) Norah Wellings girl, all original. *H&J Foulke, Inc.*

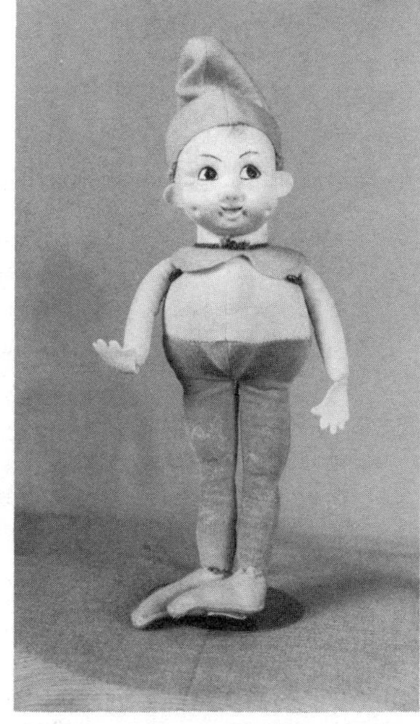

10in (25cm) Norah Wellings pixie, all original. *H&J Foulke, Inc.*

Wislizenus

Maker: Adolf Wislizenus of Waltershausen, Thüringia, Germany
Date: 1851—on
Material: Bisque head, composition ball-jointed body
Size: Various
Mark: "A.W.," "A.W." and "W," "A. W. SPECIAL.," sometimes with "Germany" added, sometimes "OLD GLORY"

Germany
A.W.
0

Wislizenus Child Doll: Ca. 1890—on. Perfect bisque head, composition ball-jointed body; good wig, blue or brown sleep eyes, open mouth; dressed; all in good condition.
22—24in (56—61cm) **$400—425**

24½in (62cm) A. W. child doll. *Dr. Carole Stoessel Zvonar Collection.*

Wislizenus Character Doll: Perfect bisque socket head, molded hair, painted eyes, open/closed mouth with molded teeth; composition toddler body; head marked only "115//Germany;" dressed; all in good condition.
12in (31cm) **$400****
**Not enough price samples to compute a reliable range.

Wood, German

Maker: Rudolf Schneider, Sonneberg, Thüringia, Germany
Date: 1914
Material: All-wood, fully jointed
Size: Various
Mark: None

"Bébé Tout en Bois" (Doll all of Wood): All of wood, fully jointed; wig, inset glass eyes, open mouth with teeth; appropriate clothes; all in fair to good condition.

16in (41cm) **$500—600****

**Not enough price samples to compute a reliable range.

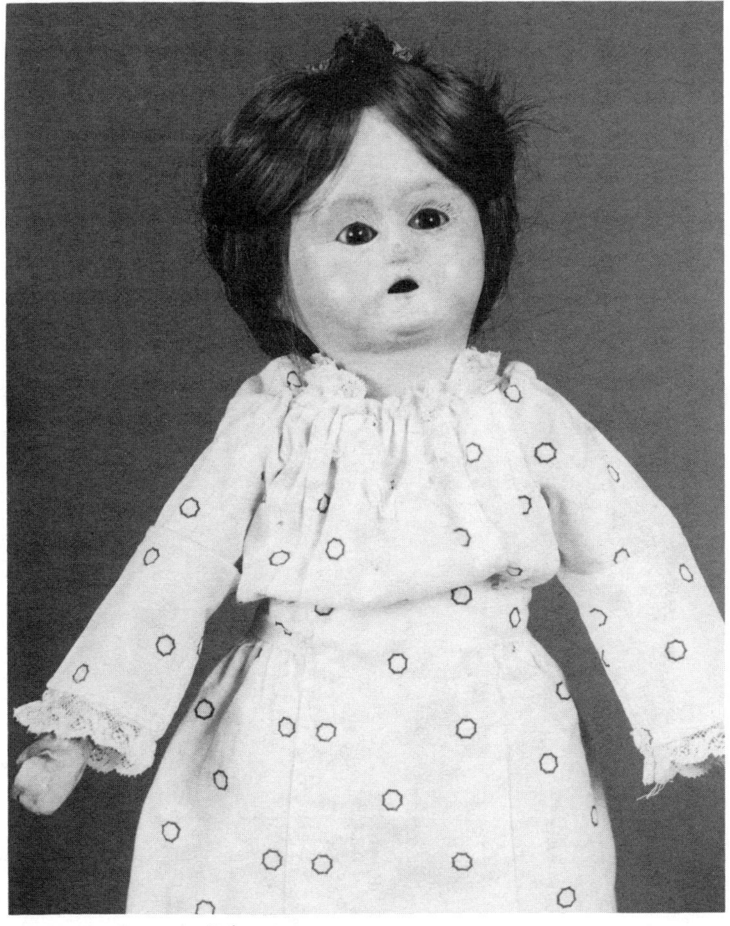

16in (41cm) ***Bébé Tout en Bois.*** *Betty Harms Collection.*

Wood, Swiss

Maker: Various Swiss firms
Date: 20th century
Material: All-wood or wood head and limbs on cloth body
Size: Various, but smaller sizes are more commonly found
Mark: Usually a paper label on wrist or clothes

Swiss Wooden Doll: Wooden head with hand-carved features and hair with good detail (males sometimes have carved hats); all carved wood jointed body; original, usually regional attire; excellent condition.

10in (25cm) **$175—200**

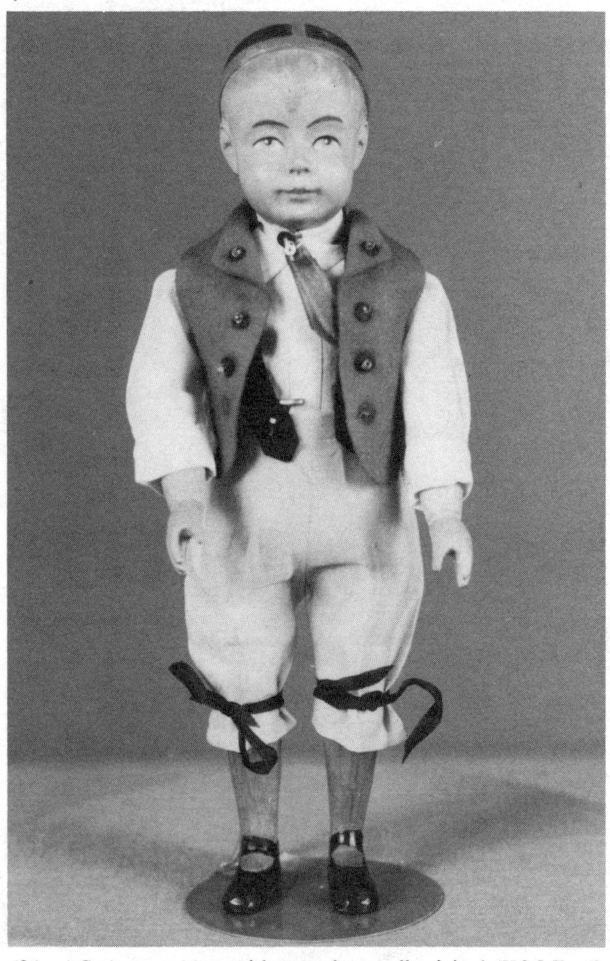

9½in (24cm) Swiss wood boy with carved cap, all original. *H&J Foulke, Inc.*

Glossary

Applied Ears: Ear molded independently and affixed to the head. (On most dolls the ear is included as part of the head mold.)

Bald Head: Head with no crown opening, could be covered by a wig or have painted hair.

Ball-jointed Body: Usually a body of composition with wooden balls at knees, elbows, hips and shoulders to make swivel joints.

Bébé: French child doll with "dolly face."

Belton-type: A bald head with one, two or three small holes for attaching wig.

Bent-limb Baby Body: Composition body of five pieces with chubby torso and curved arms and legs.

Biskoline: Celluloid-type of substance for making dolls.

Bisque: Unglazed porcelain, usually flesh tinted, used for dolls' heads or all-bisque dolls.

Breather: Dolls with an actual opening in each nostril; also called open nostrils.

Breveté (or Bté): Used on French dolls to indicate that the patent is registered.

Character Doll: Dolls with bisque or composition heads, modeled to look lifelike, such as infants, young or older children, young ladies, and so on.

China: Glazed porcelain used for dolls' heads and Frozen Charlottes.

Child Dolls: Dolls with a typical "dolly face" which represent a child.

Crown Opening: The cut-away part of a doll head.

DEP: Abbreviation used on German and French dolls claiming registration.

D.R.G.M.: Abbreviation used on German dolls indicating a registered design or patent.

Dolly Face: Typical face used on bisque dolls before 1910 when the character face was developed; dolly faces were used also after 1910.

Embossed Mark: Raised letters, numbers, or names on the backs of heads or bodies.

Feathered Eyebrows: Eyebrows composed of many tiny painted brush strokes to give a realistic look.

Fixed Eyes: Glass eyes which do not move or sleep.

Flange Neck: A doll's head with a ridge at the base of the neck which contains holes for sewing the head to a cloth body.

Flapper Dolls: Dolls of the 1920s period with bobbed wig or molded hair and slender arms and legs.

Flirting Eyes: Eyes which move from side to side as doll's head is tilted.

Frozen Charlotte: Doll molded all in one piece including arms and legs.

Ges. (Gesch.): Used on German dolls to indicate design is registered or patented.

Googly Eyes: Large, often round, eyes looking to the side; also called roguish or goo goo eyes.

Hard Plastic: Hard material used for making dolls after 1948.

Incised Mark: Letters, numbers or names impressed into the bisque on the back of the head or on the shoulder plate.

Intaglio Eyes: Painted eyes with sunken pupil and iris.

Kid Body: Body of white or pink leather.

Lady Dolls: Dolls with an adult face and a body with adult proportions.

Mohair: Goat's hair widely used in making doll wigs.

Molded Hair: Curls, waves and comb marks which are actually part of the mold and not merely painted onto the head.

Motschmann-type Body: Doll body with cloth midsection and upper limbs with floating joints; hard lower torso and lower limbs.

Open-Mouth: Lips parted with an actual opening in the bisque, usually has teeth either molded in the bisque or set in separately and sometimes a tongue.

Open/Closed Mouth: A mouth molded to appear open, but having no actual slit in the bisque.

Original Clothes: Clothes belonging to a doll during the childhood of the original owner, either commercially or homemade.

Painted Bisque: Bisque covered with a layer of flesh-covered paint, which has not been baked in, so will easily rub or wash off.

Paperweight Eyes: Blown glass eyes which have depth and look real, usually found in French dolls.

Pate: A shaped piece of plaster, cork, cardboard, or other material which covers the crown opening.

Pierced Ears: Little holes through the doll's ear lobes to accommodate earrings.

Pierced-in Ears: A hole at the doll's earlobe which goes into the head to accommodate earrings.

Pink Bisque: A later bisque of about 1920 which was pre-colored pink.

Pink-toned China: China which has been given a pink tint to look more like real flesh color; also called lustered china.

Rembrandt Hair: Hair style parted in center with bangs at front, straight down sides and back and curled at ends.

S.G.D.G.: Used on French dolls to indicate that the patent is registered "without guarantee of the government."

Shoulder Head: A doll's head and shoulders all in one piece.

Shoulder Plate: The actual shoulder portion sometimes molded in one with the head, sometimes a separate piece with a socket in which a head is inserted.

Socket Head: Head and neck which fit into an opening in the shoulder plate or the body.

Solid-dome Head: Head with no crown opening, could have painted hair or be covered by wig.

Stationary Eyes: Glass eyes which do not move or sleep.

Stone Bisque: Coarse white bisque of a lesser quality.

Toddler Body: Usually a chubby ball-jointed composition body with chunky, shorter thighs, and a diagonal hip joint; sometimes has curved instead of jointed arms; sometimes is of five pieces with straight chubby legs.

Topsy-Turvy: Doll with two heads, one usually concealed beneath a skirt.

Turned Shoulder Head: Head and shoulders are one piece, but the head is molded at an angle so that the doll is not looking straight ahead.

Vinyl: Soft plastic material used for making dolls after 1950s.

Watermelon Mouth: Closed line-type mouth curved up at each side in an impish expression.

Wax Over: A doll with head and/or limbs of papier-mâché or composition covered with a layer of wax to give a natural, lifelike finish.

Weighted Eyes: Eyes which can be made to sleep by means of a weight which is attached to the eyes.

Wire Eyes: Eyes which can be made to sleep by means of a wire which protrudes from doll's head.

Selected Bibliography

Anderton, Johana. *Twentieth Century Dolls; More Twentieth Century Dolls*

Angione, Genevieve. *All-Bisque & Half-Bisque Dolls*

Angione & Wharton. *All Dolls Are Collectible*

Borger, Mona. *Chinas/Dolls for Study and Admiration.*

Coleman, Dorothy, Elizabeth & Evelyn. *The Collector's Encyclopedia of Dolls; The Collector's Book of Dolls' Clothes*

Desmond, Kay. *All Color Book of Dolls*

Foulke, Jan. *Focusing on Effanbee Composition Dolls; Treasury of Mme. Alexander Dolls; Focusing on Gebruder Heubach Dolls - The Art of Gebrüder Heubach: Dolls and Figurines; Kestner, King of Dollmakers; Simon & Halbig Dolls: The Artful Aspect*

Hillier, Mary. *Dolls and Dollmakers*

King, Constance. *Dolls and Doll's Houses; The Collector's History of Dolls*

Merrill & Perkins. *Handbook of Collectible Dolls,* Vols. I, II, and III

Noble, John. *Treasury of Beautiful Dolls*

Richter, Lydia. *The Beloved Käthe-Kruse-Dolls*

Shoemaker, Rhoda. *Compo Dolls Cute and Collectible,* Vols. I, II and III

Jan Foulke was born in Burlington, New Jersey, and always had a fondness for dolls. Many happy hours of her childhood were spent with dolls as companions since she lived on a quiet country road, an only child for the first ten years of her life. Jan attended boarding school in Philadelphia, Pennsylvania, and then went on to college in Takoma Park, Maryland, at Columbia Union College where she was named to Who's Who in American Colleges and Universities, and was graduated with high honors.

Jan taught English for 12 years in the Montgomery County, Maryland, schools and also supervised student teachers in English for the University of Maryland, where she did graduate work.

Jan and Howard Foulke both "antiqued" for a hobby and decided to open a small shop of their own. Their daughter, Beth, rekindled Jan's interest in dolls. Their interest in old dolls naturally grew out of their love of old things. The stock in their antique shop gradually changed until one day they realized that they had an antique doll shop!

As they saw new collectors struggling to learn more about dolls and how to buy them as they once did themselves, Jan and Howard realized that there was a real need in the doll field for a good and reliable doll identification and price guide. Hobby House Press, Inc., realized this, too, and asked the Foulkes to work on the first *Blue Book of Dolls and Values*™ which came out in 1974. This book was very successful and is now in its 6th edition. The *Blue Book* is regarded by collectors and dealers as an indispensable tool in collecting, buying, and selling dolls.

Jan and Howard Foulke now earn a full-time living in the world of dolls -- writing and illustrating books and articles, appraising collections, lecturing on antique dolls, acting as consultants to museums, auction houses, and major collectors, and buying and selling dolls both by mail order and by exhibiting at major shows throughout the United States. For her work throughout the years, Jan has become recognized as a prominent authority in the doll field.

Index

Text references are indicated in alphabetical and numerical order. Often there is a photograph to accompany the text reference. References to illustrations indicate that photographs appear on a different page.

G

H

I

J

K

Mold and Mark Numbers